Human Agency in Medieval Society, 1100–1450

Human Agency
in Medieval Society, 1100–1450

Ionuț Epurescu-Pascovici

THE BOYDELL PRESS

© Ionuț Epurescu-Pascovici 2021

All Rights Reserved. Except as permitted under current legislation no part of this work may be photocopied, stored in a retrieval system, published, performed in public, adapted, broadcast, transmitted, recorded or reproduced in any form or by any means, without the prior permission of the copyright owner

The right of Ionuț Epurescu-Pascovici to be identified as the author of this work has been asserted in accordance with sections 77 and 78 of the Copyright, Designs and Patents Act 1988

First published 2021
The Boydell Press, Woodbridge
Paperback edition 2024

ISBN 978 1 78327 576 2 hardback
ISBN 978 1 83765 207 5 paperback

The Boydell Press is an imprint of Boydell & Brewer Ltd
PO Box 9, Woodbridge, Suffolk IP12 3DF, UK
and of Boydell & Brewer Inc.
668 Mt Hope Avenue, Rochester, NY 14620-2731, USA
website: www.boydellandbrewer.com

A CIP catalogue record for this book is available
from the British Library

The publisher has no responsibility for the continued existence or accuracy of URLs for external or third-party internet websites referred to in this book, and does not guarantee that any content on such websites is, or will remain, accurate or appropriate

In memoriam
Elena Pascovici

Contents

	List of Illustrations	viii
	Acknowledgements	ix
	List of Abbreviations	x
	Introduction	1
1	Articulating Human and Divine Agency: Histories and Self-Narratives	27
2	Lordship and Local Politics: The Cartulary of an Aristocratic Family	60
3	To Render an Account of One's Deeds: The *Livres de Raison*	119
4	The Social Uses of Life-Writing: The Tuscan *Ricordanze*	153
5	A Gendered Social Imaginary: The Vernacular Literature on Social Conduct	215
	Conclusions	260
	Bibliography	273
	Index	299

Illustrations

Plates

1 Cartulary of Picquigny: 'Incipiunt staciones militum'. Reproduced by permission of AN, Paris (MS R¹ 672, fol. 57r)   72

2 Register of Gérald Tarneau: 'quere infra ad istud signum'. Reproduced by permission of BFM, Limoges (MS 6, fol. 39v)   129

3 Le chastel de Labour. Reproduced by permission of The Free Library, Rare Book Department, Philadelphia (MS Widener 1, fol. 61v)   236

Map

1 Western Amiénois and the seigneurie of Picquigny, c. 1180–1250   66

Figure

1 The Picquigny family, c. 1180–1250   64

Tables

1 Armed service in the seigneurie of Picquigny   71

2 Enguerran's pious donations, 1199–1224   98

3 Esperon's sisters' dowries   146

The author and publisher are grateful to all the institutions and individuals listed for permission to reproduce the materials in which they hold copyright. Every effort has been made to trace the copyright holders; apologies are offered for any omission, and the publisher will be pleased to add any necessary acknowledgement in subsequent editions.

Acknowledgements

THIS BOOK SUMS UP A DECADE and a half of research on agency in medieval society. Its argument has been tested in several peer-reviewed articles, which have been revised and are reproduced here by permission of the original publishers: 'Conversion and autobiography: the case of Salimbene of Parma', *The Medieval History Journal*, 17:1 (April 2014), 27–55 and 'Gregorio Dati (1362–1435) and the limits of individual agency', *The Medieval History Journal*, 9:2 (October 2006), 297–325 (reproduced by permission of SAGE publishers); '*Le chemin de povreté et de richesse* and the late-medieval social imaginary', *French Historical Studies*, 36:1 (Winter 2013), 19–50 (reproduced by permission of Duke University Press); 'From moral agent to actant: conduct in *Le Ménagier de Paris*', *Exemplaria: A Journal of Theory in Medieval and Renaissance Studies*, 24:3 (Fall 2012), 214–37 (reproduced by permission of Taylor & Francis publishers); 'Local politics, social networks, and individual agency in a northern French *seigneurie*: Picquigny and its lords, c. 1190–1250', *Studies in Medieval and Renaissance History*, 3rd series, 7 (2010), 53–166 (reproduced by permission of the Arizona Centre for Medieval and Renaissance Studies Press); 'Practice and knowledge in a medieval *livre de raison*', *Viator: Medieval and Renaissance Studies*, 40:2 (Autumn 2009), 277–318 (reproduced by permission of Brepols publishers).

My warmest thanks to Paul Hyams for his generous advice and constructive criticism at the different stages of this project; and to Hirokazu Miyazaki, whose ethnographic research was the inspiration for this book and whose suggestions have been enormously helpful. For their insightful comments on earlier versions of the book's chapters, I thank Oren Falk, Robert Fredona, and Noah Guynn. My sincere gratitude to Olivier Guyotjeannin for his generous assistance and valuable suggestions during my work in the French archives. Finally, my heartfelt thanks to my brother, Cosmin, who encouraged me throughout this project.

This book is dedicated to the memory of my mother.

Abbreviations

ADHV Limoges, Archives départementales de la Haute-Vienne
ADS   Amiens, Archives départementales de la Somme
AN   Paris, Archives nationales
BA   Paris, Bibliothèque de l'Arsenal
BFM   Limoges, Bibliothèque francophone multimedia
BM   Amiens, Bibliothèque municipale
BN   Paris, Bibliothèque nationale
CCCM Corpus Christianorum, Continuatio Medieualis
CSSH *Comparative Studies in Society and History*
IRHT Paris, Institut de Recherche et d'Histoire des Textes

Introduction

HISTORICAL WRITING OVER the last few decades has been defined in large measure by an endeavour to understand the past of social realities that are so familiar today that one tends to ignore the history behind them. Historians have traced the origins of Western colonialism to the crusades or uncovered the medieval roots of human rights, seeking to historicise their subject and understand how the familiar features of modern life began to take shape and functioned according to the logic of earlier historical contexts. For all that cities are indelibly associated with modern civilisation, the history of urbanism stretches back to Mesopotamia at the end of the Neolithic. Conversely, we take the landscape for granted – it has been there since time immemorial, it seems; but research has shown that centuries of human activity created the open fields and alpine pastures. And so on: everything has a history.

What then of such a defining aspect of the Western modern world as the autonomous moral agent – how has it been historicised? Historians have documented the affirmation of the individual in the last couple of centuries and sociologists have written extensively on the subjects that remain on everyone's lips, from individualism to personal development to the self-made man. But few studies of premodern history have focused explicitly on the individual as social agent. Philosophical genealogies of the modern self occasionally go back several centuries, but they tend to focus on the intellectual elites and the inner self.[1] In turn, medievalists have seemed more interested in the chroniclers' ideas of free will and divine providence than in the social strategies of the laity. Consequently, the late-medieval and the modern social self are often contrasted as two broadly different cultural types, leaving out the continuities in social practice and everyday life and, ultimately, the medieval roots of the modern individual agent. The social history of the individual agent in the later Middle Ages remains largely to be written – a history that is of interest beyond the study of the medieval past, because it provides the context for the transition to the modern era. Central to such a history is a cluster of issues ranging from society's role in modelling individual behaviour to social networks to individual strategies and resilience. To subsume all these aspects under a convenient shorthand, the term agency is often used – from Latin *agere*, 'to act', which gave us agent and agenda.

---

[1] Notably Charles Taylor, *Modern Social Imaginaries* (Durham, NC, 2004) and *Sources of the Self* (Cambridge, MA, 1989).

The aim of this book is to understand what it meant to be an individual agent in Western European society c. 1100–1450 – a question that has rarely been at the centre of historical explorations, and then almost exclusively for the intellectual and political elites. In part this is because agency comprises a range of issues that are hard to document from the premodern evidence. To study agency is to follow an individual in his or her interactions with others and engagement with norms, ideas, and beliefs – in other words, to study the individual in relation to society and culture. Individual strategies, be they socioeconomic or cultural, are central in the study of agency, but behind every outcome there is always more than one person that has influenced it – what is known as 'co-acting'. In addition to joint action, when individuals move in concert,[2] they can also act independently, and quite often in pursuit of competing objectives. The historian is consequently called to adjudicate between the historical actors' competing claims to responsibility for a particular outcome. Assigning authorship for a course of action to specific individuals is intrinsic to the concept of agency, but it comes with its own problems: a common approach modelled on a judicial paradigm of accountability has been criticised for its narrow focus.[3] More promising has proved the analysis of agency in the context of social networks, with due attention to its transactional dimension. Agency is also a measure of societal trends, for example when individual examples are approached as test cases for a society's levels of social mobility. That an individual rose to prominent socioeconomic status by taking advantage of late-medieval states' need for entrepreneurs, as the fifteenth-century Jacques Coeur famously did,[4] says much about the society that made it possible. Consequently, a frequent question is 'how much agency' members of this or that social group have had historically. This approach reflects the widespread understanding of agency as 'the capacity of human beings to affect their own life chances and those of others as well as to play a role in the formation of the social realities in which they participate'.[5]

The popularity of the social scientific construct is not aided by the homonymy with 'agency' in the sense of organisation or institution; in many languages it does not have an equivalent or has an equally awkward one (*agentivité* in

---

[2] See Michael E. Bratman, *Shared Agency: A Planning Theory of Acting Together* (Oxford, 2014).

[3] Talal Asad, *Formations of the Secular: Christianity, Islam, Modernity* (Stanford, CA, 2003), p. 74.

[4] Michel Mollat, *Jacques Coeur ou l'esprit d'entreprise au XVe siècle* (Paris, 1988).

[5] Bruce Kapferer, 'Agency, or Human Agency', in Thomas Barfield (ed.), *Dictionary of Anthropology* (Oxford, 1997), p. 4.

French, for example). But it cannot be helped: everyday terms such as self-help are not neutral or encompassing enough to substitute for the social scientific concept, although they are used in this book in reference to specific aspects of agency. Agency is best understood as part of a conceptual triad with structure and power, which is arguably why it has not fared particularly well in the field of history, where the balance between empirical research and theoretical reflection is generally struck in the former's favour. Thus while in sociology agency stands for social action and is effectively the counterpart of structure, when historians use it as often as not it is just a fashionable synonym for power;[6] this is potentially misleading, for one because power also emanates from social structures (the crucial distinction between agency and power is explained in the next section). The study of agency differs from traditional historical subjects in that one must first make the case for it and explain why it is promising to approach the past from this angle. Until the rise of microhistory in the 1980s and of a generation of historians interested in what anthropology had to offer after structuralism, this case was rarely made. This is not say that questions about social action were ignored; whatever words one uses, some conception of the acting subject is indispensable for any meaningful reflection on society and history. But they were approached indirectly, in the tradition of research on societal structures, power, and the inner self.

Yet the social self is an equally important subject of inquiry. While human agency is shaped by society and culture, individuals' creativity in appropriating and transforming received ideas and practices remains essential. It is because of humans' capacity for reflexivity that we can talk about individuals as creators of culture and history, rather than merely reproducing existing social structures. Consequently new questions arise in the study of agency: about individuals' perception of where power lies in society, the values and beliefs that guide individual conduct, and the self-reflection preceding strategic action. What is more, one does not act only upon the world or upon others; one also acts upon oneself, hoping to change one's conduct and character – clearly an example of individual agency. On the other hand, the opposite of overt action, such as everyday resilience and especially the decision to place one's agency in abeyance, can play an important role in specific contexts. Lastly, non-human agency is a reality in many cultures,[7] and certainly in the Middle

---

[6] Mary C. Erler and Maryanne Kowaleski, 'A New Economy of Power Relations: Female Agency in the Middle Ages', in Mary C. Erler and Maryanne Kowaleski (eds), *Gendering the Master Narrative: Women and Power in the Middle Ages* (Ithaca, NY, 2003), pp. 1–16, at pp. 1–2.

[7] Dipesh Chakrabarty, 'The Time of History and the Time of Gods', in Lisa Lowe and David Lloyd (eds), *The Politics of Culture in the Shadow of Capital* (Durham,

Ages, when many believed in the effectiveness of prayers, spells, and potions, and theologians pointed out that history was the work of divine providence. This suggests that agency is best conceptualised not as a strict category but as a discursive field encompassing a range of related yet somewhat eclectic issues. Consequently, this book also discusses non-human agency, even tracing how individuals relied on written records that could take on a life of their own: because of its effectiveness the written word can be seen as a source of agency. This notwithstanding, a distinction is preserved between intentional human agents and a variety of 'actants'.[8]

As already intimated (and discussed in more detail in the next section), agency is a fundamental facet of human history and thus an impossibly vast topic – not just for one volume but even for a whole series. One way to narrow it down is through the selection of source material. This book is based on ego-documents, an inclusive category ideally suited to the study of the multi-layered topic of agency. The term might seem to designate introspective texts, but it is a social historian's construct meant to claim for the study of the individual and community a wide range of self-narratives.[9] Ego-documents include not just autobiographies, which in the Middle Ages were few and far between, but any text in which the 'ego' surfaces significantly, including chronicles that make room for the author's personal recollections, registers compiling family and personal records, account books, personal letters, memoirs, and instructional texts written for circulation within family circles. Unlike third-person accounts, ego-documents directly reflect the individual agent's perspective on social structures and interactions. Crucially, this is a socially situated perspective rather than a detached observation of society. Produced during a period when making written records was expensive and required skilled effort, ego-documents embody the concerns that the historical actors themselves defined as paramount for their participation in society. The more detailed ego-documents open a window into the process of self-interpretation through which one's agency is constituted. Most ego-documents represent their authors–protagonists engaged in their schemes and plans. Some of these texts were produced not as *ex post facto* rationales, as in the case of literary

---

NC, 1997), p. 35.

[8] This distinction is often elided in actor–network theory; see Bruno Latour, *Reassembling the Social: An Introduction to Actor-Network-Theory* (Oxford, 2005), pp. 71–2.

[9] Rudolf Dekker (ed.), *Egodocuments and History: Autobiographical Writing in Its Social Context since the Middle Ages* (Hilversum, 2002), pp. 7–15; Mary Fulbrook and Ulinka Rublack, 'In Relation: The "Social Self" and Ego-Documents', *German History*, 28:3 (2010), 263–72.

narratives shaped in part by the expectations of their intended audience, but precisely as the written instruments through which specific goals were achieved. As such clarity and accuracy were essential, as with all dispositive texts: elaborate rhetoric risked rendering the record confusing and defeating its purpose. This is notably the case of transaction records and business correspondence, but the point can be made about memoranda, both official and private, and the variety of lists and summaries that helped evaluate the opportunities for strategic action. One should never discard the possibility of administrative and legal fictions. But at the distance of more than half a millennium, these records still evoke the immediacy of the written instrument of strategic action.

The case-study method affords the in-depth focus that is needed to make full sense of ego-documents. About a dozen cases from the medieval kingdom of France and its satellites and from central and northern Italy have been selected. This choice is partly subjective and partly justified by historical contiguities and similarities, of which the most obvious is the close parallel between two types of private register, one French – the *livres de raison* – and the other Italian, the *ricordi* or *ricordanze*. This is not to imply that similar records do not exist outside France and Italy; the fifteenth-century *Familienbücher* from German cities such as Nuremberg have been compared to the *livres de raison* and the *ricordanze*.[10] The issues highlighted in this volume are of relevance for the study of agency and personal records throughout Europe. France and Italy, however, had close cultural ties, several of which are reflected in the material analysed here: echoes of Italian lawyers' work on fief-holding reached northern France while the conduct literature in French drew on translations of humanist texts. The selected ego-documents afford the opportunity to examine socioeconomic conduct in places so similar that they invite comparison, notably Paris and Florence, the late-medieval world's foremost urban centres. Much of the area covered in this study was traversed by one of the protagonists, the thirteenth-century travelling Franciscan, Salimbene of Parma.

The selection of case studies brings together texts and contexts that, owing to the division of labour among medievalists, are rarely analysed in the same monograph: from literary self-narratives to charter material and rural lordship c. 1200–1250 to the private records and conduct literature of the fourteenth- and early-fifteenth-century bourgeoisie. The imbalance in favour of the urban world notwithstanding, the case studies concern individuals of different social status and education, from modest professionals and well-off

---

[10] Karin Czaja, 'The Nuremberg *Familienbücher:* Archives of Family Identity', in Marco Mostert and Anna Adamska (eds), *Uses of the Written Word in Medieval Towns: Medieval Urban Literacy II* (Turnhout, 2014), pp. 325–38.

bourgeois to middling lords below the ranks of magnates. But what they all have in common is that they belonged to the literate minority; indeed, the sociocultural background for this study is the growth of pragmatic literacy from the twelfth century, in the context of the general demographic and economic development of the West.[11] This is a salient topic throughout the book: each chapter explores a different type of record and highlights a particular facet of pragmatic literacy, from inventorying land to keeping tabs on social connections to transmitting conduct advice. Clearly the patterns of agency identified in the ego-documents of the twelfth to fifteenth centuries should not be projected back onto the preceding period. But while pragmatic literacy and record-keeping were instrumental in the exercise of social and cultural agency, the case can be made that in many respects the middling aristocrats and town notables discussed here were not very different from their peers who did not leave behind equally rich records. 'Literate minority': the phrase used above comes naturally to the medievalist, but such had been the advances of pragmatic literacy that in the late-medieval cities of Flanders and Tuscany the literate were no longer in the minority.[12] Even the more educated among the protagonists of this study, such as the chronicler Salimbene (an ordinary Franciscan) or Gregorio Dati, the Florentine merchant with humanist ambitions, were a rung below the intellectuals whose treatises on social order, civility, arithmetic, or chess have been studied to chart the advances of (practical) reason in medieval society.[13] They can be viewed as cultural mediators,[14] immersed in a diverse urban milieu but also in touch with developments within high culture, some of which they disseminated.

Moreover, it bears emphasis that this book is first and foremost a study of practice, focusing on patterns of socioeconomic conduct, although considerable attention is also given to individuals' reflections on the possibilities for

---

[11] On this link, see Marco Mostert, 'Some Thoughts on Urban Schools, Urban Literacy, and the Development of Western Civilisation', in Marco Mostert and Anna Adamska (eds), *Writing and the Administration of Medieval Towns: Medieval Urban Literacy I* (Turnhout, 2014), pp. 337–48, at pp. 339–41.

[12] See Richard Britnell, 'Pragmatic Literacy', in Richard Britnell (ed.), *Pragmatic Literacy: East and West, 1200–1330* (Woodbridge, 1997), pp. 3–25, at pp. 5–7, and Paul Bertrand, *Les écritures ordinaires: Sociologie d'un temps de révolution documentaire (entre royaume de France et Empire, 1250–1350)* (Paris, 2015).

[13] Most notably in Alexander Murray, *Reason and Society in the Middle Ages* (Oxford, 1978).

[14] Jean-Claude Schmitt, 'Religion, Folklore, and Society in the Medieval West', repr. in Lester K. Little and Barbara H. Rosenwein (eds), *Debating the Middle Ages: Issues and Readings* (Oxford, 1998), pp. 376–88, at p. 382.

acting upon the world. The scope of this investigation extends beyond the authors–protagonists of ego-documents, with the analysis of the agency of their social partners and competitors, on which there is substantial information in the texts. While the social strategies analysed here present both similarities and differences, they were rooted in a worldview, or 'social imaginary', the core tenets of which were shared across wide swaths of urban society, which in the more advanced areas of late-medieval Europe exceeded one-fifth of the total population.[15] It is a limitation of the sources that the peasant majority can only be discussed tangentially, but the agency of marginal figures does surface from ego-documents, albeit indirectly. The sources include references to labourers, domestic servants, and marginalised family members, such as the younger daughter who remains a spinster because her sister's marriage already ensured the future of the family line and the *pater familias* decided to save the expense of another dowry, or the cadet son who unlike his elder brothers is raised in the countryside to save the cost of a city education.

The case studies are not taken as the basis for wide generalisations, but are meant to give a mosaic view of the possibilities for social action in the later Middle Ages.[16] Studying the literate laity and particularly the middle strata is a significant step forward from focusing on the views of the intellectual and political elites and presenting them as '*the* medieval culture'. Directly or indirectly, the effect of some of the church's normative practices was to encourage self-reflection and empower the individual. This is important because it shows how agency is shaped by culture, but owing to the limitations of the premodern communicational infrastructure only the key developments prioritised by the church reached even the educated laity. Individual confession, mandated for all after 1215, is a case in point. The growth of preaching in the vernacular in the thirteenth century marked an important advance in the dissemination of the core tenets of Christian moral theology. But while the core ideas and practices exercised real influence, they were appropriated and reworked in ways that reflected the laity's own priorities. In this respect ego-documents have the incontrovertible advantage of grounding our explorations *in medias res*, opening a window into what people actually believed and did. This is often different from what the student of medieval moral theology – even one sympathetic to the complexities of social experience – might expect. For example,

---

[15] Christopher Dyer, *An Age of Transition? Economy and Society in England in the Later Middle Ages* (Oxford, 2005), pp. 24–5.

[16] The alternative prosopographical approach offers broader scope but less depth, and has its own inadequacies, as acknowledged by a leading practitioner; Françoise Autrand, *Naissance d'un grand corps de l'état: Les gens du Parlement de Paris, 1345–1454* (Paris, 1981), pp. 12–15.

the case for human agency has been made on the basis of medieval authors' emphasis on the individual's role as God's coadjutor,[17] but the evidence of socioeconomic records suggests that even this approach grants too large a role to the intellectuals' doctrines. Several of the case studies analysed suggest a more radical picture: even educated laymen thought their agency was more often than not at odds with the designs of divine providence. With one or two exceptions, the individuals studied here did not make sense of their world through the categories of medieval intellectuals but through proverbs, stories, and images rooted in everyday contexts.

The focus on ego-documents can be easily misunderstood, so it bears emphasis that here they are studied not as statements of premodern individualism but as entry points into larger social dynamics, and are corroborated with a variety of other sources. Ego-documents offer an individual perspective on society that is all the more precious because it is rare for the premodern period, most of our documentation consisting of official records and third-person narratives such as chronicles. The approach proposed here has affinities with sociology's 'methodological individualism',[18] with emphasis on 'methodological' and thus an openness to intellectual pluralism. The more ample pieces of life-writing enable the historian to glimpse at the individual agent's personal development and explore the link between subjectivity and agency. This is precisely where agency stands out from the more general notion of power. Ego-documents covering several decades of one's life offer the historian the advantage of discerning patterns of actions over the long run: for instance, whether successful strategies were replicated and what lessons were drawn from personal experience. This last aspect is all the more significant because it is difficult to trace in other kinds of records, hence a certain intellectualist bias among medievalists for seeking the source of a particular behaviour or idea in the influence of a written text rather than in the individual's personal experience, even though the social sciences have made a strong case for the formative role of personal experience. A different, macrohistorical bias should also be resisted: inferring the parameters of individual agency and subjectivity from the general living conditions. To assume that because there was less private space medieval society was characterised by the 'experience of interwoven

---

[17] Philippe Buc, *Holy War, Martyrdom, and Terror: Christianity, Violence, and the West* (Philadelphia, 2015), pp. 253–61.

[18] See Raymond Boudon, *Raison, bonnes raisons* (Paris, 2013), esp. pp. 12, 19–20, 27.

selves' is simplistic to begin with,[19] but it becomes unjustifiable when there are ego-documents that present a very different picture.

Leaving aside the vast body of scholarship dedicated to institutions and large-scale historical structures, more research has been done on medieval collective action, on which there exists a classic work of synthesis, than on individual agency.[20] A preliminary clarification about individual and collective agency is apposite here; the subject will be enlarged throughout the book. Ego-documents offer substantial evidence of collective activities, but to speak of communities acting as one is to rely on a metaphor that is evocative only at one level. Underneath this, closer analysis reveals the interpersonal networks underpinning collective activities, with individuals competing for leadership roles or struggling against marginalisation. Although collective action is an important topic of historical inquiry, for the obvious reasons that it is more than the sum of its constituent parts and has wide impact, nevertheless it is not an analytical endpoint. To account for why and how individuals come together to act collectively, one can always go one step further and explore the individuals' options, since it is in individuals that we ultimately vest reflexivity and decision-making. Individual and collective agency can be contrasted in illuminating ways in specific contexts, but in most cases the two are not either–or options; they simply pertain to different levels of social interaction. A similar observation can be made about the individual and the family, a topic of some debate in medieval and early modern history.[21] There is the risk of consigning them to a zero-sum game, as if the affirmation of the individual necessarily entailed the decline of the family and vice versa. But the two do not have the same social ontological status: the family is one instantiation of the range of

---

[19] Jorge Arditi, *A Genealogy of Manners: Transformations of Social Relations in France and England from the Fourteenth to the Eighteenth Century* (Chicago, 1998), pp. 42–5, 84–5.

[20] Susan Reynolds, *Kingdoms and Communities in Western Europe, 900–1300*, 2nd edn (Oxford, 1997), whose title, Reynolds notes, might well have been 'Lay Collective Activity in Western Europe, 900–1300'; p. xii. On individual agency, David Gary Shaw, *Necessary Conjunctions: The Social Self in Medieval England* (New York, 2005), draws substantially on social theory and anthropology; in Dana Wessell Lightfoot, *Women, Dowries and Agency: Marriage in Fifteenth-century Valencia* (Manchester, 2013), the engagement with agency theory is more limited. On the Renaissance, see Paul D. McLean, *The Art of the Network: Strategic Interaction and Patronage in Renaissance Florence* (Durham, NC, 2007).

[21] See Barbara Hanawalt, *The Ties That Bound: Peasant Families in Medieval England* (Oxford, 1986), p. 9, responding to Alan Macfarlane, *The Origins of English Individualism* (Cambridge, 1979); and the nuanced position in John Jeffries Martin, *Myths of Renaissance Individualism* (New York, 2004), esp. pp. 4–6, 8–12.

relations that can obtain between individuals. The case studies analysed here show that the imperative of ensuring the future of the family line coexisted with an individual ethos, in texts commonly viewed as 'family books' no less. Solidarity between family members was an ideal frequently belied by conflicts rooted in individual self-interest and leading to exploitation, marginalisation, and exclusion.[22]

This preliminary discussion of agency as a field of study will be enlarged upon in the following section, which outlines the fundamental issues and debates in action theory, drawing on anthropology, sociology, and philosophy. But first some brief remarks are in order about the specific issues entailed by the study of medieval agency. As we shall see, structures are not necessarily constraining forces on the individual's agentive potential; they are also enabling, because an individual's capacity for action is constituted by structural conditions. For example, individuals organise their strategies around specific structural features, such as rules, patterns of resource distribution, and imbalances in social and cultural capital (stronger support networks, more prestige in the community, and so on). In the case of medieval society, however, it is the constraining aspect that has been emphasised. In addition to the argument that belief in divine intervention left little room for human agency, feudalism as a system that heavily structured social interactions is held to have drastically limited the possibilities for individual agency. This perception is strongest among non-medievalists, but the issue is far from being settled even within medieval studies. Depending on whom one asks, feudalism as a totalising system is either a construct that obfuscates medieval realities or a still serviceable approximation of them, with many shades of grey in between these two positions.[23] The related critique that 'feudal–vassalic relations', in the more narrow sense of ties between higher and lower lords, developed much later, along different lines, and were far less consequential than modern historians imagined has met with a more mixed reception.[24] Much less debated is the notion that medieval society was profoundly hierarchical and obeyed a rigid social order. The evidence in this respect may appear strong, but it comes mostly from normative and ideological sources that are not so much descriptions of social practice as elaborations of the elites' political programme. Consequently,

---

[22] On which see Martin Aurell (ed.), *La parenté déchirée: les luttes intrafamiliales au Moyen Âge* (Turnhout, 2010).

[23] Elizabeth A. R. Brown, 'The Tyranny of a Construct: Feudalism and Historians of Medieval Europe', *American Historical Review*, 79:4 (1974), 1063–88.

[24] Susan Reynolds, *Fiefs and Vassals: The Medieval Evidence Reinterpreted* (Oxford, 1994); Sverre Bagge, Michael H. Gelting, and Thomas Lindkvist (eds), *Feudalism: New Landscapes of Debate* (Turnhout, 2011).

this study asks to what extent the impression of order and hierarchy reflects the authors' investment in these ideals precisely because social realities were fluid.

The issues outlined above are fundamental in the study of medieval society and can be illuminated using the evidence of ego-documents and the insights of action theory. Social networks and gift exchange are among the social phenomena brought into the spotlight in the aftermath of the critique of feudalism and vassalage. The picture of social relations emerging from the practically orientated writings analysed here is more nuanced than that of texts serving as vehicles of elite ideology. Among the former's authors were bourgeois who did not disguise their concern with the social mobility and the ability of the seemingly disempowered subaltern classes to attain their objectives by means of effective strategising. Consequently the need for order and hierarchy was affirmed – thus emphasising social structure over agency – but it was an aspiration, expressed in response to a dynamic social world. Lastly, the slow pace of institutional consolidation has obvious implications for individuals and communities' freedom of action. It has been observed of both late-medieval England and Renaissance Florence that in the absence of strong institutions, social networks and transactional approaches tended to define social relations.[25] This study goes further. It suggests that some of the practices associated precisely with institutional professionalisation, such as record-keeping and written accountability, were equally instrumental in the perpetuation of a transactional approach to social interactions because they helped the literate elites keep better track of reciprocal exchanges and network ties. Obviously, it is not the ambition of this book to decide the debate over feudal relations or medieval social hierarchies, but to present evidence that can move the discussion forward.

One generalisation will be advanced because the case studies are consonant in this respect. The overarching argument of this book is that late-medieval ideas and practices of social interaction were primarily defined by a concern with what we call agency, rather than, as previously emphasised, power. This is not semantics: as discussed below, agency and power designate substantively different aspects of social reality. To state the case in one phrase, in a world of nascent institutions, widespread instability, and non-human agents, the interest in the possibilities for individual action took precedence over concerns with the power inherent in sociopolitical structures or predicated on the concentration of resources.

---

[25] Shaw, *Necessary Conjunctions*, pp. 93–4; Paul D. McLean, 'Patronage, Citizenship, and the Stalled Emergence of the Modern State in Renaissance Florence', *CSSH* 47:3 (2005), 638–64.

Beyond these fundamental historiographical problems, the book will delve into the rich material of ego-documents in order to bring to light the individual experience of society. The meaning with which the protagonists of ego-documents invested their social existence is revealed in their plans and actions. That their concerns were more mundane than the motifs of medieval epics and romances would lead one to expect is the sign of their lived authenticity. A caveat must be entered, however. Today we tend to privilege personality traits and personal habits and preferences in our knowledge about individuals. On this view, to understand an individual is to grasp his or her everyday persona, notwithstanding that strategic conduct stands out from a sociological standpoint because it is more consequential. But late-medieval personal records rarely permit the reconstruction of everyday life in as much detail as modern sources. As such, more space is given here to the analysis of strategic conduct, concerning the matters that weighed most heavily in the lives of individuals and families. The effort to go beyond the reflections of the medieval intellectual elites reveals a complex social imaginary. Agency, and notably one's perceived effectiveness in the world, was a fundamental building block of personal identity. At the same time, the texts tell of social competition, marginalisation, and oppression. Our modern sensibilities make it hard to empathise with some of the protagonists, such as the *pater familias* obsessed with saving on every expense and seeking to control the lives of his domestic servants and family members, particularly the women. But that is just the point: the study of agency should not be confused with a celebration of individualism.

An overview of action theory

The subject of this book is so rooted in social theory, and the use of insights from anthropology and sociology so common in medieval studies (itself an interdisciplinary field), that the case for turning to social scientific models hardly needs to be made. One might nevertheless ask what can be gained from employing notions that were alien to our protagonists, particularly since the social scientific jargon stands at some remove from the language of the historical sources. Are we not getting farther away from how the protagonists understood their world? Talking about the agency of a thirteenth-century seignior is no different than talking about Charlemagne's foreign policy or the economy of his empire: both policy and economy are terms he did not know, but the realities they designate are clearly important. The point is that we strive to understand medieval culture in its own terms but are not bound to explain it in them. The models of social theory have a heuristic role: they focus our intuitions and suggest interpretive possibilities to be tested against the evidence. They also have a mediating function that makes comparative history possible: the neutral scientific terms seem preferable to grasping substantially different historical cultures in our everyday language. Once the distance between the medieval and modern social idioms is overcome, the substance of the medieval viewpoints seems less alien and archaic. An example from an unlikely candidate, an allegorical poem analysed in Chapter 5, can be illustrative. The protagonist draws on the jargon of medieval lordship to make the point that having proclaimed his allegiance to Reason – 'homage with clasped hands'[26] – he always feels its presence inside. Is it far-fetched to interpret this statement as stressing the importance of internalising the norms of rationality – an idea familiar to any social scientist?

The following overview is limited to theoretical contributions pertaining to the societal dimension of action. Insights from other fields will occasionally inform the book's analyses. For instance, the case made in analytic philosophy for a social ontology in which events are fundamental constituents of reality is germane to the emphasis on life-changing moments in some of the medieval autobiographical texts analysed here.[27] Since the aim of this study is not social scientific exegesis but the exploration of medieval realities, modern theory is reviewed with an eye to its potential to illuminate the specific issues arising from ego-documents. There is no question of applying a particular theory to the sources and trying to fit evidence into a ready-made model. The explanatory potential of each of the contributions reviewed here is strongest for a particular aspect of agency; consequently, at the risk of methodological eclecticism, the aim of the following pages is to stake out a range of different types of social action and the interpretive models best suited to make sense of each of them. Where the models differ the most is arguably in the role granted to human reflexivity. This strongly correlates with the comparative weight accorded to agency and structure in each author's account of how society functions and historical change occurs. After some more background on the interrelation between agency, structure, and power, we move from theories that give only limited scope to reflexivity and consequently tend to emphasise structure over agency to models that prioritise self-reflection. As already indicated, the latter are better suited to make sense of the consequential matters highlighted in ego-documents; conversely, the former, notably Bourdieu's *habitus*, reviewed below, are more useful for contexts where conduct is routinised and subject to

---

[26] 'hommage … jointes mains'; Jérôme Pichon (ed.), *Le Ménagier de Paris* (2 vols, Paris, 1846), vol. 1, p. 33, col. 1.

[27] Donald Davidson, 'The Individuation of Events', in Donald Davidson, *Essays on Actions and Events*, 2nd edn (Oxford, 2001), pp. 163–80.

non-verbal self-monitoring. It is a limitation of our textual evidence that it has little to say about the body, the first tool that each individual has at his or her disposal,[28] although some aspects are discussed in Chapter 5.

The recursive character of the relation between structure and agency, best known through the work of the sociologist Anthony Giddens,[29] refers to the fact that social structures are built and maintained through human actions but then fundamentally shape human actions. History is a product of human activity, but humans are also products of history: one is the man of one's time. Take the well-known example of institutions and laws. Both are created by the agency of individuals – think of the time, effort, and creativity involved in designing legislation or a functional bureaucracy – but once in place they represent fundamental structures of society inasmuch as they shape individual conduct, prohibiting some types of behaviour while upholding others, channelling the individuals' efforts through specific procedures, and generally offering a model for how to go about achieving legitimate objectives. The same can be said of cultural structures such as language (notwithstanding that the intentional element is lower than in the case of legislating) and economic structures such as patterns of capital distribution. The example of trade routes is illustrative. Established by explorers and pioneers and consolidated with each successful convoy, the thriving route subsequently exercises a strong attraction on merchants pondering how to ship their merchandise. The route's physicality may not always be very obvious – Urdaneta's sixteenth-century sailing route across the Pacific is identified only by the fact that it was aligned with the wind patterns. But not all structures have strong materiality. Language exists as a virtual order of differences, an absent totality; conversely, action is always present in space and time.[30]

There is a larger point here about agency and structure. Any historical reality entails an agency and a structural facet, the former visible but rooted in the latter, which remains latent. Thus brokering a truce between two rival factions of medieval knights involved skilled negotiations between the main actors – that is, agency – but was also rooted in custom and shared understandings of proper aristocratic form – in other words, structure. Agency and structure are complementary ways of describing society; historical accounts need them both. But in different contexts the emphasis shifts from a narrative centred on agency to one centred on structure. Because structure manifests itself in action, one must be careful in drawing the line between the two for

---

[28] Marcel Mauss, 'Les techniques du corps', *Journal de Psychologie*, 32 (1936), 271–93.

[29] Anthony Giddens, *Central Problems in Social Theory* (Berkeley, 1979), pp. 53, 69.

[30] Ibid., pp. 70–1.

analytical purposes. In particular, it is important not to lose sight of a crucial working distinction: to a large extent, those actions that are the direct effect of structural factors can stand for structure in our descriptions. Thus agency is not normally used to describe a team that performs with statistical regularity or the workings of an impersonal bureaucracy. Rather, agency is associated with conduct that, while not necessarily the epitome of extraordinary human exertion, is rooted in individual reflection and effort.[31] This distinction goes some way towards explaining why studies of agency tend to focus on ordinary individuals, who in order to achieve strategic objectives rely on their own efforts and abilities, in contrast to those in positions of power who accomplish their goals by putting in motion institutional forces.

At this juncture it should be clarified why agency is not the same as power, the close link between them notwithstanding: first, because power also emanates from institutions and is often predicated on the control of resources – this is known as 'structural power' or 'domination'. Conversely, agency is a human capacity rooted in the individual's intellectual and physical capacities; both self-interpretation and the techniques of the body are essential for the exercise of one's capacity to act upon the world. Because meaningful action is inextricably linked with individual reflection, agency is not only about power but about culture too. Before considerations like strategies, networks, and power even come into play, the individual must feel morally authorised to act; this is part of 'the cultural construction of agency'.[32] Action is not always strategic, as entailed by the power paradigm and rational choice theory; rather, it has a substantive and expressive dimension, which touches on personal identity, feelings, and values, 'our deepest human concerns… which are constitutive of who we are'.[33] Not infrequently, 'individuals act in certain ways because it would violate their sense of being to do otherwise'.[34] It has been pointed out in a debate about medieval ritual that there are situations 'in which honour counts so much to an individual who believes he has suffered an affront that

---

[31] See Marshall Sahlins, *Apologies to Thucydides: Understanding History as Culture and Vice Versa* (Chicago, 2004), pp. 128–32.

[32] Sherry Ortner, 'Thick Resistance: Death and the Cultural Construction of Agency in Himalayan Mountaineering', *Representations*, 56 (1997), 135–62, at p. 146; cf. Shaw, *Necessary Conjunctions*, pp. 197–8.

[33] Margaret Archer, '*Homo economicus*, *Homo sociologicus*, and *Homo sentiens*', in Margaret Archer and Jonathan Tritter (eds), *Rational Choice Theory: Resisting Colonization* (London, 2000), pp. 36–56, at p. 42.

[34] Lois McNay, *Gender and Agency: Reconfiguring the Subject in Feminist and Social Theory* (Cambridge, 2000), p. 80.

he is willing to violate all the rules [and] risk everything'.[35] What is more, agency is not necessarily empowerment, because individuals do not control the outcomes of their actions, which have unintended consequences. Exercised by individuals who differ in their cultural outlook and position in society, agency yields power to degrees that vary from case to case.[36] Lastly, to attain strategic objectives individuals do not always emphasise their active involvement or take decisive action. Alternate courses of conduct involve everyday resilience, which may seem passive but can only be sustained through constant self-monitoring, and even non-action: an individual may voluntarily place his or her agency in abeyance, for moral and/or strategic reasons.[37] Individuals perform scripts of disempowerment, for instance in relation to social superiors or in specific social settings, such as the court room.[38]

The social theorists who were persuaded of the structuralist claims about the huge influence of underlying factors on individual thought and action faced the consuming challenge of explaining why reference to the individual subject remained valid. The self was so profoundly constituted by society that if one took structuralism seriously there could be little justification in giving the individual a central role in the study of society. (One answer was not to take structuralism too seriously: the philosopher Michel Foucault wrote that we are 'bodies totally imprinted by history' but it did not stop him later from developing a conception of individual autonomy or *gouvernement de soi*.[39]) What complicates matters is that merely adding agency to structure would not do; the social scientist has to offer a model of their interconnectedness.[40] One such effort, centred on Pierre Bourdieu's concept of *habitus*, became the

---

[35] Geoffrey Koziol, 'The Dangers of Polemic: Is Ritual Still an Interesting Topic of Historical Study?', *Early Medieval Europe*, 11:4 (2002), 367–88, at p. 382.

[36] Giddens, *Central Problems*, p. 88; Derek Layder, 'Power, Structure, and Agency', *Journal for the Theory of Social Behaviour*, 15:2 (1985), 131–49; Sherry Ortner, *Anthropology and Social Theory: Culture, Power, and the Acting Subject* (Durham, NC, 2006), pp. 4–8, 137–9.

[37] Saba Mahmood, 'Feminist Theory, Embodiment, and the Docile Agent: Some Reflections on the Egyptian Islamic Revival', *Cultural Anthropology*, 16:2 (2001), 202–36; Hirokazu Miyazaki, 'Faith and Its Fulfilment: Agency, Exchange and the Fijian Aesthetics of Completion', *American Ethnologist*, 27:1 (2000), 31–51, at pp. 42–3.

[38] Asad, *Formations of the Secular*, 77.

[39] Michel Foucault, *L'hérmeneutique du sujet* (Paris, 2001), pp. 241–2.

[40] Margaret Archer and Jonathan Tritter, 'Introduction', in Margaret Archer and Jonathan Tritter (eds), *Rational Choice Theory: Resisting Colonization* (London, 2000), pp. 1–17, at p. 9.

foundation of practice theory. The *habitus* refers to a set of durable dispositions acquired by the individual in the processes of interaction with the world and in turn generating new patterns of action: 'structured structures predisposed to function as structuring structures'.[41] Because Bourdieu wanted to endow the *habitus* with all the strengths and none of the weaknesses of both structuralist and subjectivist theories, the *habitus* is often said to be misinterpreted as a soft version of either structuralism or methodological individualism (the present author misinterprets it as the former). Because it emphasises non-discursive forms of knowledge and practical mastery or '*docta ignorantia*, a mode of practical knowledge not comprising knowledge on its own principles',[42] the *habitus* is not particularly apt to focus our intuitions about the more strategic socio-economic conduct documented in the ego-documents, but one illuminating case is discussed in Chapter 3. Bourdieu draws attention to 'the conjuncture which ... represents a particular state of [the] structure';[43] similarly, Marshall Sahlins points out that the cultural categories through which the individual experience of the world is organised take on specific configurations according to historical context and the interested actions of historical agents.[44]

Like Bourdieu, Anthony Giddens acknowledges that action is 'a continuous flow of conduct' orientated to a large degree by 'forms of knowledge not immediately available to discourse', but makes it clear that in one form or another social actors know what they are doing.[45] Giddens leans more towards the enabling aspect of social structures, emphasising that social actors use the structural properties of social systems as if drawing upon resources: structure is not 'a barrier to action but ... essentially involved in its production'. Viewed in this light, the traditional emphasis on the power structures of the medieval world seems misleading, because even the subaltern and seemingly disempowered individuals are apt to exploit structural properties to their advantage. In a pioneering study of everyday practices, the historian Michel de Certeau suggests that those who cannot control the field of play base their tactics on the manipulation of time, in such a way as to derive the maximum advantage

---

[41] Pierre Bourdieu, *Outline of a Theory of Practice*, trans. Richard Nice (Cambridge, 1977), p. 72. This resonates with Aquinas's concept of *habitus*; see Alain Boureau, *De vagues individus: la condition humaine dans la pensée scolastique* (Paris, 2008), p. 191.

[42] Bourdieu, *Outline*, p. 19.

[43] Ibid., p. 78.

[44] Marshall Sahlins, *Islands of History* (Chicago, 1985), pp. 144–5.

[45] Anthony Giddens, *Social Theory and Modern Sociology* (Stanford, CA, 1987), p. 63.

from the timing of their actions;[46] some apposite examples are discussed in this volume in Chapters 4 and 5.

Because for Giddens structural properties are closely involved in social action, the sociologist Margaret Archer raised concerns about the conflation of agency and structure.[47] Archer argues that each needs to be granted a certain autonomy at the analytical level the better to capture their interaction. The argument has wider implications. It is obvious that agents are engaged in the sociocultural structures of their world, and equally obvious that agents interact with other agents. Less evident perhaps but clearly consequential is the fact that logical relations obtain between the elements of a cultural system. Core ideas and beliefs can be mutually reinforcing or on the contrary incompatible, resulting in variable degrees of cultural–system integration;[48] put another way, cultural systems can have higher or lower internal coherence. When tensions and contradictions accumulate, individuals are led to question and challenge the cultural order – something that Bourdieu's theory allows only in extraordinary circumstances, whereas for Archer the relation between agency and structure cannot be understood without making ample room for individual reflexivity.[49] Reflexivity is equally important for the sociologist Franco Crespi, who argues that individuals can break their relation of unquestioned familiarity with the world.[50] The cultural structures through which one's experience of the world is mediated are too general adequately to cover all the complexities of life. One is always engaged in a non-verbal relation with the world; consequently, reference to the symbolic order always takes place in regard to specific actions for which the general cultural categories cannot offer precise guidance.[51] The inadequacy of the symbolic and normative order can become apparent to the self-interpreting individual and lead to distantiation and rejection.

'The self-interpreting individual' is at the centre of Charles Taylor's philosophy of action, which puts ego-documents in a unique position for making sense of meaningful conduct. Such conduct is predicated on a

---

[46] Michel de Certeau, *L'invention du quotidien*, repr. (2 vols, Paris, 1990), vol. 1, p. xlvi.

[47] Margaret Archer, *Being Human: The Problem of Agency* (Cambridge, 2000), p. 6.

[48] Margaret Archer, *Culture and Agency: The Place of Culture in Social Theory*, rev. edn (Cambridge, 1996), pp. 275–6.

[49] Margaret Archer, *Structure, Agency, and the Internal Conversation* (Cambridge, 2003), pp. 9–14.

[50] Franco Crespi, *Social Action and Power* (Oxford, 1992), pp. 8, 84.

[51] Ibid., pp. 64–71; also see Martin Heidegger, *Being and Time*, trans. John Macquarrie and Edward Robinson (New York, 1962), pp. 83–4.

self-interpretation 'embedded in a stream of action' and constituted through reference to 'inter-subjective and common meanings'; unlike routinised behaviour, in the case of strategic action the individual rationalises his or her moves in the language shared with contemporaries. Consequently, the initial self-interpretation that informed one's conduct and one's subsequent textual account share a great deal in common; working back from the latter, the historian can arrive at the former.[52] One criticism of this position is that individuals' accounts 'are not merely neutral guides to action but part of the discourse of self-justification';[53] the implication is that authorial agendas should be subject to careful scrutiny. Another important qualification suggested by transactional sociological approaches is that the outcomes of social interactions are best explained not by tracing them to the intentions of the parties involved but by attending to the trajectory of the relations between them, marked by adjustments and repositioning with every new exchange.[54] Because meaningful behaviour is bound up with self-interpretation Taylor suggests it can be studied as a 'language-analogue'. The idea has a longer history: the philosopher Paul Ricoeur also argued for reading meaningful action as a text, focusing on the 'marks' left in the historical record by the acting subject. With hindsight, the historian can reconstruct from the visible signs of actions – say, the building of a mill or the acquisition of a plot of land – an (ideally) dense context in which it becomes possible to understand individuals' motivations and goals.[55] Narrative texts reflect social realities in what Ricouer calls the 'mimesis$_1$' moment of narration, having to do with the fact that 'the composition of the plot is grounded in a pre-understanding of the world of action'.[56]

Taylor's insights about the shared representations in which the agent's self-interpretation is grounded are developed in his work on the social imaginary. The social imaginary consists of the shared understandings,

---

[52] Charles Taylor, *Philosophical Papers* (2 vols, Cambridge, 1985), vol. 1, p. 16 and vol. 2, pp. 25–7, 36.

[53] Webb Keane, 'Self-Interpretation, Agency, and the Objects of Anthropology: Reflections on a Genealogy', *CSSH* 45:2 (2003), 222–48, at p. 232.

[54] See Bruce Kapferer, 'Transactional Models Reconsidered', in Bruce Kapferer (ed.), *Transaction and Meaning: Directions in the Anthropology of Exchange and Symbolic Behavior* (Philadelphia, 1976), pp. 1–22.

[55] Paul Ricoeur, 'The Model of the Text: Meaningful Action Considered as Text', in Paul Ricoeur, *From Text to Action*, trans. Kathleen Blamey and John B. Thompson (Evanston, IL, 1981), pp. 144–67, at pp. 153–4.

[56] Paul Ricoeur, *Time and Narrative*, trans. Kathleen McLaughlin and David Pellauer (3 vols, Chicago, 1984–8), vol. 1, p. 54, and more generally pp. 54–64.

representations, and tacit expectations that make social interactions possible; one can think of them as 'individual knowledge systems'.[57] The social imaginary encompasses

> the ways people imagine their social existence, how they fit together with others, how things go on between them and their fellows, the expectations that are normally met, and the deeper normative notions and images that underlie these expectations.

The social imaginary is so embedded in everyday life that all members of society are possessed of it: as Taylor puts it, 'the way ordinary people "imagine" their social surroundings is often not expressed in theoretical terms, but is carried in images, stories, and legends'.[58] Particularly interesting is the programmatic dimension of the social imaginary, consisting of aspirations about what social relations ought to be (discussed here in Chapters 4 and 5). It bears emphasis, however, that the social imaginary should not be confused with the theories of the medieval intellectual elites. These enjoyed far more narrow appeal.[59] Not even the theory of the three orders – the *oratores*, *bellatores*, and *laboratores* – became part of the fabric of everyday life, even if, having been elaborated by two eleventh-century church intellectuals, it was eventually reflected in the tripartite structure of the assemblies of the realm.[60] To understand the views of the laity before the advent of printing, the public sphere, and state schooling, the social imaginary is more useful than the history of concepts (*Begriffsgeschichte*). The case for the social imaginary is buttressed by an interesting convergence: the definition of culture by the anthropologist Clifford Geertz presents notable affinities with Taylor's concept. That this definition predates the so-called 'historical turn' in anthropology and the growing interest in action theory points to the salience of notions of human agency in our thinking about society and culture. In contradistinction to the common understanding of culture as consisting of 'complexes of concrete behaviour

---

[57] Wolfgang Weber and Nicky Hayes, *Everyday Discourse and Common Sense: The Theory of Social Representations* (New York, 2005), p. 121.

[58] Charles Taylor, *Modern Social Imaginaries* (Durham, NC, 2004), p. 23; also see Otto Gerhard Oexle, 'Perceiving Social Reality in the Early and High Middle Ages: A Contribution to a History of Social Knowledge', in Bernhard Jussen (ed.), *Ordering Medieval Society: Perspectives on Intellectual and Practical Modes of Shaping Social Relations* (Philadelphia, 2001), pp. 92–143, at pp. 95–6.

[59] Furthermore, the medieval social imaginary was more emotional; Jean-Claude Schmitt, *Le corps des images: Essais sur la culture visuelle au Moyen Âge* (Paris, 2002), p. 345.

[60] Georges Duby, *Les trois ordres ou l'imaginaire du féodalisme* (Paris, 1978).

patterns', such as norms and rituals, this alternative view suggests that culture comprises symbolic schemes and scripts that inform individual conduct: 'a set of control mechanisms – plans, recipes, rules, instructions ... for the governing of behaviour'.[61] The implication is that they can be used selectively and reworked by individuals.

The case studies

The following pages offer a chapter outline of the book. Salient topics like strategising, social networks, accountability, and the instrumental role of writing and record-keeping surface in almost every chapter. Other thematic continuities may be less obvious; for instance, in their different ways, Chapters 1 and 2 address the perception that medieval cultural and sociopolitical constraints held back individuals' capacity to act autonomously and see themselves as meaningful agents. This notwithstanding, each chapter will focus more closely on a specific facet of agency while exploring a particular type of ego-document. This is meant to compensate for the fragmentary nature of the medieval evidence; rare are the cases where the documentary record is balanced enough to include both personal reflections and a tally of social partners and property investments. Both narrative texts and, less obviously, records are shaped by genre conventions: for instance, the quest for meaning affects autobiographies while the material compiled in private registers is biased in favour of acquisitions rather than alienations of land. The picture of agency emerging from conduct literature is not the same as that of personal memoirs. Consequently, the book's argument develops through an exploration of the varieties of life-writing in the later Middle Ages. As narrative texts, the twelfth- and thirteenth-century ego-documents of Chapter 1 are richer in cultural detail than the roughly contemporaneous records of a family from the middle nobility discussed in Chapter 2, but the latter open a window into the rural society. Family registers like the cartulary analysed in Chapter 2 gradually led to the development of the fourteenth- and fifteenth-century account books of the French bourgeoisie (Chapter 3). These texts take us beyond the strategies and networks on which a cartulary usually sheds light and into questions about the self-interpreting individual and the social imaginary that informs agency. The Italian equivalents of the French account books offer more detail on all of these topics, while also permitting the reconstruction of the more intriguing aspects of agency (Chapter 4). After the three middle chapters dedicated to family and personal records, Chapter 5 returns to literary texts, but of a different

---

[61] Clifford Geertz, *The Interpretation of Cultures: Selected Essays* (New York, 1973), p. 44.

kind: conduct literature, specifically instructional texts that include significant autobiographical references. Regrettably, another class of ego-documents, the collections of private letters, could not be included in this already lengthy study.

Belief in divine intervention in the world is sometimes invoked to counter the suggestion that agency can be attributed to medieval men and women in a meaningful sense. This assertion is challenged in Chapter 1 through the analysis of a text that opens a rare window into an individual's lived experience. Galbert of Bruges wrote a sizeable part of the account of political upheaval in his native city in diary fashion, recording the events as they unfolded around him. This first redaction reflects his normal view of society, which proves decidedly mundane and coloured by his legal training and political loyalties. Reading the text as a palimpsest suggests that the references to divine intervention and free will were inserted during a subsequent redaction in deference to literary conventions, as Galbert reworked the initial account into a hagiographical work. That Galbert was an educated clerk who might be expected to have internalised the doctrine of divine providence and approached his lifeworld through its prism makes this finding all the more intriguing. It suggests more caution in interpreting the views on human and divine agency expressed in the chronicles that make up so much of our medieval evidence. A medieval chronicle, but one so original that it defies the conventions of the genre, notably through the insertion of substantial autobiographical material, is analysed in the second half of the chapter. Its author, Salimbene de Adam of Parma, a thirteenth-century Franciscan and scion of a family of urban notables, strove to project an idealised image of himself, highlighting his personal achievement as a skilful agent. This reflects the influence of a model of individual agency that pervaded the Italian urban milieu. The Franciscan microcosm that emerges from Salimbene's text is more competitive than fraternal; the Franciscans asserted their knowledge and skills inside and outside the convent, emphasising their effectiveness in the secular world as mediators and interpreters. Self-assertion is not what one would expect from a monk, but Salimbene went so far as to make claims of personal initiative that went beyond the influential religious models of the time. An ordinary friar, he is an excellent example of the self-reflection and interest in individual autonomy that extended well beyond the Order's intellectual elites.

While cities spearheaded socioeconomic change, the medieval world was overwhelmingly rural; across Europe, villages were part of larger territorial units headed by a local lord, hence their name – lordships. One such lordship is explored in Chapter 2: the seigneurie of Picquigny, west of Amiens on the river Somme. Picquigny was smaller than the counties, the great lordships of the time, but it stands out because of its extant cartulary, a register compiling records ranging from sale deeds to homage charters to agreements that settled disputes. The close analysis of hundreds of records brings to light the issues that occupied the everyday life of the thirteenth-century rural aristocracy, from the management of resources through better record-keeping to maintaining and expanding networks of allies and supporters to strategic interventions when the balance of forces seemed threatened. The comparison between the life of the seigneurie during the reigns of two lords, father and son, evinces the role of human agency in shaping the regional sociopolitical structures during more than a half century. The emphasis on agency is by no means limited to these two individuals: their social partners and competitors also come into focus, from trained administrators to small aristocrats and even commoners. The different approaches to building and maintaining sociopolitical networks account to a considerable degree for the different history of Picquigny under the two lords. As late as the mid-thirteenth century feudal institutions were not significant structuring forces, much less substantial constraints on human agency. It was the planning and actions of two generations of Picquigny lords that resulted in the piecemeal introduction of new administrative practices and norms that gave more structure to relations between higher and lower lords. In parallel, the lords of Picquigny aimed to turn their castle into a noble residence and centre of the local aristocratic social life.

A century later the use of private cartularies spread to the bourgeoisie. It is plausible that some of the fourteenth- and fifteenth-century account books known as *libri rationis* or *livres de raison* evolved out of private cartularies. They shed precious light on microeconomic strategies, from the diversification of sources of revenue to calculated investments. Although these texts have been treated by modern historians as *livres de famille*, the examples analysed here entail a discourse about individual achievement and self-identity. The accounting of revenues and expenses brings up a fundamental facet of agency, the sense of personal accountability. The *pater familias* used the written record to give an account (*ratio* or *raison*, hence the genre's name) of his operations, both to himself and to the family posterity. Collective action features prominently in one of the examples studied, a hybrid text chronicling a community's struggle against predatory taxation during the Hundred Years' War but also including ample notes about the author's family. The focus on family and community, however, does not preclude the author's emphasis on his leadership role. In another *livre de raison*, the otherwise thrifty author turns the ideal of economising and rigorous accounting on its head as part of an exercise in self-representation in which he emphasises his spending for the benefit of family dependants. Some of the *livres de raison* offer a glimpse at the prospective dimension of agency, involving planning for the family future and the transmission of socioeconomic advice to future generations. The written advice had an implicit promissory note: the next generations could expect a measure of social success if they followed the lessons of their elders. The emergence of promissory notes within the domestic sphere in the later Middle Ages is significant, because they are usually associated with the programmes of political reform and modernisation of the eighteenth century. Lastly, the notes about prayers, spells, and healing potions in the *livres de raison* offer a glimpse into how individuals related to non-human agency.

A fuller picture of human agency, including aspects normally difficult to explore from the premodern evidence, emerges from the texts analysed in Chapter 4, similar to but much richer than the *livres de raison*: the *ricordi* and *ricordanze* of the premier centre of late-medieval banking and trade, Florence – hence the caveat against extrapolating unduly from these examples. The first part of Chapter 4 revisits some of the salient topics of this volume, such as socioeconomic strategies and social networks, now analysed in more detail from the *ricordi* of the Florentine merchant, Giovanni Morelli. Morelli's vivid descriptions of social scenarios make it possible to understand individual conduct in relation to the social imaginary that informed both his own actions and the detailed recommendations he formulates for his heirs. Similarly, fresh light is shed on the relation between human agency and belief in divine providence by Morelli's account of a personal religious experience. The episode opens a window into how Morelli's transactional view of social exchanges informed his idea of the individual's relation with God. The second part of the chapter capitalises on the evidence of Gregorio Dati's *ricordi* to explore the intriguing question of the alternatives to overt engagement and decisive action, from everyday resilience to the decision to place one's agency in abeyance. While in some instances Dati's choice to de-emphasise his involvement can be attributed to pragmatic calculation, others reflect the intersection of strategic and moral–religious reasons. In this context Dati made creative use of written memoranda, endowed with autonomous agency so as to evoke years later his commitment to refrain from particular courses of action.

Chapter 5 aims to capture the prospective dimension of the late-medieval social imaginary. It focuses on two related fourteenth-century vernacular texts from the Paris area that straddle the genres of self-narrative and instructional literature: the *Chemin de povreté et de richesse* and the *Ménagier de Paris*. The texts stand out from the corpus of late-medieval conduct literature in that they were authored not by professional writers but by ordinary bourgeois with modest literary ambitions who strove to articulate a viable model of individual social conduct. The texts retain a strong autobiographical component because both authors were concerned with the problems closest to them: maintaining social status while competing with unscrupulous arrivistes in the case of the *Chemin* and household management in the *Ménagier*. Gender considerations are central in both texts, and particularly in the *Ménagier*, ostensibly written to educate the author's young wife about domestic tasks. Agency, more than power, captures the authors' idea of gendered conduct, an idea that by their own account was widely shared in their milieu. The *Ménagier* is written to reaffirm the wife's material and emotional dependence on the husband and her subaltern status. In the process, however, the bourgeois anxieties about the potential of the seemingly disempowered to subvert patriarchal designs irrupt through the text. Both texts share an exacerbated sense of the individual responsibility weighing on the *pater familias*; consequently, as in the *livres de raison*, a diminished view of the wife's contribution to the family is put forth. While both texts project an ideal of social order in response to a dynamic society, the *Chemin* is innovative in its vision of a world held together by individuals' work ethic, epitomised in the allegory of the *chastel de Labour* inhabited not by knights but, in a subversion of the traditional order, by workers.

The book's conclusions relate the findings about agency to a topic suggested by both the medieval evidence and the modern social scientific literature. As research on this volume progressed it became apparent that some of the preeminent theorists of social agency are also leading contributors to the theory of modernisation, from the philosopher Charles Taylor to the sociologists Anthony Giddens and Bruno Latour. On the other hand, claims about the modernity of the later Middle Ages have been advanced by medievalists, some writing on material similar to that covered here.[62] Modernity and agency are closely related at a fundamental conceptual level, but to understand this link it is essential to re-examine our received ideas about modernity. Today modernity is often defined in all but its own terms, usually through the aggregation of different social phenomena: modernity equals urbanisation plus industrialisation plus secularism, in much the same way Lenin defined Communism as Soviet power plus the electrification of the country. Because these are hugely influential developments that mark off our late-modern world from the preceding period this indirect definition rings true. But modernity and modernisation have preserved a salient meaning ever since 'modern' – from Latin *modo*: 'now', 'recently' – was used in late-antiquity and the Middle Ages to highlight the fundamental changes separating the present from the past; thus twelfth-century humanists called themselves *moderni*, 'the men of

---

[62] Jacques Le Goff, *Saint Francis of Assisi*, trans. Christine Rhone (London, 2004), p. 55; Jean-Claude Schmitt, *Le corps, les rites, les rêves, le temps: Essais d'anthropologie médiévale* (Paris, 2001), pp. 26–7.

today', emphasising the novelty of their philosophy.[63] Modernity as a construct describing developments over the last several centuries is fundamentally predicated on the idea of change through human agency – the kind of change that is not merely incremental or largely the result of favourable circumstances. Modernity entails the idea of an open future to be shaped by new modes of agency; all modernisation projects are built on the valorisation of the acting subject and its potential to transform the world. Thus it is no accident that for two centuries the lynchpin of European modernity has been the autonomous individual, although the focus is shifting, as always in the history of modernity, towards the most recent changes. More than half a millennium ago, momentous historical change came in the form of developments such as the affirmation of the individual as autonomous social agent, the valorisation of work as part of a changing social imaginary, and the spectacular advances of literacy, record-keeping, and the vernacular languages – all of them amply illustrated in this book. Because these processes remained influential during the sixteenth to eighteenth centuries it makes sense to relate them to the early history of European modernity; some encouragement in this direction comes from the recent paradigm of 'multiple modernities'.[64] The aim is not to extrapolate from the literate and largely urban milieus analysed here so as to make the later Middle Ages modern. The critical mass needed to define a society as modern in the common understanding of the term was reached only later. But one can speak of meaningful precedents and the roots of modernity. Ego-documents help us understand the social outlook of the agents of change, from the movers and shakers who push society forward to those who struggle to keep up with a changing world.

---

[63] Hans Robert Jauss, *Pour une esthétique de la reception*, trans. Claude Maillard (Paris, 1978), pp. 163–4; Michael Clanchy, *Abelard: A Medieval Life* (Oxford, 1997), pp. 33, 39–40.

[64] Shmuel N. Eisenstadt, 'Multiple Modernities', *Daedalus*, 129:1 (Winter 2000), 1–31; Shmuel N. Eisenstadt and Wolfgang Schluchter, 'Introduction: Paths to Early Modernities – A Comparative View', *Daedalus*, 127:3 (Summer 1998), 1–18.

1

Articulating Human and Divine Agency: Histories and Self-Narratives

THE PRESENT CHAPTER IS CLOSELY circumscribed by a crucial topic, belief in divine intervention and its consequences for medieval views of social action; in addition, the second part of the chapter deals with self-fashioning and the link between identity and agency. Divine providence takes centre stage in historians' discussion of agency in a medieval context, but this is largely on the basis of normative theological sources. The present approach is different: it brings into focus the views of individuals highly familiar with religious doctrine, but who nevertheless were not theologians. The general background for the two texts analysed here is the revival of the self-narrative beginning with the twelfth century, but while well-known to medievalists, the texts analysed here are not among the canonical and well-studied examples of twelfth-century autobiography, notably by Abelard, Suger, and Guibert of Nogent.[1] Both texts are examples of history-writing in which self-referentiality and autobiographical episodes found their way; it should thus come as no surprise that both are hybrid texts that defy the conventions of medieval literary genres. They are approached as ego-documents because the individual writer and his lifeworld feature in both – ostensibly in the late-thirteenth-century chronicle of world events into which its author, Salimbene de Adam of Parma, saw fit to insert several autobiographical episodes; and more timidly in Galbert of Bruges's earlier experiment in eye-witness reporting, his account of the events surrounding the assassination of Count Charles the Good of Flanders (1127). As much as the reality of social interactions, the texts reflect the authors' notions of human agency, but since neither Galbert (a notary) nor Salimbene (a rank-and-file Franciscan friar) seem exceptional for their circles, the case can be made that they reflect worldviews shared more broadly in the urban milieu. While certainly well educated, neither author was a high intellectual.

---

[1] Aaron Gurevich, *The Origins of European Individualism*, trans. Katharine Judelson (Oxford, 1995), pp. 110–55.

The assertion of the auctorial self in twelfth-century culture has captured the medievalists' imagination because in a field concerned above all with historical and literary texts it represents a highly visible sign of the affirmation of the individual. What is indeed remarkable is that this self-assertion happened despite genre conventions and a Christian ethos of humility and self-denial. (That Salimbene's narrative self-assertion required careful handling through a series of textual strategies – as discussed below – is a clear indication that this ethos continued to shape cultural expectations). Equally remarkable is that the assertion of the auctorial self includes references to the individual's real-life context, and in this sense it also entails an affirmation of everyday life in literary culture. That the trend towards self-expression went beyond autobiography is suggested by other acts of self-inscription, such as engravings on art objects of the type *Johannes* (or *Petrus*, etc.) *me fecit*, 'made me'.[2] But the importance of the twelfth-century affirmation of the individual for the present study of human agency should not be exaggerated. In particular, the view taken in this book is that the flourishing of self-narratives does not amount to a discovery of the individual. This is not only because there are examples of self-narratives before the twelfth century, such as the well-known autobiographical writings of Ratherius of Verona.[3] The key point is that there is no reason to assume that self-reflection and the affirmation of the individual in culture and society emerged only when they were given written expression. That this assumption has been given some credence in medieval studies reflects a habit of privileging the literary expressions of self-identity and self-fashioning, although these are bound to come from elite intellectuals, at least before the thirteenth-century 'documentary revolution' in private and everyday records. Even seemingly more accommodating positions are not free of intellectualist bias: while recognising the social reality of 'empirical' individual agents independently of the affirmation of the self in medieval literature, human agency is judged of little relevance in a collective volume on the individual in medieval society.[4] But as already intimated, agency and introspection, the social and the inner self, must

---

[2] Ibid., pp. 151–3.

[3] Rather of Verona, *The Complete Works*, ed. and trans. Peter Reid (Binghamton, NY, 1991).

[4] Joseph Morsel, 'La construction sociale des identities dans l'aristocratie franconienne aux XIVe et XVe siècle: Individuation ou identification?', in Brigitte Miriam Bedos-Rezak and Dominique Iogna-Prat (eds), *L'Individu au Moyen Age: Individuation et individualisation avant la modernité* (Paris, 2005), pp. 79–100, at p. 95. This statement qualifies a previous one that beggars belief: 'l'individu, élément clé de nos représentations et institutions sociales, ne peut pas avoir existé dans la société médiévale'; ibid., p. 79.

be analysed in conjunction. As suggested in the Introduction, approaching the topic of 'the individual and society' strictly through the categories of the intellectual elites of the period restricts our understanding of the medieval practices of the self, particularly because before the advent of printing and mass schooling the cultural impact of these elites was more limited (and even today most men and women do not make sense of their lives through, say, Foucauldian theories – or even the more popular rational choice theory, for that matter).[5]

None of this is to devalue the importance of scholastic culture for our understanding of medieval society. In Galbert's time the idea of God as the author of human history was current in chronicles, and by the time Salimbene finished writing it had been enshrined in scholastic thought by Thomas Aquinas.[6] Barely two decades before Galbert wrote, the abbot Guibert of Nogent chose to highlight it in the title of his account of the first crusade, *Gesta Dei per Francos*, 'God's deeds through the Franks'; the crusade's success, largely stemming from the lack of coordinated opposition from the fragmented Islamic polities of the Near East, was widely perceived as miraculous in Europe. Guibert's title was meant to exalt rather than diminish the crusaders' achievement, in accordance with an oft-quoted passage from the early-medieval

---

[5] The present approach goes beyond the scepticism of 'la découverte de l'individu', raised by Jean-Claude Schmitt on intellectual-history grounds and emphasising 'l'absence au Moyen Âge... de la notion d'individu, au sens contemporain du terme'; *Le corps, les rites, les rêves, le temps: Essais d'anthropologie médiévale* (Paris, 2001), pp. 241–62, at p. 261. Also see Caroline Bynum, 'Did the Twelfth Century Discover the Individual?', *Journal of Ecclesiastical History*, 31:1 (1980), 1–17, for the rejection of the dichotomy between the individual and communal ethos. As Anthony Black has observed, the relation between individual and society was not a central concern for medieval theorists: 'The individual and society', in J. H. Burns (ed.), *The Cambridge History of Medieval Political Thought, c. 350-1450* (Cambridge, 1988), pp. 588–606, at p. 591. This rather suggests that historians should not privilege the categories of the medieval intellectual elites over the analytical constructs of modern social science. Thus, Stephen Rigby asks 'why should we accept what medieval people said about their own society as the basis of *our* historical description of that society?'; 'Approaches to Pre-industrial Social Structure', in Jeffrey Denton (ed.), *Orders and Hierarchies in Late Medieval and Renaissance Europe* (Toronto, 1999), pp. 6–25, at p. 11. This is not to deny the influence of medieval intellectuals' arguments on sociopolitical developments.

[6] *Summa Theologiae*, pars I, quaestio 103, in Enrique Alarcón (ed.), *S. Thomae de Aquino Opera Omnia*, https://www.corpusthomisticum.org/sth1103.html. On Aquinas's theory of action, see in general Ralph McInerny, 'Action Theory in St Thomas Aquinas', in Albert Zimmermann (ed.), *Thomas von Aquin: Werk und Wirkung im Licht neuerer Forschungen* (Berlin, 1988), pp. 13–22.

Pseudo-Dionysius, commenting on 1 Corinthians 3. 9, that to be made God's *cooperatorem* was more divine than anything else.[7] It bears emphasis that for both Pseudo-Dionysius and Guibert cooperation between human agency and divine providence was very much an ideal, attainable in extraordinary cases, for example by the glorious liberators of the Holy Sepulchre. In the everyday course of society reflection on human–divine cooperation would have occurred much more rarely, not least because a good deal of socioeconomic conduct was deemed transgressive by the church. This is an obvious point (and perhaps for this reason often passed over); but its corollary is that precisely the most consequential social matters, entailing strategic calculation and the mobilisation of support networks, were least likely to prompt the protagonists to think in terms of divine intervention in human affairs, for the simple reason that they evinced the tensions rather than congruence between human designs and divine will. Guibert of Nogent, who as a monk was apt to reflect on these sensitive matters that laymen would have been happy to ignore (and make amends for later), has left us an illustrative example in his autobiography.

After he entered the abbey of Saint-Germer de Fly at an early age, his family sought to procure for him a church prebend through money and influence, in clear violation of church regulations, as Guibert acknowledges. In the autobiography he condemns this attempt and, while admitting that he was caught up in the scheme, seeks to distance himself from it by emphasising that it was his mother's idea. Guibert's family continued to play an important role in his monastic career. He confesses that at one point he was planning to leave his monastery for a different one, 'less through the kindly authorisation of my abbot than through the pressure of my relatives'.[8] Later, around 1100–4, Guibert became involved once again in an attempt to gain an ecclesiastical benefice through the intervention of his relatives, but failed again.[9] By contrast, Guibert goes to great lengths to emphasise that when he finally became abbot (1104), it was not through personal or family efforts to influence the choice of the monks of Nogent; having abandoned all ambitions he had been

---

[7] 'omnium divinius est Dei cooperatorem fieri'; quoted by Thomas Aquinas in *Summa contra gentiles*, bk III, ch. 21, in Alarcón (ed.), *S. Thomae de Aquino Opera Omnia*, https://www.corpusthomisticum.org/scg3001.html#25723. See Etienne Gilson, *The Spirit of Mediaeval Philosophy, Gifford Lecture Series, 1931–2*, trans. A. H. C. Downes (New York, 1944), p. 44.

[8] Paul Archambault's translation: *A Monk's Confessions: The Memoirs of Guibert of Nogent* (University Park, PA, 1996), 55; cf. Guibert de Nogent, *Autobiographie*, ed. and trans. Edmond-René Labande (Paris, 1981), pp. 126–7.

[9] Guibert, *Autobiographie*, pp. 158–9.

living for months in a contemplative state.¹⁰ It was an example of election to church office *pura Dei efficientia*, 'solely through God's action'.¹¹ The profound disjunction between human efforts and divine will was not lost on Guibert, to whom it seemed as if God was saying:

> When you willed it [the election] I did not. Now you no longer will it and it displeases you. Take it, whether you will it or not!¹²

In Chapter 4 we shall explore another case of conflicting human and divine designs, in which divine will was similarly understood to manifest itself not with the individual's active cooperation but rather as one placed one's agency in abeyance, abstaining from influencing the course of events. Like Guibert, both Galbert and Salimbene were more familiar with Christian doctrine than most of their contemporaries; thus, the question asked in the following pages is not whether they believed in divine providence, but what place this belief held in the different contexts of their social existence and how it shaped their social conduct.

Galbert of Bruges: eyewitness history as a record of human agency

De multro, traditione et occisione Karoli comitis Flandriarum started as a series of notes taken some days after Count Charles's death on 2 March 1127 at the hands of a conspiracy of powerful but humble-origins aristocrats, the Erembald clan led by Bertulf, provost of the collegiate church of St Donatian of Bruges and chancellor of Flanders. The event plunged the city into civil war: the conspirators were besieged in the castle overlooking the great market of Bruges and several candidates competed for succession to the comital throne, with the king of France entering the city in April to support his favourite. These well-known events are revisited here only inasmuch as they touch upon our central topic, Galbert's views on human history and divine intervention.¹³ The present interpretation is premised on two arguments; both will be developed fully in the following pages, but it seems important to state them succinctly

---

¹⁰ Ibid., pp. 164–7; cf. Jay Rubenstein, *Guibert of Nogent: Portrait of a Medieval Mind* (London, 2002), p. 91.

¹¹ Guibert, *Autobiographie*, pp. 162–3.

¹² Archambault's translation, *A Monk's Confessions*, p. 72; cf. *Autobiographie*, pp. 164–5.

¹³ In general, see Jeff Rider, *God's Scribe: The Historiographical Art of Galbert of Bruges* (Washington, DC, 2001).

from the beginning. The first is to do with the extent to which Galbert was personally affected by the events he reports, notably the trauma of seeing his lord assassinated and his city ripped apart by civil war. Although *De multro* does not make of its author a protagonist in the events, inasmuch as these happened in his immediate microcosm his eyewitness account can be approached as an ego-document. The text speaks of his lifeworld and concerns. To borrow the phrase of British Broadcasting Corporation (BBC) journalists, Galbert did not just report the story, he lived it.[14] Furthermore, it is worth pointing out that at least when he first took up the quill, Galbert does not seem to have envisaged his notes as the basis for a future literary work; making a record of the events was not an unusual reflex for a notary – on the contrary, it helped one make sense of what was happening around.[15]

This brings us to the second argument. When his narration reaches the events of 17 March, Galbert identifies himself in the text as a notary and presents the circumstances of his writing (ch. 35).[16] But this brief authorial self-reference does not say that he started writing on 17 March, merely that he jotted down his notes in the midst of the fighting in Bruges between the Erembalds and those loyal to the count's memory. The fighting started on 8 March and from 9 March concentrated on the siege of the castle where the Erembalds were holed up. The point is that even the beginning of the fateful events was recorded with a delay of only several days.[17] But the conspiracy once defeated, Galbert's record underwent a second redaction after May 1127, when he decided to turn it into a work of hagiography weaved around Count Charles's martyr death. To this end, he added a substantial introduction which, in addition to providing background for the events he had been recording over the previous months, sets up the parameters of his literary project as he now envisaged it, with much emphasis on the workings of divine providence. A

---

[14] Cf. Marcus Bull's similar observations about Galbert and his contemporary, the chronicler Fulcher of Chartres; *Eyewitness and Crusade Narrative: Perception and Narration in Accounts of the Second, Third, and Fourth Crusades*, Crusading in Context (Woodbridge, 2018), pp. 27–8.

[15] Cf. James Bruce Ross, 'Introduction', in Galbert of Bruges, *The Murder of Charles the Good*, trans. James Bruce Ross (Toronto, 1967, orig. 1959), pp. 3–75, at p. 66.

[16] All references to *De multro* are by chapter rather than page number to facilitate consultation of the Brepols digital edition: Galbert of Bruges, *De multro, traditione et occisione Karoli comitis Flandriarum*, ed. Jeff Rider, CCCM (Turnhout, 1994).

[17] Cf. Jeff Rider, '"Wonder with Fresh Wonder": Galbert the Writer and the Genesis of the *De multro*', in Jeff Rider and Alan V. Murray (eds), *Galbert of Bruges and the Historiography of Medieval Flanders* (Washington, DC, 2009), pp. 13–38, at pp. 19–20.

third stage of writing follows the troubled succession to the county of Flanders into the summer of 1128. To arrive at Galbert's socially situated perspective during the months when civil war raged around him, it is essential to identify the changes made to the eyewitness account during the second redaction. Building on the scholarly consensus of how *De multro* was composed,[18] the argument advanced here is that these changes consist of a few interpolations identifiable as such because (1) they are brief and seem effortlessly inserted at key places in the text (the general sense is that Galbert did not systematically rework his eyewitness account) and (2) they are thematically dissimilar to the eyewitness narrative and reprise the hagiographical theme introduced in the newly added prefatory chapters.

It would be difficult to find a twelfth-century text more invested in laying bare the logic of human actions in society and politics than the eyewitness record of the events of March to May 1127. For Galbert does not merely record the events in great detail but is keenly concerned with understanding them, all the more so since they hit so close to home.[19] His everyday world was turned upside down by the assassination and the factional fighting engulfing the city's heart. As such, making sense of how the fate of his city was being decided a few streets away was part of his self-understanding.[20] Small wonder that Galbert strives to identify the individual initiative behind specific courses of action. For example, he credits one of the count's loyal advisors, now in Bertulf's power, with persuading Bertulf to hand over to the besiegers the count's archive of accounts (ch. 35). Conversely, he portrays in a few lines two of the most feared fighters who had joined the Erembalds in the castle in the hope of reward and distinguished themselves through the casualties caused among the besiegers (ch. 36). He was even more interested in the various forms of collective action, starting with rather spontaneous manifestations, such as the mobilisation of the canons of St Donatian's to save one of their circle from death at the conspirators' hands (ch. 19). But it was the formalised,

---

[18] Henri Pirenne (ed.), *Histoire du Meurtre de Charles le Bon, Comte de Flandre (1127–1128), par Galbert de Bruges* (Paris, 1891), pp. vi–xi; Ross, 'Introduction', pp. 64–5; Rider, "Wonder with Fresh Wonder".

[19] On Galbert's situated interpretation of history as an eyewitness affected by the events, see Robert Stein, 'Death from a Trivial Cause: Events and Their Meanings in Galbert of Bruges's Chronicle', in Rider and Murray (eds), *Galbert of Bruges*, pp. 200–14.

[20] This process most likely involved exchanging opinions with other participants and witnesses to the events; on this aspect, see Bull, *Eyewitness and Crusade Narrative*, p. 84. It is thus probable that some of the views on human agency articulated by Galbert during this time would have been shared more broadly.

binding alliances that appealed to Galbert's notarial *habitus*, such as the sworn agreement between the citizens of Bruges and the aristocratic faction intent on punishing the count's assassins (ch. 27). He emphasises the successful conclusion of the negotiations as the crucial moment in the campaign against the Erembalds, although the real impact of the alliance only became apparent some days later. To him, however, the siege of the conspirators in Bruges castle was a natural effect of this formal agreement. The same pattern is apparent elsewhere in the text, as Galbert records that new parties, from the magnates of the county to less significant knights, joined the faction loyal to the count's memory. For Galbert, the agreement between factions, often ratified by a written compact and the taking of mutual oaths – to which he pays special attention – is the pivotal element of political action, which thus emerges as largely collective. For instance, in describing what is now considered the beginning of the commune of Bruges on 6 April 1127 (ch. 55), Galbert's focus is not on the unprecedented nature of the agreement between the burghers and Count William (with the king of France's assent), but on the precise terms agreed upon and on what made them legally binding: the written charter (*charta conventionis*) and the exchange of oaths.

But Galbert's interest in social action was not limited to the forms it might take. He strove to make sense of the events as they unfolded, and his situated initial interpretation spotlights human causality, in contrast, as we shall see, to the providential scheme of history introduced a few months later when he laboured in the *scriptorium* to turn his record into hagiographical literature. The depiction of the events of March to May 1127 reflects Galbert's concern to explain specific actions through their causes, tracing the protagonists' motivations to the recent past and surmising about their immediate or more distant objectives, or spotlighting the impact of rumours and emotions on collective behaviour during such troubled times. Although packed with action, his eyewitness account is more than a chronicle of events: it is a window onto the sociopolitical imaginary of urban Flanders. For instance, he was quite interested in serfdom, the root cause of the Erembalds' conspiracy.[21] As a further illustration of Galbert's initial focus on society and politics, rather than divine intervention, consider the banal yet deeply historical sequence of events described in relation to Countess Gertrude of Holland's diplomatic overtures for securing her underage son's succession to the county of Flanders. As presented by Galbert, her actions are both prospective, inasmuch as she envisaged

---

[21] R. C. Van Caenegem, 'Galbert of Bruges on Serfdom, Prosecution of Crime, and Constitutionalism (1127–28)', in Bernard S. Bachrach and David Nicholas (eds), *Law, Custom, and the Social Fabric in Medieval Europe* (Kalamazoo, MI, 1990), pp. 89–112, at pp. 94–7.

that through her gifts and promises the barons would elect her son Thierry ('principes electuros filium ejus'), and rooted in an earlier nexus of events, for Gertrude decided to act in response to the proposals of the magnates and people of Flanders, who had suggested (*suggessissent*) Thierry's candidacy (ch. 34). In itself, the succession of tenses, from the pluperfect to the historic present to the periphrastic future, reflects the fundamentally historical, rather than divine, temporality and causality.[22] In other instances, it is human emotions that emerge as the motive force behind collective actions (rather in contrast to the calculated political moves described above). Many inhabitants of Bruges were greatly aggrieved ('nimis indoluerunt') by the plunder of Bertulf's property; their hearts filled with wrath ('intumuit ergo cor civium nostrorum'), they rallied to resist the attackers (ch. 45). Similarly, Galbert describes the horror that took hold of the besieged upon receiving the news of the provost's death. Here, human emotions emerge even more clearly as a kind of agent in itself: 'fear and desperation besieged them more strongly than the magnates of the siege' (ch. 58).

It bears emphasis that the absence of providential history from the eyewitness account does not imply a lack of moral concerns on Galbert's part. From the time he began writing in the immediate aftermath of the murder, he described it and the conspiracy in symbolic language without, however, turning to theology: *traditio* ('treachery'), the term he uses time and again, reflects the mindset of a notary for whom formalised political ties were a guarantee of public order, and as such their breach was particularly appalling. Equally, *traditio* has a sociomoral sense: thus Bertulf's kinsman Isaac earns himself the sobriquet *caput traditionis* because he used to be one of Charles's trusted advisors (ch. 28). In another instance, Galbert notes that the provost accused one of his clients of treachery because he had led him into the hands of his enemies through deceit (ch. 57).

If the eyewitness record is decidedly this-worldly or 'sublunar'[23] – it speaks of human political actions rooted in historical contexts, orientated towards specific objectives in the near future, informed by sociomoral values, and articulated through formalised agreements between the parties – the second redaction introduces the theme of providential history and divine intervention, which permeates the newly added prefatory and background material. This reflects Galbert's redefinition of his text as 'the record of Charles's martyrdom', 'subscriptio ... passionis' (ch. 14). From the very beginning it is stated that

---

[22] Cf. Benedict Anderson, *Imagined Communities*, rev. edn (London, 1991), pp. 22–4.
[23] See Paul Veyne, *Writing History: Essay on Epistemology*, trans. Mina Moore-Rinvolucri (Middletown, CT, 1984), pp. 28–9.

the events recorded had unfolded solely (*solummodum*) through divine ordinance (*Dei ordinatione*; Prologue). The phrase occurs once again at the crucial moment in the making of the plot against Count Charles to emphasise that the conspiracy took place 'by the necessity of divine ordination', 'ex necessitate divinae ordinationis' (ch. 11). It also occurs in the narrative of the events of March 1127, which had been written contemporaneously. Galbert notes that William of Ypres would have been well-advised to come to Bruges at once, because it would have gained him the county of Flanders (ch. 25). But because it was not so disposed by God (*a Domino disposito*), it became necessary that other magnates together with the Flemish people follow 'the divine ordinance' (*divinam ... ordinationem*) and avenge Count Charles. The use of hindsight is obvious: to write this statement one needed to know that William's candidacy had failed and the defeat of the conspirators had come about through an alliance the between magnates and citizens of Flanders. These lines are clearly a later interpolation. They show that the second redaction, characterised by emphasis on divine providence, brought about small but highly significant changes in the earlier eyewitness record. The opening line of the next section is very much in the same vein: 'God drew out the swords of divine vengeance against the enemies of his church and moved the heart of a certain knight, Gervaise, to exercise vengeance more fiercely and quickly than one expected at the time.'[24] The last words once again have a hint of hindsight, suggesting that we are in the presence of a later interpolation. Even the content matter is highly discrepant: unlike the complex view of human agency permeating the eyewitness account, in both these brief statements human actions are mere manifestations of divine causes. Gervaise is no longer given authorship of his actions: his heart has been moved to action by God. Lastly, both the clearest and lengthiest interpolation consists of several chapters that jump back from the narration of the events of 17 April 1127 to the eleventh century and the ancestors of both Count Charles and the Erembalds (ch. 68–71). Having tried his hand at theodicy in the Prologue, where the devil's intervention is invoked to explain the cataclysmic events visited upon Flanders, Galbert now revisits the issue from a different angle. Quoting Exodus 20. 5 on God's punishment of the father's sins to the third and fourth generation, he explains the assassination of Count Charles not through his transgressions – to Galbert he is now a martyr – but through those of his ancestor, Robert the Frisian (ch.

---

[24] 'Nonas Martii, feria secunda, divinae ultionis gladios evaginavit contra inimicos ecclesiae suae Deus, et commovit cor cujusdam militis Gervasii in exercendam vindictam acrius et celerius quam eo tempore aestimabatur'; *De multro*, ch. 26.

69).²⁵ Similarly, he writes of the crimes of their ancestors in order to explain within the scheme of providential history the punishment visited upon the Erembalds (which took place in early May – a clear sign that these chapters were not written around 17 April but interpolated subsequently).²⁶

Galbert does not seem to have thoroughly revised his eyewitness account, for otherwise it would be difficult to explain why viewpoints that clearly contradicted his novel hagiographical interest were not redacted. For example, having added introductory material aimed in large part at meticulously indicting Bertulf and his clan for the murder of Count Charles, Galbert did not excise from the text a conflicting perspective he had recorded in March, when the Erembalds' supporters accused a rival, Thancmar, of ultimately bearing the responsibility for the murder because he had instigated Charles against the Erembalds and thus prompted the conspiracy (ch. 45). That Galbert saw fit to record – obviously without endorsing – this accusation suggests once again that in March 1127 he was interested in this-worldly, rather than divinely ordained explanations. Also left standing is another remark highly favourable to the Erembalds in the context of the same episode: Galbert explains the burghers' opposition to Thancmar's attack on Bertulf's house through the respect and sympathy the provost and his family had inspired before the conspiracy and assassination. In sum, Galbert seems to have limited himself to inserting a few powerful statements about divine intervention at key places in the eyewitness account – such as the opening line of the chapter in which the people of Flanders begin to turn the tables on the conspirators – so as to bring this part of the narrative in line with the newly introduced providential history theme.

If the references to divine intervention are later interpolations, and considering that the contrast between the ideas of agency underlying the eyewitness account (human action) and the subsequent hagiographical project (divine providence) is very stark indeed, some obvious questions arise. Did Galbert's intellectual persona undergo a fundamental change from the spring to the summer of 1127? Was it then, as he prepared to rework his eyewitness account, that he encountered for the first time the notion that human history is shaped by divine providence? It is highly unlikely. A notary and most likely cleric in the minor orders, he was quite familiar with theology. Having embraced the providential scheme, Galbert handles it with a clear grasp of its complexities, witness the theodicy put forth in the Prologue and the interpolated chapter 69 to explain the martyr's death; and was ready to elaborate on it, for instance

---

²⁵ Cf. Rider, *God's Scribe*, pp. 56, 61.
²⁶ Ch. 70; cf. Galbert, *Murder*, p. 238 n. 10.

by including references to various omens, interpreted as God's warning to the conspirators to desist from their murderous plans (chs 2, 14). His point that the conspirators could not be 'called back' even through such divine intervention ('revocare ... per terrorem signorum') because their hearts were hardened with fervour to assassinate the count resonates with the crucial theological argument, going back to Augustine, that one sins with full knowledge and free will.[27] He even returns to the idea of providential history outside the context of the count's murder and the punishment meted on the perpetrators: *De multro*'s last chapter is Galbert's effort to explain the denouement of the battle for Flanders within the divine plan for human history. Naturally he would have conferred with peers and perhaps read up to enrich his knowledge of the subject of divine providence as he grasped the implications for his redefined hagiographical project,[28] but he clearly did not learn his Bible and core theological tenets in the summer of 1127.

To state the case clearly, for more than two months Galbert wrote almost daily of the momentous historical events unfolding around him without once mentioning divine intervention in human affairs, although he was familiar with the notion – indeed, most likely *believed* in divine providence. It is just that this belief – and this is the crucial point – did not inform his normal view of society and politics; it was not part of his everyday experience of the world. This does not imply it was not real; it is simply that belief in divine intervention was circumscribed by a highly specific setting, that of the *scriptorium* – not the street, the market, or the town hall. It belonged to the time of hagiography writing, not everyday living. Considering how effortlessly he put a transcendental spin on his earlier record of this-worldly politics through the interpolation of a mere sentence – 'God moved the heart of a certain knight, Gervaise, etc.' – it is clear that had divine providence been on his mind when he witnessed the events of March to May 1127, it would have left some trace in the record. In sociological parlance, Galbert did not internalise the theology of divine intervention and human free will. But what of his contemporaries? The hazards of extrapolation notwithstanding, Galbert's case seems exceptional only because of its circumstances, which have left us with an early-twelfth-century journal of a city's events. To ignore it because it is singular is to pass up an opportunity afforded by a rare and fortune survival

[27] Mark Stone, 'Augustine and the Discovery of the Will', *Medieval Perspectives*, 3:1 (1990), 261–70, at pp. 262–5.

[28] On the collaborative dimension of historical writing in medieval *scriptoria*, see Bull, *Eyewitness and Crusade Narrative*, p. 85. Unsurprisingly, there are more biblical and classical references in the chapters written during the second redaction; Rider, *God's Scribe*, p. 121.

of evidence. (Other relevant evidence, albeit from a later period, is discussed in Chapters 4 and 5.) If anything, Galbert's intellectual background and particularly his enthusiastic adoption of providential theology during the second redaction would have led one to expect that belief in divine agency really made a difference in the usual course of his life. Thus, this case is at the very least suggestive of the real possibility that belief in divine providence did not play a significant part in ordinary men and women's engagement with society.

Galbert's views on human and divine agency can be seen in light of Paul Veyne's discussion of the historically constituted nature of truth. Veyne notes 'the plurality of truths, an affront to logic', as when seemingly contradictory positions coexist undisturbed within the mindset of one and the same individual, such as the homeopath who 'wants to take pleasure in unorthodox medicines' but prescribes antibiotics 'in serious cases'.[29] The reason for this is that truth is a programme delineated by the accidents of history, and so there are always different programmes of truth. Thus Galbert's radically different views – the autonomous human agent versus the mere instrument of divine will – are the result of two different programmes of truth: this-worldly, legal, and political; and divinely ordained and hagiographical. On the rare occasion when the two programmes intersected, the juxtaposition of the conflicting truths reached within them – 'out of the necessity of divine ordination, through their free will'[30] – did not trouble Galbert. The matter was – and is – best left to philosophers.[31]

Salimbene de Adam of Parma: Agency and Autobiography

We owe our knowledge of a thirteenth-century Franciscan's life story to Salimbene's decision to incorporate autobiographical references in his chronicle of world events, which has been preserved in only one manuscript.[32] This was a common medieval genre, but what Salimbene offers is anything but

---

[29] Paul Veyne, *Did the Greeks Believe in Their Myths?*, trans. Paula Wissing (Chicago, 1988), pp. 86, 90.

[30] In reference to the conspirators: 'ex necessitate divinae ordinationis per liberam voluntatem'; ch. 11.

[31] On medieval and modern philosophical incompatibilism, see Scott MacDonald, 'Aquinas's Libertarian Account of Free Choice', *Revue Internationale de Philosophie*, 52 (1998), 309–28.

[32] The most recent edition is Giuseppe Scalia (ed.), *Salimbene de Adam: Cronica*, CCCM 125-6 (2 vols, Turnhout, 1998). There is a useful English translation:

conventional: much of the text is the memoir of a man who lived through most of the thirteenth century, witnessing both memorable events and minor but instructive episodes, and learning about more such cases through the network of Franciscan convents spanning the continent. The choice to write his personal history and the history of his family into the chronicle reflects a keen sense of his self-worth. His selective autobiographical recollections, however, do not amount to a coherent life-story; he dwells more on his travels through France in 1247–8 than on his time in in the convents of Romagna and does not cover his upbringing in a family from Parma's urban aristocracy.[33]

The present focus falls on the crucial autobiographical episode inserted in the chronicle, Salimbene's entrance into the Order of the Friars Minor at the age of sixteen and against the wishes of his family (1237), an event so meaningful for its protagonist that it can be described as a religious conversion.[34] Agency holds a central place in religious conversions,[35] and indeed when he wrote the chronicle late in life (c. 1283–8), Salimbene emphasised the active role that he played in the events of 1237, marginalising the part of the other actors involved and of divine providence. While Salimbene's memoirs reflect an ideal of the acting subject that is interesting in itself, the reality behind it can also be reconstructed through an examination of textual clues, leading to significant findings about late-medieval religious life. In highlighting the

---

Joseph L. Baird, Giuseppe Baglivi, and Giovanni Robert Kane (trans.), *The Chronicle of Salimbene de Adam* (Binghamton, NY, 1986).

[33] Olivier Guyotjeannin, *Salimbene de Adam: Un chroniqueur franciscain* (Turnhout, 1995), pp. 7–24.

[34] See Karl Morrison, *Understanding Conversion* (Charlottesville, VA, 1992). Salimbene's autobiographical passages have rarely been analysed, but see Gabriella Severino, 'Storia, genealogia, autobiografia: il caso di Salimbene da Adam', in *Cultura e Società nell'Italia Medievale* (2 vols, Roma, 1988), vol. 2, pp. 775–93. See also Giovanna Petti Balbi, 'Lignagio, famiglia, parentela in Salimbene', in Giovanna Petti Balbi (ed.), *Salimbeniana: Atti del convegno per il VII centenario di Fra Salimbene* (Bologna, 1991), pp. 35–47, and Luigi Pellegrini, 'Istituzione francescana e quotidianità conventuale nell'ideale umano di Salimbene', in Giovanna Petti Balbi (ed.), *Salimbeniana: Atti del convegno per il VII centenario di Fra Salimbene* (Bologna, 1991), pp. 158–73. David Foote, 'Mendicants and the Italian Communes in Salimbene', in Donald Prudlo (ed.), *The Origin, Development, and Refinement of Medieval Religious Mendicancies* (Leiden, 2011), pp. 197–238, also touches upon Salimbene's conversion.

[35] See Webb Keane, 'From Fetishism to Sincerity: On Agency, the Speaking Subject, and Their Historicity in the Context of Religious Conversion', *CSSH* 39:4 (1997), 674–93, and 'Religious Language', *Annual Review of Anthropology*, 26 (1997), 47–71, at p. 65.

effectiveness of his conduct during the contested entrance into the Order, Salimbene departed from the religious ideal of humility and the hagiographical narratives of St Francis's conversion. His case opens a new angle on the relation between medieval cultural models and individual self-fashioning. Before the well-known fourteenth-century Franciscan intellectuals, Salimbene is an example of the friars' individual ethos, with roots in the thirteenth-century Italian urban culture.

A retrospective ideal of conduct

Although he provides almost no background for his decision to join the Franciscans, nevertheless Salimbene does not cut abruptly to this crucial event of his life, but evokes at some length the history of his family line to set up the autobiographical narrative of his conversion, which can be summarised as follows. After Salimbene joins the Franciscans, a new and controversial order, his father pleads with the emperor that his son and only heir be returned to the family. This sets the stage for the climax of the conversion narrative: his father, having personally delivered to the Order's minister general the letter he secured from the emperor, is allowed one meeting with Salimbene at the Franciscan convent of Fano to which he had been assigned. In the course of this meeting Salimbene resists his father's pressures and upholds his decision to stay in the Order; the following night, he receives a divine vision. Moving forward in time a few years, the narrative recounts another vision, which Salimbene experienced in Pisa after having been confronted by a man from his native Parma. He resists attempts by agents of the family to steer him away from the religious life. The account ends with a justification of this lengthy digression from the task of the chronicle.

The emphasis on his role in the religious conversion and on the effectiveness of his actions is the defining characteristic of Salimbene's self-narrative. Of the two basic options available for describing the entrance into the ranks of the Franciscans, he emphasises the one that casts him in the role of an active subject: 'I entered the Order of the Brothers Minor.' While certainly true, this emphasis on his agency eclipses the other fundamental fact of the religious conversion, namely that the Franciscan officials made the decision to approve his request and, ultimately, received him into the Order (see further below). In this same sentence, the trope of 'the Pythagorean crossroads', the letter Y, contextualises the conversion within the coordinates of Salimbene's personal development:

> The third son was I, Brother Salimbene, who, when I arrived at the bifurcation of the Pythagorean letter, i.e., at the end of the three lustres of my life (which three lustres complete the cycle of the Indiction), entered the Order.[36]

Salimbene is at once interested in drawing attention to his own agency and in relegating the other participants to a marginal place in the crucial event of his life. His account acknowledges the political networks involved, starting with his father's appeal to the emperor. But such aspects are not brought to the fore. The narrative reduces the part of the minister general of the Order to a standard reply to the father's request, simply allowing the meeting to take place and thus delegating responsibility to the young Salimbene (the Order's Rule required spousal but not parental consent). Similarly, the narrative limits the role of the convent's custodian to merely repeating the instructions of the minister general before the crucial meeting between father and son. The friars of Fano are a passive audience for Salimbene's actions. Essentially, it is he who effects the spiritual conversion through resistance to parental pressures.

The account of Salimbene's confrontation with his father is meant to bring eloquent proof of his strength of will and effectiveness of verbal arguments. Throughout the exchange conduct appears as an instantiation of the inner state of mind, inasmuch as Salimbene does not falter but defends his decision to leave the secular world. In this sense he overcomes the problem made famous in the *Confessions* (a text familiar to Salimbene): what Augustine dramatised in the context of his own religious conversion is precisely the distance that separates will from action. Augustine wills to convert to a Christian life but this is not enough, because his is a 'fallen will' that cannot will fully.[37] The importance of intention is stressed in other contexts of Salimbene's chronicle as well.[38] But unlike those medieval theologians who emphasised the individual's intentions at the expense of the outcomes of their action,[39] Salimbene is equally concerned to make plain the effectiveness of his speech.

---

[36] 'Tertius filius ego frater Salimbene, qui, quando perveni ad bivium pycthagorice littere, id est finitis tribus lustris, que tria lustra complent cyclum indictionum, Ordinem fratrum Minorum intravi'; Scalia (ed.), *Cronica*, vol. 1, p. 56. Also see Delno C. West, Jr., 'The Education of Fra Salimbene of Parma', in Ann Williams (ed.), *Prophecy and Millenarianism: Essays in Honour of Marjorie Reeves* (Harlow, 1980), pp. 191–215, at p. 198.

[37] Stone, 'Discovery of the Will', p. 266.

[38] See, for example, Scalia (ed.), *Cronica*, vol. 1, p. 147.

[39] Notably Abelard; see M. D. Chenu, *L'éveil de la conscience dans la civilisation médiévale* (Paris, 1969), pp. 18–19, and Schmitt, *Essais d'anthropologie*, p. 251.

All this is largely retrospective idealisation. The long, carefully crafted speeches inserted in the accounts of his meeting with his father and later, at Pisa, with the man who confronts him, probably contain the gist of the shorter exchanges that had actually taken place. But they are greatly embellished and express in good measure the narrating author's ideal of what his younger alter-ego *should have said*. The large claims Salimbene makes for himself serve the goal of narrative self-assertion and reflect a process of renegotiating personal identity through life-writing. His reworking of verbal exchanges into elaborate speeches imbued with biblical references reveals the ambition to mould the crucial events of his life into a narrative that would resonate with the religious culture of the time and meet the stylistic expectations of an audience of friars and educated laymen. Tellingly, the autobiographical recollections are often followed by long theological digressions on their meaning and significance.

Even if only half-realised in the actions and decisions Salimbene took during his life, his ideal of individual agency tells us a great deal about the values of a thirteenth-century Franciscan. We shall return to the significance of Salimbene's ideal of individual autonomy in the context of the Franciscan religious movement. For the moment we should note that self-assertion represented a departure from the ideals of renunciation and fraternity.[40] Salimbene had to navigate a thin line and adjust his rhetoric.

Narrative strategies

The analysis of textual strategies is essential: to illustrate, small clues expose the author's pretension of speaking in the voice of the young Salimebene. When he conveys the anxieties sparked by the encounter with the man from his native Parma, Salimbene writes that he became concerned at the prospect of further challenges to his religious vocation, since he would spend the next *fifty years* as a mendicant.[41] But this is clearly an instance of retrospective teleology, because for the twenty-year-old even the hope of reaching the age of seventy would have been highly optimistic. The young Salimbene might also have hoped to climb up the ecclesiastical hierarchy and thus avoid begging on the streets. Most importantly, it is by recognising that he chose not to suppress sensitive or embarrassing episodes but *manipulate* them that we can draw on the text in order to go beyond Salimbene's idealisations. He does not

---

[40] On these ideals see Gordon Leff, 'The Franciscan Concept of Man', in Ann Williams (ed.), *Prophecy and Millenarianism: Essays in Honour of Marjorie Reeves* (Harlow, 1980), pp. 219–37, at pp. 220–4, and more broadly Giles Constable, *Three Studies in Medieval Religious and Social Thought* (Cambridge, 1995), pp. 185–87, 190.

[41] Scalia (ed.), *Cronica*, vol. 1, p. 65.

pass over the dramatic effects on his family of his decision to abandon secular life – quite the opposite; and he acknowledges his anxieties as a young friar. Salimbene does not appear to invent events *ex nihilo*.[42] There were practical as well as ethical reasons for this: since the autobiographical events implicated other friars and he intended the chronicle to circulate within the Order, he would have had every reason to be truthful.

The fact that his self-promoting memoirs are so carefully crafted indirectly suggests an awareness that his actions fell short of his ideal of individual agency. They needed to be brought into relief by means of a repertoire of closely related narrative strategies: shifting the emphasis; foregrounding some aspects while marginalising (rather than eliminating) others; and manipulating the narrative point of view, specifically by insisting on others' appreciative response to his actions. Salimbene's knowledge of rhetoric would have been fine-tuned by his authorship of several religious and literary texts, now lost.[43] Thus, Salimbene professes to depart from the chronicle of historical events merely to narrate his family's distinguished history – in which he really did take pride – but this merely serves to emphasise the significance of his decision to leave the secular world, because in so doing he, the last male descendant, effectively ended the family line. The gradual transition from European events to individual biography reflects an understandable narratological concern, considering Salimbene's unconventional choice of inserting autobiography into a chronicle.[44] But more importantly, the interpolation of family history as a way of transitioning to autobiography serves the author's aims of self-assertion because it culminates with his religious conversion, making this event the apex of the intriguing excursus from the chronicle of political events. When at last the narrator signals the return to the course of European history, the reader is left with the overwhelming impression that the reason for the lengthy digression was Salimbene's own life story.

Not that Salimbene says this much; manifest self-assertion was problematic because it conflicted with the Christian ideal of humility. This is why he prefers to advance his agenda in a less emphatic but highly effective way, bringing to the fore those moments that spotlight his agency. Fond of drawing attention to his own actions and their effectiveness, he does so not by erasing others' involvement from the record but by marginalising it. Having emphasised his role as the active subject of his religious conversion, he adds a few lines further, after the crucial statement has been delivered, that Brother

[42] Cf. Paul and D'Alatri, *Salimbene*, p. 191.
[43] See Guyotjeannin, *Salimbene*, pp. 28–32.
[44] Severino, 'Storia, genealogia, autobiografia', pp. 787–9.

Elias – the minister general – received him into the ranks of the Franciscans: 'Receperat enim me frater Helias.' Furthermore, this took place at Parma, before Salimbene's much-vaunted confrontation with his father at Fano. By bringing up the role of the Franciscan official who made the decision to accept Salimbene, this statement disturbs the earlier narrative and its emphasis on individual agency, but it is an incidental reference. The acknowledgement that the formal reception into the Order had already taken place before the meeting at Fano is made in passing, without any elaboration. This event implicated the institutional structures of the Order and entailed an element of chance, in the sense that Salimbene's religious turn, even if in the making for some time, was finally triggered by a circumstance, the minister general's passage through Parma. Bearing in mind these implications and Salimbene's auctorial agenda of emphasising his exemplary conduct at Fano, it is no wonder that the Parma episode is marginalised. Salimbene also fails to acknowledge any spiritual influence on his decision from his elder brother Guido, already a member of the Order. Not even his assignment to the convent of Fano, quite some distance away from Parma, is attributed to the fact that Guido was residing there. While Salimbene does not go as far as suppressing such details, they emerge as bits of incidental information supplied before or after the account of the confrontation with his father, which is given the central place as the true moment of the conversion simply because Salimbene played the decisive role in it.

Another interesting detail is added *after* the description of the confrontation between father and son, almost as a sort of marginal comment that cannot change the reader's mind. When his father first passed near Fano on the way to the emperor – that is, before Salimbene was given the freedom to make his own choice – the friars took the initiative of hiding both Salimbene and Guido in the house of Martino of Fano, a professor of law. Once again, the episode disturbs the earlier narrative sequence. It now appears that the friars of Fano and their associate were instrumental in Salimbene's conversion. We do get a sense of the social context of Salimbene's complicated entrance into the Order, but only through a detail that is purposively marginalised in the text. Similarly, at a different juncture in the chronicle, when his immediate auctorial agenda is not to portray himself as the maker of his own destiny but to evoke a former mentor, Salimbene acknowledges, once again in passing, the intercessory role of Gerardo of Modena, who pleaded his case with the minister general when he joined the Order at Parma.[45] The statement is reiterated in another context, in relation to the minister's life, and this time Gerardo's

---

[45] Scalia (ed.), *Cronica*, vol. 1, p. 109.

intercessory role appears more clearly, the wording suggesting basically that Salimbene was accepted into the Order because Gerardo's plea was heeded.[46] This is quite different from the author's previous effort to emphasise his conduct at Fano over the formal entrance into the Order at Parma. Lastly, it seems that a religious movement, 'the Hallelujah', produced a great impression on the young Salimbene, influencing his decision to join the Franciscans.[47]

Finally, the role of the audience is crucial in Salimbene's efforts to highlight the effectiveness of his replies to his father. His answers make the witnessing friars rejoice and marvel; encouraged by his remarks, they even permit his father to meet with him privately. The narrative sequence does not lack the ring of authenticity, as when it mentions that the friars of Fano listened behind the door to the private conversation.[48] During the face-to-face meeting, Salimbene resists his father's last attempt to make him change his mind. His firmness makes his father despair and, before leaving 'troubled beyond measure', throw himself to the ground in the presence of both the friars and his lay companions, as if to acknowledge his defeat. The friars are 'greatly comforted'; even the laymen depart the scene greatly edified by Salimbene's determination ('valde edificati de constantia mea').[49] At the narrative level, the audience offers a space on which the effects of Salimbene's speech are registered. To further emphasise the effects of his conduct, Salimbene adds that the minister general showed his appreciation by offering him the privilege of choosing the province in which to begin his novitiate.

Cultural models reworked: St Francis's conversion

It has been observed that Salimbene's dialogue with his father is modelled on St Francis's quarrels with his own father, similarly reluctant to accept his son's decision to abandon secular life.[50] What is more, Christ was a model for both St Francis and Salimbene. Salimbene draws that comparison by casting his father in the role of Satan tempting Christ: 'come with me, and all mine I shall give to you', is one of his father's lines during their exchange – to which Salimbene replies, 'Go, go, father!' (cf. Matthew 4. 9–10: 'All these will I give

---

[46] 'Et erat ibi frater Ghirardus de Mutina cum receptus fui, qui etiam rogavit pro me ut reciperer, et exauditus fuit'; ibid., vol. 1, p. 140.

[47] Ibid., vol. 1, p. 104.

[48] On Salimbene's efforts to enliven his chronicle by reproducing witty exchanges, see Giuseppe Baglivi and Joseph L. Baird, 'Salimbene and Il Bel Motto', *American Benedictine Review*, 28:2 (1977), 201–9.

[49] Scalia (ed.), *Cronica*, vol. 1, p. 65.

[50] Ibid., vol. 1, p. ix.

thee' and 'Begone, Satan!').[51] St Francis had called for the imitation of Christ, making him the model for believers. While his explicit statement to this effect in the First Rule of the Order was not retained in the Second, the *imitatio Christi* became an influential cultural model.[52]

This notwithstanding, my argument is that the *differences* between the narratives of St Francis's conversion and Salimbene's are significant and revealing. A key distinction lies in the moment and nature of the divine visions each experienced. Salimbene notes that the night after the meeting with his father the Holy Virgin rewarded him with a vision: 'remuneravit me Virgo beata'. She appeared to him holding the infant Jesus and encouraging Salimbene to kiss him as a reward for having confessed him in front of everyone the previous day ('coram hominibus confessus fuisti': the audience again plays a vital role in registering Salimbene's actions). The Virgin's reward appears as the effect of Salimbene's commendable conduct; the spiritual gift is prompted by his merits in defending the Franciscan way, the *imitatio Christi*.

Our sources for Francis's spiritual turn are his *vitae*, from Thomas of Celano's *Vita prima* (1228) and *Vita secunda* (1246–7) to St Bonaventure's *Legenda maior* (1263) – adopted as the saint's 'official life' – to Jacopo de Voragine's *Legenda Aurea*, a popular late-thirteenth-century hagiographical collection, which Salimbene used. It is striking that in all these accounts Francis renounces his earthly possessions and confronts his father *after* he experiences two nocturnal divine visions, to which the hagiographical tradition added, starting with the *Vita secunda*, the famous vision received in St Damian's church, in which Jesus urges Francis to take on the task of correcting the corrupt church.[53] This is consistent with Francis's autobiography: in his *Testament* he attributes his religious vocation to divine inspiration.[54]

---

[51] Biblical wording aside, the promise was real because Salimbene was the last heir to the estate; see Petti Balbi, 'Lignaggio, famiglia, parentela', p. 38.

[52] Jacques Le Goff, *Saint Francis of Assisi*, trans. Christine Rhone (London, 2004), pp. 11, 16.

[53] *Legendae S. Francisci Assisiensis saeculis XIII et XIV conscriptae*, Analecta Franciscana 10 (Quaracchi, 1941), pp. 8–15, 137, 563; Jacopo de Voragine, *Legenda Aurea*, ed. Th. Graesse, 3rd edn (Osnabrück, 1965), p. 663. On the *Vita secunda* as a hagiographical turning point, see Chiara Frugoni, *Francesco e l'invenzione delle stimmate* (Turin, 1993), pp. 11–12. Francis De Beer, *La conversion de saint François selon Thomas de Celano* (Paris, 1963), pp. 75–9, 210–11, makes clear Celano's emphasis on divine grace rather than Francis's role in the conversion.

[54] 'Dominus ita dedit mihi fratri Francisco incipere faciendi poenitentiam … et ipse Dominus conduxit me'; *Opuscula Sancti Patris Francisci Assisiensis* (Quaracchi, 1949), p. 77; Théophile Desbonnets, *From Intuition to Institution: The Franciscans*, trans. Paul Duggan and Jerry du Charme (Chicago, 1988), p. 11.

In Salimbene's self-narrative the sequence of events is noticeably different. He first decides to join the Franciscans and rejects his father's entreaties, and then receives the divine vision. Whereas Francis acts prompted by divine intervention, Salimbene presents himself as acting on his own initiative and receiving the 'great sweetness' of the divine vision as a reward for his efforts. Thus, not only does Salimbene claim exclusive initiative for his conversion – marginalising, as we have seen, the intercessory role of his brother Guido and Gerardo of Modena. He also gives no place in his account to divine inspiration as the cause of his spiritual turn – a move all the more remarkable because it represented a break with a highly influential cultural model.

Did Salimbene deliberately set out to put himself in a favourable light in comparison to St Francis, whom he revered?[55] It is more likely that he ends up making such large claims for himself as a result of the unrelenting narrative pursuit of an ideal of individual initiative and agency. For one, the divine vision was something too important for the devout Salimbene to invent *ex nihilo*. Perhaps he was praying before the altar at night, fell asleep, and experienced this vision. He suspected that some might think of it as a dream, so he interjects a personal anecdote to prove that 'sometimes dreams are true'.[56] Most likely Salimbene did not expect the readers of his chronicle to take away from it the idea that his conversion was in some sense more remarkable than St Francis's. Nevertheless, when writing the narrative of his conversion he is quite ready to depart from cultural models so as to affirm his own worth and uphold an ideal of individual autonomy and agency.

This ideal is qualified in the report of a second vision, experienced some four years later at Pisa. Salimbene was rebuked by a man from Parma for begging for bread while he could have lived in prosperity with his family. Typically, Salimebene's memoirs stress that his reply – as he admits, much embellished in the text – put the man at a loss for words and made him retreat (*recessit confusus*). Speech once again represents Salimebene's key mode of agency.[57] Nevertheless, he began to doubt his choice of the religious life. At this juncture, he received a dream vision in which Christ, accompanied by the

---

[55] In a now-lost work he discussed the ways in which St Francis resembles Christ; Scalia (ed.), *Cronica*, vol. 1, p. 296; Le Goff, *Saint Francis*, p. 44.

[56] Scalia (ed.), *Cronica*, vol. 1, p. 60. On the church's ambivalence towards dreams, see Jean-Claude Schmitt, *La Conversion d'Hermann le Juif: Autobiographie, Histoire, et Fiction* (Paris, 2003), pp. 108–9.

[57] By contrast, the text has little on the techniques of the body, which were fundamental for the ascetic Franciscans who, like Salimbene, followed Joachim's teachings. The effectiveness of speech is highlighted elsewhere in the chronicle, e.g., Scalia (ed.), *Cronica*, vol. 1, pp. 103–4.

Holy Virgin and Joseph – His human family – comforted him. Christ appears as a model for Salimbene inasmuch as He had left His home and inheritance to bring salvation to mankind. The moral of the vision was not lost on Salimbene: 'Then I understood that *where human aid ends, it is necessary that divine help step in*.'[58] While the sense of individual agency is now tempered, this is by no means a vigorous statement of the role of divine providence. Human efforts remain central and divine agency appears to be complementing them – not the other way around, as Christian doctrine asserted. Interestingly, in other contexts the chronicle reflects the dominant paradigm, in which divine grace played the crucial role while making some room for free will.[59] But as regards his own actions, Salimbene wanted to highlight human initiative and effectiveness.

The reasons why the departure from St Francis's conversion model should detain us go beyond the issue of self-representation. Salimbene's perspective on his conversion, although personal and idealised, leads us back to thirteenth-century values.

Social and cultural contexts

The events at Fano are separated from the moment of narration by half a century, but while the text reflects first and foremost the values of the elderly Salimbene who projects an ideal of conduct into his personal past, there are indications that he remained in touch with the world of his youth. He preserved an appreciation for his family's prominent social status – he refers on two occasions to the lands he used to own – and his civic pride as a son of Parma was not displaced.[60] The tension between Salimbene's assertion of individual agency and the religious values of humility and self-renunciation is a complex issue, complicated by the early history of the Franciscan Order. The well-known narrative of the institutionalisation of the fraternal, communitarian movement started by Francis has in this case limited analytical purchase. While he opposed the movement of the spiritual Franciscans, Salimbene greatly respected St Francis and his legacy, all the more so since he had known personally some of Francis's companions.[61] Furthermore, Salimbene lived his formative years in the couple of decades after Francis's death in 1226, when the

---

[58] Ibid., vol. 1, p. 65; Scalia traces the quote to the *Ecclesiastical History* of Eusebius of Caesarea and to Sedulius Scottus.

[59] See, for example, ibid., vol. 1, p. 161.

[60] Guoytjeannin, *Salimbene*, p. 13; Lodovico Gatto, 'Il sentimento cittadino nella *Cronica* di Salimbene', in *La coscienza cittadina nei comuni italiani nel Duecento* (Todi, 1972), pp. 365–94, at pp. 370–2, 378–9.

[61] Scalia (ed.), *Cronica*, vol. 1, p. 56.

saint's legacy still resonated strongly.[62] Salimbene's life in the Order entailed both private meditation and common activities such as group reading.[63] Lastly, it does not seem that Salimbene owed his ideas about social agency to the influence of Bonaventure's subtle theological reworking of Francis's message of fraternity and humility from an ideal of social relations merely to an inward disposition ('esse ergo mitem et humilem *corde*' – 'meek and humble in *heart*', emphasis added).[64]

Without seeking to fit Salimbene into one of the several directions within thirteenth-century Franciscanism, his interest in individual agency can be related to St Francis's cultural legacy, but not to the saint's ethos of humility and self-denial, which did not appeal to him.[65] Another approach pioneered by the saint found adherents, doubtless because it resonated with the background of many Franciscans. The spirited claim to personal initiative that characterises the account of Salimbene's conversion is echoed by a near-contemporary text, the *Meditations on the Life of Christ*. The *Meditations*' textual history is complicated but it is usually accepted that it was authored by the Franciscan Giovanni de Caulibus and intended as a guide for preaching in the

---

[62] On the 'clericalizzazione' of the Order, see Edith Pàsztor, 'L'esperienza francescana nella *Cronica* di Salimbene', in *Salimbene da Parma. Curiosità umana ed esperienza politica in un francescano di sette secoli fa: Studi in occasione delle celebrazioni nel VII centenario della morte di Fra Salimbene da Parma (1221–1287)*, Zenit Quaderni, Supplemento al IV numero del 1987 (Bologna, 1987), pp. 13–21, at p. 14; Rosalind Brooke, *Early Franciscan Government: Elias to Bonaventure* (Cambridge, 1959), pp. 45–55. The narrative of decline from the founder's fraternal ethos has been recognised as problematic; Caroline Bynum Walker, 'Franciscan Spirituality: Two Approaches', *Medievalia et Humanistica*, 7 (1976), 195–7.

[63] See Bert Roest, *A History of Franciscan Education (c. 1210–1517)* (Leiden, 2000), pp. 252–4.

[64] Michael F. Cusato, '*Esse ergo mitem et humilem corde, hoc est esse vere fratrem minorem*: Bonaventure of Bagnoregio and the Reformulation of the Franciscan Charism', in Giancarlo Andenna, Mirko Breitenstein, and Gert Melville (eds), *Charisma und religiöse Gemainschaften im Mittelalter* (Münster, 2005), pp. 343–82, at p. 375. Salimbene's affirmation of individual agency is at odds with the idea of social *minoritas*, which still found adherents among Italy's Franciscans; ibid., p. 380. When he does come out in defence of humility his point is self-interested: the Order's hierarchy should be more humble towards ordinary friars; Scalia (ed.), *Cronica*, vol. 1, pp. 166–7.

[65] Cf. Foote, 'Mendicants and Italian Communes', pp. 203–17: 'the social and political vision that shapes Salimbene's narrative is fundamentally incompatible with the spirituality of St Francis'.

vernacular.⁶⁶ As Daniel Lesnick argues, the text, although drawing on an older homiletic tradition, is quite innovative in the emphasis on 'active participation in the life of Christ and the Virgin'.⁶⁷ The reader is encouraged to use his or her imagination creatively in order to visualise and partake in the crucial moments of Christ's life, for example, embracing and kissing the newly born Jesus – a passage reminiscent of Salimbene's vision, in which, however, the emphasis falls on the divine reward of his meritorious conduct.⁶⁸ The *Meditations* ultimately urges the believer to take the initiative even in relation to Christ. As Lesnick put it:

> As is typical in the *Meditations on the Life of Christ*, the lay person initiates the interaction. While God's freely given grace is in no way denied, de Caulibus's point in such passages is the efficacy of the Christian's own initiative and action.⁶⁹

The two texts, Salimbene's chronicle and the *Meditations*, were written independently of each other. Their emphasis on individual action echoes what Jacques Le Goff has called St Francis's 'spirituality of initiative': his plea for the active life – in opposition to the old ideal of monasticism – exemplified by the decision to send the friars into the cities. Francis also attached great importance to the individual's spiritual conversion, seen as the starting point of a new life.⁷⁰ Both the *Meditations* and Salimbene's self-narrative elaborated on this cultural legacy, taking it considerably further – in Salimbene's case, as we have seen, transcending the hagiographical model of St Francis's spiritual conversion by emphasising individual rather than divine agency. Francis was a social innovator;⁷¹ little wonder that those who

---

⁶⁶ For a different view of the text's authorship, see Sarah McNamer, 'The Origins of the *Meditationes vitae Christi*', *Speculum*, 84:4 (2009), 905–55.

⁶⁷ Daniel Lesnick, *Preaching in Medieval Florence: The Social World of Franciscan and Dominican Spirituality* (Athens, GA, 1989), pp. 144, 177.

⁶⁸ 'Accipias eum, et inter brachia tua retine. Intuere faciem eius. Diligenter ac reuerenter deosculare, et delectare in eo confidenter'; Iohannis de Caulibus, *Meditaciones vite Christi*, ed. M. Stallings-Taney, CCCM (Turnhout, 1997), p. 35. On the role of the reader's power of imagination, see Holly Flora, *The Devout Belief of the Imagination: The Paris 'Meditationes Vitae Christi' and Female Franciscan Spirituality in Trecento Italy* (Turnhout, 2009), pp. 18–22.

⁶⁹ Lesnick, *Preaching in Medieval Florence*, p. 170.

⁷⁰ Le Goff, *Saint Francis*, p. 103.

⁷¹ A *homo novus*, as Thomas of Celano called him; see Luca Bianchi, '*Prophanae novitates* et *doctrinae peregrinae*: la méfiance à l'égard des innovations théoriques aux

found inspiration in him were not content to enact received cultural models but articulated their own perspectives.

Salimbene's self-esteem was bolstered both by descent from a family of the urban aristocracy and membership in an ultimately successful religious order.[72] Even the circumstances of his entrance into the Order were apt to foster a strong sense of his own achievements. At Fano, structural conditions empowered Salimbene, setting the stage for the exercise of his agency, even if he does not recognise it. Surrounded by the convent's friars, with the imperial mandate allowing his father nothing more than the opportunity of a meeting, Salimbene was in the rare position of being able to carry the day simply by reaffirming his earlier decision. With some gentle encouragement from his peers, like the one who later suggested that he change his name from Ognibene to Salimbene because he made a 'good leap' into the Order,[73] in effect starting a new life, the young friar was apt to retrospectively cast himself as the idealised protagonist of his religious conversion, an autonomous agent who barely needs others' support. Indeed, what would be surprising is if he did not believe in the mixture of fact and fiction of his autobiographical narrative. For instance, he did not feel he had a debt of gratitude towards Brother Elias,[74] a fact that resonates with the negligible part given him in the account of the confrontation at Fano. Furthermore, the emphasis on his resistance to his father made for an edifying conversion narrative for would-be friars facing family opposition. Indeed, among the professed reasons for writing the family genealogy is the desire to instruct his niece Agnes, a nun in the Order of St Clare. But whereas such thirteenth-century edifying narratives were generally hagiographical,[75] Salimbene offers his own conduct as a model.

Beyond these circumstances, which, like the Franciscan spirituality of initiative, go some way towards explaining Salimbene's claims of individual agency, a crucial explanation is rooted in the family context of his entrance

---

XIIIe et XIVe siècles', in H.-J. Schmidt (ed.), *Tradition, Innovation, Invention: Fortschrittsverweigerung und Fortschrittsbewusstsein im Mittelalter* (Berlin and New York, 2005), pp. 211–29, at p. 212.

[72] Pellegrini, 'Istituzione francescana e quotidianità', p. 163; Cinzio Violante, 'Motivi e carattere della *Cronica* di Salimbene', *Annali della Scuola Normale Superiore di Pisa: Lettere, Storia, e Filosofia*, 22 (1953), 108–54. On Salimbene's cultural affinity with the urban elite, see Gatto, 'Sentimento cittadino', pp. 368–9.

[73] Scalia (ed.), *Cronica*, vol. 1, p. 56.

[74] See Brooke, *Early Franciscan Government*, pp. 45–6.

[75] Anne M. Schuchman, 'The Lives of Umiliana de' Cerchi: Representations of Female Sainthood in Thirteenth-Century Florence', *Essays in Medieval Studies*, 14 (1997), 15–28.

into the Order. For Salimbene, autobiographical writing was a way of coming to terms with his past. His individualist stance builds on a keen sense of personal responsibility for the end of his family line. Unlike the accounts of St Francis's encounter with his father, in which some sense of the saint's ideal of peace-making persists,[76] in Salimbene's confrontation with his father there is no attempt at conciliation. St Francis's resistance to parental pressure is somewhat passive: he docilely lays his clothes at his father's feet in a well-known scene of their confrontation, to make complete his abandonment of the material world. By contrast, the autobiography depicts Salimbene as quite bellicose towards his father.

Having been subjected for so long to his family's recriminations over the dramatic impact of his conversion on the Adam line, Salimbene adopts in his memoirs a judicial paradigm of agency. In this paradigm, agency is about attributing responsibility and '*forcing* a person to be accountable, to answer to a judge in a court of law ... In that sense agency is built on the idea of blame and pain'.[77] Salimbene was familiar with the legal culture of the Italian cities and the friars' role as arbitrators.[78] His perspective on the consequences of his religious conversion includes both blame and reward – note the explicit recognition of its dramatic effects on the Adam family:

> ... I, Brother Salimbene, and Brother Guido de Adam, have destroyed our house in both the male and female line by entering the religious life, so that we may build it in heaven. May He deign to give this to us, Who forever lives and reigns with the Father and the Holy Spirit! Amen.[79]

Salimbene acknowledges his parents' accusations regarding the extinction of the family line. He concludes the autobiographical excursus with biblical and recent examples of family lines that have ended abruptly, to imply that the end of a family is not quite the tragedy it might seem, because in fact it occurs

---

[76] Le Goff, *Saint Francis*, pp. 56–7.

[77] Talal Asad, *Formations of the Secular: Christianity, Islam, Modernity* (Stanford, CA, 2003), p. 77.

[78] On which see André Vauchez, *Francesco d'Assisi e gli Ordini mendicanti* (Assisi, 2005), pp. 172–3; Jacques Dalarun, *François d'Assise ou le pouvoir en question: Principes et modalités du gouvernement dans l'ordre des Frères mineurs* (Paris, 1999), pp. 131–4.

[79] 'Porro ego frater Salimbene et frater Guido de Adam domum nostram destruximus in masculis et feminis, religionem intrando, ut eam in celis edificare possemus. Quod nobis prestare dignetur qui cum Patre et Spiritu Sancto vivit et regnat in secula seculorum! Amen'; Scalia (ed.), *Cronica*, vol. 1, p. 81. The invocation of divine aid indisputably brings up the limits of human agency.

quite frequently.⁸⁰ Yet in the end he does not eschew responsibility, for example through a detailed rebuttal of the family's accusations. Rather, he claims authorship of his actions and their effects, and wards off blame by emphasising the spiritual merits of his decision. Salimbene's formula about the destruction and rebuilding of the Adam house turns his father's indictment on its head by shifting the ground from this-worldly to spiritual. He probably rationalised that as friars, he and his brother could play the intercessory role that was the privileged domain of the clergy, thus gaining the spiritual salvation of their family. In other words, he hoped to rebuild the Adam house in heaven by cleansing it of sin. He had already taken some steps in this direction: concerned for his mother's spiritual salvation, he procured a letter from the pope for her entrance into the Order of St Clare and later made arrangements for her burial in the sisters' convent at Parma.⁸¹

The defining themes of the religious conversion are also reflected in a number of smaller autobiographical episodes interspersed throughout the chronicle, which offer important clues about Salimbene's cultural development. That the friars saw in edifying, effective speech a fundamental way of making their mark on the world is confirmed by an exchange that Salimbene chose to highlight because it shows him comforting a notable ecclesiastic, Martino of Parma, bishop of Mantua. Salimbene stresses that his words of solace helped dispel the bishop's doubts about his religious vocation. Once again he highlights the effects of his intervention, turning the spotlight on the bishop's acknowledgement of the usefulness of his consolatory speech: 'May God reward you (*retribuat*), Brother Salimbene, for you have greatly comforted me.'⁸² Reward, as in the case of the divine vision he received at Fano, is an effect of the individual's agency. Yet another experience from his life in the Order was included in the chronicle on similar considerations. Salimbene shows how his wisdom saved the life of his ailing companion, Brother Johannino, who finally decided to heed his advice and leave the unhealthy climate of Provence. He thus escaped a fate that befell six other friars who over the winter passed away from illness. In this instance as well, Salimbene makes it a point to record Johannino's profuse gratitude upon learning of the fate of the friars.⁸³ As part

---

⁸⁰ Ibid., vol. 1, p. 86.

⁸¹ Ibid., vol. 1, p. 80.

⁸² Ibid., vol. 2, p. 657.

⁸³ 'gratias referebat michi, quod eruissem eum de faucibus mortis'; ibid., vol. 1, pp. 478–9.

of the ideal of *curialitas*, praise was a symbolic good in which the friars habitually trafficked. Salimbene says this much in reference to his own exchanges with the friars of Sens, during his travels through France: 'the French brothers received me gladly everywhere, on account of the fact that I was a peaceful and happy youth and because I praised their deeds'. Such praise-giving was strategic, considering the value of a friendly reception in the wide network of Franciscan convents.[84] The thirteenth-century Franciscan world pictured in the chronicle could be quite competitive, mirroring the urban culture with which it interacted rather than its founder's ideals of fraternity and self-denial.[85] It was within this milieu that Salimbene's sense of individual agency developed. Several passages from the chronicle suggest that he was strongly attached to a model of social relations rooted in reciprocal exchanges: thus, he recalls the exchange of gifts (*exenia*) between his father and the bishop of Parma, and condemns the wandering 'false apostles' because they give nothing in return for the alms they receive.[86]

The case for the complexities of, and tensions within, thirteenth-century Franciscan culture builds not only on Franciscan sources but also on the evidence of the mendicants' medieval critics. They were well aware of the distance between the professed self-renunciation and the individualistic values practised by the mendicants, although they construed it merely as proof of the friars' hypocrisy. Of the many charges levied against the friars in the 1250s and 1260s by William of Saint-Amour, particularly relevant here is the ambition to affirm their status in society through knowledge and effective speech. As Penn Szittya has shown, William alluded to the mendicant orders' determination to have their theologians recognised as *magistri* at the University of Paris, where he was teaching. Working from biblical references to the Pharisees'

---

[84] 'fratres Gallici libenter ubique tenebant me, eo quod essem pacificus et alacer iuvenis et quia commendabam facta eorum'; ibid., vol. 1, p. 320. On the ideal of socialisation or *curialitas* in Salimbene's chronicle, see Vecchio, 'Valori laici' and Maureen Miller, 'Religion Makes a Difference: Clerical and Lay Cultures in the Courts of Northern Italy, 1000–1300', *American Historical Review*, 105:4 (2000), 1095–1130, at pp. 1124–6.

[85] The mendicants also competed for the resources that attracted them to the cities; Antonio Rigon, 'Mendicant Orders and the Reality of Economic Life in Italy in the Middle Ages', in Donald Prudlo (ed.), *The Origin, Development, and Refinement of Medieval Religious Mendicancies* (Leiden, 2011), pp. 241–75, at pp. 248–9, n. 32.

[86] Scalia (ed.), *Cronica*, vol. 1, pp. 100, 437; on Segarello's 'apostles', see Maria Pia Alberzoni, 'Un mendicante di fronte alla vita della Chiesa nella seconda metà del Ducento: Motivi religiosi nella Cronaca di Salimbene', in Giovanna Petti Balbi (ed.), *Salimbeniana: Atti del convegno per il VII centenario di Fra Salimbene* (Bologna, 1991), pp. 7–34, at pp. 10–11, 13.

ambition to be seated first at table and be greeted *in foro* (which he chose to construe as the law court), William denounced the friars' habits of courting the company of secular and ecclesiastical magnates and using their skills in the legal arena (compare with Salimbene's *curialitas* and his role in the dispute between Bologna and Reggio, below; Salimbene also notes that his brother Guido used to be a judge before joining the Order and that his protector, Gerardo of Modena, served as *podestà* of Parma with a mandate to reconcile the rival factions).[87] While the biblical trope of the *homines seipsos amantes*, the self-loving men, could be understood as a general criticism – indeed in 2 Timothy 3.2 it is part of a list of moral failings – its use by William and later Jean d'Anneux against the friars makes sense considering what this chapter has found about the appeal of individual values to Franciscans.[88]

Salimbene was careful to highlight the instances in which he participated in the model of reciprocity – for example, acquitting himself of the debt towards Martino of Fano by designating him as arbitrator in the negotiations between Bologna and Reggio (1256).[89] For him as well as his contemporaries reciprocity, quite calculated at times, represented a fundamental societal bond.[90] The patterns of agency we can identify from Salimbene's recollections resonate with contemporary social practices. For the friars, offering advice, putting one's knowledge in another's service, and giving morally edifying and socially effective sermons were among the most important ways of participating in the life of society. Salimbene even intended some of the chronicle's pages as *materia predicabile*, material on which preachers might draw as they prepared their sermons.[91]

A keen interest in human agency informs Salimbene's participation in the culture of reciprocity. In medieval society reciprocity informed even exchanges between human and divine agents: thus 'the [pious] gift permitted the lay

---

[87] Scalia (ed.), *Cronica*, vol. 1, pp. 107–8.

[88] Penn R. Szittya, *The Antifraternal Tradition in Medieval Litterature* (Princeton, 1986), pp. 20–3, 35–9, 53, 58, 90. In William's 'false preachers' both critics and supporters recognised the friars.

[89] A fact confirmed by the *Memoriale Potestatum Regiensium*; Ludovico Antonio Muratori (ed.), *Rerum Italicarum Scriptores*, 1st ser. (25 vols, Milan, 1723–51), vol. 8, cols 1120–1.

[90] On reciprocity, see George Homans, 'Social Behavior as Exchange', *American Journal of Sociology*, 63:6 (1958), 597–606.

[91] Scalia (ed.), *Cronica*, vol. 2, p. 827. On Salimbene's interest in preaching, see Lucia Lazzerini, 'Fra Salimbene predicatore', in Giovanna Petti Balbi (ed.), *Salimbeniana: Atti del convegno per il VII centenario di Fra Salimbene* (Bologna, 1991), pp. 133–41; Paul and D'Alatri, *Salimbene*, pp. 181–99; Roest, *Franciscan Education*, pp. 277–8.

donor ... to take part in exchanges with God'.[92] While in Salimbene's autobiography the fundamental asymmetry of such exchanges remains in place,[93] the individual is more fully engaged in a relation of reciprocity with the divine, drawing a response that recognises his achievements (thus, the divine vision rewards Salimbene's conduct). Three centuries later the idea that humans can impinge on divine will, even inasmuch as their meritorious behaviour might seem to demand the divine reward, became one of the strongest imputations against Catholic practice made by Protestant theologians.[94] In view of Salimbene's interest in human agency, the numerous references to divine providence in his chronicle cannot simply be read as evidence that widespread belief in God's intervention in everyday life 'reduced the person's margin of freedom'.[95] Rather, divine intervention as Salimbene understands it is not about the inscrutable will of an omnipotent God but about bringing people their just deserts.[96] As for Salimbene's reflections on demons' meddling in human affairs, similarly invoked as evidence of a limited conception of human agency, they were meant to provide readers with the mental equipment for fighting off demons' deception, and as such reflect an ideal of self-empowerment and individual autonomy. Salimbene the chronicler of political and religious events expresses much the same views of human and divine agency as Salimbene the autobiographer.

Several themes that emerge from the analysis of Salimbene's religious conversion have a broader relevance in the study of late-medieval culture. His affirmation of individual autonomy and agency, particularly inasmuch as it entailed a departure from the doctrine of divine providence famously

---

[92] Eliana Magnani S.-Christen, 'Transforming Things and Persons: The Gift *pro anima* in the Eleventh and Twelfth Centuries', in Gadi Algazi, Valentin Groebner, and Bernhard Jussen (eds), *Negotiating the Gift: Pre-modern Figurations of Exchange* (Göttingen, 2003), pp. 269–84, at p. 279.

[93] For example, Salimbene censures a friar for believing that he could work miracles without God's help; Scalia (ed.), *Cronica*, vol. 1, p. 111.

[94] 'In a profound sense, the religious reformations of the sixteenth-century were a quarrel about gifts, that is, about whether humans can reciprocate to God, about whether humans can put God under obligation'; Natalie Zemon Davis, *The Gift in Sixteenth-Century France* (Madison, 2000), p. 100. Also see Heiko Oberman, 'Via Antiqua and Via Moderna: Late-Medieval Prologomena to Early Reformation Thought', *Journal of the History of Ideas*, 48:1 (1987), 23–40.

[95] Mariano D'Alatri, 'La religiosità popolare nella Cronaca di fra Salimbene', *Collectanea Franciscana*, 60:1–2 (1990), 175–90, at p. 190.

[96] The sense that the divine reward is tied to the individual's merits is quite clear, for instance, in the lines about Brother Jacopino; Scalia (ed.), *Cronica*, vol. 1, pp. 103–4.

illustrated in St Francis's hagiography, suggests that cultural attitudes did not simply mirror the dominant models but resulted from individuals' reworking of them. For example, a recent study of the origins of modernity asserts that Joachimism, a millenarist heresy, inhibited the individuals' confidence in their capacity for autonomous action that is the defining mark of modernity.[97] The evidence analysed here, however, suggests otherwise: while pursuing an ideal of individual agency that resonates with modern attitudes, Salimbene never completely abandoned his Joachite beliefs.[98] Any sense of a sharp dichotomy between individual and communitarian values dissolves as one attends to the complexity of Salimbene's position. He was attached to the Franciscan community, his home for half a century. Yet this did not inhibit a strong sense of his personal worth and impact upon the world, which he was eager to affirm through his writing. This was shaped in part by an urban culture in which individual values were increasingly affirmed and by developments within the Franciscan milieu. But these factors should not overshadow Salimbene's personal efforts at self-fashioning. He supported the so-called clericalisation of the Order during the thirteenth century, whereby Franciscans gained a firm status within the church hierarchy. But where he departed most significantly from St Francis's ideal of self-renunciation and humility it was not for the material reasons that animated the Order's aggrandising leaders, but for the sake of a model of individual autonomy inspired in part by Francis's own ethos of initiative but carried even further.

Franciscans' interest in the individual is sometimes portrayed as originating with luminaries like Ockham, whose path-breaking philosophical thought, it is suggested, helped usher the world into modernity. This focus on fourteenth-century Franciscan philosophy and its nominalist and individualist theses exemplifies a broader scholarly trend that privileges the influence of elite intellectuals at the expense of the cultural improvisations of more ordinary individuals.[99] Everyday manifestations of individual autonomy and agency, well-documented since at least the twelfth century, are largely neglected in

---

[97] Michael Allen Gillespie, *The Theological Origins of Modernity* (Chicago, 2008), p. 4.

[98] On his Joachimism, see Alison Williams Lewin, 'Salimbene de Adam and the Franciscan Chronicle', in Sharon Dale, Alison Williams Lewin, and Daniel J. Osheim (eds), *Chronicling History: Chroniclers and Historians in Medieval and Renaissance Italy* (University Park, PA, 2007), pp. 87–100, at pp. 91–9.

[99] As Roest points out, it 'is almost automatically assumed that the other members of the order would have shared the views' of the Franciscan regent masters; *Franciscan Education*, p. 189. On Ockham, see Louis Dumont, *Essays on Individualism: Modern Ideology in Anthropological Perspective* (Chicago, 1986), p. 63, and specifically on his idea of individual autonomy, see Takashi Shogimen, *Ockham and Political*

this approach.¹⁰⁰ Notwithstanding the originality of Salimbene's reworking of dominant cultural models and his literary culture, he remained an ordinary friar who was never part of the Order's hierarchy. He seems a better candidate than many a bishop or university master for informing us about thirteenth-century cultural practices. Case studies should not be generalised, but they can be suggestive. Salimbene's example points to a different trajectory for the Franciscans' defence of individual values, rooted in thirteenth-century contexts that owe little to nominalism and the debates among philosophers. As a suggestion for further research, following the example of Joel Kaye's exploration of the influence of economic trends on fourteenth-century natural philosophy,¹⁰¹ it might prove interesting to investigate what fourteenth-century Franciscan intellectuals who advocated individualist positions owe to the broader cultural climate to which Salimbene's memoirs bear witness.

Discourse in the Late Middle Ages (Cambridge, 2007), pp. 250–3. On Duns Scotus and his influence, see Roest, *Franciscan Education*, pp. 191–3.

[100] Gillespie, *Theological Origins*, pp. 26–9.

[101] Joel Kaye, *Economy and Nature in the Fourteenth Century* (Cambridge, 1998).

2

Lordship and Local Politics: The Cartulary of an Aristocratic Family

THE URBAN MILIEU OF MEN like Galbert and Salimbene has been the predilect focus of studies of 'the medieval individual', but the overwhelming majority of the medieval population lived in villages and farms. In part, this imbalance reflects the availability of evidence. The historical record is richer for the cities, which is in itself significant: the higher literacy levels and more intense social competition of the urban world are conducive to the development of a stronger sense of personal identity and effectiveness in the world. But the paucity of non-urban evidence should not be exaggerated. As discussed in the Introduction, the revival of the self-narrative among twelfth-century intellectuals was paralleled by the exponential growth and increased diversity of administrative, private, and even everyday records in the thirteenth century. Such documents open new perspectives on life in the lordships that dotted the medieval landscape. The early-medieval evidence is often limited to monastic cartularies – registers in which land deeds and records about an abbey's patrimony were compiled through a selection that left out the documents pertaining strictly to the lay world. For twelfth-century France a dossier that reaches the critical mass needed for studying an individual's social strategies – some twenty documents, perhaps – cannot normally be put together for men below the ranks of magnates.[1] By contrast, for the period 1190–1250, the lay cartulary at the centre of this chapter compiles close to two hundred deeds, homage charters, and notes covering two generations of lords of a seigneurie encompassing no more than a third of the county of Amiens in northern France; other records surviving independently of this register increase the documentary tally.[2] Much of this material concerns the relations between the head of the seigneurie and his aristocratic subjects, but

---

[1] Some sixty charters survive from the renowned viscountess of Narbonne; Frederic Cheyette, *Ermengard of Narbonne and the World of the Troubadours* (Ithaca, NY, 2001), p. 5.

[2] A small illustrative sample is edited and translated in Ionuț Epurescu-Pascovici, 'Local Politics, Social Networks, and Individual Agency in a Northern French

many of the latter, though styling themselves knights, were little more than village notables.³ Commoners also surface in the documentary record, some based in the town that developed near the lord's residence, the socioeconomic centre of the seigneurie.

Arguably the more significant reason why lay charters and cartularies were rarely explored in the study of individual agency and identity is that they were so heavily used for a different task: the study of local lordship. There is no good reason why the two should be competing rather than complementary research directions. The point, however, is that the study of the seigneuries, even more than medieval historiography in general, has privileged sociopolitical structures over human agency. The emphasis on feudal institutions in so much scholarship – a trend that has abated after the critiques of the last decades⁴ – is both cause and symptom of this historiographical state of affairs. The enduring appeal of feudal models reflects the structuring role with which medievalists have invested them.⁵ Unlike the social and critical theories of the last few decades, whose aim was to show that texts and contexts are more complicated than the positivist reader would expect, feudalism was meant to explain medieval society at the expense of local and chronological diversity and nuance. It aimed to provide medieval society with a basic social cell: the fief (*feudum*), a conditional possession, usually a landed estate, received and held by a vassal from an overlord in exchange for performing military and political service. The relatively early date – the Carolingian age – advanced for the genesis of feudal relations through the union of fief-holding and vassalic fidelity greatly

---

Seigneurie: Picquigny and Its Lords, c. 1190–1250', *Studies in Medieval and Renaissance History*, 3rd ser., 7 (2010), 53–166, at pp. 148–66.

³ Titles such as *dominus* or *miles* are mere approximations of one's economic and political position and were not used consistently in the thirteenth century; see the examples in Dominique Barthélemy, *Deux ages de la seigneurie banale: Coucy (XIe–XIIIe siècle)*, 2nd edn (Paris, 2000), p. 199; also see Susan Reynolds, *Fiefs and Vassals: The Medieval Evidence Reinterpreted* (Oxford, 1994), pp. 22–3, 32–4, 45, and Robert Fossier, *Hommes et villages d'Occident au Moyen Age* (Paris, 1992), p. 323.

⁴ Brown, 'The Tyranny of a Construct'; Alain Guerreau, *Le féodalisme: un horizon théorique* (Paris, 1980); Reynolds, *Fiefs and Vassals*.

⁵ Elizabeth M. Hallam and Judith Everard, *Capetian France, 987–1328*, 2nd edn (Harlow, 2001), p. 20; Chris Wickham, 'Le forme del feudalesimo', in *Il feudalesimo nell'alto medioevo* (Spoleto, 2000), pp. 15–52, at pp. 42–3; Jean-François Nieus, 'Avant-Propos', in Jean-François Nieus (ed.), *Le vassal, le fief et l'écrit: pratiques d'écriture et enjeux documentaries dans le champ de la féodalité (XIe–XVe siècle)* (Louvain-la-Neuve, 2007), pp. 5–9, at p. 5; Hélène Débax, *La féodalité languedocienne, XIe–XIIe siècles: Serments, hommages et fiefs dans le Languedoc des Trencavel* (Tolouse, 2003), p. 182.

facilitated the structuring role they were called on to play in histories of the Middle Ages. Local governance and lordship in the eleventh to the thirteenth centuries could be explained in terms of a sociopolitical system with a few hundred years of history behind it – a strong structural factor if there ever was one. Within this timeframe historical change was also viewed as largely structural, a function of the system's capacity to reproduce itself and generate mutations in the nature of feudal society. Rarely was a historiographical subfield more interested in norms and institutions at the expense of human agents and their strategies. The whole point was to explicate the functioning of a system: the focus was on the quasi-autonomous operation of feudal institutions, not on the social interactions and strategies through which fiefs and vassalage were negotiated and transformed. The technical norms governing tenure in fief were frequently seen as more important than the meaning with which they were invested by individuals pursuing competing goals. Within this paradigm human agency was marginalised by design. The exception was the leading political actors, the counts and princes, whose initiative and planning, though more rarely negotiation with social subalterns, were emphasised. In France, a historiographical trend evolved positing the historical region and county as the proper unit of analysis in the study of lordship,[6] thereby reinforcing the emphasis on both the ruling elite and power structures such as norms and institutions. Only in recent decades, after microhistory emerged as a vital research direction, the shift towards a more focused level of analysis, the castellany and the seigneurie, brought about increased attention to individuals' role in relation to social structures,[7] although even the recent studies have not taken advantage of the insights of practice theory. More generally, when medievalists turned to social theory and anthropology, not in direct connection to fiefs and vassals but to related issues such as dispute resolution, the models

---

[6] Notably Georges Duby, *La société aux XIe et XIIe siècle dans la region mâconnaise* (Paris, 1953) and Dominique Barthélemy, *La société dans le comté de Vendôme, de l'an mil au XIVe siècle* (Paris, 1993).

[7] E.g., Pascale Verdier, 'La construction d'une seigneurie dans la Champagne du XI-IIe siècle: Renier Acorre, seigneur de Gouaix (1257–1289)', in *Seigneurs et seigneuries au Moyen Age* (Paris, 1993), pp. 99–110; Dominique Barthélemy, *Deux ages de la seigneurie banale: Coucy (XIe–XIIIe siècle)*, 2nd edn (Paris, 2000); Annie Renoux, 'Aux sources du pouvoir châtelain de Geoffroi "seigneur de Mayenne, le plus fort homme du Maine" (c. 1040–1098)', in Dominique Barthélemy and Olivier Bruand (eds), *Les pouvoirs locaux dans la France du centre et de l'ouest (VIIIe–XIe siècles): Implantation et moyens d'action* (Rennes, 2004), pp. 61–89; Elizabeth Haluska-Rausch, 'Transformations in the Powers of Wives and Widows near Montpellier, 985–1213', in Robert F. Berkhofer III, Alan Cooper, and Adam J. Kosto (eds), *The Experience of Power in Medieval Europe* (Aldershot, 2005), pp. 153–68.

on which they settled made only marginally more room for human agency, because they focused less on practices and strategies and more on the norms structuring social interactions.

Because the local politics and networks on which much of this chapter dwells were framed by the prominent seigneurie of the western Amiénois area, this chapter engages not only with the historiography of 'the individual in the Middle Ages' but also with that of medieval lordship. In particular, the chapter explores how foregrounding agency can advance the study of medieval lordship in the aftermath of the critique of the feudal paradigm. The sociopolitical life of the seigneurie of Picquigny is examined during a span of sixty years when it was ruled by two individuals, father and son: Enguerran (1192–1224) and Gérard III (1224–1248/9) (see Figure 1). Their ruling styles shared common features but differed in significant respects; comparing the two evinces both the role of individuals in shaping their world and the influence of structural factors.[8] Close attention is also paid to the agency of social partners and competitors – a task that involves examining many minute interactions.

The lordship of Picquigny, first attested in the first half of the eleventh century, was located in western Amiénois and by 1190 occupied a territory south of the Somme roughly between the rivers Selle and Saint-Landon, extending north of the Somme into the Vicogne region (Map 1). Its lord was the *vidame* or *vicedominus* of Amiens, a position that purports to designate him as the bishop's secular arm, obliged to represent the bishop in his dealings with the secular powers and generally to protect the church of Amiens. However, at the beginning of the thirteenth century the *vidame*'s office carried no real duties.[9] In the half century following the annexation of the county of Amiens to the royal domain (1186), with the royal power slow to consolidate in the region, the *vidame*'s power in the Amiénois was rivalled only by that of the bishop, although the castellan of Amiens also remained a force to be reckoned with. In the royal lists of military service, the *vidame* was placed in an intermediary category, *Barones*, below counts and above castellans.[10] In addition to the

---

[8] For a similar approach, see Simon Walker, *Political Culture in Later Medieval England*, ed. Michael J. Braddick (Manchester, 2006), pp. 39–67.

[9] Chantal de Tourtier, 'Les seigneurs de Picquigny, vidames d'Amiens et leur famille: des origines la fin du XIVe siècle', *Positions des theses, École nationale des chartes* (1954), 135–8, at p. 137; Felix Senn, *L'institution des vidamies en France* (Paris, 1907), pp. 119–55.

[10] Leopold Delisle (ed.), *Recueil des historiens des Gaules et de la France* (24 vols, Paris, 1869–1904), vol. 23, p. 683. Similarly, in a charter of the countess of Boulogne, Gérard of Picquigny, who stood surety for her, is listed third, preceded only by the counts of Saint-Pol and Ponthieu; Alexandre Teulet (ed.), *Layettes du Trésor des*

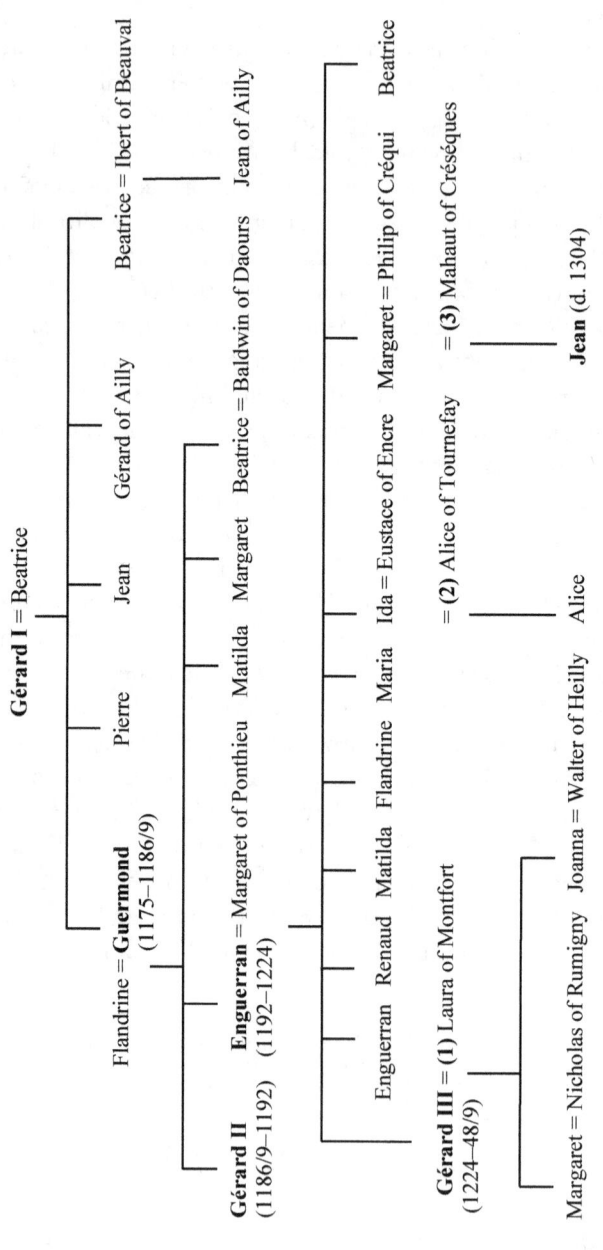

Figure 1. The Picquigny family, c. 1180–1250

family's landed estates in western Amiénois, an important source of revenue were the customs taxes on the river Somme trade at the toll 'of the bridge of Picquigny',[11] while the *pesage* and *sesterage*, tolls and measuring dues, were collected by the *vidame* at Amiens. Besides the castle of Picquigny, the *vidame* held several smaller fortifications in key points of western Amiénois. The *vidame* and his lord, the bishop, generally cooperated on matters of mutual interest.[12] The cartulary includes a letter sent by the bishop to King Philip II asking him not to collect the revenues of the church of Amiens while the episcopal seat was vacant but to let the *vidame* do it. The letter alluded to the normative framework, which had been intended to make of the *vidame* the protector of the church's patrimony.[13] Philip gave his agreement in 1208;[14] the episode is an instance of local cooperation against a royal government that was not fully accepted in the Amiénois two decades after the annexation. The potential for disputes between bishop and *vidame*, however, remained very real because they were the largest landowners in western Amiénois and moreover the church sought to wrest back from secular lords the tithes it had lost to them in the last two centuries.[15]

The source of most of our information, the cartulary of Picquigny, underwent two redactions, of which the first, c. 1250, is of interest here. With the exception of a few earlier records, it consists of material pertaining to the rule of Enguerran and Gérard III. The context for this first redaction is the

---

Chartes (2 vols, Paris, 1863–6), vol. 2, pp. 281–2. This position was shared with, e.g., the ambitious lord of Coucy, who sought elevation to the rank of count; Barthélemy, *Deux ages*, pp. 413–16.

[11] Chantal de Tourtier, 'Le péage de Picquigny au Moyen Age', *Bulletin philologique et historique*, 1 (1960), 271–94.

[12] Enguerran submitted a homage charter to the bishop in 1218; Victor de Beauvillé (ed.), *Recueil de documents inédits concernant la Picardie* (4 vols, Paris, 1860–81), vol. 4, pp. 40–1.

[13] 'vices domini debeat agere bona episcopi conseruando seu non dissipando'; Paris, AN, MS R^1 672 (Cartulary of Picquigny), fol. 2v.

[14] Amiens, ADS, MS 3 G 405. Philip turned down a similar request by the *vidame* of Châlons (1203), who had reportedly availed himself of an old custom to plunder the goods of his deceased bishop; John W. Baldwin, *The Government of Philip Augustus: Foundations of French Royal Power in the Middle Ages* (Berkeley, 1986), p. 161; Bernard Guillemain, 'Philippe Auguste et l'épiscopat', in Robert-Henri Bautier (ed.), *La France de Philippe Auguste: Le temps des mutations* (Paris, 1982), pp. 365–84, at p. 374.

[15] In the 1170s Enguerran's grandfather had to compensate the church of Amiens at the end of a long and bitter conflict; J. Roux (ed.), *Cartulaire du chapitre de la cathédrale d'Amiens* (2 vols, Amiens, 1905–12), vol. 1, pp. 75–6.

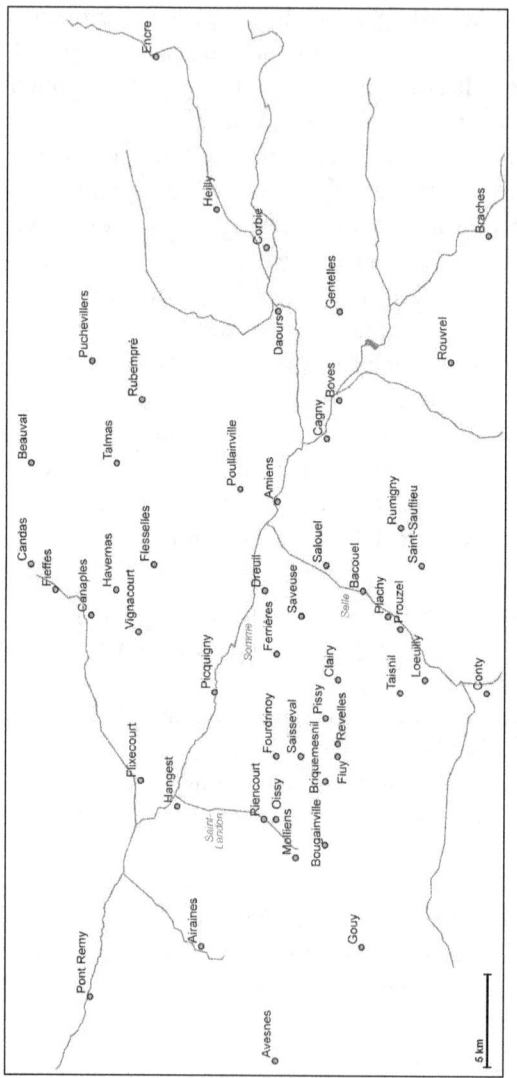

Map 1. Western Amiénois and the seigneurie of Picquigny, c. 1180–1250

aftermath of Gérard's death, when the seigneurie was administered on behalf of his underage son by tutors who would have found a complete record of the *vidame*'s rights and claims instrumental in their task. To this end the services of a specialist scribe were enlisted.[16] Half a century later material pertaining to the rule of Gérard's son Jean was added to the cartulary in a second redaction; later still, the occasional document would be copied on the folios left blank by the two main redactions. The largest section of the first redaction of the cartulary compiles the written recognitions of the *vidame*'s preeminence submitted by the local aristocrats. While the details and specific wording of each charter vary, in essence the local aristocrat acknowledged the *vidame* as lord, often declaring himself his man (*homo*); this subordinate status was expressed through one of two technical terms, *lizanchia* or *hominium*, reflecting the medieval vocabulary of allegiance and homage, but deployed in specific ways at Picquigny. What exactly was entailed in the recognition of the *vidame*'s superior status has to be reconstructed in the specific context – it cannot be deduced from a putative standard medieval practice because for centuries oaths of homage had been used in very different ways. In the Carolingian and post-Carolingian era homage emerged as a key practice for structuring the relations between members of the political elite and between them and their social subalterns. Part of its success as a social form stemmed from its malleability: oaths of homage and allegiance were often demanded of social subordinates, but could also be used to cement an alliance between aristocrats who were essentially social peers.[17] The specific usage to which homage was put in the Amiénois c. 1200 is inextricably linked to the locally prominent practice of castle guard service: with a few exceptions, the homage charters submitted by the local aristocrats included the provision that they could be summoned to Picquigny for castle guard. Other material copied in the cartulary pertains to rights of jurisdiction, various arrangements with local aristocrats, and the occasional disputes and the agreements that ended them. Furthermore, whereas alienations of property were merely summarised in a few words, the

[16] 'hic incipiunt rubrice cartarum Pinconii quas Quintinus cumpilauit'; Paris, AN, MS R^1 672, fol. 40r. Quintinus had more cartulary work to his credit; see Jean-François Nieus, 'Les quatre travaux de maître Quentin (1250–1276): cartulaires de Picquigny et d'Audenarde, *Veil rentier* d'Audenarde et *Terrier l'évêque* de Cambrai. Des écrits d'exception pour un clerc seigneurial hors normes?', *Journal des Savants* (2012), 69–119, at pp. 71–81, and '"Et hoc per meas litteras significo": Les débuts de la diplomatique féodale dans le nord de la France (fin XIIe–milieu XIIIe siècle)', *Cahiers de civilisation médiévale*, 58 (2015), 43–64.

[17] See Paul R. Hyams, 'Homage and Feudalism: A Judicious Separation', in Natalie Fryde, Pierre Monnet, and Otto Gerhard Oexle (eds), *Die Gegenwart des Feudalismus* (Göttingen, 2002), pp. 13–49.

documents concerning acquisitions of land and land-rents were copied with particular care; one section of the cartulary consists of sale deeds confirmed by the chapter of the cathedral of Amiens, as a precaution against possible challenges by the seller's family.[18] These records bring up the agency of professional administrators. The successful transfer of a piece of property depended on the *vidame*'s aides drafting a clear – and ideally unassailable – charter.[19] The seller's wife's approval was sought and recorded in detail. Because it was not always clear what constituted the wife's dower, the aides aimed to eliminate possible grounds for future challenges by explicitly stating that the wife was compensated with land or revenues oftentimes identified with precision,[20] although in many cases such compensation would have been only nominal.

Approaching medieval charters as ego-documents might seem to stretch the boundaries of the concept. True, after a period in the eleventh century when a charter's prologue occasionally narrated a story as background for the subsequent dispositive clauses, charters became terse and formulaic, a sign of documentary professionalisation. This notwithstanding, charters are the 'ego-document' par excellence, inasmuch as most of them begin with a statement in the first-person singular, such as 'Notum sit quod *Ego* donaui…' (*Ego* is occasionally capitalised in the middle of a sentence, a visual clue that underscored the lord's agency). Charters might offer little insight into the individual's inner thoughts,[21] but they tell us a great deal about the individual's social persona and role as social agent – the subjects at the centre of this book. Although not written by them, charters reflected the views and expressed the

---

[18] *Emptiones ab ecclesiastica curia confirmate*; Paris, AN, MS R^1 672, fol. 40r.

[19] See Richard Britnell, 'Pragmatic Literacy', in Richard Britnell (ed.), *Pragmatic Literacy: East and West, 1200–1330* (Woodbridge, 1997), pp. 3–25, at p. 4.

[20] At Picquigny it is difficult to distinguish between two possible meanings of *dotalicium*: the husband's marriage gift to the wife (*donatio propter nuptias*) and the 'property to which a widow is entitled at the death of her husband', which often included both the dowry and the marriage gift; see Régine Le Jan-Hennebicque, 'Aux origines du douaire medieval (VIe–Xe siècle)', in Michel Parisse (ed.), *Veuves et veuvage dans le haut Moyen Age* (Paris, 1993), pp. 107–22; Laurent Feller, '*Morgengabe*, dot, *tertia*: rapport introductif', in François Bougard, Laurent Feller, and Régine Le Jan (eds), *Dots et douaires dans le haut Moyen Age* (Rome, 2002), pp. 1–25; Paul Ourliac, 'Législation, coutumes et coutumiers au temps de Philippe Auguste', in Robert-Henri Bautier (ed.), *La France de Philippe Auguste: Le Temps des Mutations* (Paris, 1982), pp. 471–87, at p. 475; Jack Goody, *The European Family: An Historico-Anthropological Essay* (Oxford, 2000), pp. 86–9, 187.

[21] But see Geoffrey Koziol, 'Is Robert I in Hell?', *Early Medieval Europe*, 14 (2006), 233–68, for a notable exception.

interests of the people on whose behalf they were drafted,[22] and who by the thirteenth century possessed the rudiments of literacy.[23] As discussed in the Introduction, Ricouer's and Taylor's models of reading strategic action – of the kind outlined in charters, say, about building a mill or having an aristocrat perform homage – as a text or language analogue of meaningful behaviour are particularly helpful here. This is because in a very real sense, a charter is not merely the account of a transfer of property but also a crucial element of the transfer itself. Because they were fully embedded in the stream of action – unlike narrative sources written years after the events – charters open a unique window into the individual agent's motivations and attitudes.

This chapter begins with a picture of the relations between the aristocracy and the *vidame*, built from the local sources rather than a priori notions about feudal relations and lordship. The analysis then turns to the management of the resources of the seigneurie, a fundamental dimension of agency in medieval society, because considerable time and effort went into consolidating property and revenues with the help of administrators and supporters that needed to be cultivated. Notwithstanding the continuities and similarities between Enguerran and Gérard, they exemplify different patterns of ruling a seigneurie, precisely because of their respective ways of building social ties.

Local governance and relations with the Amiénois aristocracy

That so much of the material compiled in the cartulary pertains to relations between higher and lower aristocrats suggests their importance in the eyes of the protagonists. These relations were circumscribed by a local political framework, but notwithstanding its normative role in structuring social interactions, it remained relatively fluid and was shaped by the designs of the lord of Picquigny and the negotiations with the local aristocracy. A keen recognition of individuals' agency was required to maintain the balance of power in the Amiénois.

A comprehensive picture of the aristocracy from the orbit of the seigneurie of Picquigny is provided by the lists of castle guard or *estages*. The earliest, known by its modern title the *Livre des stages*, is a roll of parchment consisting of three pieces sewn together; based on internal evidence it can be dated to

---

[22] This issue is problematised in an earlier, eleventh-century context by Brigitte Miriam Bedos-Rezak, *When Ego Was Imago: Signs of Identity in the Middle Ages* (Leiden, 2011), pp. 134–7.

[23] See Michael Clanchy, *From Memory to Written Record: England 1066–1307* (Oxford, 1993).

or shortly after 1192, the year when Enguerran took over.[24] The list is divided into four sections: castle guard (*staciones*) at Picquigny, at Ailly-sur-Somme, and at Clairy-Saulchoix, and service without guard (*seruiciis sine stacione*; see Table 1). The typical entry lists the name, length of service, type of homage owed, liege or plain, and sometimes the main lands of the *vidame*'s man. The two subsequent sets of homage charters have been compiled in the cartulary of Picquigny (beginning on fol. 57r; see Plate 1).[25] The first set of charters was produced between June and October 1223, towards the end of Enguerran's life. Thirty-two people recognised the homage and service they owed and many are said to have affixed their seals to the charters; five more did so at different times during Enguerran's life. The second set, of fifteen charters,[26] was produced between March and July 1244, under Gérard's rule; eleven other aristocrats submitted homage charters at different moments between 1229 and January 1250. The difference in numbers between the roll of *estages* and the sets of homage charters are in part the result of different methodologies and in part reflect changes in the function of castle guard.

At first glance, the terse list of guard service and the slightly more detailed homage charters seem hopeless for studying the individual perspective on society and sense of agency. Closer examination, however, opens a fascinating window into the sociopolitical imaginary that informed the protagonists' strategic decisions. The caveat is that we cannot ascertain the extent to which the *vidames*' views on the social and political stage of the Amiénois were shaped by their aides. To begin with, a vision of territorial hegemony underlies the texts that formed the normative basis of the lord of Picquigny's relations with the local aristocracy. The *vidame* insisted that within the territory under his control those with substantial lands or land-rents had to recognise his lordship and, at least nominally, a duty to perform certain services. This was typically done through homage, which often included the obligation to perform some armed service. This is interesting because Picquigny was not a political unit with a history going back to the Carolingian age, like many French counties; rather, it was a seigneurie carved out relatively recently by an ambitious family. The clearest expression of this vision of territorial lordship comes from outside lords who owed homage to the *vidame* for property that is specifically described as held by them in western Amiénois. A few examples are

---

[24] Paris, AN, R^1 675, dossier 1; on the dating, see Epurescu-Pascovici, 'Picquigny and Its Lords', p. 62 n. 22.

[25] Paris, AN, MS R^1 672, fols 40v–41v; 57r–63v. A third list was drawn up in 1279; ibid., fols 72v–85.

[26] Plus one person who owed homage but did not submit a charter.

Table 1. Armed service in the seigneurie of Picquigny: 1) *Livre des stages*; 2) homage charters issued for Enguerran (1210–24); 3) homage charters issued for Gérard (1229–50); 4) charters with no date (y.= year; m.= month)

	Armed service in the seigneurie of Picquigny									Total
	Castle guard							Other armed service	Homage, no service	
	Picquigny				Ailly		Clairy			
	1y.	3–7 m.	1–2 m.	other	9 m.–1y.	1–2 m.	1–2 m.			
1) 1192–7	28	12	13	5	4	6	4	14	31	117
2) 1210			2							37
1220								1		
1223	15	5	7			2	1	2		
1224	1			1						
3) 1244	4	4	4		2				2	27
1229–50	3		3						5	
4) No date				1		1				2

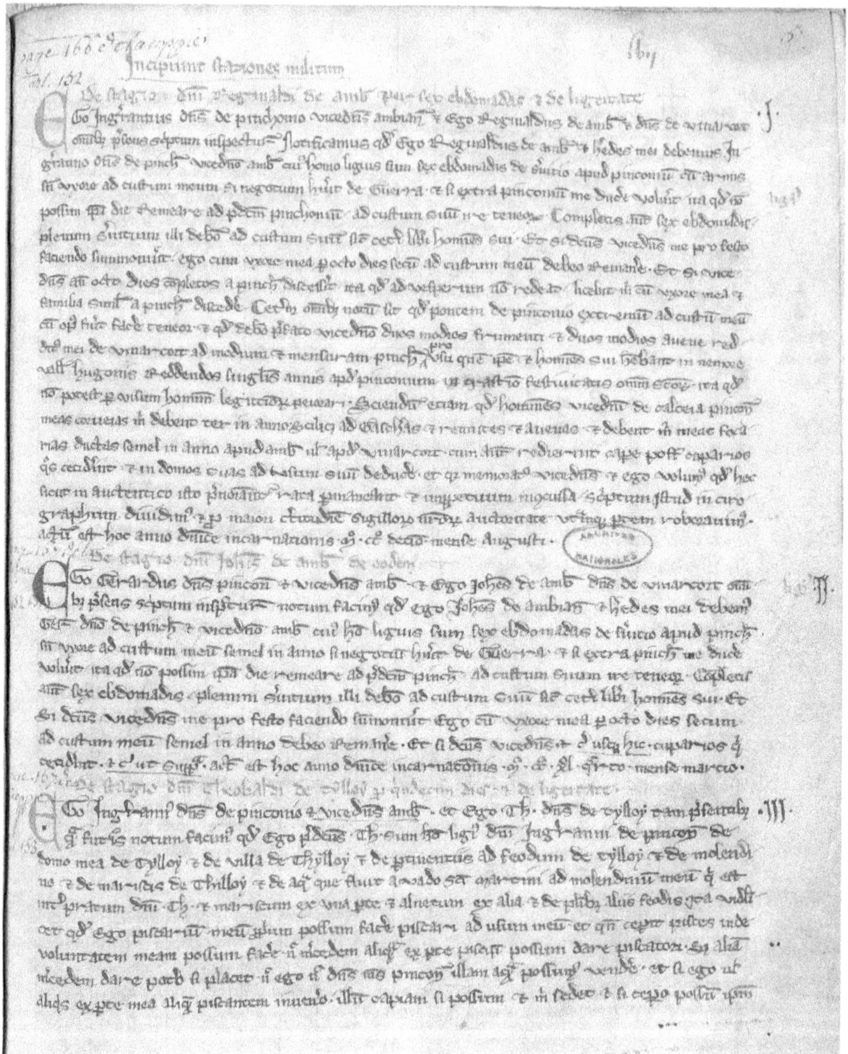

Plate 1. Cartulary of Picquigny: 'Incipiunt staciones militum'. Reproduced by permission of AN, Paris (MS R^1 672, fol. 57r).

illustrative. The lord of Fouilloy in eastern Amiénois had close ties to the abbey of Corbie, which it recognised as lord,[27] but because he held part of a tithe at Ailly (a mile up the Somme from the town of Picquigny), he was listed on the roll of *estages* with one month of service; his name was crossed out when the *vidame*'s aides decided it was unrealistic to demand it, when they did not even know the name of the current lord of Fouilloy. In other cases, the border of the seigneurie of Picquigny was defined with remarkable precision. Robert of Orville (northern Amiénois) is recorded in the roll of *estages* to have performed homage together with his son. It is significant that Robert did homage for specific lands, 'that part of Beauquesne that is in Vicogne and the two measures of land possessed in the same Vicogne'.[28] This statement makes clear that Robert entered into a relation of subordination to the *vidame* because he had land in an area – Vicogne – that fell under the latter's lordship. Orville, Robert's patrimonial land, was north of the perceived border of the seigneurie of Picquigny. Similarly, renewing the terms of his father's homage, Baldwin of Beauval specified which of his lands were under the *vidame*'s authority (1234). Among them were Baldwin's possessions in Vicogne as well as his residence at Beauval. Beauval itself was included up to the well in the middle of the villa and to the church tower. The implication is that the rest of the village was outside the lordship of Picquigny, along with Baldwin's lands north of Vicogne.[29] Although smaller than even the smallest counties, the seigneurie of Picquigny could be described as a 'land' – Robert of Orville promised to serve the *vidame* 'in terra sua' – incorporating not just the town of Picquigny but the whole territory controlled by the *vidame*. This view of Picquigny as a larger territorial unit is expressed in a charter exempting the men of the *vidame*'s land, 'homines de terra sua', from a toll tax in Picardy[30] – a case that illustrates how the collective identity of the denizens of western Amiénois came to be tied to the *vidame*'s political construction. The language of lordship was far

---

[27] Paris, BN, Fonds latin, MS 17758, fol. 180r.

[28] 'de illa parte de Belcaisne que est in Viconia et de duabus carrugatis terre in eadem Viconia possessis'.

[29] Paris, AN, MS R¹ 672, fol. 63r. Similarly, in the *Livre des stages* the lord of Heilly in eastern Amiénois owed homage on account of his ancestress's dowry near the river Selle ('de matrimonio Gile auie sue quod est in riuo Salaia'); Paris, AN, R¹ 675, dossier 1; and see William M. Newmann, *Le personnel de la cathédrale d'Amiens* (Paris, 1972), pp. 44–5. In 1248 the lord of Mailly in north-eastern Amiénois owed 'plain houmage et plain seruice' on account of a land-rent purchased at Beauval; Paris, AN, MS R¹ 672, fol. 62r. See below for the duties imposed on outsiders who recently acquired land in the seigneurie of Picquigny.

[30] Paris, AN, MS R¹ 672, fol. 52v.

from standardised at the end of the twelfth century: referring to Enguerran's donations throughout the seigneurie in a charter drafted on his behalf, the vice-prior of the abbey of Gard wrote 'in omne *potestate* mea',[31] literally 'in all my *power*', possibly reflecting the medieval French *poesté*, of which one attested meaning is lordship. Modern historians face their own terminological predicament. No single label fits the the aristocracy of the *estages* perfectly: not exactly subjects, because Picquigny was a small lordship without a long history as a political–territorial entity; not truly followers, because many found themselves in the orbit of Picquigny but were not too keen about the *vidame*'s hegemony and kept merely nominal ties, such as the submission of a homage charter.

The political geography enshrined symbolically in the *Livre des stages* was apt to reinforce the *vidame*'s territorial hegemony. A sense of centre and periphery is clearly discernible in the list of castle guard. The lords of villages around Picquigny and the strategically important valley of the Selle were on call for castle guard for the full year – men like the lords of Belloy, Crouy, Dreuil-lès-Amiens, Ferriéres, Fluy, Oissy, Saisseval, Salouel, Taisnil, and the castellan of Picquigny. Those whose lands were farther away from the perceived centre of the seigneurie of Picquigny owed considerably less service, generally only a few months. Because the length of service had become largely nominal this geography was largely symbolic, but it shaped political identities. How the *vidame* and his aides viewed the strategic map of western Amiénois can be gauged from the structure of the list of *estages*, which opens with Enguerran of Saint-Sauflieu, followed by Walter the castellan of Picquigny and Pierre the lord of Vignacourt and castellan of Amiens: two of the *vidame*'s closest supporters and his most powerful lay rival. It should also be pointed out that the length of castle guard generally correlates with the size of one's estates. This trend is not absolute, because the lord of Picquigny could not impose his terms on the local aristocracy but negotiated them. One case is illustrative. In 1223, Pierre of Dreuil owed one year of castle guard at Picquigny, because he had inherited an entire half of Dreuil-lès-Amiens. But Pierre Quartier and Dreux of Dreuil, who only had some land in the village, owed just two months each. Pierre's younger brother, who did not inherit any of the patrimonial lands at Dreuil and had to settle for land at Briquemesnil, was not even selected to be at Picquigny with the *vidame*'s leading men but merely owed *residentiam continuam* at Molliens-Vidame.[32]

Lastly, it is worth asking what the whole point of castle guard was. Guard service, sometimes prescribed for one year, would have actually been performed

---

[31] Amiens, ADS, MS 13 H 4, vol. 2, fols 420–1.

[32] Paris, AN, MS R^1 672, fols 58v–59v.

only at the *vidame*'s express request and presumably for shorter terms, as stated in the *Livre des stages*: 'Let it be known to those present and future that all those written above must do castle-guard annually at Picquigny [or Ailly and Clairy] *when ordered by the vidame*'.³³ The roll of *estages* does not give the name of each of the *vidame*'s men; in twelve cases the person is simply identified as someone's heir – clearly some of the homages had not been renewed for some time. Furthermore, with one notable exception, the text does not mention the actual performance of homage. This suggests that the list was a compilation of past custom, drawn from older records or verbal agreements. It reflected older practices, from a period when a viscount's or castellan's knights lived in his castle; in the twelfth century, six-month or even one-year terms of service might have made sense. But to Enguerran when he took over as lord of Picquigny, the list provided an overall assessment of the aristocratic ties that could potentially be mobilised in support of his designs (more on this in the next section). Of course, in late-twelfth-century Amiénois there were good reasons to maintain an armed force ready for action. The charters also mention service with one or more armed men in the case of higher lords, and the *Livre des stages* includes a fourth section, 'Service without guard', consisting of fourteen men assigned to 'service with horse' or 'knightly service'. These men would have been needed to defend Picquigny; memory of 1186, when Philip II and the count of Flanders took their armies to Amiens before signing a treaty there, would have inspired prudence.³⁴ The *vidame*'s territorial hegemony entailed an obligation to protect the locals by rallying the local knights under his banner.

By the time of the homages of 1223, however, the main purpose of castle guard was clearly social and symbolic, reinforcing the political function of homage as the acknowledgement of the *vidame*'s lordship. This is reflected in the homage charters of Hugo of Beauval and Renaud of Amiens in 1210.³⁵ Hugo's charter stressed the symbolic importance of having the lord of Beauval at the castle of Picquigny by requiring him to send no fewer than five knights if he could not come himself. He was also expected to bring his wife to Picquigny, but could send her home if the *vidame* needed his services and bring three other knights to assist him – here, military service is mentioned as a

---

33 'notum sit tam presentibus quam futuris quod omnes supra scripti annuatim proprias staciones *ad iussionem vicedomini* debent facere apud Pinconium' (emphasis added); Paris, AN, R¹ 675, dossier 1.

34 Robert Fawtier, *The Capetian Kings of France*, trans. Lionel Butler and R. J. Adam (New York, 1960), pp. 112–13.

35 Paris, AN, MS R¹ 672, fols 57r–57v.

mere contingency. The charters of 1223 similarly required the wife's presence at Picquigny – a clause that was not in the roll of *estages*. Armed service was not abandoned in 1223 and armed conflict was still present in the aristocrats' imagination: in 1238 the lord of Saint-Sauflieu envisaged the possibility of an attack against his residence.[36] But the obligation to bring along one's wife indicates an emphasis on socialising.[37] The members of the aristocracy were expected to interact with the *vidame* and with each other in a manner that evokes the courtly society. The clearest expression of this fact comes from Renaud of Amiens's homage charter, prescribing in addition to armed service eight days of presence at Picquigny with his wife when summoned to the *vidame*'s banquet, *pro festo faciendo*. Enguerran intended to rescue some of the conviviality of the twelfth century by adjusting it to the new social realities. The new castle guard was a means of reinforcing the social bonds between the *vidame* and his men and symbolically asserting his preeminence.[38] Similar but much larger lists survive from twelfth- and thirteenth-century Champagne,[39] but the direct inspiration for the *estages* of Picquigny might well have been Flemish – and quite possibly also in regard to the insistence that lords be accompanied by their wives: at least one aristocrat is known to have performed castle guard for the count of Flanders in Picardy accompanied by his wife, before the treaty of 1186.[40]

Quite how successful the courtly society of Picquigny turned out cannot be gauged from the charter evidence; we are more fortunate, however, in the case of the *vidames*' other strategy for tightening their grip on the local aristocracy: better records and more rigorous administration. The 1192 list of castle

[36] 'si contingat guerram moveri versus villam de Sessollieu'; Roux (ed.), *Cartulaire de chapitre*, p. 333.

[37] It remains unclear what games, if any, were held on 'the day of jousting' ('in die hastiludii': a common name for the first Sunday of Lent) mentioned in a couple of charters; Paris, AN, MS R¹ 672, fols 6v, 57v, 4v; Pierre-Nicolas Grenier, *Introduction à l'histoire générale de la province de Picardie*, ed. Ch. Dufour and J. Garnier (Amiens, 1856), pp. 108–9.

[38] See Robert Fossier, *La terre et les hommes en Picardie jusqu'à la fin du XIIIe siècle* (2 vols, Paris, 1968), vol. 1, pp. 669–71.

[39] Theodore Evergates, *Feudal Society in the Baillage of Troyes under the Counts of Champagne, 1152–1284* (Baltimore, 1975), pp. 11–12.

[40] 'Domina Margarita dixit quod fecit estagium cum domino suo'; 'Guerricus de Fillcines ... vidit dominum Jobertum de Firmitate et Margaritam uxorem suam que adhuc vivit facere estagium ad Ribemontem'; John W. Baldwin (ed.), *Les registres de Philippe Auguste* (Paris, 1992), vol. 1, pp. 81–2. Also see Olivier Guyotjeannin, 'French Manuscript Sources, 1250–1330', in Richard Britnell (ed.), *Pragmatic Literacy: East and West, 1200–1330* (Woodbridge, 1997), pp. 51–71, at pp. 54–5.

guard, the series of homage charters of 1223 and 1244, and the first draft of the Picquigny cartulary c. 1250 were the work of professional administrators retained by the *vidame*, sometimes at significant cost. Occasionally bearing the title of *magister*, they had more to offer than record-keeping skills: in particular, they were trained to work out the complexities of land-holding and lordship in more rigorous ways, and proved instrumental in the dissemination in Picardy of new ideas and practices regarding land ownership and its place in the relations between higher and lower lords, inspired in part by Italian developments in academic law from the early twelfth century.[41] Until recently these developments have been seen as emblematic of the feudal relations allegedly underpinning medieval society. Just what 'feudalism' refers to has been notoriously difficult to agree on, which has not helped to focus the debate: the proponents of a given paradigm could plead exception, arguing that the critique did not apply to their, 'true', version of feudal relations. Briefly, feudalism is sometimes evoked in historical accounts in a general, Marxist sense, to designate a largely agricultural society of non-salaried labour and land-based elites.[42] Many societies, not just the West c. 800–1400, fit this description. Another usage of the term, as a synonym for political anarchy and a weak state, also quite general in principle, nevertheless tends to occur more frequently in descriptions of the post-Carolingian period, as in the 'feudal anarchy' of the tenth and eleventh centuries. Most often, however, medievalists deal with a more specific feudal model, known as feudal–vassalic because it places at its centre the union of fief and vassalage (usually dated to the Carolingian period), whereby the relation between a higher lord and his followers (vassals) was given a material basis, the fief (*feudum*), a piece of land held on condition of performing service. On this view the dyadic relation formed between lord and vassal on the basis of the fief becomes the underlying structure of medieval society.[43] There is some hesitation in defining this relationship as either affective or legalistic, or somehow both. But because it is more precise, this model is more easily falsifiable: much of it hinges on whether *feudum* was used consistently with the meaning of conditional possession and whether relations between higher and lower lords changed substantively because of the introduction of tenure in fief. Lastly, a recent and geographically limited

---

[41] Reynolds, *Fiefs and Vassals*, esp. pp. 258–9, 265.
[42] Wickham, 'Forme del feudalesimo', pp. 29–34.
[43] The classic view is François-Louis Ganshof, *Feudalism*, trans. Ph. Grierson, repr. (Toronto, 1996), pp. 65–155.

variation bears the label 'feudalism without the fief'.[44] Even more so than the standard feudal–vassalic model, this approach deals with relations among the elites rather than between lower-rung lords and the peasants who worked their lands.

It is striking that three of the four versions of feudalism retain in their name the medieval notion of *feudum* while abandoning it in substance (openly so in the recent 'feudalism without the fief'). Beyond this contradiction and the confusion sown by the different feudalisms, the crucial issue is that these labels fail to describe the realities to which they are affixed. If the point is to contrast, in the most general terms, the modern capitalist state with an agricultural society of landed aristocrats and weak institutions, why not use this concise and fairly accurate characterisation of Europe c. 900–1200? The argument for maintaining the feudal label out of deference to a tradition of scholarship – be it Marxism or the previous generation of medievalists – is untenable. Respect for an intellectual tradition – a reasonable proposition – means carrying forward its spirit while revising its notions in step with the progress of knowledge. The embrace of feudalism, particularly after Susan Reynolds's critique grounded in a thorough reading of the medieval sources has questioned the core of this model, the role of fiefs and vassalage up to 1300,[45] speaks of a desire for a unifying model, no matter its flaws and inconsistencies. Approaching medieval society through the feudal lens is fundamentally different from trying to make sense of the sources in local contexts with the aid of the heuristic models that the evidence itself calls for – which is what testing modern social scientific models against the medieval sources is all about. (Ironically, a defence of Marxist feudalism that draws inspiration from the social sciences misses the fundamental fact that a definition applicable to most of the societies between the Roman Empire and the modern capitalist state does not have any real heuristic force: vague and general, it cannot guide research into specific contexts.[46]) Ultimately, however, the crucial difference between the various feudal paradigms and the present study is that the former see feudal–vassalic relations as an *explanans*, a known quantity that can explain other historical realities, whereas here they are approached as an *explanandum*, a social form whose coming into being – albeit later and with lesser consequences than

---

[44] Hélène Débax, 'L'Aristocratie languedocienne et la société féodale: Le témoignage des sources (Midi de la France: XIe et XIIe siècles)', in Sverre Bagge, Michael H. Gelting, and Thomas Lindkvist (eds), *Feudalism: New Landscapes of Debate* (Turnhout, 2011), pp. 77–100.

[45] Reynolds, *Fiefs and Vassals*.

[46] Wickham, 'Forme del feudalesimo', pp. 35–6, 46.

generally believed – needs to be elucidated by studying the motives and strategies of the individuals that implemented it. This is important to bear in mind in the case of the recent 'feudalism without fief', which gestures towards the social sciences with its redefinition of the fief not as an estate but as the relationship that landed property enables between individuals.[47] This perspective is more self-serving than analytical: for one thing, it is tailored to suit the evidence of southern France, where references to fiefs are rare. Most importantly, while the redefinition of the fief in relational terms calls for a methodological approach inspired by the social sciences – network analysis, for example[48] – this is by no means the step taken by 'the feudalism without fief' position, which instead falls back on a normative notion of vassalage.[49] The effort speaks to the allure of feudal models for medievalists in search of unifying explanations: more troubling than the failure to reconstruct the specific meaning of *feudum* in varying contexts is the commitment to show some kind of feudalism at work even when the sources barely mention fiefs at all.

Whereas feudal–vassalic relations have traditionally been approached as an eminently structural and normative development, the story told here is one of individual initiatives, administrative professionalisation, and negotiation between the political actors. The aim is to restore human agency as fundamental in the transformations in land tenure and local governance. To begin with, what do terms like fief (*feodum*), liege homage (*lizanchia, ligensia*), and 'to hold from' (*tenere de*), which were a natural choice for the *magister* familiar with the recent legal developments, tell us about social realities? What was entailed precisely in a knight's acknowledgement that he was the *vidame*'s *homo*? Local lords were said to owe homage and castle guard for specific lands that were sometimes termed fiefs, but more frequently were identified simply by village name,[50] which they 'held from' the *vidame*. In these cases as throughout France, *feodum* was used to designate noble property with no suggestion of 'conditional possession', as in the feudal model; the *vidame*'s fief was his land, the seigneurie of Picquigny, as explicitly stated on occasion: 'in terra mea et

---

[47] Débax, 'Aristocratie languedocienne', p. 96.

[48] Luigi Provero, 'Vassallaggio e reti clientelari: Una via per la mobilità', in Sandro Carocci (ed.), *La mobilità sociale nel medioevo* (Roma, 2010), pp. 437–51, is a rare example of network analysis applied to vassalage.

[49] The focus on the 'norme morale et sociale de la fidélité' obviates the analysis of *strategic manipulation* even when this is explicit in the sources (e.g., 'nec per suo ingenio'); Débax, *Féodalité languedocienne*, pp. 101, 110.

[50] 'pro feodo de Calceia', 'de feodo meo de Foucaucourt et de pertinentiis eiusdem feodi'; compare with 'pro eo quod teneo apud Hamevile et apud Sasseval', 'de Prousel et de Donvilla', etc.

feodo meo', 'de feodo meo', etc.[51] Because castle guard was correlated to the size of one's estates, it made sense to name fiefs in the homage charters, but this does not imply that homage and service were owed in exchange for land. The lands of the local aristocracy had been in their family for generations and the *vidame* made few donations to his followers.[52] The importance of homage, with or without castle guard, was political: it was the recognition of the *vidame*'s territorial preeminence. Occasionally this aspect is made explicit in the sources: in his homage charter of 1233 Walter of Belloy declares himself Gérard of Picquigny's liegeman, *and therefore* (*ergo*) 'holds from' him all which he has at Belloy.[53] That aristocrats owning land within the territory controlled by the lord of Picquigny should acknowledge his political preeminence was becoming an accepted principle. But a recurring form of words suggests that the *vidame*'s ambitions of territorial hegemony occasionally needed to be couched in nuanced language; thus property was said to 'regard' or 'look to' (*spectare*) the seigneurie of Picquigny.[54] The connotations are positional (compare with the logic of centre and periphery informing the *estages*), designating one's political orientation towards the *vidame* and not some other lord.

Naturally lords of seigneuries such as Picquigny were apt to take a maximalist view of the effects of homage, arguing that holding in fief fundamentally changed the ties that bound their aristocratic subjects to them. The modern advocates of feudalism have accepted this case and turned homage and fief-holding into the fundamental structuring forces of medieval society. But the convergence between the views of the medieval nobility and modern

---

[51] Reynolds, *Fiefs and Vassals*, p. 258; Paris, AN, MS R^1 672, fol. 21v; L. E. Deladreue, 'Histoire de l'abbaye de Lannoy, ordre de Cîteaux', *Mémoires de la Société académique d'archéologie, sciences et arts du département de l'Oise*, 10 (1878), pp. 405–84, 569–696, at p. 693. Similar phrases were used by other aristocrats, e.g., 'in feodo et demanio'; Paris, AN, MS R^1 672, fol. 63r.

[52] See Reynolds, *Fiefs and Vassals*, p. 268, for a comparison with the aristocracy of Champagne.

[53] 'Ego sum homo ligius Gerardi militis domini de Pinconio vicedomini Ambianensis et ergo teneo de ipso omnia que habeo apud Beeloy'; Paris, AN, MS R^1 672, fol. 59r. But Walter did not surrender his lands only to receive them back in fief, as in the modern model of the *fief de reprise*.

[54] 'Hoc concessit vicedominus de Pinchonio ad cuius feudum predicta terra spectat'; Amiens, ADS, MS 13 H 4, vol. 2, fol. 420; 'me [Enguerran] presente et concedente, ad cuius feodum predicta decima spectabat', Paris, AN, MS R^1 672, fol. 7; same phrase as regards other local lords: of Boves – 'ad cuius feodum dicta terra spectabat'; Amiens, ADS, MS 65 H 88 (Cartulary of Paraclet), fol. 77r – and Belloy, 'qui decimam illam ad feodum suum spectare dicebat'; Amiens, ADS, MS 13 H 4, vol. 1, fol. 6.

scholars leaves out the lesser aristocrats who had competing ideas about what their subordination through homage charters or fief-holding effectively entailed. It is consequently essential to ask in each specific context what real limitations on the use of land, mills, or castles were brought about by homage and holding in fief – and notably, how the freedom to inherit and alienate property was affected in practice.

The evidence indicates that Enguerran and Gérard's territorial hegemony and efforts towards better record-keeping and clearer rules had a very limited impact on the property rights of local aristocrats.[55] In real terms, the aristocratic generation of the *Livre des stages* owed the *vidame* loyalty and castle guard. The approval for alienations of lands was not a requirement that applied uniformly, but it was generally sought because it entailed the *vidame*'s warranty of the sale or donation. It was exceptionally rare that a lord from the Amiénois would withhold his approval of his man's donation.[56] Just as rare are the references to other restrictions on property: only two charters mention that the Picquigny family might reclaim the property of its aristocratic men if they failed to perform their duties (1198–9). The clauses were hypothetical and regarded two aristocrats of little weight in respect to their donations to an abbey, the church having pioneered many of the changes in the status of property.[57] Only in 1239 was a similar clause entered again in a donation charter. That it concerned a family recently arrived to western Amiénois is in itself significant.[58] For such newcomers were the first – and, as it turns out, by and large the only – targets of Enguerran and Gérard's effort to impose new duties – the relief tax and the so-called aids – on land held from them.

The small pecuniary contributions demanded by the lord on such occasions as the knighting of his son or his daughter's marriage are sometimes called 'feudal aids', but originally need not have had a feudal character: throughout

---

[55] A question posed by Elizabeth Magnou-Nortier, 'La féodalité en crise: Propos sur "Fiefs and Vassals" de Susan Reynolds', *Revue historique*, 600 (1996), pp. 253–348, at p. 294.

[56] I found only one case, and it does not involve the *vidame*; Paris, BA, Ms 5259, fols 20v–21r.

[57] See Reynolds, *Fiefs and Vassals*, pp. 142–3; Amiens, BM, Ms 781, fols 21r–21v, 34v–35r; the charters were drafted by Saint-Jean abbey on behalf of its benefactors with the purpose of excluding the donations from the property that the benefactor might forfeit to his lord.

[58] Paris, AN, R^1 634, dossier 4 (Le Gard). I have consulted the records from AN, R^1 634, under the old shelfmark R^1 114, dossiers 1–3; for the updated references I have used the AN correspondence file: http://www.archivesnationales.culture.gouv.fr/chan/chan/pdf/sa/R1_concordance.pdf.

France they initially applied not to lords but to lesser people and obtained not only in the secular world but also within the ecclesiastical hierarchy. In time, however, the practice of demanding the aids spread more widely as lords and their professional administrators saw an opportunity to tighten their grip on their subjects.[59] The *estages* of 1223 include one case in which a payment was owed to the *vidame* in the event of the owner's death without direct heirs; this due was mentioned explicitly, in addition to the traditional 'customs that a noble man owes to his lord' (on which more below). It was imposed on an outside lord from the neighbouring Ponthieu who recently acquired land at Picquigny.[60] Similarly, when a bourgeois of Amiens acquired land near the abbey of Saint-Jean, the *vidames*' foundation, and thus entered the orbit of Picquigny, Enguerran received him as his man, requiring him to attend his court (*placita*) three times a year, under fine of 10 *solidi* (1219). Such attendance was not mentioned in the *Livre des stages* or the homage charters of the traditional local aristocracy. In view of his profession (*monetarius*) he understandably did not owe any service, except 'these three just and right aids', that is, 10 *solidi* each on the knighting of the *vidame*'s first-born son, the marriage of his first-born daughter, and the *vidame*'s ransom.[61] The phrasing of the duties in value-laden language was meant to eclipse their uncustomary nature; importantly, there is no mention of them in the charters of the *vidame*'s traditional aristocratic subjects. Lastly, a relief-tax of 10 *solidi* was also owed. By 1239 the aids were referred to generically (*de auxiliis*) when they were imposed, together with the relief-tax on another newcomer not mentioned in previous charters or the *Livre des stages*, who had recently acquired certain unspecified lands in the lordship of Picquigny.[62] Better-off people were able to negotiate more favourable terms: another 'citizen of Amiens', but this time from the family of lords of Conty, purchased a sizeable land-rent at Val-de-Maisons in the lordship of Picquigny, but managed to owe only five *solidi* as relief tax, no aids at all, and was required to attend the *vidame*'s *placita* only once a year (1239).[63] The *vidame* would have wanted a man of such social weight at his court of

---

[59] Reynolds, *Fiefs and Vassals*, pp. 312–14.

[60] Paris, AN, MS R¹ 672, fol. 58r; he is not in the *Livre des stages*.

[61] 'pro cuius donatione terre sibi facta, idem Thomas est et erit homo meus'; 'exceptis tribus iustis et rectis auxiliis … pro milicia primogeniti mei filii, et pro maritagio primogenite filie mee, et pro redemptione corporis mei si forte captus essem in guerra comuni'; ibid., fols 15r–15v.

[62] Ibid., fol. 21v.

[63] The land-rent cost him 250 *livres* – a significant sum; Paris, AN, MS R¹ 672, fol. 14r.

justice at least as often as he wanted a bourgeois, but imposing uncustomary demands on people of higher social standing proved difficult. Enguerran and Gérard aimed to emulate magnates like the neighboring count of Saint-Pol in demanding the aids and relief payments,[64] but they could not change the customs that obtained between them and the local aristocracy for generations, and were content to impose the new duties on those who were recently arrived in the seigneurie of Picquigny. At roughly the same time, in places where the aids had been long collected from the general population by powerful rulers (such as the king of England), there was growing resistance against them.[65]

As the changes in the regime of property gained currency in western Amiénois, we encounter in 1248 the sale of a fief by the lord from whom it was held, but the fief-holder was compensated with perhaps around half of the sale price (see below). By the middle of the century homages could be transferred in return for a financial compensation – a sign of commodification, if not necessarily institutionalisation. Sometimes it was merely the legal jargon of fiefs and homage that was stamped on a social relationship that remained the same. Thus, in 1228 Simon of Beaussault granted Gérard of Picquigny an annual rent of 30 *livres* to incentivise him as his ally; the size of the military aid owed by the *vidame* was not specified and the language of gift-giving was preferred over legalese: 'I have given' (*dedi*), stated Simon in the sentence immediately after the charter's salutation. There was no question of identifying the *vidame* as 'the man' of the lord of Beaussault. When Simon's son renewed the agreement in 1230, the new charter, drafted by a scribe more inclined towards neat categories, announced from the very beginning that Gérard was his man, 'est homo meus', on account of the annual rent.[66] The change in language did not imply a transformation of the relationship, whose terms remained the same. The new charter exemplifies how the jurists' legal categories were imposed on social realities.

But if the new norms about fiefs and homage began to shape social realities, it was also by being adjusted to them at the initiative of the political actors assisted by their professional aides. *Lizanchia*, liege homage, is a good example of a notion that underwent significant changes when it was put to

---

[64] He demanded the aids from the town of Encre as early as 1188, but in return granted it a communal charter; J. Estienne (ed.), *Chartes de l'hôpital et de la ville d'Albert (Encre)* (Amiens, 1942), p. 14.

[65] Elizabeth A. R. Brown, *Customary Aids and Royal Finance in Capetian France* (Cambridge, MA, 1992), pp. 44–5, 48–9.

[66] Paris, AN, MS R¹ 672, fol. 52r; sixty years later, the compilers of the cartulary preferred to see the annual rent as a gift, copying the two charters in the section *De donis*, under the title *De dono triginta librarum*, etc.

work. In the roll of *estages* liege homage was contrasted with *hominium*, plain homage: of the 117 people, sixty-three were listed as owing *lizanchiam* and fifty-three *hominium*, with one case unspecified. *Hominium* was used for people who presumably owed (liege) homage to a lord other than the *vidame*,[67] but this cannot be verified in each case. They were not expected to provide extensive aid, either owing no military service at all (thirty names), owing non-guard military service (four), or a mere one or two months of castle guard (nineteen) – and predominantly in the smaller strongholds: half of the knights serving at Ailly and all of those at Clairy owed *hominium*. Yet of the people who owed liege homage the majority were firmly entrenched in the seigneurie of Picquigny and did not have another lord.[68] This shows a different usage from our general view of liege homage as referring to the precedence given to one among a man's multiple lords. At Picquigny *lizanchia* was appropriated to designate the more important type of homage,[69] performed by the people who mattered most to the *vidame*, notwithstanding that they did not have another lord.

The notion of liege homage underwent further modifications; in the *Livre des stages* and the charters of 1223 it was adjusted to fit the political reality of the *vidame*'s alliance with the lord of Saint-Sauflieu, Enguerrran (d. by 1197), followed by his heir Dreux. While under obligation to serve in the guard of Picquigny for one year, they enjoyed a special status in that they were permitted to retain a number of lesser lords as their liege men, who owed one year of castle guard to both the lords of Picquigny and Saint-Sauflieu, in the sense that while doing castle guard for one they could be summoned by the other. In the *Livre des stages* this was called *lizanchiam communitatis*, 'liege homage of the joint type', while the charters of 1223 referred to 'the liege man of the

---

[67] E.g., Robert of Orville; Baldwin of Daours, who was connected to the counts of Ponthieu and Saint-Pol (Fossier, *La terre et les hommes*, vol. 1, p. 518 n. 208); and Walter of Heilly, whose family held lands from the abbey of Corbie and the count of Saint-Pol, whom it owed military service; Paris, BN, Fonds latin, MS 17758 (Cartulaire 'noir' de Corbie), fols 22v, 174r; Jean-François Nieus, 'Un exemple précoce de répertoire féodal: le livre des fiefs de la châtellenie d'Encre (nord de la France, ca. 1245)', *Bulletin de la Commission Royale d'Histoire*, 168 (2002), 1–70, at pp. 25, 53–4.

[68] Only in some cases can we surmise that the *vidame* managed to claim the status of liege-lord over men who had multiple loyalties: e.g., Enguerran of Gentelles and Willard of Cottenchy, both from the orbit of the lord of Boves, or Garin of Belloy.

[69] See the similar findings about the *liegei homines* of Corbie abbey; Laurent Morelle, 'La notice des plaids generaux de Corbie: une revision', in Elisabeth Mornet (ed.), *Campagnes médiévales: l'homme et son espace: études offertes à Robert Fossier* (Paris, 1995), pp. 573–86, at pp. 576, 582.

lord of Picquigny and of the lord of Saint-Sauflieu jointly (*communiter*)'.⁷⁰ This was not liege homage in any classical way. Notwithstanding that the lord of Saint-Sauflieu himself could in principle be summoned to serve for a full year at Picquigny, the joint liege homage offered him the means to assert symbolically his dominance over a group of some ten local aristocrats and affirm his special status among the *vidame*'s men. The idea was probably discussed between Enguerran or Dreux of Saint-Sauflieu and Enguerran of Picquigny, and put into practice with the help of the *magistri* who bent the legal forms to fit the political situation.⁷¹ The practice was abandoned by Gérard of Picquigny, who did not enjoy the same close relationship with the lord of Saint-Sauflieu. The alterable nature of liege homage warns against approaching the world of thirteenth-century seigneuries in normative terms.⁷²

Another development that testifies to the adaptation of legal notions to social realities is the way in which the *vidame* and one of his men, Hugo of Beauval, owed *each other* homage for land acquired by the former within an area controlled by the latter. This reflected Hugo's role in brokering Enguerran's purchase of land at Fieffes (1206). In keeping with custom, the owners first offered the land for sale to Hugo as their neighbour, then, following protocol, formally resigned it to him, and it was Hugo who issued the sale charter to the *vidame*. Notwithstanding Hugo's general homage in the 1190s, 1210, and 1234 to the *vidame* – whom he calls 'his lord' in the sale charter – as far as their rights at Fieffes were concerned the two remained on equal footing, owing each other homage in a circular way that is at odds with the classical model of feudal–vassalic relations. Enguerran was even received as Hugo's man in respect of the estate of Fieffes, notwithstanding that otherwise Hugo was the man of the lord of Picquigny. Homage was a malleable form that reflected the designs of the sociopolitical agents. Finally in 1243 Baldwin of Beauval quit his right to the homage of Fieffes.⁷³

The point of the foregoing discussion is not to redraw the geography and chronology of feudal relations, notwithstanding that this is a valuable endeavour in its own right. Western Amiénois was a small corner of medieval France,

---

⁷⁰ 'sum homo ligius domino Pinconii et domino de Sessauliu communiter'; Paris, AN, MS R¹ 672, fol. 58r. Hugo of Belloy's charter was exceptional in stating explicitly that he could not be summoned by the lord of Saint-Sauflieu while on the *vidame*'s castle guard; ibid., fol. 57v.

⁷¹ See the somewhat similar examples of *salva ligeitate* in Charles du Fresne Du Cange, *Glossarium Mediae et Infimae Latinitatis*, new edn by Léopold Favre (10 vols, Niort, 1883–7), vol. 5, p. 105.

⁷² Cf. Guerreau, *Féodalisme*, p. 179.

⁷³ Paris, AN, MS R¹ 672, fols 48r–48v.

and the present microhistorical approach does not lend itself easily to extrapolation. While the fief as a 'restrictive' tenure[74] with enough strings attached that it can be contrasted with full ownership was barely in evidence in western Amiénois by 1250, in other regions a distinction was being drawn around this date between allods and fiefs,[75] with consequences for local politics. The chronological and geographical diversity points not to a uniform process across Western Europe but to a series of transformations in land-holding and relations between greater and lesser lords which, notwithstanding a shared background of administrative professionalisation and influence of Italian legal models, unfolded according to the logic of local contexts. The present findings are valuable for understanding one of several scenarios of how the new ideas about fiefs and homage charters were appropriated and adapted, and with what effects. The nature of the twelfth- and thirteenth-century changes in aristocratic land tenure, lordship, and local governance cannot be understood outside the designs of the individuals who implemented them, from ambitious lords like Enguerran of Picquigny to their aides.

This picture of sociopolitical relations would not be complete without emphasising that custom and tradition limited the *vidame*'s freedom of action. This explains the remarkably stable terms of castle guard over the sixty years, with very few changes.[76] It also explains why Enguerran and Gérard took the pragmatic approach of a gradual tightening of their grip on the local aristocracy through homage, castle guard, and dues such as the aids and the relief. The general trend for tenure in fief and homage charters, in the Amiénois and elsewhere in the thirteenth century, was to make the ties between lower lords and the head of a territorial seigneurie such as Picquigny more normative and institutionalised; less a matter of practice, negotiation, and strategising, and more a matter of rules rooted in written agreements. Achieving this transformation, however, took a good deal of time. Reciprocity, however asymmetrical, informed the relations between the *vidame* and his men, whom he had a duty

---

[74] Evergates, *Feudal Society*, pp. 63–4.

[75] For instance in Savoy; see Bernard Andenmatten, *La maison de Savoie et la noblesse vaudoise (XIIIᵉ–XIVᵉ s.): Supériorité féodale et autorité princière* (Lausanne, 2005).

[76] E.g., Raoul of Bacouel, who owed one year of castle guard both in 1223 and 1244, but while in 1223 he was equipped at the *vidame*'s expense, in 1244 he was required to serve 'with [his] men', which reflects a real increase in status that Raoul was expected to match by providing more service; Paris, AN, MS R^1 672, fols 58r, 59r. Castle guard was more often reduced, e.g., from one year to two months, or, when only one month was owed, simply eliminated.

to assist. On several occasions the *vidame* gave his protection in regard to lands threatened by attacks or litigation.[77]

The local aristocracy offer a good example of collective agency in their dealings with the dominant seigneurie of western Amiénois. The *vidame*'s men agreed to serve under the conditions that customarily applied to free, noble men. In some sense this went without saying, but lesser aristocrats made sure that they were given in their homage charters the same terms as their better-off peers. One declared in his charter of 1223 that he owed liege homage and such service as a free man owes to his lord; another obligated himself, in addition to castle guard, to all other customs that a free man owes to his lord.[78] The key formula, *homo francus*, was intended to make the subordination more easily acceptable.[79] Through it, the *vidame*'s men asserted their place as members of a privileged group. The castle of Picquigny was one site of production of this social identity, because the custom of Picquigny castle, referred to explicitly in several charters, set a standard for the type of noble service that defined the aristocracy.[80] The custom consisted of shared expectations about the manner of service, some of which made their way into the homage charters, but many probably remained unwritten. The point was that a lord could not be subjected to conditions radically different from those that applied to his peers. *Francus homo* referred to a status shared first of all with one's immediate social peers, the *vidame*'s aristocratic men. This sense of belonging was made explicit in a homage charter of 1244; quite possibly recording the preferences of the two lords involved, the scribe noted that they each owed one year of castle guard as full peers, *ut par integer*. Others, owing six or seven months, had the status of *semipar*, serving 'in the manner and according to the customs of the other semi-peers of the said castle' of Picquigny.[81] As a group, the peers of Picquingy could look after each other and ensure that the *vidame* did not bring uncustomary demands on them.[82]

---

[77] Several references in the *Livre des stages* ('de custodia terre sue', etc.) and the homage charters ('de tutela et garandela de terra mea', 'pro custodia terre mee', 'de custodia bonorum meorum omnium'); Paris, AN, MS R¹ 672, fols 58v, 59v, 60v.

[78] 'debeo etiam ligeium et tale seruitium quale francus homo debet domino suo'; 'et totas alias consuetudines sicut liber homo debet domino suo'; ibid., fols 58r, 57v.

[79] Cf. Reynolds, *Fiefs and Vassals*, p. 263 n. 24.

[80] 'istud feodum debet deduci ad usus et consuetudines castelli Pinchonii'; Paris, AN, MS R¹ 672, fol. 21v.

[81] 'seruitium ad usus et consuetudines aliorum semiparium casteli sepedicti'; ibid., fols 59r, 61r, 61v.

[82] On the twelfth-century 'pairie de château', see Barthélemy, *Deux ages*, pp. 153–6; cf. Magnus Ryan, 'Feudal Obligation and Rights of Resistance', in Natalie Fryde,

Collective agency was particularly favoured by small aristocrats and better-off commoners. In 1217 four peasant families or some fifteen people, of which two families were bound by marriage ties, unsuccessfully contested the construction of Gard abbey's mills.[83] More successful in acting together to defend their interests were the millers of Picquigny, who made a written agreement with respect to the *vidame*'s donation of free milling to the hospital of Picquigny so that they could collect their due every third time the hospital brought its grains for grinding (see below).[84] This is all the more significant considering that the *vidames* did not hesitate to pressure the aristocrats of their entourage to contribute to their pious donations. On the other hand, the rural–communal movement made only modest inroads at Picquigny: only Molliens was granted a communal charter, fashioned on the model of the commune of Amiens (1209).[85]

Conversely, aristocrats of higher socioeconomic standing negotiated individually for more favourable terms. Renaud, the castellan of Amiens – the rival family in western Amiénois – was bound to serve a short term of six weeks and, more significantly, was tasked with guarding the northern end of the bridge of Picquigny. Although a vanguard post, it reflected the castellan's interests: from the northern bank of the Somme he could keep a closer eye on the lands north of the Somme where his lordship lay and intervene or retreat there more easily. Unlike the lesser aristocracy who handed in their homage charters, Renaud of Amiens and Hugo of Beauval were issued chirograph charters, thus retaining one original of the document for themselves, which stressed the contractual nature of their relation to the *vidame* and affirmed symbolically their status as autonomous agents. In general, lords from the vicinity of the counties of Saint-Pol and Ponthieu and the abbey of Corbie could not be fully integrated in the orbit of Picquigny through long terms of service. Robert of Orville used his status and proximity to Saint-Pol to negotiate only one month of castle guard with four knights; in a clause that epitomises the arithmetical habits of mind of the seigneurie's administrators, he was given the option to serve for

---

Pierre Monnet, and Otto Gerhard Oexle (eds), *Die Gegenwart des Feudalismus* (Göttingen, 2002), pp. 51–78.

[83] Amiens, ADS, MS 13 H 4, vol. 1, fols 47–9.

[84] By comparison, the bishop had to excommunicate the millers of Amiens before an agreement was reached on the division of the revenues (1191); Roux (ed.), *Cartulaire du chapitre*, pp. 106–8.

[85] Alcius Ledieu, 'La carte de commune de Molliens-Vidame', *Cabinet historique de l'Artois et de la Picardie*, 8 (1893–4), 156–201. Urban communes such as Arras and Amiens suppressed the initiatives of neighbouring villages seeking enfranchisement; Fossier, *Hommes et villages*, p. 223.

half that time with more than twice as many knights. The same arithmetical logic dictated that the lord of Tilloy, peripheral but important, owed a mere fifteen days of service but, as if to compensate for this short term, was required to provide one other knight to serve with him.[86] Even such people, however, realised the advantages accruing from membership in the group of castle peers; Hugo of Beauval, having negotiated specific terms of service, had it stated in his homage charter that he was to serve like his peers, the *vidame*'s free men ('sicut pares mei et liberi homines sui faciunt').[87] The individual's ability to exploit his strategic assets did not preclude the possibility of future collective action.

Finally, Enguerran and Gérard's success depended on the capacity to react to potentially damaging developments in the network of aristocrats tied by homage to them. Theirs was a world of strategic agency. Recognising the position of Hugo of Beauval and Renaud the castellan of Amiens, Enguerran secured their homages as early as June and August 1210, far in advance of the systematic renewal of homages of in 1223. Similarly, Gérard made sure to secure the homage of the new lord of Saint-Sauflieu shortly after his succession, notwithstanding that their fathers had been allies and friends.[88] A more complex episode involved Maria, the lady of La Ferté, an outsider who by 1220 had extended her influence in western Amiénois from some land at Molliens in the *Livre des stages* (for which she owed *hominium* to the *vidame*) to the point that the castellan of Hangest and lord of Bougainville ended up holding lands from her. Since both were his liegemen, Enguerran was concerned with this situation of double loyalties, not least because the lady of La Ferté escaped his direct control. To reinforce his ties to the men from the western part of his seigneurie, he procured Maria's recognition that she held from him whatever lands or revenues the lords of Airaines, Bougainville, *Ceruels*, and the castellan of Hangest held from her.[89] In effect, Maria did not abandon her claim to a position of authority vis-à-vis these four lords but recognised the *vidame*'s superior authority. Similarly, Gérard purchased the homages of three small aristocrats from Jean of Hangest as a preemptive

[86] Paris, AN, MS R^1 672, fols 57r–57v.

[87] A cadet branch of the counts of Saint-Pol, the lords of Beauval had land near the border with the Amiénois and in Vicogne; Jean-François Nieus, *Un pouvoir comtal entre Flandre et France: Saint-Pol, 1000–1300* (Bruxelles, 2005), pp. 125–6, 148–9.

[88] Dreux of Saint-Sauflieu was succeeded by his son Enguerran at some date after July 1228; the latter submitted a homage charter in February 1230; Paris, AN, MS R^1 672, fol. 59v.

[89] Paris, AN, MS R^1 672, fol. 62r. On Airaines and La Ferté, see Fossier, *La terre et les hommes*, vol. 1, pp. 520–4.

measure, establishing his direct control over the men (a similar case involving the castellans of Amiens is discussed below).[90]

A path to consolidation: building connections

A second son, Enguerran owed his position at the head of the lordship of Picquigny to an accident in the norm of primogeniture, the death of his elder brother Gérard II, childless, during the third crusade. The ambitions he would have fostered in the shadow of the heir apparent arguably explain his consequential initiatives and vigorous start as lord of Picquigny. He not only set the *vidame*'s authority over the local political actors on clearer and more solid bases through written instruments like the records of homage, but also financed a building programme, pursued opportunities to acquire land, and sought to expand his power base by drawing more distant lords into the orbit of the seigneurie of Picquigny. Crucially, to bring these initiatives to fruition Enguerran relied on human capital, building a small network of local supporters and allies who, like the professional aides he retained, were closely implicated in his projects (in some cases the line between hired aide and local supporter is hard to draw). That this instrumental network was much smaller and maintained through different means than the looser network of aristocrats who recognised the *vidame*'s authority through charters points to the limited role played by homage and fief-holding. The significance of social ties and 'co-acting' notwithstanding, the case for Enguerran's agency as an individual rests on his role as the architect of both the network and the specific initiatives that were pursued through it.

Of this smaller circle of kin, allies, and close aides on whom Enguerran relied – his support network – his wife Margaret stands out, although her role cannot be fully reconstructed. She would have played an important part alongside her husband in the banquets held at the castle, where the aristocracy were asked to bring their wives. The mother of nine, she presumably took an active role in her children's education. Margaret was the daughter of the count of Ponthieu, and while hypogamy was a common trend in the aristocratic marriages of the time,[91] it says something about the importance of the seigneurie of Picquigny that the second in line of inheritance received her hand in marriage. The corollary of hypogamy was Margaret's small dowry, but the marriage ensured good relations with a powerful neighbour and brought the lord of Avesnes into the *vidame*'s network 'on account of the fief of the

---

[90] Paris, AN, MS R¹ 672, fols 48v–49r.
[91] Barthélemy, *Deux ages*, p. 121; Fossier, *Hommes et villages*, p. 329.

count of Ponthieu'.⁹² Margaret was frequently associated with Enguerran's pious donations, which she approved as his wife. Enguerran also had a close relationship with his sister Matilda, whom he entrusted with some of the business of the seigneurie: assisted by a knight, she received the oath of one of the two *vavassores* who had challenged a donation of Jean of Picquigny (1197); she also appears on the witness list of a donation charter of 1200, after which date she is no longer mentioned. In 1213 Enguerran funded religious services in her memory with a donation to the abbey of Gard.⁹³

Notwithstanding the importance of kinship in medieval society, it may be that medievalists have exaggerated its sociopolitical role over that of social ties with local allies, supporters, and aides,⁹⁴ which at Picquigny proved more instrumental both in the management of the regular business of the seigneurie and in the *vidames*' larger projects. One must not lose sight of the frequency of conflicts among kin in medieval society. Gérard bargained hard with his brother and Enguerran even clashed with his uncle over the family inheritance. Both, however, made a conscious choice of allies and collaborators.

Enguerran was a man animated by ambitions of development who seized the opportunity of his elevation to the head of the seigneurie; compiled shortly after he took power, the *Livre des stages* was an assessment of resources, fundamental for the execution of his plans.⁹⁵ To carry them out he also needed the support of the local elites. Apparently before he even became lord of Picquigny, he took a non-returnable loan of 60 *livres* from the bishop of Amiens in order to finance the completion of fortification work at Loeuilly.⁹⁶ Loeuilly was probably the dowry of Enguerran's daughter Maria, married to Eustace of Encre: it is listed in the *Livre des stages* as Eustace's possession and he was to hold it from the bishop as part of the agreement for financing the construction work undertaken by Enguerran. The relations between the families of Picquigny and Encre were quite close in the 1190s: leaving on crusade, Gérard II left Eustace in charge of the seigneurie rather than his own brother

---

⁹² 'item de feodo comitis Pontiui'; Paris, AN, MS R¹ 672, fol. 59v.

⁹³ Amiens, ADS, MS 13 H 4, vol. 1, fols 25–8.

⁹⁴ See John S. Ott, review of Heather J. Tanner, *Families, Friends, and Allies: Boulogne and Politics in Northern France and England, c. 879–1160* (Leiden, 2004), *Speculum*, 81:2 (2006), 615–16.

⁹⁵ Cf. the count of Champagne's use of similar lists as 'a powerful administrative tool'; Evergates, *Feudal Society*, p. 10.

⁹⁶ Roux (ed.), *Cartulaire du chapitre*, p. 129.

Enguerran.[97] In 1197, Eustace's relation, Enguerran of Encre, founded a chapel at Picquigny – a significant gesture of good will between the families.[98]

A strategic reorientation occurred, however, during the final years of the twelfth century (Eustace was dead by 1197); Enguerran developed a close relationship with Dreux, lord of Saint-Sauflieu, who came to play an instrumental role in Enguerran's projects, in effect replacing the lord of Encre at the pinnacle of the *vidame*'s support group as his main local ally.[99] Dreux's logistical aid was first of all needed for Enguerran's major project as lord of Picuiqgny: by 1199 he had built a second mill at Picquigny, doubling the milling capacity inherited from his predecessors. Mills were an important source of income because of the *vidame*'s monopoly over the grinding of grains, one of the few seigniorial impositions documented in the cartulary of Picquigny. In one of Gérard II's charters only one mill is mentioned, but in 1199 Enguerran granted the hospital of Picquigny the privilege of free milling 'at our two mills at Picquigny'.[100] The privilege explicitly involves Dreux of Saint-Sauflieu as co-donor, and its subsequent confirmation again mentions that free milling was given with Dreux's express approval inasmuch as it regarded his possession.[101] This suggests that in order to cover the costs of building the mill Enguerran had turned to the lord of Saint-Sauflieu who, in exchange for his aid, retained a share of the mills' income and the corresponding rights over the adjacent waters of the Somme.[102]

This rapprochement was facilitated by the history of good relations between the families of Picquigny and Saint-Sauflieu, but it was also a personal option. To reconstruct the trajectory of the relationship between Enguerran and Dreux we have only the terse charter evidence, but it seems that the personal character of their relationship developed over time. Each transaction involving the mills of Picquigny became an instance when Enguerran and Dreux came together and issued a common charter. By virtue of his share in the mills,

---

[97] Eustace witnessed two of Gérard's charters in 1190, on the eve of the departure; Paris, AN, MS R^1 672, fol. 47v; Amiens, ADS, MS 13 H 4, vol. 1, fols 8–9.

[98] Paris, AN, MS R^1 672, fol. 7r.

[99] Enguerran of Encre's heir, Otto, had no known dealings with the *vidames*.

[100] 'de censu molendinii Pinchonii' vs 'in duobus nostris molendinis Pinchonii'; Paris, AN, MS R^1 672, fol. 3.

[101] Same phrasing in another donation charter to a local church (1200); ibid., fols 3v, 6v.

[102] Building a new mill required a substantial investment that was often met by the association of several parties; Jean Gimpel, *The Medieval Machine: The Industrial Revolution of the Middle Ages* (New York, 1976), pp. 12–13.

Dreux became associated with many of Enguerran's pious donations. In time he began to emulate the *vidame*'s donations, as if learning from and aspiring to the model offered by his lord and ally. In 1205 he voluntarily added his own donation to the abbey of Gard, although this was not required of him in the same way as approval of the free-milling privilege was. In 1211 Dreux's donation to Notre-Dame de Gard of fishing rights on the Somme near Picquigny was even more clearly his initiative, only inspired by Enguerran's similar gift to the abbey in 1201.[103] The donation represented a gesture of good will between friends; no doubt that Dreux was performing the socially scripted role of the reliable friend, but all friendship is socially defined. The charters of thirteenth-century Amiénois commonly identify friends as a valuable source of aid and advice.[104] An indirect testimony of the close relations between Enguerran and Dreux is that the former's second son established his residence at Saint-Sauflieu with his part of the inheritance. The personal character of the relationship is brought into sharp relief by the fact that Enguerran's and Dreux's successors had no dealings with each other beyond the submission of the standard homage charter. While Dreux enjoyed, like his father, the 'joint liege homage' of a group of local lords, this privilege was denied by Gérard of Picquigny to the new lord of Saint-Sauflieu.

The rest of Enguerran's support network consisted of aides, including professionals like the *magister* rewarded by his brother, and a group of local aristocrats. A series of donations testify to the effort of retaining a circle of administrators: Enguerran's *camerarius*, bailiff, and professional clerk (*magister*) were all rewarded in this way. The donations were small in the case of the former two aides,[105] who were men of modest origins. Their roles were flexible; for example, during Enguerran's early years, his bailiff also carried his seal on occasion.[106] In addition to their regular duties at the castle and their dealings with the peasants, Enguerran's aides occasionally represented him in transactions involving people of some standing. For example, the bailiff was invested on Enguerran's behalf with an annual rent purchased from the chapter of Amiens,[107] and another aide received the oath of a *vavassor* in the matter of a challenged pious donation ('fide data in manu Maloth servientis mei').[108]

---

[103] Amiens, ADS, MS 13 H 4, vol. 1, fols 9, 21–4.

[104] Paris, AN, MS R^1 672, fols 49r, 55r, 57v; Amiens, ADS, MS 13 H 4, vol. 1, fol. 7.

[105] Alan got some land at Foucaucort and Gérard an annual rent of one *modius* of wheat; Paris, AN, MS R^1 672, fols 1r, 4r.

[106] Amiens, ADS, MS 13 H 4, vol. 2, fols 420–1.

[107] 'inuestiuimus ... ad opus ipsius vicedomini'; Paris, AN, MS R^1 672, fol. 49v.

[108] Roux (ed.), *Cartulaire du chapitre,* pp. 124–6.

The management of a lordship the size of Picquigny required administrators that could be trusted to act with some autonomy. In particular, property transactions were being conducted with increasing involvement from legal professionals. Thus, to retain the services of *magister* Fulk of Cagny without drawing on his patrimonial revenues, Enguerran gave him a substantial annual income, consisting of the tithe of Fouilloy. To do this Enguerran engaged in a long dispute with the tithe's rightful owner, the abbey of Saint-Fuscien,[109] at the end of which he had to renounce the tithe but not before ensuring that it would be returned to the abbey only after Fulk's death, in effect ensuring Fulk's continuing services. Additionally, Enguerran secured the services of other *magistri* when the situation demanded it.[110]

The other group, the *vidame*'s entourage of small local aristocrats, stands out from the charter witness lists in that unlike the *vidame*'s aides its members were identified as knights. Some overlap between this entourage and the aides was inevitable, as in the case of Bernard, serving Enguerran as seneschal and later castellan of Molliens, who seems better-off and in the context of a more substantial donation to Notre-Dame of Molliens was even called a knight. The witness lists of fifteen charters drafted between 1197 and 1208 include, in addition to Enguerran's family and other notable figures who added the weight of their social position to guarantee the transactions, a number of lesser lords who were called upon to endorse the charters, and possibly to assist the *vidame* with their counsel. By and large they formed a compact group, with several presences on the witness lists, for instance Enguerran of Hédicourt (six), Garin of Belloy (three), and Allermus of Roemont (two). These three were also on Gérard II's witness lists in 1190, and they each owed one year of castle guard, suggesting the strength of their links to the Picquigny family. On the other hand, Giles of Clairy (seven) owed only two months of castle guard for a meagre quarter of a manse; described as a *vavassor* in one charter, his status was closer to that of the *vidame*'s aides. Overall a pattern of attracting loyal men from modest backgrounds, sometimes in competition with rival local lords, is discernible. At a time when the situation of many a small landowner was turning precarious – in the 1220s and 1230s many were forced to sell lands and revenues to the *vidame* and the bishop to survive – Giles was a man in search of a patron who would appreciate his services. In 1183 he was the guarantor (*fidejussoris*) of the castellan of Amiens in a pact with the church of Amiens, but by 1195 the two had fallen out: Giles contested the castellan's donation of 104 *jornalia* of land to

---

[109] Paris, AN, R¹ 634, dossier 4 (Saint-Fuscien); Paris, BA, Ms 5259, fol. 22r.

[110] E.g., in 1216, *magister* Bernard 'tunc agentis vices domini Ambianensis'; Roux (ed.), *Cartulaire du chapitre*, p. 196.

Saint-Jean's abbey but the bishop's arbitration decided against him. The episode explains Giles's strategic reorientation towards the *vidame*.[111]

The exchanges between the *vidame* and this entourage of kin, allies, aides, and aristocratic supporters far outweigh his dealings with the rest of the local lords who owed him homage. It was the former, not the latter, that formed his support network and proved instrumental in his plans; personal ties were established with members of this smaller circle, not with the tens of aristocratic men who did homage. The exchanges should be understood in an inclusive sense, notably encompassing pious donations to the vidame's religious foundations, which can be read as an indicator of the relations between the vidame and local aristocrats. That the lords of Belloy, Molliens, and even the more remote Beauval directed some of their pious donations to Notre-Dame de Gard and the leprosarium of Picquigny reflects Enguerran's influence over them. On a couple of occasions he went further: to spare his own resources, Enguerran called upon the lords from his entourage, such as Garin of Belloy, to join him and donate their own land, conveniently bordering his, to the churches associated with the Picquigny family. It is possible that the aristocrats were compensated subsequently and we do not know about it owing to the accidents of document survival. Garin was no petty lordling and had his own men and the option to realign himself with his powerful neighbour, the castellan of Amiens, from whom he held some lands. That he found this arrangement acceptable suggests that the association with the *vidame* was overall worthwhile for local aristocrats, in spite of its occasional material costs. Significantly, Garin was also a remote family relation of the vidame.

Enguerran was apt to capitalise on his position in the political networks of the Amiénois beyond the western area where he enjoyed a position of political preeminence. He offered himself as the guarantor and pledge of the lord of Querrieux (eastern Amiénois) in his transfer to the church of Amiens of the tithes of Querrieux and Allonville for 300 silver marks (1205). It bears emphasis that this was a complex deal rather than a straightforward sale: Fulk of Querrieux was entitled to buy back the tithes after six years and it was stipulated that the annual tithes would be paid to the church by Fulk's men, with the bishop's agent merely supervising the collection from a residence provided by Fulk. These provisions point to tension over the collection of the tithes, and it is the high potential for dispute that suggests what Enguerran could gain from the deal by virtue of his role as guarantor. Because both parties relied on him to settle the potential disputes the *vidame* had leverage on both of them. In particular, the bishop and chapter of Amiens, Enguerran's powerful

---

[111] Roux (ed.), *Cartulaire du chapitre*, pp. 91–2; Amiens, BM, Ms 781, fols 51–51v.

neighbours, were well aware that an open conflict with the *vidame* left them on their own to deal with Fulk and his family, their only weapons ecclesiastical censures of uncertain efficacy. That no open conflict broke out between the *vidame* and the church of Amiens goes some way towards establishing the case. This and similar examples explain why the *vidame* was in a strong position to negotiate acceptable compromises on those rare occasions when the chapter and bishop brought heavy charges against him. The point to make is that in this affair Enguerran acted from the position of a network gatekeeper: while not directly above Fulk (who was not his man) or the bishop, his unique position to guarantee the deal was essential for both parties.[112] His role in this case is reminiscent of what had been envisaged as the *vidame*'s function two centuries earlier, before he became an autonomous seignior rather than the bishop's secular arm.

The flipside of the active cooperation extended by smaller lords from Dreux of Saint-Sauflieu to Garin of Belloy was the effort of a few local aristocrats to limit their interactions with Enguerran, in effect removing themselves as much as possible from the *vidame*'s orbit. A leading role was played by a cadet branch of the Picquigny family that clashed with Enguerran over the division of their patrimony. This is another indication that kinship was not always instrumental in the strategic designs of late-medieval sociopolitical actors – quite the contrary at times, which explains the importance of diversified support networks like Enguerran's. By 1210 Enguerran had successfully claimed his uncle Pierre's inheritance in Vicogne from Gérard of Ailly, Pierre's brother. Since Gérard had enjoyed possession of the lands for a time, Enguerran's intervention understandably vexed both him and his heir.[113] His son Jean, Enguerran's cousin, surfaces only twice in the documentary record, and even then not in charters preserved in the cartulary of Picquigny, which collected material deemed relevant to the *vidame*'s interests. He did not even submit a homage charter. This fact should be interpreted in light of the observation that in principle one did not do business with one's rivals, and certainly did not buy or sell precious commodities like land and rents.[114] Jean's influence extended over some of the *vidame*'s liegemen, and he was tied through a double marriage

---

[112] Roux (ed.), *Cartulaire du chapitre*, pp. 149–50. Fulk was not the *vidame*'s man but his ancestor had been in the 1170s; Fossier, *La terre et les hommes*, vol. 1, p. 515 n. 206; Amiens, ADS, MS 13 H 4, vol. 1, fol. 7.

[113] Paris, AN, MS R^1 672, fols 48v, 54v–55r; Amiens, BM, Ms 781, fol. 87v.

[114] See Chris Wickham, *Community and Clientele in Twelfth-century Tuscany: The Origins of the Rural Commune in the Plain of Lucca* (Oxford, 1998), esp. pp. 23–5, 28–46, 125–6.

alliance to Robert of Saveuse who,[115] significantly, also did not submit a homage charter to either Enguerran or Gérard and did not have any dealings with them, although his ancestor Raoul had been listed in the *Livre des stages*. The repercussions of this pole of local aristocratic opposition to the *vidame* were not consequential enough to register in the documentary record.

Enguerran's modus operandi was not shared by Gérard, but before turning to the latter's rule, one point of convergence between father and son is worth exploring in some detail: they both display a pragmatic, quid-pro-quo attitude towards the religious foundations of the Amiénois and the church in general. Pious donations, systematically promoted by the church for centuries, were embedded in the aristocratic way of life. They ensured the performance of commemorative services, and as such were linked to achieving salvation. While engaging in this key social practice of the time, Enguerran and Gérard acted as autonomous agents, seeking to derive the maximum advantage from their donations to religious houses. Because a church was a central site of social life, a lord's privileged relation to it would reinforce his status and his donations would signify his social position. Enguerran's pious donations started in 1199–1201, after the seigneurie's finances recovered from Gérard II's crusade – always a costly enterprise – and Enguerran's investments (see Table 2). The newly built mill apparently did good business, for in 1216 Enguerran and Dreux of Saint-Sauflieu could afford to grant the abbey of Gard the right to welcome all patrons to its mills, with the exception of their subjects – had the mills been short on customers Enguerran would not have encouraged such competition.[116]

Enguerran made a calculated choice to associate the Picquigny family with Notre-Dame de Gard, an abbey located in the heart of the seigneurie of Picquigny, where he decided to transfer the last remains of his father and grandfather. His pious donations privilege it by far, followed at some distance by the hospital of Picquigny: Gard received a total of one hundred *jornalia* of forest and thirty-three of meadow, twelve *livres* in annual income, an annual rent of three *modii* of wheat, as well as fishing rights and the use of the Somme for its mills.[117] Enguerran also intervened in support of the abbey. In 1215 he

---

[115] Amiens, BM, Ms 781, fols 26r–27r.

[116] On the use of mills, see Fossier, *Hommes et villages*, p. 334.

[117] Enguerran also granted a charter encouraging donations to the abbey; Paris, AN, MS R¹ 672, fol. 1v; Amiens, ADS, MS 13 H 4, vol. 1, fols 9–15, 25–8, 41–6; Roux

Table 2. Enguerran's pious donations, 1199–1224 (● for donations, ○ for confirmations)

	1199–1201	1205–11	1213–19	1223–24
Gard	●	● ○ ○	● ● ● ○ ○ ○	● ● ○
Hospital	●	● ○	○	
Molliens		● ○		●
St-Jean		● ○	○	
Hangest	●			
Bishop				●
Other[1]	●		● ● ●	

1. Notre-Dame of Fontaine; the abbey of Cherlieu (Gard's mother-house); Notre-Dame de Parco (Cistercian); the abbey of Saint-Lucien of Beauvais.

brokered a compromise favourable to Gard in its dispute with the abbey of Saint-Pierre of Gouy over their mills, and in 1219 he mediated an agreement in another dispute between the two abbeys, retaining the right to enforce its terms on behalf of Notre-Dame de Gard.[118] His generosity was calculated, for Enguerran exercised a large degree of influence over the abbey. He saw to it that the abbey match from its own revenues the donation he made when his ancestors' bodies were moved to Gard.[119] This eased his financial contribution to an event for which he would nevertheless get the credit, namely the monks' banquet on St Catherine's feast, instituted by his donation and at which his name would have been recalled with gratitude and his ancestors commemorated; the same goes for his donation of eight *livres* for the monks' soup, also matched by the abbey. Similarly, Enguerran insisted that the Eucharist be made from the wheat of his donation, thus scoring a major symbolic point inasmuch as he inscribed himself in a central part of liturgical life. He went further still: he treated the lands donated to Gard and the hospital as if they continued to belong in some sense to his seigneurie. He forbade the monks

(ed.), *Cartulaire du chapitre*, p. 160.

[118] Amiens, ADS, MS 13 H 4, vol. 1, fols 30–1.

[119] Paris, AN, MS R^1 672, fol. 1v.

to sell for the extraction of peat the meadows donated by him at Dreuil,[120] made use of the hospital's land to help a local bourgeois build his household, and disposed of the lepers' house at Clairy.[121] Although the hospital was later compensated, the point is that when necessary the *vidame* was able to draw on the hospital's resources; the subsequent compensation was itself described as his pious donation.[122] In contrast with Notre-Dame de Gard, the abbey of Saint-Jean at Amiens, the *vidames*' twelfth-century foundation, had its earlier privileges confirmed but received only one donation from Enguerran.[123] At the outskirts of Amiens, Saint-Jean was bound too closely to the city and the bishop to fit Enguerran's purpose, a church he could control.

Gérard's donations similarly came with strings attached, but he made fewer of them. The donation to Gard in August 1237 probably rewarded its cooperation in Gérard's settlement with his brother earlier that month. It included an unprecedented clause in the family's relations with Gard, explicitly requiring the monks to read aloud the charter at the annual visitation as a reminder of the *vidame*'s generosity.[124] He made two small donations, one to Saint-Jean abbey and one to the church of Saint-Denis at Fouilloy, the burial place of his daughter Alice, and confirmed the donation of his first wife, in which the abbey of Gard was only given an intercessory role, the distribution of money to the poor by its porter – a significant development.[125] Also intriguing is Gérard's donation to the abbey of Paraclet early in his reign, which might have been an overture for securing good relations with a recently founded and prosperous abbey known for offering loans to secular lords[126] – if so, it shows a seigneur keenly aware of financial matters.

Gérard's minimalist policy of pious donations makes sense in view of his disputes with the bishop of Amiens (see below), but can also be viewed in a broader context. Many of the features that have been identified in thirteenth-century Castile as part of a general trend in Western Europe towards

---

[120] Amiens, ADS, MS 13 H 4, vol. 1, fols 62–3.

[121] Paris, AN, MS R^1 672, fol. 4v.

[122] Paris, AN, MS R^1 672, fol. 4r.

[123] Amiens, BM, Ms 781, fols 21r, 35r.

[124] Paris, AN, MS R^1 672, fol. 1v.

[125] Amiens, ADS, MS 13 H 4, vol. 1, fol. 104; Amiens, BM, Ms 781, fol. 40v. Gérard also confirmed Saint-Jean's privileges; Amiens, BM, MS 781, fol. 31r; Paris, AN, MS R^1 672, fol. 62r.

[126] Paris, AN, MS R^1 672, fol. 5r; Amiens, ADS, MS 65 H 88, fol. 45r; Fossier, *La terre et les hommes*, vol. 1, pp. 629–30. Some of the *vidame*'s men followed their lord's example and made donations; Amiens, ADS, MS 65 H 88, fols 42v, 45v.

'laicisation' are amply in evidence in Enguerran's and particularly Gérard's approach to pious donations:[127] the more tight control over the destination of gifts and their increasingly quid-pro-quo nature – tied to strategies for commemoration or economic interests – and ultimately the diminishing interest in pious donations.

This approach underwent a significant blow in 1246, when Gérard had to consent to the relocation of the canons of Picquigny from St Martin's church, located on the hilltop just near his castle, to a new church to be built in the valley of Picquigny, on the site where the hospital then lay. The new church, dedicated to St John the Baptist, was to replace St Martin's as the parish church of Picquigny. Gérard donated the site, including the lots for the canons' houses, and 200 *livres* for the foundation, promising to procure another 100 *livres* from the peasants and townsfolk, and as much as he could from his aristocratic men (an indirect recognition of their autonomy vis-à-vis the *vidame*'s coercive powers). Lastly, the relocation of the hospital also fell upon Gérard. All this was brought about by the papal legate to France, Odo of Chateauroux, bishop of Tusculum, who had come to the Amiénois to preach the crusade when he was approached by the canons of Picquigny to complain about the inadequacy of their location atop the hill and away from the town.[128] Might the canons have also resented living next door to the castle, under the *vidame*'s control?[129] The charter's rhetoric cites the townsfolk's complaints to the bishop about the difficulty of accessing the parish church as the reason for building a new church. Gérard would not have been happy to see the canons leave the vicinity of his castle, where their presence helped confer the appearance of a magnate's court and their knowledge could be put to good use in administrative and legal matters. So why sponsor the new church? Odo's success in securing Gérard's support involved a good understanding of the *vidame*'s social world and reasons for acting. While the charter's rhetoric exaggerates Gérard's enthusiasm for the new foundation (*ardenti desiderio cupiebat*, etc.), it acknowledges that his

---

[127] Teofilo Ruiz, *From Heaven to Earth: The Reordering of Castillian Society, 1150–1350* (Princeton, 2004), pp. 10, 131–2.

[128] Per the church's foundation charter, Paris, AN, MS R^1 672, fols 55v–56r; Marie-Madeleine Lebreton, 'Eudes de Chateauroux', in M. Viller et al. (eds), *Dictionnaire de spiritualité: ascétique et mystique, doctrine et histoire* (17 vols, Paris, 1932–95), vol. 4:2, pp. 1675–8, at p. 1675.

[129] The thirteenth-century castle was rebuilt in the fourteenth century on the same site; St Martin's church is located so close to the castle walls that it was connected to it by a subterranean corridor; *Picquigny: le château-fort, la collégiale, la ville* (Amiens, 1987), p. 19.

consent came only after the initiative had been taken by Odo, at the canons' request and with the bishop of Amiens's approval, and hits the mark in stating that the *vidame* 'wanted to pose as the patron of the church'. Odo had left Gérard with little choice, because patronage of the town's church had great symbolic value and reaffirmed the *vidame*'s lordship. Although commonplace, his claim that Gérard eagerly petitioned him ('a nobis cum instantia postulabat') for the building of the new church is a noteworthy attribution of agency. In the same vein, the bishop's confirmations of donations to religious houses or sales of tithes to the chapter were expressly said to have been demanded by the secular lords, while in fact the confirmations were needed first of all by the church, their direct beneficiary. The aim of this discourse was to articulate a model of how a lord should behave towards the church. Its rhetoric brought intentionality to the fore, representing action as an instantiation of the individual's inner state.

Lastly, it is significant that the canons found a solution to their problems only with the arrival of an outsider. During previous disputes with the church, the *vidames*' knowledge of the Amiénois political stage worked, with greater or smaller success. But in this case Gérard could not anticipate that the canons would gain an important ally. With respect to the itinerant papal legate his local knowledge was of no help. If he did know in advance about Odo's passage, Gérard seems to have expected at worst some pressure to join the crusade, which, as an ageing seigneur recently remarried in the hope of producing a male heir, he could have declined elegantly. Another way to put this is in terms of one's range of vision inside the network. Nominally aware of the ecclesiastical network of which the canons were part, Gérard failed to see that one of the canons' distant connections in the network, a papal legate, could be mobilised in their support.

Managing resources and preserving the gains

Unlike his father, Gérard did not rely on negotiation and compromise, preferring to rule in a more impersonal manner. The instances of cooperation with the regional aristocracy were fewer and the disputes more numerous; with fewer clients and allies, he had to use force and money. Gérard's is a good example of how one's social world is structured by the actions of one's predecessor: after the seigneurie had prospered under his father, his strategy was to buy land and revenues. But because the growth also brought tensions with the neighbouring aristocracy, his major disputes were either inherited from, or rooted in, his father's final years.

Gérard inherited solid finances – just a few months after he assumed power he was able to buy back his sister Ida's dowry for a considerable sum[130] – but also a complicated family situation. His father, whose views on primogeniture were probably shaped by his experience as a second son, made sure his younger son received a sizeable share of lands and revenues. Pursuing a strategy of consolidation, Gérard bought back his brother's possessions at Picquigny as he had bought back his sister's dowry (1237).[131] The practice was common: the heir of an aristocratic estate would try to reassemble lands alienated through inheritances and marital endowments. The settlement eliminated a possible source of embarrassment in running business at Picquigny, but Gérard was not willing to sacrifice much in exchange. He gave his share of a forest and marsh near Picquigny and persuaded the neighbouring owners, a local lord and the canons of the church of Picquigny, to give up theirs for a compensation;[132] in effect, Gérard replicated his father's strategy of capitalising on his influence over local landowners so as to preserve the family lands. With the addition of 93 *livres* to be paid from the revenues of the toll of Picquigny, the transaction was acceptable for the cadet brother. A few years later, when Enguerran received his annual revenue of 100 *livres* from Amiens according to his father's last will,[133] Gérard similarly worked out an advantageous deal that spared as much as possible his main source of revenue in the town, the *sesterage*. Enguerran's share was a patchwork of small revenues, each requiring a separate effort to administer; they included fines and tolls and a strictly defined portion of the *pesage*. Gérard also retained the option to buy back Enguerran's share of the wheat from the *sesterage* (15½ *livres*) from harvest time until the first of October.

Other purchases of land and annual revenues followed as Gérard capitalised on both his position of political preeminence and the prosperity achieved under his father. The financial difficulties of many a landowner created a

---

[130] For his daughter's endowment Enguerran had used recently acquired properties, rather than patrimonial lands; cf. Georges Duby, 'The "Youth" in Twelfth-century Aristocratic Society', repr. in Frederic Cheyette (ed.), *Lordship and Community in Medieval Europe: Selected Readings* (New York, 1968), pp. 198–209, at p. 202; Le Jan-Hennebicque, 'Origines du douaire', p. 118. For the buy-back, Paris, AN, MS R^1 672, fol. 48; the sum can be deduced from Ida's compensation, an annual revenue of 100 *livres*.

[131] With the exception of his brother's house; Paris, AN, MS R^1 672, fol. 15v.

[132] September 1237; ibid., fol. 54r.

[133] Ibid., fol. 8r.

favourable context for the acquisition of lands and land-rents.[134] The *vidame* was not the only person in the region with money – many purchases were made by the church of Amiens – but he had preemption rights by virtue of his lordship and, what is essential, could back them with his political influence. It is instructive to compare the sums paid by Gérard with contemporary prices, even if these were not the expression of purely economic factors: for instance, a tithe held by a secular lord was sold back to the church at a low price (below); furthermore, the quality of the land was a huge factor. As regards land, the abbey of Gard paid 3½ *livres* per *jornalium* of arable land (1224) and the chapter of Amiens paid 7 *livres* (1238); by contrast, Gérard paid 1.15 *livres* and again 1½ *livres* per *jornalium* (1247); exceptionally, he bought land for as little as 0.6 *livres* per *jornalium* (1248; discussed below). More numerous, of course, are the cases in which either the size of the land or the sum of the transaction was not recorded. As regards annual revenues of wheat (where the quality of the land is no longer a factor), the chapter of Amiens bought back the revenue of a tithe for 15 *livres* per *modium* of wheat in annual revenue (1238), and the abbey of Gard paid 40 *livres* per *modium* of wheat and oats in annual revenue (1239). The price of the produce itself, according to a surviving estimation from 1241 was 1.875 l. per *modium* of wheat.[135] But the *vidame* paid 7½, 4.2, and 5 *livres* per *modium* (1224, 1243, and 1245).[136] Clearly the *vidame* bought far more cheaply: both arable land and annual revenues in wheat, from a mere one tenth to less than half the price paid by the churches. Even at a conservative selling price of one *livre* per *modium* of produce (well below the 1241 estimate), an annual land rent purchased by the *vidame* in perpetuity for 5 *livres* paid for itself in a mere five years. The conclusion is straightforward: the *vidame* took advantage of his position to buy from the needy landowners of the seigneurie at very low prices.

That Gérard did not buy all the lands offered for sale indicates selection, which was based on price and the potential for profit. He did not use his preemption rights vis-à-vis the lord of Rivery, whose sale to Saint-Jean's abbey

---

[134] Fossier argues that the years 1215–45 saw the decline of many families from the Amiénois aristocracy, as the sales to the *vidame* by needy local aristocrats also suggest, but the method of relying on titles such as *miles* and *dominus* as clear indicators of social status is problematic; *Hommes et villages*, pp. 306–7.

[135] For the prices paid by the churches: Paris, AN, R¹ 634, dossier 4 (Le Gard); Amiens, ADS, MS 13 H 4, vol. 2, fols 219–20; Roux (ed.), *Cartulaire du chapitre*, pp. 332, 335–6; by the *vidame*: Paris, AN, MS R¹ 672, fol. 51v.

[136] Paris, AN, MS R¹ 672, fols 49v, 50r, 51r.

he approved and confirmed as lord (1228).[137] Most likely Bernard stuck to the price, 190 *livres*, which was considerably more than what Gérard normally paid. That after some early acquisitions (1224 and 1228), most of Gérard's purchases took place in the 1240s suggests that he continued his father's competent management of the seigneurie's finances. He pursued a focused policy of acquisitions, not unlike his father's interest in the lands from Fieffes. Between 1243 and 1247 he made three purchases at Gornay, which indicates a strategy of consolidating property.[138] Similarly, his purchase of the land-rents and taxes of Clairy in 1228 was intended to consolidate the family's hold on the village, coming a few years after Enguerran's acquisition of a land-rent there.[139] The purchase of an annual income of 10 *modii* of wheat from the revenue of the mill of Hangest in 1237 was likewise followed by the acquisition of another two *modii* annually from the mill's revenue in 1245, as well as other lands and revenues in the village, in 1244 and 1247.[140]

In one case, Gérard took advantage of the precarious position of a small landholder to buy at an extremely low price: a mere 72 *solidi* for 6 *jornalia* of land in July 1248. Furthermore, the price of a much larger purchase of land from the same owner, although not recorded, must have been quite similar since it took place the previous month; the man holding in fief 20 of the 74 *jornalia* sold was compensated with 100 *solidi*.[141] There was a history behind the purchase and the landowner's financial woes: he had proved unable to transport to the agreed delivery point the wheat he owed Gard abbey from his land, and Gérard stepped in, buying the land for 40 *livres* only to sell it to the abbey for 55 (1243).[142] The 15 *livres* profit might seem modest, but the finances of medieval lordships rested on the management of small but numerous and diverse sources of revenue[143] – a recurrent pattern for both Enguerran and Gérard, and well worth emphasising. Conversely, prompted perhaps by shared expectations about what constituted a fair price, Gérard renegotiated

---

[137] Paris, AN, R¹ 634, dossier 4 (Saint-Jean d'Amiens); and Amiens, BM, MS 781, fols 48v–49v, 53r–53v.

[138] Paris, AN, MS R¹ 672, fols 50–51v.

[139] Ibid., fols 48r, 49v.

[140] Ibid., fols 48v, 50r, 51r. In 1247 the seller's lands were under the *vidame*'s protection and he got a slightly better deal: 25 *livres* for an annual revenue of 3½ *modii* of wheat and 12 *solidi*.

[141] Ibid., fols 48v, 49v, 50v.

[142] Amiens, ADS, MS 13 H 4, vol. 2, fols 217–20.

[143] Fossier, *Hommes et villages*, p. 332.

another land transaction, paying the owner 18 *livres* for some 9 *jornalia* of land, three times the initial price.[144]

Like other seigniors of their time, Enguerran and Gérard achieved their success through a careful management of many different small assets.[145] This attention to seemingly small details was facilitated by their investment in human resources: the circle of administrators and aides. On the other hand, the charter material has relatively little on cultural values and the symbolism of property and land, beyond the attachment to patrimonial land. The professionalisation of seigniorial administration had done away with many of the symbolic gestures attendant upon transfers of property in earlier centuries, replacing them with legal jargon.[146]

The standing of the seigneurie of Picquigny in northern France is reflected in matrimonial alliances. The first of Gérard's three marriages, to the second daughter of Simon, count of Montfort, was arranged by his father, who participated in Simon's campaign against the Albigensians. It is indicative that even after her death Gérard remained part of the Montforts' orbit, receiving 15 *livres* annually from the count;[147] clearly the *vidame* was a welcome addition to the count's network. Gérard also preserved the alliance forged by Enguerran's marriage to the daughter of the count of Ponthieu, standing surety for Simon of Dammartin and his wife Maria, heiress of the late count of Ponthieu (1231): he promised to deny Simon 'auxilium vel consilium' and join the king's host against him if Simon broke his agreement with the king.[148] But while Gérard sought to maintain good relations with the magnates of Picardy, Simon does not seem to have invested in the relationship with the *vidame*, reaching instead a matrimonial alliance with the *vidame*'s traditional rivals, the family of castellans of Amiens.[149]

---

[144] Paris, AN, MS R^1 672, fols 51r–51v.

[145] Daniel Pichot, 'Une famille de la petite aristocratie du Bas-Maine', in Elisabeth Mornet (ed.), *Campagnes médiévales: l'homme et son espace: études offertes à Robert Fossier* (Paris, 1995), pp. 477–80; Verdier, 'Construction d'une seigneurie'.

[146] See Aaron Gurevich, 'Représentations et attitudes à l'égard de la propriété pendant le haut Moyen Age', *Annales: Économie, Sociétés, Civilisations*, 27:3 (1972), 523–47.

[147] Paris, AN, MS R^1 672, fol. 54v.

[148] Teulet (ed.), *Layettes*, vol. 2, p. 197; Jean Richard, *Saint Louis: Roi d'une France féodale, soutien de la Terre sainte* (Paris, 1983), pp. 72, 112.

[149] In 1239 he was paying an annual rent of 60 *livres* to the nephew of the castellan of Amiens, Bernard of Estrées, whom he called his 'family relation' (*consanguineo nostro*); Ernest Prarond (ed.), *Le cartulaire du comté de Ponthieu* (Paris, 1898), pp. 79–80.

Little is known about Gérard's second and third marriages, but we find out about his role as *pater familias* from the convention regarding his second daughter's marriage with Walter of Heilly, from a family close to the *vidames*.[150] Joanna's dowry would normally have consisted of her part of the inheritance from her mother, but Gérard chose to keep the land that his wife had brought him through marriage and compensate Joanna with 100 *livrées de terre* in annual revenue from the *sesterage* of Amiens, plus 20 *livrées*, which represented the compensation for acquisitions made by him during his wife's lifetime by drawing on her assets. The charter included some elaborate clauses regarding Gérard's legacy, which covered a number of contingencies: that his first-born daughter Margaret would inherit the seigneurie or conversely that a son would be born to him and Margaret would die childless. In either event Joanna received all the maternal land but was required to give back 80 *livrées de terre* from her compensation; the point was that the heir of Picquigny – either his or Margaret's son – should enjoy full possession of the patrimonial right to collect the *sesterage* at Amiens. While acknowledging that the two sisters' maternal land was governed by inheritance rules (*jure hereditario*), Gérard felt entitled to bend the norms and confer it entirely on Joanna in the event that Margaret inherited the seigneurie; presumably his logic was that by bestowing on Margaret the lordship of Picquigny he could dispose of her maternal legacy. To enforce his will from the grave Gérard relied on the authority of the written word and the agency of the party directly interested: he directed Joanna to claim Clairy and Molliens if Margaret refused to hand over their mother's land. Above all, Gérard's testamentary dispositions privileged a male heir: if the seigneurie passed to Margaret, Joanna was to receive an additional payment of 2,000 *livres*, drawn over ten years from the revenues of the forest of Ailly; but if a son was born to him and inherited the seigneurie, Gérard did not want to deprive him of this large sum. Notwithstanding that charters often aimed to cover even remote possibilities, this speaks to something that rarely surfaces in the records: an emotional hope – here, that a son would be born to an aging father.

We know less about Gérard's network of local supporters because after the first decade of the thirteenth century the local charters rarely include a list of witnesses. But it is clear that he did not continue the close relationship with the lord of Saint-Sauflieu that had been so important for his father. Equally revealing is the fact that the major effort to consolidate his network came at a price. At first glance, the purchase of Jean of Hangest's land at

---

[150] Paris, AN, MS R^1 672, fols 62v–63r; this charter of 1246 postdates the marriage but recapitulates previous agreements.

Rouvroy-lès-Abbeville (1237) might seem a routine acquisition, surprising only because of the distance from Picquigny, given Gérard's strategy of consolidating holdings in the heart of the seigneurie. In fact, it was the first step in a calculated and complex move aimed at securing the loyalty and services of a local aristocrat.[151] Gérard then exchanged the 100 *virgas* of meadowland for 24 *virgas* of meadowland that the lord of Rouvroy owned near the residence of Jean of Fourdrinoy.[152] The explanation for the imbalance comes indirectly from the charter, which specifies that the 24 *virgas* were to be held by Jean of Fourdrinoy from the *vidame*. In other words, the point of Gérard's purchase of land at Rouvroy was to make a gift to Jean of Fourdrinoy after having exchanged it, however disadvantageously, for land situated near Jean's home. Although Jean's previous services are unknown, the investment paid off and he served as bailiff to Gérard's son, on whose behalf he concluded a deal with the chapter of Amiens in 1263.[153] His family may not have been prosperous,[154] but because it was part of the local aristocracy, Jean was a substantial improvement from Enguerran's agents. This explains the higher costs of retaining his services and suggests that Gérard needed men of higher station as his agents in order to deal more effectively with the local lords. In another case, it was probably the need to preserve a traditional pillar of his network of aristocratic supporters that led the *vidame* to come to the aid of Garin of Bougainville through a loan of 30 *livres* on highly favourable terms.[155] The decision reflected the model of 'good lordship', which underscored the moral value of giving aid to one's subjects. Lastly, there is only one case reminiscent of the good relations Enguerran had enjoyed with his aristocratic men: a few years after he was permitted to divert the Somme's waters to the moat surrounding his residence on condition that it did not adversely affect the fishing and milling, Gérard of Dreuil reciprocated by donating a small revenue to the *vidame*'s hospital.[156]

---

[151] Ibid., fol. 48v.

[152] Ibid., fol. 63v.

[153] Ibid., fol. 43v.

[154] In 1224 he and his elder brother had to sell 39 *jornalia* to raise 136 *livres*; Paris, AN, R^1 634, dossier 4 (Le Gard).

[155] Paris, AN, MS R^1 672, fols 49r–49v; similarly, in early-modern Europe a family member might receive aid in the form of the purchase of his land at a high price; Giovanni Levi, *Inheriting Power: The Story of an Exorcist*, trans. Lydia Cochrane (Chicago, 1988). On the lord of Bougainville's donation to the *vidame*'s monastic foundation, see Paris, AN, MS R^1 672, fol. 4r.

[156] Paris, AN, MS R^1 672, fols 5r, 16r.

This meagre tally of cooperation with the local elites is matched by a series of disputes with both smaller lords and the two other powerhouses of the region, the bishop and the family of castellans of Amiens. Mutual mistrust, which accounts for the absence of close relations with the local aristocracy, probably played its role. Raoul of Fluy must have perceived Gérard as a weaker lord than his father, to whom he did homage in 1223, for he seized the revenues of the tolls of Hangest and Molliens. It is easy to see how Gérard's reaction to take back the revenues by force would have alienated Raoul and perhaps estranged other local aristocrats as well, especially since Raoul's claims had merit. Towards the end of his life ('enfaine vie'), Gérard showed remorse and promised to compensate Raoul, but this was only done in 1266 by his son Jean.[157] Gérard's dealings with his son-in-law, Nicholas of Rumigny, display a similar trajectory of mistrust and politics of force likely to alienate the local aristocracy, while seemingly lacking the late-life change of heart. Gérard did not deliver the promised dowry of his daughter Margaret, admittedly three times higher than that of her younger sister Joanna: 300 *livrées de terre* annually. It was his wife Mahaut, shortly after his death and at the advice of friends, who compensated Nicholas.[158]

Gérard's more important conflicts were clearly inherited from his father.[159] With an outsider like Raoul of Braches, from south-eastern Amiénois, Gérard found it difficult to deal from a position of force and had to reach a compromise (1242): in exchange for a revenue of 9 *livrées de terre* Raoul abandoned all the disputes between them, going back to their ancestors, and did homage.[160] The homage proved inconsequential: years later, the compilers of the cartulary were at a loss as to where exactly the lord of Braches fitted in the *vidame*'s network and copied his homage charter four times in different sections – including 'homage with service' and 'without service' – before crossing out three of the entries.[161]

With the family of castellans of Amiens there had been some instances of cooperation in Enguerran's early years, when he was still establishing himself

---

[157] Ibid., fol. 8v.

[158] Ibid., fol. 52v.

[159] Medieval conflicts 'were more *structures* than *events* ... often enduring generations'; Patrick Geary, 'Living with Conflicts in Stateless France: A Typology of Conflict Management Mechanisms, 1050–1200', repr. in Patrick Geary, *Living with the Dead in the Middle Ages* (Ithaca, NY, 1994), pp. 125–62, at p. 139.

[160] 'controuersiis, querelis et aliis, habitis inter predecessores meos, etc.'; Paris, AN, MS R^1 672, fol. 57r.

[161] Ibid., fols 56v, 57v, 61v, 63v.

as lord of Picquigny. Enguerran and some of his men endorsed the agreement that put an end to a conflict between the castellan and the bishop and chapter of Amiens.[162] In turn, the castellan endorsed Enguerran's donation charter to the hospital of Picquigny a few years later (1199). But during the next twenty-five years, only the homage charter submitted by the castellan to the *vidame* and the two men's homage to the king in 1211, when each stood as guarantor for the other – the castellan as the *vidame*'s leading subject and the *vidame* as the castellan's lord – can be documented.[163] This points to a rift, most likely caused by apprehension at Enguerran's increased presence north of the Somme in Vicogne, where the castellans' lands and interests lay (see above for Enguerran's acquisition of land at Fieffes, successful claim of Pierre of Picquigny's inheritance, alliance with the lord of Beauval, and extension of authority over the lord of Orville). The tensions, however, only broke out in 1241–3, when Gérard intervened promptly against a cadet branch of the castellans' family in order to prevent a potential shift in the balance of power in Vicogne. The problem arose from Matthew of Beauval's sale to Theobald of Amiens, lord of Canaples, of the homages owed to him by two aristocrats from Vicogne. Matthew eventually acknowledged that he held these homages 'from', if not 'of' Gérard, who was not his lord ('tenebam *a* domino Gerardo'; a rare formula: *de* was normally used). This had not been a problem as long as the homages were owed to Matthew – probably a relative of Baldwin of Beauval, the *vidame*'s man – but now that they ended up in the hands of a lord from the rival family of castellans of Amiens the allegiance of the two aristocrats from Vicogne was at issue. The purchase of the two homages was intended to consolidate Theobald's position in Vicogne, because the lands of the two aristocrats lay near Canaples. So Gérard intervened and took back the homages, 'homagia in manu sua cepit et saisiuit'. The move suggests the attention to details required of the head of a medium-sized seigneurie: even relatively minor changes in the strategic configuration commanded one's attention. Theobald's response is unknown, and it may well be that between 1241 and 1243 Gérard remained in uncontested possession of the homages as he claims in the charter putting an end to the whole affair through Matthew's formal transfer of the homages to him for an unspecified sum.[164] As always in such cases an appearance of legitimacy remained important. Matthew justified this reversal by appealing to custom: following the advice of honourable men,

---

[162] Roux (ed.), *Cartulaire du chapitre*, pp. 119–20.

[163] Teulet (ed.), *Layettes*, vol. 1, p. 372.

[164] Edited and translated in Epurescu-Pascovici, 'Picquigny and Its Lords', pp. 160–1; on Canaples, see Fossier, *La terre et les hommes*, vol. 1, p. 584.

he realised that Gérard had the better preemption right on grounds of kinship and lordship, 'racione parentele et dominii'.

Gérard's actions with regard to the northern half of the seigneurie were clearly dictated by his father's strategy: after expansion in Vicogne driven by Enguerran came preservation and consolidation of the gains. Following another dispute between Gérard and Jean, castellan of Amiens, a charter of arbitration of May 1248 was meant to clarify and distinguish more sharply each party's rights in Vicogne, and specifically in the village of Flessell.[165] That Gérard and Jean agreed to share control over the village was an implied recognition of the *vidames*' successful consolidation north of the Somme. They disagreed, however, on how the lands and land-rents should be divided among three local aristocrats whose loyalties were now at issue. The arbitrators chose the most simple and economic solution for the *vidame* and the castellan: one half of the lands and land revenues was assigned to a local lord who was declared the *vidame*'s man, and the other half to the other two lords henceforth identified as the castellan's men. In doing so, the arbitration paid little attention to the potential disruption for the peasant landholders, of whom one ended up owing lands rents to both the *vidame*'s and the castellan's men precisely so that the two lords' holdings might be balanced.

Lastly, a consequential dispute with the church of Amiens was inherited directly from Enguerran, who in June 1224 agreed with the chapter of Amiens to submit to the arbitration of a council of three: the bishop, the dean of the chapter, and another canon.[166] Drafted by the chapter and pervaded by the rhetoric of church documents, the charter was also endorsed by the *vidame* who, following his aides' review, consented to the terms of the agreement and had his seal affixed to it. The first knot of contention was the chapter's use of the waters of the river Selle, whose steep gradient made it heavily used for mills; however, dikes and water gates affected the river's discharge and thus the mills' productivity, as well as fishing and fluvial navigation.[167] In 1222 Enguerran granted a canon of Amiens permission to divert the Selle's waters at Plachy for his own use for as long as he held the village, on condition that this *ad vitam* privilege to an individual not be turned into the chapter's

---

[165] Paris, AN, MS R¹ 672, fols 53r–53v.

[166] Ibid., fol. 43. In December 1223 relations were still good, judging by Enguerran's donation to the bishop; Beauvillé (ed.), *Recueil de documents inédits*, vol. 4, pp. 47–8.

[167] Albert Demangeon, *La plaine picarde* (Paris, 1905), p. 160. In the twelfth century fishing rights on the lower Selle were also granted by the *vidame* to the abbey of Saint-Jean; Amiens, BM, Ms 781, fol. 24v.

customary right.[168] What triggered the confrontation in 1224 is unknown but quite possibly the canons refused to remove the dikes upon being notified by the *vidame* as per the agreement of 1222; in the charter of 1224 they also raised the issue of their right to wash cloth in the river (*arroagium*); lastly, fishing rights were also submitted for arbitration. Other outstanding issues included the division of the *vidame*'s and chapter's lands around the Selle's confluence with the Somme near Amiens, and their respective rights over the forest of Gisonville; like similar proceedings between the *vidame* and other lords, these issues speak to the trend towards a clearer definition of property rights. Lastly, a decision also had to be reached on the fine the *vidame* had to pay for his transgressions against the church of Revelles. Enguerran had good reason to expect the arbitration to end in a compromise, which explains why he accepted two canons on the three-man arbitration commission. He probably expected the bishop to defend his interests to some degree, because the bishop and the cathedral chapter did not always agree, while on the other hand he and the *vidame* were closely bound by a relationship in which they guaranteed each other's donations, sales, and loans; furthermore, the *vidame* controlled a sizeable part of the lesser aristocracy of western Amiénois, not to mention several religious houses. Perhaps Enguerran brought up matter of the dikes as a bargaining tool; his crisis management strategy centred on damage control and preventing new claims from the church of Amiens. In August he procured the bishop's admission that his one-time military aid could not be turned into a custom, and in October his donation of a fishery on the Selle to Saint-Fuscien ensured that the abbey would not join the chapter of Amiens in its claims. It was in this context that Gérard took over; the bishop's confirmation of the deal with Saint-Fuscien, in November 1224 shortly after Enguerran's death, shows that he and the new *vidame* were working together towards reaching a compromise.[169] Thus, although Gérard inherited a crisis from his father, he was also given a strategy for solving it. The dispute with the chapter ended through a final agreement in July 1226. On the key issues, Gérard donated

---

[168] 'Nos quicquid de ipso Thome contingat siue dimittat locum de Placeio siue quocumque alio modo de ipso deficiat, in consuetudinem non trahemus, quod aqua illa debeat ibidem ulterius currere, nisi fiat de voluntate vicedomini'; Paris, AN, MS R^1 672, fol. 55r; original charter in AN, R^1 634. Thomas, a scion of the family of lords of Boves and promoted to provost of the chapter in 1225, probably inherited Plachy from his kin but was expected to leave it to another canon; Newmann, *Personnel*, p. 7. With the exception of Margaret of Picquigny's marriage to Nicholas of Rumigny, the son of Isabelle of Boves, the *vidame* and the family of Boves did not have significant interactions; William M. Newmann, *Les Seigneurs de Nesle en Picardie, XIIe–XIIIe siècle* (Paris, 1971), pp. 95–7.

[169] Paris, AN, MS R^1 672, fol. 54r; Paris, AN, R^1 634, dossier 4 (Saint-Fuscien).

the forest of Gisonville as well as fishing rights near the Somme's confluence but reserved free navigation for his fishermen.[170] In addition, the chapter received its *arroagium* and the existing dikes were allowed, but it promised not to build new ones and accepted that its rights did not extend beyond the lower course of Selle. Finally, Gérard was absolved of any compensation for his father's harassment of the church of Revelles (the fact that this was even considered is another indication that one's social world was shaped by the actions of one's predecessor).

In the long run, the convention of 1226 signalled the *vidame*'s failure to control the resources of the Selle valley. The chapter's interest in the area persisted and Gérard leased out segments of the Selle to be exploited by the chapter, including more fishing rights and the collection of the passage tax at the bridge of Saleux (1244), a deal reworked by his son Jean in 1263, when he also farmed out the Selle from Bacouel to Prouzel. Despite provisions that limited the duration of the concession, the chapter's investment in the area points towards a more enduring presence.[171] Gérard seems to have settled on the idea that he would share control of the Selle with the church of Amiens, but no others: the canons, it was stipulated, could not in turn sell the fishing rights to a third party.

Conflicts lingered, however, around the village of Revelles, where the church of Amiens was opposed by the leading lay landowners, backed by the *vidame*. The problem was the chapter's systematic policy of acquisitions of land from the 1190s to the 1210s, which threatened the balance of power in the village.[172] In all likelihood, some of the men had been reluctant sellers, forced by financial difficulties to part with their lands. When two agents of the chapter apprehended the man of Enguerran of Revelles, the *vidame*'s *vavassor*, on account of some missed payments, his two sons freed the man and injured one of the agents: they broke into the mayor's house where the man was held, and one of the brothers, named Robert, head-butted (with his helmet on!) the chapter's man and punched him in the face.[173] The brothers were subsequently excommunicated by the chapter's dean, and it was only through Gérard's intercession that an agreement was reached in January 1235, whereby they pledged their property to the church awaiting fuller investigation and a definitive judgement; Gérard's brother Renaud guaranteed the agreement by pledging his own lands. Robert accepted the chapter's version

---

[170] Paris, AN, MS R^1 672, fol. 43v.

[171] Ibid., fols 43r, 54r.

[172] Roux (ed.), *Cartulaire du chapitre*, vol. 1, pp. 175–6, 196.

[173] Ibid., vol. 1, pp. 301–3.

of the events and centred his defence on the absence of premeditation, hoping for a mitigated judgement. He claimed he initially wanted to release the man by giving pledges but changed his mind upon hearing that he had been treated badly. In medieval society, the public rumour that Robert referenced was closer to our 'common knowledge' and approached the status of a legal category.[174] In this case as well, Gérard sought a strategy of compromise with the church of Amiens. With the chapter claiming Revelles as its village, he focused on limiting the damage to his influence by holding on to whatever foothold he still had through his men there, like the *vavassor* and his sons.

That relations between the church and the *vidame* soured is confirmed by the 'numerous altercations' alleged against Gérard in respect to the *sesterage* or due on grains that both parties claimed was theirs to collect at Le Hocquet. The episode is important because it reveals the difficulties Gérard faced trying to preserve his father's acquisitions. In an arbitration charter of 1235,[175] Gérard emphasised that he and his father had enjoyed possession of this revenue, whereas the bishop argued that the *vidame* did not have the right to collect the *sesterage* because it had been wrongly acquired. The bishop had managed to seize the revenue – a classic move whereby one made one's claims known – and was in possession of it at the time of the agreement. Despite the bishop's allegations, Gérard's response had been limited and adjusted to the logic of a game in which the first move had been made by the bishop. Strategic agency was also constructed culturally. Whereas a disproportionate reaction might have eliminated the chance of a compromise, the chosen course of action apparently created only enough trouble so that a more balanced arbitration commission could be selected. For the dispute over the river Selle had driven home forcefully the need to select truly neutral arbitrators. In a first stage this consisted of an official of the chapter and a notable of Amiens, named Firminus. The latter was not the *vidame*'s man but he was not the bishop's either: some nine years later he was the mayor of Amiens's surety in a conflict with the bishop.[176] The bishop realised that Firminus might not rally to the canons' findings, hence the provisions for a second stage of the arbitration, when a third man, Enguerran of Heilly, would join the commission. Although a canon of Amiens, he held lands at Val-de-Maisons from Gérard and his family had been closely linked with the lords of Picquigny; he was an acceptable solution

---

[174] See Chris Wickham, 'Fama and the Law in Twelfth-Century Tuscany', in Thelma Fenster and Daniel Lord Smail (eds), *Fama: The Politics of Talk and Reputation in Medieval Europe* (Ithaca, NY, 2003), pp. 15–26, at pp. 16–17, 25.

[175] Paris, AN, MS R^1 672, fol. 54v.

[176] Roux (ed.), *Cartulaire du chapitre*, vol. 1, p. 382.

for both parties. The bishop's limited confidence in a favourable arbitration surfaces in the provision that either party could appeal the decision in his court with respect to permanent ownership of the *sesterage*.[177] While the final decision in the arbitration is not preserved, on the whole the *vidame* procured a better arrangement than ten years previously.[178]

In sum, fifty or more years after the annexation of the county of Amiens to the royal domain, local affairs were settled through the agency of the main political actors, the bishop and the *vidame*, increasingly drawn into conflict with each other by their plans of expansion and consolidation but still willing to compromise because too much was at stake in their close relationship to risk escalation. The persistence of a mode of dispute resolution going back to the 'stateless France' of the tenth and eleventh centuries reflects the very limited role played by the king's *prevôt* in the *vidame*'s and bishop's affairs.[179] The first royal *prevôt* appointed to Amiens, Pierre of Béthisy, was involved only occasionally in the arrangements of the leading men of the Amiénois; he never reached enough social standing to pose a challenge to the preeminence of *vidame*, from whom he held a tithe in Vicogne.

The goal of this detailed study of a seigneurie smaller than a county for a period of little more than half a century is not to extrapolate unduly at the expense of local and chronological diversity, but to offer an anthropologically

---

[177] The larger political context in France was not favourable to such a sentence; backed by the king, the magnates, including Gérard's relations, the counts of Montfort and Ponthieu, had resolved not to accept ecclesiastical judgements in civil cases; see Richard, *Saint Louis*, p. 79.

[178] In 1302 the inventory of the bishop's possessions and rights listed the tithe and mills of Le Hocquet but not the *sesterage;* M. J. Garnier, 'Dénombrement du temporel de l'évêché d'Amiens, en 1301', *Mémoires de la Société des Antiquaires de Picardie*, 2nd ser., 7 (1860), 107–310, at pp. 156, 161, 164. The inventory included Jean of Picquigny's homage charter detailing what he held from the bishop, including the collection of the *sesterage* 'in the city as well as the suburbs and hinterland of Amiens' ('en le chité d'Amiens et en le banliue d'Amiens et es appartenanches de ches lieus'), which may well have Le Hocquet; ibid., p. 294.

[179] See Frederic Cheyette, 'Giving Each His Due', repr. in Lester K. Little and Barbara H. Rosenwein (eds), *Debating the Middle Ages: Issues and Readings* (Oxford, 1998), pp. 170–9; Stephen D. White, 'Pactum ... legem vincit et amor judicium: The settlement of disputes by compromise in eleventh-century Western France', repr. in Stephen D. White, *Feuding and Peace-making in Eleventh-century France* (Aldershot, 2005), pp. 281–308, esp. pp. 289–90.

informed perspective that brings to light crucial aspects of medieval rural society that have been obscured by the focus on the structures of power. Individual strategising, negotiation, and exchanges within the frame of local sociopolitical networks have been brought into view by a microhistorical investigation attentive to nuance. Conversely, kinship ties, structural power or domination, and feudal relations, the battle horses of so much scholarship on medieval lordship, appear less consequential.

Mobilising kinship ties was not Enguerran and Gérard's preferred means of achieving strategic objectives; rather, they relied on professional administrators, detailed record-keeping, and the networks of local supporters in which they invested so much of their time and resources. The fact that we only know this thanks to the exceptionally detailed evidence of the Picquigny cartulary suggests that in less well-documented cases the prominence of kinship ties may be a distortion caused by fragmentary evidence. The *vidame* might find in his family a source of support (Enguerran's sister, Margaret, being the prime example), but also of resistance – witness the dispute between Enguerran and his uncle Gérard of Ailly, followed by cold relations with Gérard's son.

Homage and fief-holding were shaped in the interactions and dialogue of power between the political actors. These were not limited to the leading noblemen of the region, but included village notables styling themselves knights, as well as well-off commoners, such as the millers. Notwithstanding his position of power, the lord of Picquigny was attentive to the agency of less powerful competitors, notably the lords of Vignacourt, and even social subalterns. This is particularly true of Enguerran, whereas Gérard, who relied more on the resources accumulated during Enguerran's rule rather than a network of supporters, met with less success. This difference in patterns of agency notwithstanding, the viability of the seigneurie of Picquigny rested less on structural power – be it the concentration of economic resources or the institutional position of *vidame* of Amiens – and more on building networks of supporters, investment in professional administrators and record-keeping, negotiation, and strategic action. Power was constituted through these practices; the agency of the lords of Picquigny and their supporters and competitors accounts for the balance of power in the Amiénois. This may seem banal but it is a corrective to the perspective of a good deal of scholarship on medieval lordship that takes power for granted, with little attention to how it was built; not infrequently, the point is merely to show how forcefully power was wielded by those at the top of the social hierarchy. Similarly, relations between the *vidame* and the bishop of Amiens are best approached from the perspective of social network analysis, rather than in institutional terms. Their reluctance to escalate occasional conflicts makes better sense from this perspective: connected through multiple network ties and involved in common enterprises, the *vidame* and the bishop depended on each other.

The focus on agency brings to light the human dimension of the larger historical processes that Picquigny exemplifies. Enguerran, Gérard, and their entourage channelled a good part of their efforts towards a political design that is part and parcel of the sweeping transformations of the twelfth and thirteenth centuries. Like higher lords around them, they aimed to control more closely the local elites by combining two increasingly prevalent but fundamentally different strategies: extensive record-keeping and clearer legal norms on the one hand, and courtly sociability on the other. The latter approach, manifest in the *vidames'* insistence on the local elites' attendance at the banquets organised at their castle, resonates with a general social trend going back at least two centuries in Western Europe and known as 'the civilising process'.[180] The former tends to be associated unreflexively with 'feudalisation' because some of its aspects resemble the core tenets of one or another of the feudal paradigms popular fifty years ago. But of feudal relations in any meaningful sense this comprehensive survey of the records of the Amiénois has found only a few traces. Formulas such as 'I am the man of the *vidame* of Amiens' and the stipulations regarding the dues owed for property or attempting to restrict its alienation did not produce substantial changes in local politics. The modest beginnings made in this respect by Enguerran and Gérard picked up pace in the ensuing half century, but because by the fourteenth century local power relations were shaped by the growing power of the French monarchy, it does not seem that by then feudal relations were strong structural factors any more than in the first half of the thirteenth century. The historical significance of Enguerran and Gérard's initiatives lies less in the consolidation of the normative framework of lordship along 'feudal' lines and more in the gradual bureaucratisation of local governance and society through trained administrators, extensive record-keeping, and more methodical procedures.[181]

The new aristocratic sociability was advanced within the accepted frame of the older castle guard service that it fundamentally transformed. Similarly, the norms regarding fiefs were appropriated and transformed by the lords of Picquigny – witness the complex arrangement known as 'joint liege homage' with

---

[180] Norbert Elias, *The Civilising Process*, rev. edn, trans. Edmund Jephcott (Oxford, 2000).

[181] The 'feudal' crisis alleged by Nieus in connection with the *estages* – but ignoring the evidence of land acquisitions – rests on the assumption that homage charters were a last-ditch attempt to replace an earlier putative 'feudalism' of the interpersonal, affective kind; 'Débuts de la diplomatique', p. 86. From the 1190s to the 1230s and Gérard's minor setbacks, Picquigny was a thriving seigneurie.

the key family ally, Dreux of Saint-Sauflieu; or the reciprocal, circular homage exchanged between the lords of Picquigny and Beauval. Both examples testify to the adaptability and creativity required of territorial leaders in a changing society. Some of the *vidames*' schemes were remarkably complex, as in the case of the land deal aimed at ensuring the services of Jean of Fourdrinoy. Notwithstanding the instrumental role of administrators and key supporters, the strategic decisions were made by the lord of Picquigny. This much is clear from the different strategic designs pursued by Enguerran and Gérard: development and expansion for the former, consolidation for the latter. Gérard's social world and courses of action were shaped in good measure by Enguerran's achievements. This offers another illustration of the limits placed on the agency of the leading territorial lord, not just by peers and subordinates, but also by a predecessor.

Notwithstanding that cultural aspects are harder to study from charters, this chapter has reached some significant findings, worth highlighting as a corrective to the bias in favour of strategising in the sources. We have formed an idea of Enguerran's and Gérard's worldviews, particularly of where they sensed that power lay, as reflected in the organisation of the lists of castle guard according to the social weight of the aristocrats and a logic of centre and periphery. Their worldviews were shaped by family tradition: as elsewhere in premodern Europe, patrimonial land was prized for more than just economic reasons. Enguerran and Gérard acted as autonomous moral agents even in matters touching on religion: their pious donations came with strings attached and were aimed at deriving symbolic gains through the association with religious houses that were important centres of local social life, and economic gains by drawing on church resources for their own projects. Local knowledge could account for success but relying on it alone could spell failure, as when an outsider like the papal legate arrived at Picquigny. The *vidame*'s network of key supporters and allies was not merely strategic but entailed a cultural dimension as well. However terse, the records afford a glimpse into the development of the friendship between Enguerran and Dreux of Saint-Sauflieu – a relationship at once personal and socially scripted. Dreux's gestures of good will – the donations to Gard abbey – can be seen as giving expression, in a shared cultural idiom, to his genuine regard for a friend and desire to emulate a cultural model: to be more like his noble friend, we might say. That the donations also served the strategic purpose of consolidating the alliance between the two lords points to the convergence of instrumental and expressive rationality. Strategic interests and sociocultural values were often aligned. The dispute regarding the *sesterage* of Le Hocquet, for example, brings to light not just divergent interests, but divergent worldviews as well. The secular viewpoint drew attention to the fact that the *vidames* enjoyed unchallenged possession of the *sesterage* for many years; thus it emphasised custom and tradition. Conversely, the ecclesiastical perspective singled out the fact that the *sesterage* had been wrongly acquired in the first place. Against the empirical viewpoint that that practice creates rights and uncontested possession leads, after a time span, to ownership, the bishop's argument asserts the primacy of more abstract reasoning, operating in terms of right or wrong regardless of the realities on the ground. Undoubtedly the material stake of the dispute reinforced each party's commitment to its own perspective on justice and society, but it is as likely that the genuine attachment to their divergent worldviews also reinforced the decision to pursue the case.

Reconstructing sociocultural perspectives from charters may seem to yield meagre results, but it must be stressed that the foregoing analysis has discerned the lived values of the Picard aristocracy. The attention received by minute matters of local politics and economics tells us what occupied much of the time of thirteenth-century lords.[182] Whereas their ancestor met his end in the third crusade, Enguerran and Gérard III rode into battle only on some rare occasion.[183] The endemic private wars and knightly violence of *Raoul de Cambrai*, the celebrated epic poem completed and circulated during their lifetime, could hardly have resonated in their world of careful management of resources, investment in professional administrators, and calculated action – a fact that suggests more caution in abstracting cultural models from literary texts on the basis of arguments for the verisimilitude of medieval literature.[184]

---

[182] Cf. the investigation of seigniorial microeconomics in Catherine Goldmann, 'La seigneurie de Fontenay-le-Marmion (Calvados): analyse d'une comptabilité seigneuriale (1377–1380)', in *Seigneurs et seigneuries au Moyen Age* (Paris, 1993), pp. 275–87. On the monastic side, see Constance Brittain Bouchard, *Holy Entrepreneurs: Cistercians, Knights, and Economic Exchange in Twelfth-century Burgundy* (Ithaca, NY, 1991) and Robert Berkhofer, *Day of Reckoning: Power and Accountability in Medieval France* (Philadelphia, 2004).

[183] E.g., in 1242 Gérard and other Picard lords were in the king's army assembled against the count of Marche; Delisle (ed.), *Recueil*, vol. 23, pp. 726–7.

[184] See, e.g., Stephen D. White, 'Service for Fiefs or Fiefs for Service: The Politics of Reciprocity', in Gadi Algazi, Valentin Groebner, and Bernhard Jussen (eds), *Negotiating the Gift: Pre-modern Figurations of Exchange* (Göttingen, 2003), pp. 63–98.

3

To Render an Account of One's Deeds: The *Livres de Raison*

THE PICQUIGNY WERE AMONG the very first French aristocrats to commission a private cartulary, but by the fourteenth century such records became more widespread and were even adopted by better-off bourgeois.[1] Private cartularies provided some of the inspiration for a new kind of register that took root among legal professionals and merchants: the *liber rationis* or *livre de raison*,[2] kept by the *pater familias* and often passed on from father to son over several generations. It compiled all manner of material deemed crucial for the management of the family patrimony, from accounts of receipts and disbursements to transcripts of sale deeds, in French, Occitan, or Latin. Indeed, some *livres de raison* are little more than accounting and patrimonial lists, quite close to private cartularies.[3] However, the inclusion of notes on family events, notably births and marriages, became a defining feature of the genre. The more elaborate *livres de raison* combine features of family chronicle, account book, and diary; by the end of the fifteenth century more than one such register might be kept by the *pater familias*.[4] Exceptionally, even a family

---

[1] See Lucie Fossier and Olivier Guyotjeannin, 'Cartulaires français laïques: seigneuries et particuliers', in Olivier Guyotjeannin, Laurent Morelle, and Michel Parisse (eds), *Les Cartulaires: Actes de la table ronde organisée par l'Ecole nationale des chartes* (Paris, 1993), pp. 379–410, at pp. 392–7.

[2] Jean Tricard, 'Qu'est-ce qu'un livre de raison Limousin du XVe siècle?', *Journal des savants* (1988), pp. 263–76.

[3] Marie Rose Bonnet (ed.), *Livres de raison et de comptes en Provence: Fin du XIVe siècle – début du XVIe siècle* (Aix-en-Provence, 1995). But one of the earliest extant *livres de raison* includes notes on personal and local events in addition to copies of charters and entries on payments; Joseph Petit (ed.), *De Libro Rationis Guillelmi de Erqueto* (Paris, 1900).

[4] Thus the opening line of the Roquet *livre de raison* (1478–) indicates that its focus was material that did not belong in 'the great account books': 'lo libre de las memorias, en lo qal ha escrichas pluzors cauzas las qalas no so pouhont escrichas en los grans libres de sayns'; Louis Guibert (ed.), *Nouveau recueil de registres domestiques limousins et marchois* (2 vols, Paris, 1895), vol. 1, p. 118.

of illiterate peasants might pay to have their records kept.⁵ Most of the extant medieval *livres de raison* are from Limousin and Provence, and it is unlikely that this is merely the effect of the accidents of survival, although the *livres'* poorer archival conservation compared to official records explains why only some twenty-odd have been preserved for the period before 1500. Having said this, the medieval *livres de raison* are something of a textual experiment, unaffected by the constraints of a genre, and as such particularly valuable for the sociocultural historian. By contrast, from the late sixteenth century manuals provided guidelines on keeping a *livre de raison*, a development that speaks to the standardisation of the genre.⁶

Not all registers that today are grouped under this category were identified by their compilers as *livres de raison*. This notwithstanding, the name is appropriate because accounting and accountability were crucial in all of them, whether or not the title included the term *ratio* or *raison*, in the sense of account or rationale. The term referred both to the ubiquitous accounting of revenues and expenses as well as to the moral accountability of the *pater familias* towards the family and its posterity. Both aspects are directly relevant for the study of agency: the former for its strategic dimension, inasmuch as socioeconomic agency was predicated on a correct assessment of limited resources; the latter in a broader cultural sense, as illustrated in Chapter 1 by Salimbene's acceptance of responsibility for the effects of his actions on the family line. Medieval practices of accountability have been studied mostly in relation to the development of administrative and financial institutions, which, however, were informed by sociomoral ideas. This is epitomised by the widespread use in twelfth-century administrative documents of a phrase with biblical echoes, *reddere rationem*, 'to render an account'. It suggests an act of judgement and thus carries an implication of responsibility to a social superior.⁷ As literacy became more widespread among the middle urban strata, by the fourteenth century such notions were grafted on the customary role of

---

⁵ Florent Hautefeuille, 'Livre de compte ou livre de raison: le registres d'une famille de paysans quercynois, les Guitards de Saint-Anthet (1417–1526)', in Natacha Coquerie, François Menant, and Florence Weber (eds), *Écrire, compter, mesurer: vers une histoire de rationalités pratiques* (Paris, 2006), pp. 242–6. For an Italian parallel, see Duccio Balestracci, *The Renaissance in the Fields: Family Memoirs of a Fifteenth-century Tuscan Peasant*, trans. Paolo Squatriti and Betsy Merideth (University Park, PA, 1999).

⁶ Sylvie Mouysset, *Papiers de famille: Introduction à l'étude des livres de raison (France, XVe–XIXe siècle)* (Rennes, 2007), p. 39.

⁷ Thomas Bisson, *The Crisis of the Twelfth Century: Power, Lordship, and the Origins of European Government* (Princeton, 2008), p. 324, and more generally pp. 322–49.

the *pater familias*. Another use of the *livres de raison* is noteworthy: the transmission of conduct advice to one's heirs, from lessons about making the right business decisions to tips about travel, medicine, and keeping track of one's records. In the area analysed here, Limousin, the authors of *livres de raison* often hailed from small towns and were in touch with rural life, a fact that accounts for a mix of learned and popular knowledge on miraculous remedies, from potions to prayers and incantations. This opens a new angle on beliefs in non-human agency – not from theology but from a popularising magical–religious literature and, importantly, the everyday experience of the natural world. Lastly, the *livres de raison* offer a grassroots perspective on some of the crucial developments of the fourteenth and fifteenth centuries. Beyond the obvious growth of pragmatic literacy, of note is the rise in status of a socioprofessional group of lawyers, notaries, and judges, to which can be added in the case of Limousin the reconstruction of the rural economy affected by the Hundred Years' War, a process that involved microeconomic strategies down to the level of the heads of individual households.

Agency and accountability in the register of Gérald Tarneau

The *livres de raison* have not received the attention that their Italian counterparts, the *ricordi* and *ricordanze*, have enjoyed for several decades now. They have mostly been used for studies of historical demography and the medieval family,[8] with the occasional exploration of family 'memory'.[9] As we have seen, there are solid grounds for the association between the *livres de raison* and the history of the family. Equally, however, an individual voice emerges from each record: that of the *livre de raison*'s author or compiler, as a rule the *pater familias*. Thus, the *livres de raison* occasionally functioned as the medium for a discourse about the self. It bears emphasis that in the *livres de raison* the focus can be both more narrow and wider than the family. On the one hand, although the *livres* are circumscribed by the family sphere, they amount in large measure to a record of individual agency, as the initiatives of the *pater familias* are disproportionately represented to the detriment of the domestic

---

[8] E.g., Jean-Louis Biget and Jean Tricard, 'Livres de raison et démographie familiale en Limousin au XVe siècle', *Annales de démographie historique* (1981), pp. 321–63.

[9] Jean Tricard, 'La mémoire des Benoist: livre de raison et mémoire familiale au XVe siècle', in Bernard Guillemain (ed.), *Temps, mémoire, tradition au Moyen Age* (Aix-en-Provence, 1983), pp. 119–40. The *livres* are rarely discussed in English-language scholarship; see, e.g., Kathleen Ashley, 'Creating Family Identity in Books of Hours', *Journal of Medieval and Early Modern Studies*, 32:1 (Winter 2002), 145–66, at p. 147.

labour of other family members. The authors' occasional reflections on their achievements open a window onto one's sense of acting on behalf of others, specifically in the service of the family – a subject that also occupied Salimbene, as we have seen. On the other hand, in the *livres* the family is reflected in its wider social context. The accountability goes beyond the family head's responsibility to heirs and includes a record of his exchanges with social partners and involvement in the community, from representing it in local politics to the collection of taxes. Both scenarios are illustrated by the *livre de raison* of Etienne Bénoist,[10] as well as by the first case study explored in this chapter.

In 1425 Gérald Tarneau, royal notary in Pierre-Buffière, used the middle folios of a notarial register inherited from his father to write an account of the events in which his town and himself as a local notable had been embroiled for several months.[11] Pierre-Buffière was a strategically located fortified town of some commercial importance, some 20 kilometres south of Limoges. The community had received its charter of franchise in the thirteenth century, but Pierre-Buffière remained the seat of a regionally significant seigniorial family.[12] Gérald Tarneau was a trained lawyer, signing his notarised charters as *magister* and *bacallarius in legibus* and at one point in the narrative calling himself *judex vicecomitatus* (it was not uncommon for legal professionals to hold more than one appointment).[13] By his own account he was on good terms with both the lord of Pierre-Buffière and the family of viscounts of Limoges, originally from Brittany. He soon expanded the scope of his writing to include important family events, notably births, in line with the practice of *livres de raison*. He continued to use the rest of the register, after the chronicle and

---

[10] Benoist recorded how he discharged himself, as consul of Limoges, of the collection of a tax from his fellow citizens in 1427; Louis Guibert (ed.), 'Le livre de raison de Etienne Benoist', *Bulletin de la Société Archéologique et Historique du Limousin*, 29 (1881), 225–318, at p. 258.

[11] The first charters transcribed in the register are not only signed by his father but written in a different hand from the local chronicle penned by Gérald; Limoges, BFM, MS 6, *Registre d'Aimeric et Gérald Tarneau, notaires à Pierre Buffière*. The paper register numbers 58 folios. The narrative of events and the family notations are edited in A. Leroux and A. Bosvieux (eds), *Chartes, chroniques et mémoriaux pour servir à l'histoire de la Marche et du Limousin* (Tulle and Limoges, 1886), pp. 203–37. References to the manuscript use Leroux's numbering of the folios, where the chronicle of local events begins on fol. 35r (or fol. 39r, according to the numbering in the lower corner).

[12] Jean-Michel Desbordes, 'Les origines de Pierre-Buffière (Haute-Vienne)', *Revue archéologique du Centre de la France*, 17:3–4 (1978), 169–76.

[13] Limoges, BFM, MS 6, fols. 49v, 50; Leroux and Bosvieux (eds), *Chartes*, p. 228.

family notes inserted in the middle, for his notarial work, transcribing the contents of various charters (from fol. 43r).

It all started with a tax.[14] A *taille* had been agreed by the three estates of Limousin in 1424, to be collected by the king of France's lieutenant in the province, Guillaume d'Albret. Pierre-Buffière's share was 80 francs but when the officials in charge of collection came to the town the people gathered 'cum gladiis et fustibus', refusing to pay (December 1424); they even put on a show of defiance on the occasion of d'Albret's passage through the town some days later. As a town notable who furthermore was in the good graces of the local lord, Gérald Tarneau is at pains to emphasise that all this was done against the better counsel of Louis of Pierre-Buffière, who became 'multus iratus contra gentes' once he learned of their actions. The result was that d'Albret delegated the collection of the *taille* to a Gascon soldier of fortune who with his henchmen terrorised the countryside from the hilltop castle of Châlucet. That was when the troubles really started for the people of Pierre-Buffière. One of the two local notables tasked with collecting the *taille* refused to get involved – presumably because he sensed that the mood in town had not changed and the collection would be difficult – and the other was absent (Easter 1425). Nothing was collected and the Châlucet gang proceeded to attack the town by surprise but were repelled. This helped focus the denizens' minds, who assembled in the presence of Louis of Pierre-Buffière and his nephew, the lord of nearby Châteauneuf-la-Forêt, and following Gérald's presentation of the facts the decision was reached to collect and pay the *taille*. After this was done some inhabitants of Pierre-Buffière who had been held prisoner in Châlucet were released. But some of the Châlucet-based raiders remained a threat even after the payment of the *taille* to their lord, because as a condition for peace they demanded reimbursement for their losses in the attack, notably a horse, whose price was quite probably inflated. After another attack claimed the life of an inhabitant of Pierre-Buffière (and the loss of another horse for the attackers), negotiations and an attempted arbitration in which Gérald played a key role proved unsuccessful. After a failed attempt to storm the town by deceit, another round of negotiations took place, again with Gérald among the representatives of Pierre-Buffière, and again to no avail. Pierre-Buffière even suffered the destruction of a tower when the prisoners held therein tried to escape. Finally, through the involvement of Guillaume d'Albret, who had been given a recitation of the events from the locals' perspective by the same Gérald, a compensation was fixed for four of the fighters from Châlucet. But this was

---

[14] Brief overview of the events in Jean Tricard, *Les campagnes limousines du XIVe au XVIe siècle: originialité et limites d'une reconstruction rurale* (Paris, 1996), pp. 3–4.

strongly resented at Pierre-Buffière and consequently nothing was paid. The matter seemingly went quiet for a while and Gérald interrupted his narrative.

He resumed it some months later, by which time the local context had become more complicated. In August 1426 Jean de l'Aigle, the brother of the viscount of Limoges, lay siege to the city of Limoges for two weeks, with Louis of Pierre-Buffière joining the sieging army and the people of Limoges enlisting the services of the mercenary captain of Châlucet and his men, including several protagonists of the yet unsolved conflict with Pierre-Buffière. The narrative now reaches the climax of the *guerra*: on the night of 31 January 1427 a raiding party from Châlucet managed to enter within the walls of Pierre-Buffière; one of their first targets was Gérald's house, attacked by some 17 men 'bene armati' who cried 'Ad domum magistri Géraldi!' He successfully defended his home until dawn, barricading the entrances and establishing firing posts for the three crossbows he had at hand, aided by family and friends, including the town schoolmaster. His brother and the lord of Pierre-Buffière joined forces with the inhabitants and at the end of a night's fighting the *latrones* retreated, having failed to take control of either the town tower or the castle, but carrying with them what they had looted from the denizens' houses. As news of the attack spread, Jean de l'Aigle sent a letter of support to the lord of Pierre-Buffière, copied by Gérald in his account. De l'Aigle and his troops, some of them English, spent a night in Pierre-Buffière; de l'Aigle himself was hosted in Gérald's home. In his account, Gérald is at pains to stress that he opposed their arrival and that in the end they caused no disturbance and paid for their victuals. A truce was agreed through the exchange of several letters of agreement (*sufferta*), duly included by Gérald in his register; he had continued to play a part in the negotiations and drafted the first letter sent by de l'Aigle to the captain of Châlucet. The peace that was concluded between de l'Aigle and the mercenaries of Châlucet in May 1427 was funded through a new *taille* imposed on Pierre-Buffière, in excess of 600 *écu* (approximately five times the *taille* paid in 1425), a fact that Gérald, who was involved in the apportioning of the tax among the inhabitants, avows to have deplored even as he dared not complain in view of the powerful lord de l'Aigle's involvement in the matter.

Self-references abound in Gérald's chronicling of these events, mostly in the first person, for example, 'ego respondi sibi quod ego non habebam mandatum ad hoc'.[15] Their number and narrative significance mark an important difference from Galbert de Bruges's otherwise similar piece of local history in which writing about one's community in crisis amounts to narrating one's own

---

[15] Leroux and Bosvieux (eds), *Chartes*, p. 215.

predicament and thus, in a sense, narrating the self. Gérald's autobiographical insertions are more redolent of Salimbene's chronicle but, crucially, without the tone of retrospective, narrative self-assertion. Rather, Gérald's writing is forensic even as he seeks to present himself in a positive light; far from embellishing his role in the events, he is content to document it meticulously. There is a simple reason for this: from beginning to end Gérald was truly instrumental in the community's resistance against the Châlucet mercenaries, in particular playing a leading role, as town notable and trained legal professional, in the successive rounds of negotiations. But the denouement left many in the town unhappy – Gérald himself makes plain his discomfort – and although the logical explanation, then and now, is that the people of Pierre-Buffière were no match for the forces fighting for control of Limoges and its hinterland, Gérald found it prudent to produce a comprehensive record of the events and his role in them. He did not write to make himself stand out among his fellow men as knowledgeable and influential, which is largely Salimbene's motivation in narrating several autobiographical episodes, but wrote about himself because he *had been* so important in the events of his community. This observation finds its corollary in the contrast between the use of rhetorical strategies in Salimbene's narrative self-fashioning – the creation in the text of a favourable self-image – and Gérald's evidential approach aimed at producing an unembellished record of his actions, with special emphasis on the precise words exchanged during the negotiations. He is careful to record Louis of Pierre-Buffière and the community's approval of his part in the negotiations, but does it forensically, without aggrandisement: 'ego repportavi quod feceram. Et fuerunt domnus et gentes contenti quod non feceram [compensation under the terms of an agreement that excluded d'Albret], dicentes quod non facerent residuum, quia jam esset causa decisa'.[16] His writing is similarly understated when he points to those behind ominous decisions. Acknowledging his presence among the notables to whom the request for the *taille* had been put, the second time around, by the captain of Châlucet, Gérald wards off personal responsibility not emphatically but matter-of-factly. Although terse, the account unmistakably implies that the collection failed because of the two locals assigned as tax officials, one absent and the other one simply refusing to get involved: 'Sed Guillemus Hugonis dixit quod non se intromitteret, et ibidem remansit commission'.[17] Only once does Tarneau defend his actions

---

[16] Ibid., p. 215.
[17] Ibid., p. 207.

in rather impassionate language, calling God as his witness that he did not consent to d'Albret's English troops' entrance into Pierre-Buffière.[18]

The tone of Tarneau's account is more than a lawyer's reflex; it speaks to a well-defined project underlying the chronicling of local events. To understand its nature two more considerations are essential. First is Tarneau's care not only to identify by name as many as possible of the participants to the multiple rounds of fighting and negotiations, but also to document in forensic detail their precise actions – who fired the first crossbow shot, for example – and verbal arguments in the negotiations. Second is the minute attention to the damage caused and sustained by both parties, the locals and the Châlucet raiders: the war horses lost and how the financial compensation demanded for them evolved during negotiations; the prisoners and the length of time they spent in detention; and obviously the damage to property in Pierre-Buffière. In view of these facts, I argue that the text is fundamentally an account, at once financial and, inasmuch as it seeks to trace individual responsibility, moral. It resembles both a legal memorandum and a tally – both of them in narrative form. This conclusion is supported by the verbatim copying of legal documents and more generally the over-abundance of detail, which would seem out of place in a conventional narrative concerned above all with reaching its denouement. The same accounting mentality underpins the *livres de raison*, a fact that explains the ease with which Tarneau moved from chronicling local events to making notations about family events of the kind commonly encountered in the *livres*. The chronicle of local events should thus be viewed as an ego-document not merely for the obvious but rather superficial reason that Gérald uses the pronoun *ego* quite often, which is merely a reflex of the use of *je* in his native French.[19] Rather, it is an ego-document by design, inasmuch as the narrative of local events is inseparable from the record of Gérald's own involvement in them, and shares the same underlying accounting logic as the *livres de raison*, which Gérald emulated through the family notes interspersed through the chronicle's folios.

Gérald's forensic identification of the specific contribution of each individual, friend or foe, in a conflict he clearly understood as between collective entities, reflects a worldview that prioritises individual agency; conversely, collective agency is reduced to the sum of individuals' interventions – a far cry from the emphasis it receives in modern historiography. This is not

---

[18] 'Ego quidem assero, et sic sit michi Deus testis, quod non consentii neque ante neque post'; ibid., p. 227.

[19] There are many other calques from French in his Latin, from 'erat diu' ('il y a longtemps'), to numbers such as 'quatuor viginti' ('quatre-vingt'); ibid., pp. 211, 205.

because Tarneau failed to grasp the importance of collective action; quite the contrary, as a notary he was keenly aware of what it meant. For instance, he stresses he had been chosen (*electum*) by the lord and 'others' (presumably the leading citizens) of Pierre-Buffière to make their case in the first round of negotiations, 'de precepto dicti domini et voluntate et consensu aliorum de Petrabufferia'.[20] More emphatically still, during a second round of negotiations, he declined to accept a proposed solution because it went beyond the limits imposed by the lord and people of Pierre-Buffière on his negotiating mandate: 'domnus de Petrabufferia et habitatores ejusdem ville constituerant terminos legacionis mee et non audebam extendere fines mandati'.[21] As the last words indicate, Gérald was acutely aware of the limits of an individual's freedom of action, which makes it all the more revealing that throughout his narrative he remained deeply interested in individual agency. This finding is worth emphasising in view of medievalists' emphasis on collective agency, from the family to the village or town community. Gérald's interest in individual agency is closely tied to a conception of individual responsibility that reflects his legal background. Specific legal notions shaped his perspective on sociopolitical conduct: for instance, during a proposed arbitration, he invites the knights of Châlucet to make the opening statement because 'ipsi erant actores'.[22] Gérald's personal concern with legal form and proper procedure is evident, but it is clear from his account that by the early fifteenth century legal notions were more present in the life of communities, from conflict settlement to tax collection. The same can be said about the judicial conception of agency, built around individual responsibility. Lastly, the legal habit of documenting in detail the circumstances of key actions leads to the inscription of domestic scenes in the local chronicle. Gérald records that the night of the attack on Pierre-Buffière, as the brigands surrounded his house, he was sleeping in bed with his wife and son Gérald: 'Egoque eram in lecto cum Mariota Bondusona uxore mea, Geraldo filio meo, in domo quam construi.'[23]

The notes on family events ('Nota quod…'), typical of the *livres de raison*, occupy less space than the local chronicle. How Gérald came to record them illustrates a different path to creating one's *livre de raison* than the passage from a register of charters and lists (a private cartulary, *grosso modo*). Having begun writing the chronicle on fol. 35r, Gérald must have found it a short step from writing about his involvement in the community's affairs to taking down

---

[20] Ibid., p. 211.

[21] Ibid., p. 215.

[22] Ibid., p. 210.

[23] Ibid., p. 223.

notes on the events of his family. Accordingly, he left the space of several folios to finish his account, and inserted the first family notes on fols 39v–41v, not in perfectly chronological order but taking advantage of the available space on the folio. Thus, having recorded on fol. 40r the births of his children between 1424 and 1427, he returned in 1438 to the space left at the bottom of fol. 39v to record the birth of his son Hugo. (The space from fols 35r to 39v proved insufficient for his very detailed chronicle and he had to continue it on fols 41r to 42v; on fol. 39v the note 'quere infra ad istud signum' sends the reader to a sign on fol. 41r. where the narrative is resumed – see Plate 2). The notes are almost all about births. Gérald is careful to record the social ties mobilised on these important occasions, starting with the names of the women present to assist in the delivery, both relatives and friends of the family. While such information is rare in the *livres*, the other names recorded in this context, of the baptism sponsors (the *compater* and *commater*), are a normal feature of the genre. A preferred arrangement was that one of the sponsors came from the extended family while the other was either a professional connection – a fellow jurist – or someone of higher social rank, such as the wife of a local aristocrat,[24] whose involvement brought prestige to the Tarneau family. Occasionally family and social ties were embodied by the same person: the godmother of Gérald's first born was the daughter of Gérald's late sister and wife of a lawyer ('licenciatus in legibus') from Limoges.[25] To what extent this accounting of services rendered by kin and friends was utilitarian – recorded in the expectation of further exchanges between the protagonists or their descendants – or merely expressive – put into writing as a record of the social standing of the *pater familias* and the family – remains difficult to ascertain. The former reading makes sense in relation to one episode chronicled in Gérald account, in which he identifies those who helped him defend his home during the night of the attack on Pierre-Buffière.[26] Generally terse, the notes about family events occasionally shine a light on the less readily documented topic of agency within the domestic sphere, as when Gérald's mother-in-law and her sister decided to act quickly and baptise his premature-born daughter a few hours after birth, fearing she might die unbaptised – clearly an example of initiative and mobilisation under exceptional circumstances (shortly afterwards she was baptised a second time by the rector of the hospital of Pierre-Buffière in the church of a near-by monastery; she died eight days later).[27]

[24] Ibid., p. 237.
[25] Ibid., p. 220.
[26] Ibid., p. 225.
[27] Ibid., p. 204.

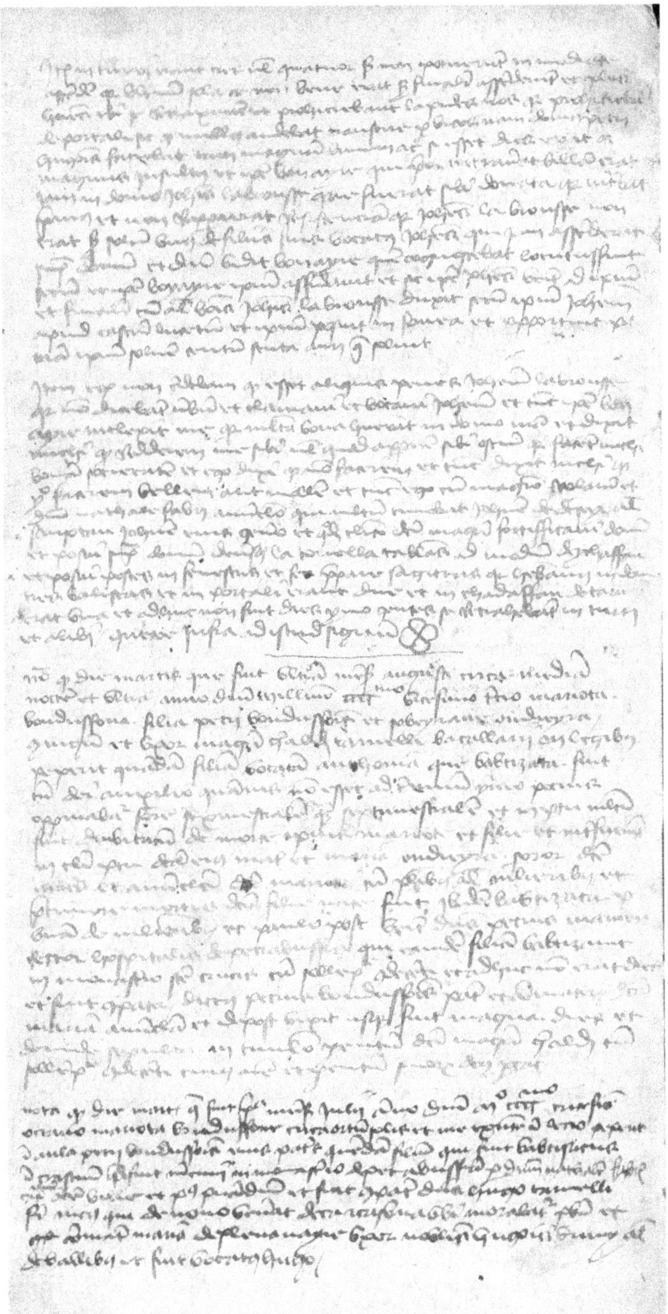

Plate 2. Register of Gérald Tarneau: 'quere infra ad istud signum'.
Reproduced by permission of BFM, Limoges (MS 6, fol. 39v).

A few other notes pertain to a relative's visit to Pierre-Buffière in August 1425; the prices of wheat and rye during the penury of 1434; and the beginning of Gérald's second son's schooling. The last two entries occasion some personal remarks, brief but nevertheless revealing of the desire to inscribe the self in the family history. Gérald emphasises that notwithstanding the large size of his household ('magnam familiam') he was well provisioned with wheat during the penury: 'ego ... eram bene provisus' (note the first-person statement, a marker of his responsibility for the family). He also makes it a point to note that he took his son Jean to school and gave him the first lesson himself ('ego ipsum').[28] As the record of the family's history these notes were not meant for their author alone as aide-mémoire but also for his heirs. Inferences about the envisaged uses of the chronicle of local events are more problematic, but it seems that, recorded in the same register as the family notes, it served a similarly dual purpose: a memorandum of the events and Gérald's role in them both for his own *and* his heirs' use, should the contentious history be brought up against the family by their rivals within the community. In such a case the account would have provided a wealth of evidence in Gérald's defence. That Gérald envisaged his account reaching a broader audience than his family and heirs is suggested by the way he identifies himself in the text on a couple of occasions: 'Egoque Geraldus Tarnelli intereram' or 'domnus de Petrabufferia precepit michi Geraldo Tarnelli quatinus responderem'.[29]

The exemplary *livre de raison* of Pierre Esperon

This section focuses on one of the most well-rounded late-medieval *livres de raison*. It seeks to offer a detailed picture of the sociocultural microcosm of a small-town legal professional with ties to the rural world, a local notable to be sure, but not a member of the aristocracy. Almost everything we know about Pierre Esperon comes from his *livre de raison*. His family had a small estate in Cognac,[30] but he married the heiress of a legal professional and moved to nearby Saint-Junien (some 30 kilometres west of Limoges), where he combined a legal career with diverse businesses, many based around his wife's inheritance. Initially a clerk ('scriptor curie ville Sancti Juniani'), in 1392 he was promoted to judge of the town of Saint-Junien on behalf of the bishop

---

[28] Ibid., p. 236.
[29] Ibid., p. 210.
[30] Called *l'Esperonie*; André Lecler, *Dictionnaire historique et géographique de la Haute Vienne* (Marseille, 1976), p. 310.

of Limoges, who had jurisdiction over the town. He had two daughters and appears to have died shortly after the last diary entry of October 1417. Only a couple of the numerous charters that he must have authored in his career survive independently of the *livre de raison*.[31] Except for a couple of later additions made after Pierre's death by his son-in-law and grandson, the *livre* covers the years 1384–1417.[32] It consists largely of transcriptions of contracts, accounting lists, and the typical notes on births and marriages; a few contracts and pieces of correspondence have been preserved with the *livre*. More interestingly, the *livre* includes a memoir in which Esperon reviews his life-long achievements and a section on extraordinary remedies, from prayers to potions.

Microeconomics

Esperon lived during a turbulent period of the Hundred Years' War, when Limousin suffered devastations, famine, and disease, which puts into perspective his attention to even meagre sums of money. In 1370 the countryside from Limoges to Châlucet was ravaged by three armies (two French and one English);[33] in 1373 the generalised insecurity led the bishop of Limoges to appoint a captain at Saint-Junien to protect the town and enforce order.[34] In 1394 the seneschal of Limoges found that the number of Saint-Junien households capable of paying tax to the crown had been more than halved.[35] After the armistices of the 1390s brought a brief respite, the devastations resumed in the 1400s.[36] War, brigandage, and plague remained on Pierre Esperon's mind and are alluded to in the *livre*, but no mention is made of raids on the town, as at Pierre-Buffière.

---

[31] Louis Guibert (ed.), *Documents, analyses de pièces, extraits et notes relatifs à l'histoire municipale des deux villes de Limoges* (2 vols, Limoges, 1897–1902), vol. 1, pp. 306–8; probably attributable to Esperon is also the record of an agreement between the bishop of Limoges and the chapter of the church of Saint-Junien; Limoges, ADHV, MS 1 G 162.

[32] Guibert (ed.), *Nouveau recueil*, vol. 1, pp. 13–81. The manuscript must be counted among the lost or privately owned *livres de raison*; see Tricard, 'Qu'est-ce qu'un livre de raison', p. 263 n. 1.

[33] Tricard, *Campagnes limousines*, p. 18.

[34] 'speciale mandatum ad faciendum excubias et custodias in eadem villa nostra de die et de nocte'; ADHV, Limoges, MS 1 G 163.

[35] François Arbellot (ed.), *Chronique de Maleu, chanoine de Saint-Junien: Suivié de documents historiques sur la ville de Saint-Junien* (Saint-Junien and Paris, 1847), pp. 183–4.

[36] Tricard, *Campagnes limousines*, pp. 27–8.

The bulk of Esperon's revenue was generated by his land, much of it brought in marriage by his wife. Its successful management was not an unproblematic task. More so than in a stable society, in the turbulent late-medieval Limousin ownership of land and land-rents did not simply lead to prosperity; rather, the success of even the better-off individual depended on his efforts. The foundations of Esperon's prosperity lay in a pattern of diversification of sources of income that required his close monitoring. To understand the importance of his management skills, consider the diary entry of 1403 that lists no fewer than 16 revenues and land-rents, which Esperon collected from some 12 tenants. The largest of these were only 5 *solidi* and 2 *sextarii* of wheat, respectively.[37] The list was subsequently annotated – the *livre de raison* functioned as a managerial tool, similar to seigniorial registers[38] – to reflect the changes that Esperon made in order to ensure the collection of the revenues. In two cases he had to reduce the land-rent ('laxata fuit') when the new tenants took over. Furthermore, comparing the entries of 1403 and 1384 it is apparent that in yet another case the tenant had changed and the annual rent of the plot was reduced.[39] This was a measure often employed by the landlords of Limousin in order to attract tenants and ensure that the lands remained cultivated and produced some revenue.[40] Sometimes it did not work and the landlord faced the abandonment of the land by the tenants,[41] as it happened to Esperon in three cases.[42] Farming was supplemented with a variety of other lucrative activities. Esperon's remuneration, even after his promotion from clerk to judge, brought a mere 100 *solidi* annually.[43] Even his salary had to be collected from as many as 13 locals (1392) who owed moneys to the bishop.[44] Looking for every opportunity to augment his income, he also ran a real-estate business, leasing

---

[37] Guibert (ed.), *Nouveau recueil*, vol. 1, pp. 45–6. Also see the brief survey of Esperon's holdings in Jean Tricard, 'Livres de raison et présence de la bourgeoisie dans le campagnes limousines (XIVᵉ–XVᵉ siècle)', in Elisabeth Mornet (ed.), *Campagnes médiévales: l'homme et son espace: études offertes à Robert Fossier* (Paris, 1995), pp. 709–22, at pp. 714–15.

[38] See, e.g., Catherine Goldmann, 'La seigneurie de Fontenay-le-Marmion (Calvados): analyse d'une comptabilité seigneuriale (1377–1380)', in *Seigneurs et seigneuries au Moyen Age* (Paris, 1993), pp. 275–87, at p. 280.

[39] Guibert (ed.), *Nouveau recueil*, vol. 1, pp. 26–7; 46.

[40] Tricard, *Campagnes limousines*, pp. 48, 66–9.

[41] Ibid., pp. 49–50.

[42] Guibert (ed.), *Nouveau recueil*, vol. 1, p. 46.

[43] Ibid., pp. 27, 30, 33, 76.

[44] Ibid., pp. 27, 35–6.

several houses and occasionally taking in as lodgers the young boys sent to study at Saint-Junien.[45] At the same time that he leased out his land to others, Esperon was also a farmer of land (*receptor*): a small garden from the bishop of Limoges and the domain of Chavagnac from the bishop of Poitiers.[46]

Strategies of economic diversification and small but varied investments have been documented from late-medieval lords – including, as we have seen, the Picquigny – to early-modern ordinary households.[47] This was also the approach of Tuscan merchants; famously, Francesco di Marco Datini derived his financial success from the moderate returns of diversified investments.[48] These otherwise very different examples can be read as a form of risk insurance through hedging one's economic bets. To find a contrasting approach one need look no further than present-day capitalism, where the drive to identify the single most promising venture has raised doubts regarding the value of diversification for corporations.[49] The avoidance of the single path to prosperity had important implications for one's social agency. It required a more nimble, context-sensitive approach, and mastery of different skills. Farming land from the bishops of Limoges and Poitiers Esperon had to perform in relation to them the social role that he sometimes would have needed to counter in dealing with his own tenants and farmers. He needed to know enough about agriculture to exploit his lands effectively, but also act the part of the educated legal professional in front of the parents looking for a suitable host for their children studying in Saint-Junien.

The *livre de raison* bears witness to a coherent strategy of acquisitions, whose main objective was the consolidation of the family assets. First, before 1384, Esperon bought back an annual rent in rye that weighed on the family estate in Cognac, shortly after the rent passed from his uncle to a third party. Second, in 1397, he bought back three-fifths of another annual rent in wheat due from

---

[45] Ibid., pp. 47, 48–9, 58.

[46] Ibid., pp. 34–5, 77.

[47] Laurence Fontaine and Jürgen Schlumbohm, 'Household Strategies for Survival: An Introduction', in Laurence Fontaine and Jürgen Schlumbohm (eds), *Household Strategies for Survival, 1600–2000: Fission, Faction, and Cooperation*, International Review of Social History, supplement 8 (Cambridge, 2000), pp. 1–18, at pp. 3, 11.

[48] Iris Origo, *The Merchant of Prato: Francesco di Marco Datini, 1335–1410* (New York, 1957), p. 149.

[49] See, e.g., John G. Matsusaka, 'Corporate Diversification, Value Maximization, and Organizational Capabilities', *Journal of Business*, 74:3 (2001), 409–31, and Edith C. Busija, Hugh M. O'Neill, and Carl P. Zeithaml, 'Diversification Strategy, Entry Mode, and Performance: Evidence of Choice and Constraints', *Strategic Management Journal*, 18:4 (1997), 321–7.

the same estate of l'Esperonie.⁵⁰ The emancipation (*exonerare*) of the estate from the obligations that weighed on it on behalf of outsiders was a priority because while Pierre may have lived in Saint-Junien, he had high regard for l'Esperonie as the land of his ancestors. The two deals reveal a modus operandi in which time was crucial, starting with the timing of the first transaction: Esperon tied the buy-back to the seller's request for the repayment of the expenses he made on the funeral of Esperon's uncle. In other words, Esperon found the moment propitious to strike a deal because the seller depended on his willingness to accept the funerary expenses as accurate and repay him:

> First, I bought from Pierre d'Alvernhia or de Collibus, in his role as executor of my late uncle Jean's last will, *as well as for reimbursing him* for my uncle's funeral, four of the ten *sextarii* of rye in annual rent which Jean claimed in my household on account of the division [of the patrimonial estate]; these cost 16 *livres* (emphasis added).⁵¹

In 1397, it is the partial character of the acquisition that needs emphasis: Esperon was in no hurry to buy all of the annual rent that weighed on his estate. He must have realised that the purchase opened the way for the acquisition of the other two-fifths of the rent and included in the contract a clause that allowed him to buy them 'at a price in accordance with the usage and custom of the parish of Cognac'.⁵² Esperon might have hoped that the remainder could be redeemed even more cheaply when the right opportunity presented itself. 'Time would work in my benefit,' he apparently reasoned. In the end it did: at an unspecified date he acquired the other two-fifths *titulo donationis*, presumably as a gift. Here, it was the deferment of action that saved Esperon some money; his intuition in deciding to let things unfold at their own pace paid off. Similarly, Esperon became interested in the property lying between another recent land purchase and his vineyards. But he could only acquire it in 1393, after it had devolved to the owner's widow.⁵³ Once again Esperon realised that he could achieve his goal simply by waiting and outliving an owner too reluctant to sell. Another case of good timing involved Esperon taking advantage of the minority of two brothers to purchase an annual

---

⁵⁰ Guibert (ed.), *Nouveau recueil*, vol. 1, p. 42.

⁵¹ 'Primo, emi a Petro de Alvernhia, alias de Collibus, tanquam excequtore testamenti Johannis Esperonis, quondam patrui mei, et pro solvendo funerarias excequias dicti patrui, quatuor sexatarios siliginis renduales, de decem sextariis siliginis rendualibus quos idem Johannes dicebat habere racione partagii sui in hospicio meo; constiterunt xvi'; ibid., p. 53.

⁵² Ibid., p. 42.

⁵³ Ibid., p. 36.

rent in cash.⁵⁴ Finally, by his own account, Esperon helped an elderly couple from Cognac with food and clothing in 1399. Apparently he targeted their inheritance, and indeed was designated the husband's heir in his last will and testament of November 1399. Esperon supported the widow financially, but she did not remain a burden for him for long and passed away the following year.⁵⁵ Esperon gained the inheritance, which admittedly was not large, with a minimal investment. His anticipation of the elderly owners' demise was so well calculated that he only provided for them for a short while. Timing was once again of the essence.

This broad pattern of action can be grasped as a way of *manipulating time*. While the temporality of action is a key aspect more generally, the manipulation of time refers specifically to strategies in which time is the central element. In some of the example above it was all about knowing when to act, while in others it was all about waiting, but what they all have in common is the conscious exploitation of the possibilities that time opens up. If time was on Esperon's side, it is because his business interests encompassed more than one front and he could afford to wait until the opportune moment for a deal while making use of his resources in a different business. As Michel de Certeau has observed, the manipulation of time is employed particularly by those who cannot control the field of play (see the Introduction). Rather than simply rely on his landed power and the authority conferred by his office, Esperon developed his own socioeconomic strategies.

Networking and social capital

These business transactions took place within a social context in which ties of support between kinsmen, friends, and allies could prove decisive. The way in which several of Esperon's affairs implicated the same people is notable. He cultivated a special relationship with the Roserio brothers, who belonged to the lower echelons of the aristocracy (one of them was described as *domicellus* or squire).⁵⁶ Although taking advantage of the brothers' underage status, Esperon's first transaction with them was not a rip-off (see above), for otherwise they would have frozen their relations. Instead, in 1391 one of the brothers and Esperon absolved one another of the annual rents that each held on the other's land, and in 1392 the other brother, Jean, purchased a horse from Esperon at the expensive price of 12 *livres* – five times the price of another horse sold in the same year by Esperon, who occasionally traded animals to augment his

---

⁵⁴ Ibid., pp. 28–9.

⁵⁵ Ibid., p. 54.

⁵⁶ Ibid., pp. 34, 39.

revenues.⁵⁷ To make such a sale one needed to be on good terms with well-off locals who could afford the price. Indeed, the following year Esperon helped Jean with a seemingly long-term loan of 25 *livres*, a gesture aimed clearly at consolidating their relationship.⁵⁸ A few years later, Jean was Esperon's witness, alongside another notable, a town's consul, in his acquisition of a house.⁵⁹ These ties developed into a family relationship extending over generations: in 1422 Jean's son served as witness for Esperon's son-in-law.⁶⁰

The other pillars of Esperon's support network were characters of more modest status, such as a neighbour, Jean Javerlhac, who was entrusted with accompanying Esperon's grandson and his nurse to the feast of St Maxence at Ansac (1416), and served the Esperons as witness in two transactions (1417, 1427).⁶¹ Similarly, Esperon's clerk, Jean Montjon, aided him outside office duties: he kept some of Esperon's private papers and witnessed his private contracts.⁶² Most importantly, he was instrumental in the complex transaction that brought Esperon a neighbouring property, the house of the late Jean Toquat.⁶³ On 17 March 1395 Esperon, acting as a notary, delivered to a local the sum of 3 *écus* on behalf of his son living in Paris; the money was received from the son of the late Jean Toquat, also named Jean, who now lived in Paris but had kept contacts at Saint-Junien.⁶⁴ This contract brought Esperon in touch with the heir to the late Jean Toquat's inheritance (Jean was also the tutor of his late sister's children). He might have been eyeing the neighbouring house for a while, which required a good deal of repairing and its new owner lived far away in Paris – two factors conducive to an advantageous purchase. But the price might have gone up if Toquat realised that the prosperous Esperon was interested in the house – hence the benefit of resorting to a proxy, the loyal Jean Montjon. There is no evidence that Esperon advanced him the money to buy the house, but this is most likely what happened, for through a donation charter of 30 March 1395 Esperon received the house as a gift from Montjon, who professed to repay him for the benefices and services bestowed on him

---

⁵⁷ Ibid., pp. 31–2.
⁵⁸ Ibid., p. 34.
⁵⁹ Ibid., p. 39.
⁶⁰ Ibid., p. 74.
⁶¹ Ibid., pp. 61, 62, 79.
⁶² Ibid., pp. 26, 31, 51.
⁶³ Ibid., pp. 38–9.
⁶⁴ Ibid., p. 37.

('remunerare ... de bonis et benefficiis antedictis').[65] The episode is revealing for Esperon's calculated way of capitalising on his professional position. Its aftermath is also instructive: putting his standing in the community to good use, he convinced his neighbours to contribute to the repairs to the house, which moreover started immediately. The masons' bill eventually came to 22 *livres*, but of these only 12 *livres* was paid by Esperon, with the rest covered by three neighbours (he paid separately 14 *livres* for other work on the house).[66] The works benefited the neighbours' properties – the back of the house had collapsed in large part – but the episode speaks to Esperon's ability to mobilise his social capital so as to spare his finances.

The acquisition of the house is the most obvious example of how Esperon's professional knowledge benefited his private aims. Most of his social partners were drawn from the legal milieu: Monjon; the Roserios, descendants of a *jurisperitus*;[67] his father-in-law, master Bernard Goudiou;[68] and lastly his only son-in-law, Pierre Davinaud, a law clerk from a neighbouring town.[69] In marrying off his daughter Jeanne to a legal professional Esperon replicated his personal experience, especially since Jeanne was sole heiress to the estate as her mother had been when she married him. The search for a suitable son-in-law appears to have been a meticulous process, for Jeanne was married when she was at least 24, older than many a bride in late-medieval France.[70] This pattern of social networking reflects solidarities within the legal profession, reinforced by its social success in late-medieval France, particularly in the south, where it played a major role in the renewal of the urban elites.[71] Having increased his material base through his marriage to an heiress, Esperon was interested in marrying off his daughter to a competent, educated individual who would succeed in administering the family estate. In the volatile context of the Hundred

---

[65] Ibid., p. 38.

[66] Ibid., pp. 39–42.

[67] Limoges, ADHV, MS 1 G 8, fol. 27v (register of the bishop of Limoges, compiled in the sixteenth century and known as 'Ac singularem').

[68] Guibert (ed.), *Nouveau recueil*, vol. 1, p. 52.

[69] Ibid., p. 55.

[70] See Biget and Tricard, 'Livres de raison et démographie', pp. 327–8.

[71] Bernard Chevalier, 'Le pouvoir par le savoir: le renouvellement des élites urbaines en France au début de l'âge moderne (1350–1550)', in Claude Petitfrère (ed.), *Construction, reproduction et répresentations des patriciats urbains de l'Antiquité au XXe siècle* (Tours, 1999), at p. 75; Chevalier, 'L'état et les bonnes villes en France', pp. 71–85; Albert Rigaudiere, 'Hiérarchie socioprofessionnelle et gestion municipale dans les villes du Midi français au bas Moyen Age', in *Gouverner la ville au Moyen Age* (Paris, 1993), pp. 167–214.

Years' War, the individual's agency mattered more than structural assets such as wealth or noble status.

Esperon's rapports with his son-in-law were a mix of cooperation and self-interest. As an heiress, Jeanne did not bring Davinaud a dowry; however, as if to compensate, Esperon paid for the wedding feast – which his father-in-law had not, three decades earlier – and made a couple of gifts to his son-in-law. Davinaud moved to Saint-Junien and entered the Esperon family as an uxorilocal son-in-law (1408). The *livre de raison* documents a few of the more significant instances when Esperon assisted Davinaud, making two trips to Limoges in order to recover a debt owed to him and also buy him some medicine; a woman was even sent on a pilgrimage to Rochechouart with propitiatory offerings meant to bring about his recovery.[72] Davinaud's transactions, with Esperon's occasional assistance,[73] were recorded in the *livre de raison* because they were viewed as pertaining to the family's affairs. But Davinaud remained something of a stranger within the family, as Esperon took far more interest in the well-being of Davinaud and Jeanne's son Junien (born in 1411), whom he saw as the family's future; for example, Junien was sent to St Maxence's feast at his grandfather's expense.[74] The entry in the *livre de raison* recording his birth makes clear that in the absence of male children – 'cum nullos liberos masculos habeam' – Esperon promptly regarded him as his direct heir.[75] Indeed, in 1422 a contract was signed by Davinaud 'both on my own behalf, and as legitimate administrator of my son Junien and of Jeanne Esperon'.[76] By 1443 Junien seems both to have completed his studies in (what else?) law and acceded to his maternal inheritance, for a charter refers to him as 'nobili viro magistro Juniano Davinelli, baccalario in legibus, domino de *Lesperonia*'.[77]

Each man seems to have achieved what he had been hoping for from the matrimonial alliance: Esperon a compliant and reliable, if perhaps impecunious, grandson, and Davinaud social elevation at no financial cost. Behind this compromise there would have been much negotiation that is not recorded in the *livre de raison*, but we have learned about some of Esperon's concessions: paying for the wedding feast, making some gifts, and later granting a loan. Perhaps the greatest concession was designating Jeanne as sole heiress: with

---

[72] Guibert (ed.), *Nouveau recueil*, vol. 1, pp. 59–60.

[73] Ibid., p. 63.

[74] Ibid., p. 61.

[75] Ibid., p. 56.

[76] 'Ego Petrus Davinelli, pro me, quantum me tangit, et ut legitimus administrator Junianii, filii mei, et Johanne Esperone'; ibid., p. 74.

[77] Ibid., p. 75.

the younger daughter, Lucia, remaining a spinster, Davinaud would not have had to worry about sharing the inheritance with a brother-in-law. Equally, this might not have been a concession at all but Esperon's preference as well; with the family's future ensured through Jeanne's marriage he might not have seen the point of providing a dowry for Lucia. The attitude was common enough in late-medieval Limousin.[78] A textual clue confirms the impression that Lucia remained a marginal figure within the family: recording her death in 1417 Esperon could not remember her age.[79] She is a reminder of the darker side of the family line's success.

To sum up the analysis, Esperon's social network was rather limited in scope – or at least that is the impression created by the evidence of the *livre de raison*. But the ties were strong, as evidenced by the recurrent interactions with the same handful of people. The importance of distant ties in one's social network, however sporadically used, is emphasised because they give access to resources outside one's milieu. This was not, however, Esperon's case, because his professional milieu offered access to precious contacts and information.[80] Esperon might have found the limited range of his network satisfactory, for he does not seem to have made social overtures – such as through small gifts on festive occasions[81] – aimed at expanding his support group. He merely acquitted himself of the social and moral responsibilities he incurred as inheritor of the estate of his father-in-law, for example providing for the funeral of Margaret's mother and stepfather.[82] Fulfilling these duties helped Esperon establish his place in the community to which he had moved, because the funerals were important social events and traditionally shows of prestige. A similar case of conspicuous consumption involved Jeanne's wedding feast, which Esperon describes in some detail in the *livre de raison*, dwelling on the varied victuals and emphasising that it was well attended by 'many nobles and notable persons and a great multitude of [common] people of both sexes'.[83]

---

[78] Biget and Tricard, 'Livres de raison et démographie', pp. 329, 349–50.

[79] Guibert (ed.), *Nouveau recueil*, vol. 1, p. 62.

[80] Mark Granovetter, 'The Strength of Weak Ties', *American Journal of Sociology*, 78:6 (1973), 1360–80. Esperon is an example of the weight of close ties; see Michael Eve, 'Qui se ressemble s'assemble? Les sources d'homogéneité à Turin', in Maurizio Gribaudi (ed.), *Espaces, temporalities, stratifications: exercises sur les réseaux sociaux* (Paris, 1998), pp. 43–69.

[81] See Natalie Zemon Davis, *The Gift in Sixteenth-Century France* (Madison, 2000), pp. 23–33.

[82] Guibert (ed.), *Nouveau recueil*, vol. 1, p. 52.

[83] 'in quibus nupciis fuerunt multi nobiles multeque notabiles persone et magna populi multitudo utriusque sexssus'; ibid., p. 55.

Esperon's focus on the strength of social ties rather than the scope of the social network becomes more readily understandable once the broader social context is considered. His position as judge of the bishop of Limoges provided not only the advantages identified above but also liabilities. On the whole, this makes his real but not spectacular socioeconomic success more the result of human agency than structural advantages. The bishop ran into occasional disputes over land, revenues, and jurisdiction with the chapter of the collegiate church of Saint-Junien, in which the scions of leading local families were well represented. Such disputes were current in the towns of late-medieval France.[84] In the case of Saint-Junien, compromises were periodically reached but in between the tensions ran high. An agreement reached in Paris in 1407 describes the dispute as going back forty years.[85] It was certainly alive in the 1390s,[86] and amplified by another contested issue, the bishop's right to an annual visit and inspection, which was submitted to the arbitration of the bishop of Poitiers in 1400,[87] but apparently with no success, for before the settlement of 1407 the bishop of Limoges threatened the confiscation of the chapter's properties and revenues.[88] Esperon was caught between his lord the bishop and the chapter of the church of Saint-Junien, but how far the division strained social relations in town is hard to assess from the *livre de raison*. It is not even clear that the chapter rallied together the notables of Saint-Junien behind its cause, because during the final phase of the dispute bishop of Limoges was Hugh of Magnac, scion of a family of Saint-Junien nobles.[89] On the other hand, there is some evidence of overlap between the families represented in the town's consulate and in the chapter of the church of Saint-Junien. Both high and low justice belonged to the bishop,[90] which may have been resented by the consuls, who had good reasons to limit his influence

---

[84] Such conflicts over jurisdiction were frequent; Bernard Chevalier, 'L'état et les bonnes villes en France au temps de leur accord parfait (1450–1550)', in Neithard Bulst and Jean-Philippe Genet (eds), *La ville, la bourgeoisie et la génese de l'état moderne (XIIe–XVIIIe siècles)* (Paris, 1988), pp. 80–2.

[85] Limoges, ADHV, MS 1 G 11 (cartulary of the bishop of Limoges titled 'Tuae hodie'), fol. 93r.

[86] Limoges, ADHV, MS 1 G 14 (Livre des hommages), fol. 4r.

[87] Leroux and Bosvieux (eds), *Chartes*, p. 241.

[88] Limoges, ADHV, MS 1 G 162.

[89] Three decades previously, the elected bishop of Limoges continued to serve as *prévôt* of the chapter of Saint-Junien; Vital Granet, *Histoire de la ville de Saint-Junien* (Saint-Junien, 1926), p. 102.

[90] 'consules nullos clamores recipient nec causas aliquas audient'; Limoges, ADHV, MS 1 G 11, fol. 37v.

in town, exercised in legal matters through Esperon. But the consuls did not openly challenge the bishop's power, one reason being because half of them (three) were designated by the bishop. At any rate, it is perhaps suggestive that the man who would not sell his land to Esperon was from the Boaresse family represented in the town's consulate.[91]

It certainly seems that the knightly aristocracy in and around Saint-Junien, powerful through its lands and connections, was ambivalent towards the bishop's judge. Esperon managed to cultivate good relations with some local aristocrats. His position and legal expertise were valuable assets; we know about the services that his predecessor in office rendered to the seneschal of Limousin in an inquiry into local land registers conducted in 1378,[92] a mere decade before Esperon took over. Esperon received a small donation of land near l'Esperonie from the lord of Cognac (1404),[93] and other occasional small favours: in 1416 he travelled to Limoges in the company of the viscount of Rochechouart and the lord of Mortemart, and was hosted by them in the city for several days.[94] But far more aristocratic families whose presence at Saint-Junien is confirmed by the evidence of charters of homage and land transactions did not interact with Esperon in any significant way, from the knightly Montvallier family, who secured the services of another legal professional,[95] to the Magnac, whose members were among the canons and consuls of Saint-Junien throughout the fourteenth century,[96] to the lord of Chabaneix,

---

[91] Arbellot, *Chronique de Maleu*, p. 244. The land was eventually sold by Boaresse's widow – see above.

[92] 'selont les rolles et terriers anciens des dits lieux de Veyrac, etc.'; Paris, AN, Q^1 1620; discussed briefly in Jean Tricard, 'Confiscation et conaissance d'une seigneurie: l'état de "biens et héritages" du seigneur de Veyrac en 1378', in *Seigneurs et seigneuries au Moyen Age* (Paris, 1993), pp. 123–39, at p. 126.

[93] Guibert (ed.), *Nouveau recueil*, vol. 1, pp. 43–4.

[94] Ibid., p. 59. The viscount had lands at Saint-Junien, for which it did homage to the bishop; Limoges, ADHV, MS 1 G 6, fol. 465.

[95] Limoges, ADHV, MS 1 G 9 (cartulary of the bishop of Limoges titled 'O Domina'), fol. 96v; MS 1 G 11, fol. 14v; MS 1 G 12 (Livre des hommages), fol. 13v; MS 1 G 14, fol. 5v.

[96] Limoges, ADHV, MS 1 G 14, fol. 7r; Arbellot, *Chronique de Maleu*, p. 115; Leroux and Bosvieux (eds), *Chartes*, p. 241; Granet, *Histoire de la ville de Saint-Junien*, pp. 74–6, 102, 103.

with lands at both Saint-Junien and Cognac[97] (I leave aside those without an active presence in town).[98]

Life-writing

The memorandum or memoir – I use both terms in order to avoid a univocal translation of *memoria* – written in the *livre de raison* in November 1409 offers precious insight into Esperon's personality.[99] His elder daughter married and the family's future assured, he was entitled to think that his last major task had been fulfilled. He did not have a grandson yet for whom he might enumerate his achievements, so he wrote the memorandum as a reminder for a general family posterity. That he wrote it in Latin – when switching between languages was not unusual in the *livres* – suggests that Esperon envisaged his heirs (as yet unborn!) as students of this language, quite obviously as part of their legal training, in keeping with the family tradition.

Written in the first-person singular, the text is a prime example of life-writing in the *livres de raison*. It is also highly particular: Esperon chose to portray himself in a distinct light. The memorandum 'causa eterne memorie' of his life-long achievements is basically a list of expenses, as made explicit from the second paragraph: 'I, Pierre Esperon, clerk, have made in my times many disbursements and paid many costs, and I wish that among others the following should be remembered…'.[100] The next folios list in great detail the expenses caused by his sisters' marriages, followed by the costs of the funerals of his parents and his wife's mother and stepfather; then come the prices paid for various acquisitions of land and revenues, and in the end the expenses caused by his daughter's recent marriage.

Esperon did not write of personal or family matters, even though it would have been entirely appropriate to have shared some with his posterity. Unlike the Florentine Gregorio Dati (Chapter 4), he did not think it important to highlight in the memoir that he was appointed to a significant office, judge of Saint-Junien – although at the time of the appointment he had indeed considered it an event very much worthy of record. What he chose to emphasise in his piece of life-writing was his spending. Living in times of prolonged crisis, Esperon made a habit of augmenting his incomes in just about every way

---

[97] Limoges, ADHV, MS 1 G 11, fol. 81r.

[98] Such as the Prunh family; Emmanuelle Billac, *Une famille de vassaux des vicomtes de Rochechouart (1260–1388): les Prunh* (Limoges, 1990), pp. 216–17.

[99] Guibert (ed.), *Nouveau recueil*, vol. 1, pp. 50–5.

[100] 'Ego, Petrus Esperonis, clericus, feci temporibus meis multas misias, sumptus et expensas, et volo quod inter cetera sit memoria de sequentibus…'; ibid., p. 50.

possible, kept careful records even of seemingly small expenses, and obviously tried to save every penny; these, of course, were common strategies at the time.[101] What then could be more meaningful, from a perspective predicated on the creative reversal of the terms of his engagement with the world, than to show in great detail what he spent, all the money he gave away – almost sacrificed, one might say? Throughout the memoir, the same pattern is repeated with slight variations: an opening note in the first-person singular about Esperon's particular achievement, mirrored by a precise statement of costs at the end of the entry. A few examples may illustrate the point:

> First, I married off my three sisters, namely Mariotte, Jeanne, and Catherine, for whom I have made payment as follows:

> To Pierre de Beauregard, husband of said Mariotte, with respect to the dowry promised her in the marriage contract, among others, 18 *livres* and nine *solidi* (this can be established by receipts); likewise, for her trousseau, 18 *livres*; likewise, for my share of the wedding-feast expenses, four *livres*; likewise, I have delivered to said Mariotte a good and proper bed, with sufficient bed linen, worth 15 *livres* and more [...]

> Now follow other charges for the burial of the dead:

> First, I took care of the proper burial of the lord my father and of the lady my mother – may their souls rest in peace! Their funerals cost: my father's, including the liturgical services in the octave of the Ascension and at the beginning of the year, 40 *livres*; likewise, my mother's, in all, 30 *livres*.

> *Item*, I have arranged for the burial of my wife's stepfather, Jean Solio; whose funeral cost 17 *livres* [...]

> *Item*, I had a new gate built to the house which used to belong to Jean Solio, looking towards the fountain. It cost, both for the masonry and all that goes with it, as well as for the carpentry and all that goes with it, with the lock and the hinges, 10 *livres*.[102]

---

[101] Gabriela Signori, '"Family traditions": Moral Economy and Memorial "gift-exchange" in the Urban World of the Late Fifteenth Century', in Gadi Algazi, Valentin Groebner, and Bernhard Jussen (eds), *Negotiating the Gift: Pre-modern Figurations of Exchange* (Göttingen, 2003), pp. 285–318, at pp. 286–7.

[102] Guibert (ed.), *Nouveau recueil*, vol. 1, pp. 50, 52, 54.

The memorandum's structure makes plain the equivalence between Esperon and his expenditure. Put simply, Pierre Esperon was what he spent.

The fact that his wife brought valuable property to the family estate is not acknowledged as such in this survey of *his* achievements. Esperon acknowledges that he married an heiress, but only to draw attention to the fact that on this account he paid for the wedding feast.[103] He does not state that he inherited a house from his wife and another one from her stepfather – we only learn this from a passing reference – but he does state with precision the additions that *he* made to the houses, and gives the expenses in detail.[104] Spending as a measure of individual achievement is elevated to such heights as to exclude not only personal accomplishments like his appointment to office, but also acquisitions of material goods that did not cost him money. The augmentation of the estate of l'Esperonie, clearly important because it added to the patrimonial lands, is not mentioned in the memoir because it was a donation from the lord of Cognac. Never mind that this was no pure gift, but more likely a strategic move prompted by Esperon's rise in social status. Esperon also had no intention to tell his posterity how hard he had worked to make the money he spent. In this image of himself that he created, his actions as dispenser of money, either for immediate causes such as his sisters' dowries or for the family's long-term prosperity in the case of his acquisitions, completely eclipse his arduous work to earn this money – in the same way they eclipse his social achievements and his wife's contribution to the prosperity of the family through her inheritance and labour.[105] In the *livre de raison* her domestic work is acknowledged only exceptionally and in passing, in regard to looking after the student lodgers, a service for which she was due a mere piece of fabric.[106] Similarly, Esperon records that he hosted and supported his sister Héloïse for a year, inflating the costs to 10 *livres*, but does not acknowledge her domestic labour during this time.[107]

---

[103] Ibid., p. 52.

[104] Ibid., pp. 53–4.

[105] I borrow the trope from Marilyn Strathern, who argues that in Papua New Guinea gift-exchanges the participants 'eclipse their *own* productive activities' to bring to the fore their role as ceremonial gift-givers; *The Gender of the Gift* (Berkeley, 1988), p. 155.

[106] Guibert (ed.), *Nouveau recueil*, vol. 1, p. 58.

[107] Ibid., p. 51.

By contrast, analogies with nineteenth-century evidence suggest a complex picture of women's roles in rural households.[108]

As an exercise in textual self-fashioning this is quite original and makes a powerful case for Pierre's keen sense of self. The standard which he chose for measuring his achievements, namely spending, was a personal construct. It did not simply reproduce contemporary social models; quite the contrary, it reworked them in a way that evinces his intellectual creativity through the figurative reversal of the meaning of his life-long economic practices. Inasmuch as he did not simply accept the valuation schemes of society but devised his own, Pierre Esperon stands out as a self-reflexive, self-fashioning agent – and also quite modern. While the memoir stands out from the rest of the *livre de raison* as a coherent self-narrative, it is built around the facts of Esperon's existence, not so much distorted as cast in a favourable light. The ethos of personal achievement and responsibility towards the family is real, but Esperon's attachment to family values is expressed from the standpoint of the individual, the *ego* explicitly foregrounded from the opening lines of the memoir. To be an agent often meant to act with someone else in mind;[109] the language of many of the contracts copied in the *livre*, although formulaic, expresses the idea that one acts for one's family and posterity: 'pro se et suis', 'pro se et suis heredibus et succesoribus quibuscumque'.[110] While the memoir opens with the foremost obligations incumbent upon the *caput familias*, marrying off his sisters and providing for his parents' funeral, Pierre selects only his achievements, stating explicitly that he would not delve into the dowry arrangements of his elder sister Héloïse because these had been made by his father. The whole memoir chronicles Esperon's impact on the family scene; in it the family functions as the field on which the effects of his actions are registered. 'I have married three sisters'; 'I have buried the lord my father' ('maritavi tres sorores'; 'sepelivi dominum patrem meum'): Pierre is the author of the actions and his family their object. In this way a sense of individual achievement emerges even within the familial, communal sphere. One's effectiveness in the world represented a crucial source of the self and a building-block of identity.

A final remark on numbers and money in the memorandum. The sums spent by Esperon for the benefit of the family are not just rounded off but clearly exaggerated, as one might expect in a discourse about individual

---

[108] Gertrud Hüwelmeier, 'Gendered Houses: Kinship, Class, and Identity in a German Village', in Victoria Goddard (ed.), *Gender, Agency, and Change: Anthropological Perspectives* (London, 2000), pp. 122–41.

[109] Strathern, *Gender of the Gift*, p. 272.

[110] Guibert (ed.), *Nouveau recueil*, vol. 1, pp. 28, 38.

achievement. For example, at 15 *livres* 'and more', the value of Mariotte's bed and bed-linen trousseau was overstated; by comparison in a note in the *livre de raison* three beds 'meliores aliis' were valued at only 6 *livres* and 2 *solidi*.[111] But the dowries are not rounded off, and Esperon even refers to the receipts for them, which suggests that the numbers are accurate. The dowries, trousseaus, and wedding-feast expenses are all in the same range (see Table 3).

Table 3. Esperon's sisters' dowries (*including, for comparison, Héloïse's, although not provided by him)

	Mariotte	Jeanne	Catherine	*Héloïse (arranged by her father)
Dowry	18.5 l.	26 florins = c. 21 l.		
Trousseau	18 l. + bed, c. 15 l.	20 l. + bed, c. 15 l.		
Wedding	4 l.	4.75 l.		
Total	c. 55.5 l.	c. 61 l.	80 l.	*100 l. (promised)

Similarly the annual charges for hosting the students are more or less the same, 40 to 60 *solidi* and 6 to 8 *sextarii* of wheat. Now the dowries involved three different parties, and the boarding deals another four, but significantly none of these people procured a substantially better arrangement than the norm; only Catherine's dowry is higher, because she married later, when Esperon was more prosperous and had reached a higher status. The minor variations in the price of basically the same deals suggest that there was little room for negotiation, although one would have expected the opposite inasmuch as the transactions were not about commodities that could be sold or bought in the open market. The price was set in a tacit fashion, but not without a logic of its own, as suggested by the more or less constant outcome. The parties' manifest involvement in setting the price seems minimal; rather, the prices appear adjusted to the particulars of each transaction somewhat unreflexively. This works not only for Catherine's dowry but also for the funerary expenses, which show an unmistakable gradation: 40 *livres* for Esperon's father, 30 for his mother, 22 for his wife's mother, 17 for his wife's stepfather. The variations are not random but obey a tacit logic that is both social, privileging the male parent and blood kinship, and individual: Esperon's parents are worth

[111] Ibid., p. 49.

more than his wife's. These findings are arguably best understood in light of Pierre Bourdieu's concept of the *habitus*, the 'generative principle of regulated improvisations' manifest through a set of dispositions that tacitly guide action towards goals anticipated by the objective socioeconomic conditions.[112]

The efficacy of forms: from prayers to miraculous remedies

Late in life Esperon added to the *livre de raison* a mix of prayers, recipes for miraculous potions, and other such notable matters (in 1417). His grandson would have been the primary addressee of these pieces of wisdom. I list them here in the order in which they were recorded: verses that insured personal salvation if recited devoutly; a prayer to be said during Mass; remedies against disease of the eyes; a prayer for protection against sudden death and epidemics; Bacchic verses; a prayer to chase away tempests; a prayer to protect against highwaymen; a prayer for extracting an iron from a wound; remedy for inflammations; notes on the miraculous virtues of rosemary; the uses of the snake's skin; a wolf's blood potion and other recipes, including an aphrodisiac; the properties of *aqua ardens*; the special import of certain days; potion for getting rid of flies; and finally notes about the Indiction and the dating of documents.[113]

The provenance of all this remains difficult to elucidate. The complex structure of some of the prayers suggests they were copied from prayer books and treatises. The verses that ensured personal salvation came from the psalms. Esperon might have been instructed to say the Mass prayer by a priest; indeed in late-medieval England believers were encouraged to say whatever prayers they knew if they could not follow the priest's recitation.[114] The note regarding rosemary might have come from medieval pharmacological treatises such as the one by Mathaeus Platearius.[115] Esperon notes that he read about the magical significance of certain days, but does not give the source. The prayer for extracting an iron from a wound was a variant of a well-known invocation.[116] Esperon insists that after using snake skin as an unguent for the hands people – presumably with whom one shook hands – will find you generous and kind, and his avowal that this was a tried-and-tested method – 'experiencia docebit' – has a personal ring. Some of the grammatical and

---

[112] Pierre Bourdieu, *Outline of a Theory of Practice*, trans. Richard Nice (Cambridge, 1977), p. 78.

[113] Guibert (ed.), *Nouveau recueil*, vol. 1, pp. 64–74.

[114] Keith Thomas, *Religion and the Decline of Magic* (London, 1971), p. 33.

[115] Jean Tricard, 'Maladies et médicines en Limousin à la fin du Moyen Age', in Elisabeth Mornet and Franco Morenzoni (eds), *Milieux naturels, espaces sociaux: études offertes à Robert Delort* (Paris, 1997), pp. 741–9, at p. 748.

[116] Richard Kieckhefer, *Magic in the Middle Ages* (Cambridge, 1989), p. 71.

orthographical errors in this specific entry suggest that he was not copying it from a manuscript in front of him. Some of the potions seem to reflect orally transmitted therapeutic practices, which makes sense considering Esperon's contacts with the rural world. They certainly look quite different from the sophisticated recipe in the *livre de raison* of the Massiot family.[117] In fact, of the four Limousin *livres de raison* that include natural medicines, Esperon's alone touches upon magic as well.[118]

The heterogeneous character of these notations is evident. They combine more or less orthodox prayers with material that church figures would have regarded as spurious. But the border between magic and Christian piety was thin in general.[119] Unlike demonic magic, natural magic generally invoked plant remedies and was thus close to medicine.[120] Theological condemnations, however, often ignored such distinctions.[121] At the end of the fourteenth century church intellectuals were taking more distance vis-à-vis incantations and the idea of the natural effectiveness of powerful words.[122] The prayer for extracting an iron from a wound begins with a common motif in the medieval literature on magic, 'Longinus miles ebreus fuit', which reflects both the emphasis on Christ's corporeality in late-medieval piety and the laity's liberties with the letter of the Scriptures. The usage of even Christian formulas was at times condemned by the church.[123] Other remarks would have been considered superstitious, such as the belief in the magical significance of certain days of the year. Lastly, some of the practices clearly ran counter to Christian moral theology, from the aphrodisiac ('pulvis … redactus in cibo et potu, generat amorem et dilectionem') to the belief that through snake skin powder it was possible to extract others' secrets while they were sleeping.

Esperon probably believed in some of these formulas more than in others, but the fact that he wrote them down for posterity suggests that on the whole he took the matter seriously. This was a significant part of his cultural universe. Notwithstanding his borrowings from diverse sources with little reworking,

---

[117] Tricard, 'Maladies et medicines', p. 746.

[118] Ibid., p. 747.

[119] See Thomas, *Religion and the Decline of Magic*, pp. 42–3, for a similar case.

[120] See Kieckhefer, *Magic in the Middle Ages*, pp. 8–17.

[121] Ibid., pp. 181–93.

[122] Béatrice Delaurenti, *La puissance des mots, "Virtus Verborum": Débats doctrinaux sur le pouvoir des incantations au Moyen Age* (Paris, 2007), p. 150.

[123] H. A. Kelly, 'Canon Law and Chaucer on Licit and Illicit Magic', in Ruth Mazo Karras, Joel Kaye, and E. Ann Matter (eds), *Law and the Illicit in Medieval Society* (Philadelphia, 2008), pp. 211–24.

Esperon could claim authorship of the final selection of material. The unifying principle of this eclectic construct is directly relevant for the study of agency. The prayers and potions were all written down on account of their perceived efficacy.[124] When he could not vouch for it through personal experience, Esperon would note that it was 'firmly believed' to be so. In other cases, a qualification such as 'if one says it devoutly', 'if both [the wounded and the person who pulls the iron] are repentant and have confessed [their sins]', shows a concern for the orthodoxy of the practices, resonating with the emphasis on the inner state of the believer in Christian doctrine. Equally, however, this served a more practical function as an implicit justification for the cases when the prayer failed.

The writing process behind this compilation, specifically the order in which these assorted pieces were written, offers some clues as to the value Esperon attached to each of them. He began with an orthodox prayer, aimed, traditionally, at ensuring personal salvation. He continued in the same vein with the prayer to be said during Mass, which would bring *magna indulgentia*. The following entries, however, reflect specific circumstances: the pharmaceutical remedies for eye ailment – an obvious concern for both Esperon and his grandson as legal professionals; the prayer for protection against sudden death and epidemics, such as the 1361–3 plague that Esperon would have remembered from his childhood;[125] the prayer against tempests, of interest to a family owning vineyards and arable land; and the prayer against highwaymen, which would have brought some comfort to the traveller on the brigand-infested roads of Limousin.[126] The fact that Esperon did not throw in all the marvellous remedies that he chanced to hear about but operated a selection adjusted to the particulars of his situation suggests that he entertained serious thoughts about their effectiveness. This slowly led him away from the orthodox beginnings of the list. The practical logic that took hold of Esperon's writing brought together Christian prayers, aphrodisiacs, and snake-skin powder with magical properties. Pitted against each other by theologians and inquisitors, they peacefully coexisted in the mind of the bishop's judge in Saint-Junien. Thus, Esperon's case fits with Alexander Murray's argument that 'everyone, intellectual or rustic, actually accepted both modes of thinking, magical

---

[124] Cf. Tricard, 'Maladies et medicines', p. 749. As Richard Kieckhefer put it, 'what mattered was whether a remedy worked, not how'; *Magic in the Middle Ages*, p. 67.

[125] On epidemics in late-fourteenth-century Limousin, see Tricard, *Les campagnes limousines*, pp. 40–2.

[126] See ibid., pp. 19–21; René Morichon (ed.), *Histoire du Limousin et de la Marche*, vol. 1 (Limoges, 1982), pp. 136–7.

and non-magical, but in ratios widely differing, and, in each person, with a boundary of uncertainty between what they did and did not believe',[127] and with similar observations about the boundaries between sacred and profane in early-modern culture.[128] Esperon certainly remained critical of some of the received knowledge of this kind. The last entries in the list are something of a tack-on. He had reached the *cul de sac* in his search for consequential pieces of practical knowledge and now began to add, hesitantly, other assorted bits and pieces. He ended with an entry that he did not endorse, simply noting that it was something he read, and, at the very bottom of the list, a plant recipe for driving the flies away from the house.

The specific cases when Esperon might have resorted to such prayers were unlikely to turn up in the *livre de raison*. But we have already encountered an entry on a pilgrimage, which can offer an analogy because both prayer and pilgrimage were intended for similar practical ends: in 1416 the family hoped that a pilgrimage to St Paul's feast in Rochechouart would restore Davinaud's health. This appeal to divine help, it bears emphasis, was made only after medical remedies had been tried, apparently without much success. Conversely, the author of an earlier Limousin *livre de raison* focused on medical aid for his ailing wife, in the forms of a doctor, an apothecary, and a barber.[129] The fact that a proxy who was not even a family member was sent on pilgrimage on Davinaud's behalf (see above), suggests that Esperon was less concerned with the inner state of the individual believer than he professed in his notes on the use of prayers. The point about pilgrimage was that someone would go, make an offering to St Paul, and procure in return Davinaud's recovery – no surprise that Esperon recorded the precise amount of the offering, which included a large candle.[130] This was commerce with the saints.[131] This example of the laity's appropriation of religious practices resonates with the findings of ethnographic research. Thus, in a study of nineteenth-century Karelia pilgrimage 'comes across … as a type of exchange or transaction with a specific aim or reward in mind'; '[pilgrims] fulfilled their obligations and asked for

---

[127] Alexander Murray, 'Missionaries and Magic in Dark-Age Europe', repr. in Lester K. Little and Barbara H. Rosenwein (eds), *Debating the Middle Ages: Issues and Readings* (Oxford, 1998), pp. 92–104, at pp. 103–4.

[128] Piero Camporesi, *Bread of Dreams: Food and Fantasy in Early Modern Europe*, trans. David Gentilcore (Chicago, 1989), p. 22.

[129] Tricard, 'Maladies et medicines', p. 744.

[130] Guibert (ed.), *Nouveau recueil*, vol. 1, p. 60.

[131] Cf. Thomas, *Religion and the Decline of Magic*, p. 34.

aid in return'.¹³² Supernatural agencies presented great appeal to the medieval subaltern classes.¹³³

As argued above in relation to his managerial approach, Esperon relied on his agency, redeploying his skills and efforts across diverse investments and business schemes. This might explain why other advice he might have shared with his descendants, on business, family, and networking, did not find its way into the list – in contradistinction with the inclusion of such pieces of wisdom in the *livres de raison* of Etienne Benoist and Jean Massiot.¹³⁴ For Esperon these were complex matters, dependent on the individual's intuition and too context-bound to lend themselves to facile summaries. Conversely, in the list he concentrated on formulas whose mysterious modus operandi and efficacy rendered human efforts minimal: when turning to 'magic' only knowledge of the exact formula mattered.¹³⁵ The agent was the invocation or potion itself. For all the list's eclecticism, Esperon tacitly acknowledged a distinction: between human and non-human agency.¹³⁶

Town notables though they were, Tarneau and Esperon did not control the economic and social field of play; their stories are about agency more than structure. To cope with the vicissitudes of the Hundred Years' War they developed specific strategies, from conflict resolution to managing an agrarian economy in need of reconstruction. To this end they drew on both social

---

¹³² Laura Stark, *Peasants, Pilgrims, and Sacred Promises: Ritual and the Supernatural in Orthodox Karelian Folk Religion* (Helsinki, 2004), pp. 58, 60.

¹³³ Michael Goodich, 'The Multiple Miseries of Dulcia of St Chartier (1266) and Cristina of Wellington (1294)', in Michael Goodich (ed.), *Voices from the Bench: The Narratives of Lesser Folk in Medieval Trials* (New York, 2006), pp. 99–126, at p. 116.

¹³⁴ Guibert (ed.), 'Livre de Benoist', pp. 250–3; Louis Guibert (ed.), *Livres de raison, registres de famille et journaux individuels, limousins et marchois* (Paris, 1888), p. 145.

¹³⁵ Similarly, in late-medieval courts of justice, knowledge of the exact legal formulas could win or lose a case; Esther Cohen, *The Crossroads of Justice: Law and Culture in Late Medieval France* (Leiden, 1993), pp. 62–5. Yet, somewhat surprisingly, Esperon wrote down only one piece of legal advice, on the dating documents and the change of the Indiction. Since this is his penultimate entry in the *livre*, it is possible that he simply did not live to write more advice on legal matters.

¹³⁶ Cf. Bruno Latour, *We Have Never Been Modern*, trans. Catherine Porter (Cambridge, MA, 1993), p. 12.

experience and learned knowledge. Their mastery of literacy and accounting in the *livres de raison* was instrumental for their success as heads of family; in this sense, both cases, documented here in some detail, illustrate the rise in social status of the legal profession. The written word also facilitated their efforts to fashion a sense of self, built on their perceived effectiveness in society.

4

The Social Uses of Life-Writing: The Tuscan *Ricordanze*

More elaborate than the *livres de raison*, the *ricordi* and *ricordanze* of the Florentine merchants and urban professionals shed precious light on some of the more intriguing questions in the study of agency.[1] Thus, this chapter delves in greater detail into how culture and the social imaginary shape individuals' agency: how one's personal values as well as ideas about social interactions lead to specific patterns of acting upon the world. A topic of particular interest is the codification of social knowledge so as to pass down to the family posterity successful patterns of agency. The second half of the chapter explores the other side of agency, from the seemingly passive resilience in the face of overwhelming odds, but which actually requires the mobilisation of considerable energy, to individuals' decision to place their agency in abeyance. The patterns of agency discussed here reflect one of the most advanced late-fourteenth-century milieus: Florence was the continent's financial heart, a major hub of long-distance trade, and a republic in which thousands of citizens were coopted into communal governance but politics remained controlled by an oligarchy.[2]

The *ricordi* and *ricordanze*'s eclectic material covers business and family affairs as well as important events in the history of Florence; personal reflections were also included more frequently than in the *livres de raison*. Many of the notes open with a formula, 'ricordanza sia', 'let it be recalled', that echoes the wording of the entries in Benoist's *livre de raison*, 'renembranssa sia', and became so popular that it gave the name of the genre: *ricordanze*. While a distinction has been proposed between *ricordi*, construed more strictly as records or deeds of the kind transcribed or summarised in private cartularies and registers, and *ricordanze*, referring mainly to notes and memoranda to posterity, in practice the two terms were used interchangeably – a usage that

---

[1] The two genres have been compared most recently by Jean Tricard, 'Les livres de raison français au miroir des livres de famille italiens: pour relancer une enquête', *Revue historique*, 307:4 (2002), 993–1011.

[2] John M. Najemy, *A History of Florence, 1200–1575* (Oxford, 2006), pp. 96–118.

is retained by modern scholarship.³ The *ricordi* and *ricordanze* have survived in much larger numbers than the *livres de raison*, proof that the practice of keeping such registers was more common in Tuscany than in Limousin and Provence.⁴ Around 1400, when the two texts analysed here were produced, the *ricordi* are clearly more elaborate than the *livres de raison*, with many including substantial narrative material, in contrast to the latter's itemised lists. Their beginnings, however, bear more resemblance to the *livres de raison*: in the second half of the thirteenth century a merchant's register might be used to record in detail a transaction for which no deed or charter had been drafted. A key development was the addition of notes about family affairs, marking the rapprochement between the business and domestic spheres that is the hallmark of the Tuscan social imaginary. As late as the end of the fourteenth century, the *ricordi* might include full transcriptions of sale deeds, notably pertaining to the enlargement of the family patrimony.⁵ By that time, however, the *ricordi* also make numerous references to documents kept in the family archive (usually a coffer). Not only is the creation of family archives among the urban elites significant,⁶ but the notion of merely referencing documents, instead of copying them verbatim in a register, is a departure from the practice of private cartularies and *livres de raison*. What is more, cross-referencing took hold in the register of *ricordanze* so as to centralise information first recorded in several other ledgers. Sometimes known as the *libro segreto*, this register

[3] Giovanni Ciappelli, 'La memoria degli eventi storici nelle ricordanze private fiorentine (sec. XIII–XV)', in Claudia Bastia and Maria Bolognani (eds), *La memoria e la città: Scritture storiche tra Medioevo ed Età Moderna* (Bologna, 1995), pp. 123–50, at p. 141; Leonida Pandimiglio, 'E in fine ci sono le "Ricordanze"?', *Testo e Senso*, 12 (2011), http://testoesenso.it/article/view/46; Mark Phillips, *The Memoir of Marco Parenti: A Life in Medici Florence* (Princeton, 1987), p. 34.

[4] More than 300 *ricordi*, *ricordanze*, family chronicles, and other memoirs, from the thirteenth to the seventeenth century, are inventoried in Fulvio Pezzarossa, 'La tradizione Fiorentina della memorialistica', in Gian-Mario Anselmi, Fulvio Pezzarossa, and Luisa Avellini (eds), *La 'memoria' dei 'mercatores': Tendenze ideologiche, ricordanze, artigianato in versi nella Firenze del Quattrocento* (Bologna, 1980), pp. 39–149.

[5] Giovanni Ciappelli, *Memory, Family, and Self: Tuscan Family Books and Other European Egodocuments* (Leiden, 2014), pp. 14–15; Christian Bec, *Les marchands écrivains: affaires et humanisme à Florence, 1375–1434* (Paris, 1967), p. 50. On the trajectory from account book to memoir, see Isabelle Chabot, 'Reconstruction d'une famille: Les Ciuriani et leurs *Ricordanze* (1326–1429)', in Jean-André Cancellieri (ed.), *La Toscane et les Toscanes autour de la Renaissance: Cadres de vie, société, croyances* (Aix-en-Provence, 1999), pp. 137–60, esp. pp. 138–9, 145.

[6] Christiane Klapisch-Zuber, 'Les archives de famille italiennes: le cas florentin, XIVe–XVe siècles', in *L'autorité de l'écrit au Moyen Âge* (Paris, 2009), pp. 361–78.

also included notes to self and posterity. Specific circumstances and individual motivations were often decisive in the decision to start keeping such a register or take over the recording from the previous generation. This gesture, reserved to the *pater familias*, signalled an important moment in a young man's development as a moral agent.[7]

To explain the development of the *ricordi* into private records unparalleled in their number and level of detail by either the French *livres de raison* or the so-called *libri di famiglia* from other regions of Italy, one must turn to the backdrop of socioeconomic change in fourteenth-century Florence. The commercialisation of Tuscan society, part of a broader Italian trend, led to increased literacy rates and the proliferation of administrative, business, and domestic records.[8] Accounting habits entered the domestic sphere from the realm of business. The increasingly complex record-keeping practices required by the growing business ventures – short-term companies involving multiple partners, some of them posted abroad – left their mark on the merchants' private records. Their influence is most evident in the structure of a sizeable part of the *ricordi*. While about half of the more than one hundred texts surveyed in a recent analysis consist of diverse entries in chronological order, a substantial number adopted a business-inspired structure, organising their entries into receipts and disbursements (*avere* and *dare*), followed by a third section consisting of notes and memoranda, that is, the *ricordanze* proper. In the second half of the fifteenth century, this kind of *ricordi* adopted the double-entry structure of business registers, starting with the city's uppermost merchant aristocracy.[9]

By itself, however, the impact of commercial record-keeping and accounting practices does not account for the singular evolution of the Tuscan *ricordi*. Long-distance trade and banking flourished elsewhere in central and northern Italy, yet in the other major cities, such as Genoa and Venice, private records were fewer and less complex. A similar case can be made for the influence of humanism, which explains in part why many *ricordi* grew into elaborate

---

[7] See Phillips, *Memoir of Marco Parenti*, p. 37.

[8] Thomas Behrmann, 'The Development of Pragmatic Literacy in the Lombard City Communes', in Richard Britnell (ed.), *Pragmatic Literacy: East and West, 1200–1330* (Woodbridge, 1997), pp. 25–41, at pp. 28–9; Bonvesin de la Riva, *De magnalibus urbis Mediolani*, ed. M. Corti (Milan, 1974), pp. 64–7.

[9] Christiane Klapisch-Zuber, 'Comptes et mémoire: l'écriture des livres de famille florentins', in Caroline Bourlet and Annie Dufour (eds), *L'Écrit dans la société médiévale: Divers aspects de sa pratique du XIe au XVe siècle* (Paris, 1991), pp. 251–8, at pp. 252, 255.

textual accounts.[10] From Paolo da Certaldo in the mid-fourteenth century to Leon Battista Alberti in the first half of the fifteenth, the humanist literature in the vernacular encouraged the merchants to busy themselves making written records and keep them in good order.[11] But while Florence stands out as the birthplace of civic humanism, Padua was the cradle of early Renaissance humanism and fifteenth-century Venice was home to a respectable cohort of humanists – yet neither produced anything like the *ricordi*.

A more likely explanation focuses on the role that family history played in the public life of the Florentine commune. The constant renewal of the ruling elites is a defining feature of Florentine politics. Facing tremendous competition, the notable families turned to history to reassert their identity.[12] The upward social mobility experienced by 'newer' families pushed their opponents into shifting the competition onto the terrain of cultural and symbolic capital by asserting their illustrious lineage. The *ricordi*, in which ample room for domestic matters had already been made, were ideally placed to serve as depositories of family tradition. Consequently, many *ricordi* dedicate considerable space to genealogy and family history, with short biographies of the ancestors emphasising their achievements – above all holding communal office, a key source of social prestige. Some *ricordi* were intended from the very beginning not as account books but as genealogies and histories of the family.[13] Accomplished *ricordi* authors like Buonaccorso Pitti and, as discussed below, Giovanni Morelli, did their own research the better to document their families' history. Even those *ricordi* that kept the format of the account book made reference to family history. This kind of open competition among families for preeminence in public life was not paralleled by other mercantile cities, which consequently did not produce private records as elaborate as the Florentine *ricordanze*. The upshot is that although we think of the *ricordi* as private records, they could also be used to inform public debate. Morelli hints at the political uses to which a record of family history might be put – specifically,

---

[10] Bec, *Marchands écrivains*, p. 444.

[11] Leon Battista Alberti, *The Family in Renaissance Florence: Book III*, trans. Renée Neu Watkins (Prospect Heights, IL, 1994), p. 67; Bec, *Marchands écrivains*, p. 51.

[12] James Grubb, 'Libri privati e memoria familiare: esempi dal Veneto', in Claudia Bastia and Maria Bolognani (eds), *La memoria et la città: Scritture storiche tra Medioevo ed Età Moderna* (Bologna, 1995), pp. 63–72, at pp. 65–6; Ciappelli, *Memory, Family, and Self*, pp. 17–19; Pezzarossa, 'Tradizione Fiorentina', p. 43.

[13] Anthony Molho et al., 'Genealogia, parentado e memoria storica a Firenze nel XV secolo', in Claudia Bastia and Maria Bolognani (eds), *La memoria et la città: Scritture storiche tra Medioevo ed Età Moderna* (Bologna, 1995) pp. 253–70, esp. pp. 236, 258–70.

to provide evidence of the family's historical support of the Guelf establishment. To this end, he tells in his *ricordi* the story of how a thirteenth-century ancestor exiled by the Ghibellines, the Guelfs' rivals, was granted in Arezzo a charter permitting him to bear weapons, a privilege reserved to the Guelfs.[14] Furthermore, the references to local history are a measure of the authors' investment in their civic identity, as members of a self-governing city that competed for preeminence in Tuscany. Such mentions can be found even in the memoirs of modest artisans.[15]

The corollary of the focus on family history was ensuring its future. Keeping tallies remained important when chronicling a family's history because it recorded for posterity the services rendered in the past by friends and allies, since family alliances based on reciprocity ran their course over several generations.[16] Accounting was thus extended beyond material possessions and into the realm of social capital. Accounting was particularly sophisticated in those *ricordi* that retained the structure of business accounts: a piece of information, say, regarding a payment, would be recorded under several different accounts in the first part of the register (receipts and disbursements), and cross-referenced in the second section of memos. As Christiane Klapisch-Zuber has argued, this fact reflects the realisation that a particular expenditure has multiple ramifications, from the obvious immediate financial impact to the consequences for the family's future in the case of an investment in the children's education. The implication is that *ricordi* authors were future-oriented and keenly aware of the potential implications on multiple planes of one and the same transaction.[17] The *pater familias* increasingly turned to the *ricordi* to transmit to posterity the socioeconomic lessons of his experience. Sometimes the case was made from the very beginning: in the opening of his *ricordi*, Filigno de' Medici rationalised his recording of events from the recent past as essential for the instruction of future generations. Conversely, Buonaccorso Pitti left for the final folios of his celebrated *ricordi* the exhortation to the family posterity to heed the lessons of his experience.[18] Literacy opened new possibilities for

---

[14] Vittorio Branca (ed.), *Mercanti scrittori: ricordi nella Firenze tra Medioevo e Rinascimento* (Milan, 1986), pp. 129–30.

[15] Franco Franceschi and Josiane Tourres, 'La mémoire des laboratores à Florence au début du XVe siècle', *Annales: Histoire, Sciences Sociales*, 45:5 (1990), 1143–67, at pp. 1156–9.

[16] Ciappelli, 'Memoria degli eventi', p. 146.

[17] Klapisch-Zuber, 'Comptes et mémoire', pp. 256–7.

[18] Ciappelli, *Memory, Family, and Self*, p. 23; Buonaccorso Pitti, *Cronica*, ed. Alberto Bacchi della Lega (Bologna, 1905), p. 177; Leonida Pandimiglio, 'Pigliate esempro

agency, as the individual with access to written material was less dependent on the community for conduct advice.[19]

The foregoing remarks point to the duality at the heart of the *ricordi* genre, which included both an accounting of receipts and disbursements, business-style even when it pertains to domestic matters, and the chronicling of a family's achievements, with its corollary transmission to posterity of the lessons of experience. The duality is illustrated here by the selection of two texts that have in common a good deal of standard *ricordanze* material, yet in each of them the emphasis is different. Both Giovanni di Pagolo Morelli (1371–1444) and Gregorio Dati (1362–1445) were members of the seven major guilds from which the magistrates were predominantly selected and late in life served terms in office, including as Standard Bearer of Justice, the commune's highest office. Because of the two-month term of office this was not an uncommon experience for their milieu; significantly, it did not carry the power to effect real change, since the electoral system and the policy consultations were controlled by the wealthiest and most powerful families. The benefits of holding office were symbolic, enhancing one's standing in the community; as such, communal offices were used to reward non-elite members of the major guilds for their loyalty to the oligarchy. In this and other respects Morelli and Dati are representative for their microcosm. Dati's commercial ventures were a mix of success and failure. Little is known about Morelli's business efforts, but a general sense of decline in family fortune emerges from his *ricordi*. The 1427 fiscal survey gives Morelli's wealth at some 9,100 florins (ranking 122nd in Florence) and Dati's at around 3,300 florins. Both fortunes consisted mainly of private and public investments, the two elderly men having largely retired from their merchant careers.[20] Finally, there is no doubt that both Dati and Morelli were more in touch with humanism than the average Florentine merchant. But exposure to humanist culture did not yield uniform results: it is

---

di questo caso: l'inizio della scrittura di Bonaccorso Pitti', *Lettere italiane*, 40:2 (1988), 161–73, at pp. 170–3.

[19] Roger Chartier, 'The Practical Impact of Writing', in Roger Chartier (ed.), *A History of Private Life*, vol. 3, *Passions of the Renaissance*, trans. Arthur Goldhammer (Cambridge, MA, 1989), pp. 111–61, at pp. 116–17.

[20] Leonida Pandimiglio, 'Giovanni di Pagolo Morelli e la continuità familiare', *Studi Medievali*, 3rd ser., 22 (1981), 128–81, at p. 150; David Herlihy, Christiane Klapisch-Zuber, R. Burr Litchfield, and Anthony Molho (eds), *Online Catasto of 1427*, version 1.3, machine-readable data file based on D. Herlihy and C. Klapisch-Zuber, *Census and Property Survey of Florentine Domains in the Province of Tuscany, 1427–1480* (Providence, RI, 2002), s.v. Giovanni Pagolo Morelli and Goro Stagio Dati, http://cds.library.brown.edu/projects/catasto/.

Morelli's *ricordi* that are more elaborate, although Dati was the more accomplished humanist as the author of a history of Florence.[21] Morelli's text stands out as one of the three or four most fascinating *ricordi*, and has been seen as paradigmatic – highly accomplished, but illustrating the range of concerns that defined the genre.[22]

Giovanni di Pagolo wrote primarily to make the case for the illustrious genealogy of the Morellis and instruct his family posterity about socioeconomic conduct. Much of the text has a narrative structure, moving from biographies of the ancestors to a chronicle of the main events in the life of the Florentine community and their consequences for the Morellis. While the socioeconomic advice is obviously prospective (aimed at the future Morelli generations), it also looks back to the recent family history: Giovanni reflects on the vicissitudes that marked his youth and his father's life and draws consequential lessons. A personal vision of the continuity and success of the family line underlies the entire project. Conversely, the family past commanded Gregorio Dati's attention to a lesser extent. He focused more on personal affairs and the present, making frequent entries into the *ricordi* to keep track of his business partnerships and successive marriages, and occasionally recording other significant events. The step to diary-style entries was a short one: two personal memoranda open a fascinating insight into his sense of agency. By contrast, the inward reflections of Morelli's *ricordi* were a late addition, sparked by the trauma of losing his son; only in a few other instances does he put his personal feelings in writing.

The first part of this chapter explores the ideas of agency that dominate in each of the different kinds of writing that Morelli engaged in: the portraits of the family ancestors, the advice for posterity, and the account of his religious experience in the wake of his son's death. This approach can evince how writing in different genres, from biography to conduct literature, leads to different nuances in one's views of human and divine agency. Because Morelli's text

---

[21] And possibly of *La Sfera*, part cosmographic treatise and part pilot-book, sometimes attributed to his brother Leonardo; Filiberto Segatto, 'Un'immagine quattrocentesca del mondo: la *Sfera* del Dati', *Atti della Academia Nazionale dei Lincei. Memorie. Classe di Scienze morali, storiche e filologiche*, 8th ser., 26:4 (1983), 147–82, at p. 172. On Dati's humanism, see Hans Baron, *The Crisis of the Early Italian Renaissance* (2 vols, Princeton, 1955), vol. 1, pp. 140–60.

[22] Ciappelli, 'Memoria degli eventi', p. 124. Excerpts from Morelli's text are translated into English in Vittorio Branca, *Merchant Writers: Florentine Memoirs from the Middle Ages and Renaissance*, trans. Murtha Baca (Toronto, 2015), and from Dati's in Gene Brucker (ed.), *Two Memoirs of Renaissance Florence: The Diaries of Buonaccorso Pitti and Gregorio Dati*, trans. Julia Martines, repr. (Prospect Heights, IL, 1991).

illustrates the range of issues taken up in the Tuscan *ricordi*, it will also serve to further introduce the genre, beyond the foregoing remarks. The second half of this chapter, on Gregorio Dati's *ricordi*, focuses on alternatives to decisive action, such as everyday resilience and even placing one's agency in abeyance. The in-depth focus on specific aspects of individual agency is facilitated by the substantial amount of scholarship on the *ricordi*.[23]

Biography, autobiography, and conduct advice: Giovanni Morelli's *ricordi*

At different stages between 1393 and 1421 Giovanni di Pagolo Morelli wrote about family and personal events in a register which grew in size to voluminous proportions. During these three decades his life changed tremendously and his priorities as a writer of *ricordi* evolved accordingly, but this notwithstanding, the prologue of the text is an excellent starting point for understanding his idea of a book of *ricordi* and *ricordanze*. The main goal, highlighted in the opening paragraph, was to write the history of the family so as to instruct 'our people', and in particular so that the truth about their venerable ancestry might be established at a time when many a 'no-name' (*ogni catuno*) claimed descent from an ancient family line. This statement should be read against the background of political turmoil in Florence: Giovanni Morelli took up writing the year his protectors and relatives by marriage, the once-powerful Albertis, were exiled and consequently the Morellis faced a good deal of hostility and were forced to move to a different neighbourhood to avoid fiscal persecution. The prologue sets up a highly structured project, divided into four parts: the description of the Morellis' ancient homeland in Mugello, north of Florence; the Morellis' implantation in Florence; the family's history in Florence; and a record (*memoria*) of the great events affecting both the city and the Morelli family during his lifetime, of which he had solid knowledge, either directly or from reliable sources.[24]

---

[23] Notably several of Christiane Klapisch-Zuber's essays in historical anthropology reprinted in *Women, Family, and Ritual in Renaissance Italy*, trans. Lydia G. Cochrane (Chicago, 1985), esp. pp. 68–93; even in these studies, however, agency is not the focal point. The focus on participation in social structures in Richard Trexler, *Public Life in Renaissance Florence* (New York, 1980), is germane to the present study of agency. Gene Brucker, '"The Horseshoe Nail": Structure and Contingency in Medieval and Renaissance Italy', *Renaissance Quarterly*, 54 (2001), 1–19, does not deal with the *ricordi*.

[24] 'avvenuti alla nostra cittá e a noi, cioè in nostra particularitá propria'; Branca (ed.), *Mercanti scrittori*, p. 105. On the *ricordi*'s manuscripts, see the remarks in the earlier

This structure owes something to the scholastic habits of rigorous organisation that influenced humanist writing and in Florence reached even the merchant milieu. In accordance with an old *topos*, Morelli professes his limited literary talent, which further suggests he gave serious consideration to his audience. His project was shaped by the cultural expectations associated with the increasingly popular genre of *ricordi*. Aware that the *ricordi* ought to be grounded in material from the family archive, he refers to ancient documents illustrating the family's respectable history, complemented by orally transmitted but well-established information ('per iscritture o per vera fama'). His reluctance to embellish the family past reflects the common standard of the *ricordi* genre. Giovanni was ready, however, to brush aside the modest steps taken by his father towards keeping a record of family affairs, so as to assert his own status as the first chronicler of family history. The text opens with a misleading statement: 'Because in this book no matter has been written before, I, that is, Giovanni di Pagolo ... have decided to write about our lineage and ancient condition.' In reality, this was not a blank register: his father had used it to copy a few family records, without, however – and this is the key point – starting a book of *ricordanze*.[25]

Advice for posterity was an essential part of Morelli's design. In the prologue, he states his aim to instruct (*ammaestrare*) the family posterity through real examples (*per vero asempro*), drawing on the events that marked the family's destiny. He hoped that by examining his record of the events 'our sons and indeed our descendants' might gain practical knowledge and foresight (*buono provvedimento*).[26] What he ended up writing, having finished the family history some ten years after he first took up the pen, was a substantial segment on the lessons of his orphaned childhood, a period he came to identify as the roots of the family's declining fortunes. It is tempting to suspect that in drawing this conclusion Morelli sought to deflect attention from his own responsibility for forging a marriage alliance that backfired. But his detailed and passionate treatment of the topic suggests he became genuinely convinced that the seeds of the family's decline had been planted in the years following his father's untimely death. It is intriguing then that his focus is less on the seven ills or harms (*danni*) suffered by the orphans and more on the possible

---

edition, Giovanni di Pagolo Morelli, *Ricordi*, ed. Vittorio Branca (Firenze, 1956), pp. 55–63.

[25] Leonida Pandimiglio, 'Giovanni Morelli e le strutture familiari', *Archivio Storico Italiano*, 136 (1978), 3–88, at pp. 16–25, 54–88.

[26] Branca (ed.), *Mercanti scrittori*, p. 105; and see Leonida Pandimiglio, 'Giovanni di Pagolo Morelli e la ragion di famiglia', in *Studi sul Medioevo Cristiano* (2 vols, Rome, 1974), vol. 2, pp. 553–608, at p. 555.

remedies. The formulation of advice for posterity becomes indistinguishable from a textual exercise that replays the dramas of Morelli's childhood so as to devise an intricate arrangement of measures capable of preventing it. For Morelli the written text opened an alternative world in which the problems that had plagued his life could be sorted out by developing appropriate remedies. His autobiographical obsession haunts a discussion ostensibly orientated towards the future. The conduct advice is entirely circumscribed by the vicissitudes of his orphaned childhood. The first harm to the children is that they remained without a father at an early age; the second, that they subsequently also lost their mother, who remarried; the third, that they were left in the care of tutors, a poor substitute for a father; the fourth, that in a few years the tutors squandered a quarter of the children's inheritance; the fifth, that the tutors' continued management of the children's business interests led to further losses against third parties; the sixth, that the tax assessment of their estate was unfair and heavy; and the seventh, that they were deprived of the traditional paternal teachings.[27]

This list draws on a *topos* made popular by the vernacular treatises that matched seven sins with destabilising social consequences with as many remedies rooted in a particular virtue – Temperance as the antidote to Wrath, for instance. This lends a clear structure to the instructional discourse, but the impression is that the taxonomy is forced onto overlapping realities: the second and third pairs of harms and remedies, involving the children's tutors and mother, are quite similar; likewise the fourth, fifth, and six all reflect the tutors' disregard for the children's financial interests. As Morelli became absorbed by the writing process, the advice for posterity grew into a florid exposition of instructions and practical tips about trade and social networking, retaining the initial subheadings as organising categories but going well beyond them in the actual contents. In a departure from the formalism of the seven *danni* and *remedi*, some guidelines on running commercial affairs are offered in the section purportedly dedicated to countering the fourth harm to the orphan, having to do with the expenses that he incurs after the death of the father, such as unpaid debts. General principles become interspersed with highly specific instructions. The best example is the statement that might serve as Morelli's motto in both business and communal politics: 'Before all else, do less but do safely.'[28] This general principle is not set out at the beginning of the section; rather, it comes in the middle of specific advice on investing one's capital in commercial ventures, choosing reliable business partners, and

---

[27] Branca (ed.), *Mercanti scrittori*, pp. 165–6.
[28] 'Inannzi fa meno, fa tu siguro'; ibid., p. 177.

deciding on business opportunities – all very concrete matters, illuminated through particular examples. The transition from retrospective solutions to the dramas of Morelli's youth to more general socioeconomic advice is generally smooth, and it is only towards the end that it becomes evident that the initial design has been relegated in favour of general conduct advice. For instance, in the fifth subheading, about exploitative relatives and business partners of the deceased father who press for money under various pretexts, Morelli acknowledges that there is little the orphans can do. Consequently, the discussion turns to advice for the *pater familias* on how to choose reliable business associates with an eye to the possible consequences for his children in the event of his untimely death. This is followed by advice on a related topic, how to navigate the webs of social connections. Lastly, a whole new discussion is added at the end of the advice section: the remedies against the plague,[29] clearly a timely subject but not on the initial list.

The proliferation of advice beyond the initial design is doubly significant. First, it suggests that Morelli fostered a vibrant internal conversation on society and the hot issues of the day; consequently, when the opportunity presented itself the step to a fully fledged instructional discourse was an easy one. Second, it brings everyday life into in the text through myriad particular situations, calling into question the neat categories inspired by scholastic literature. The evolution of the segment on social advice replicates the text's general trajectory from the conventional description of the ancestral world of Mugello as befitted a piece with literary pretensions to a hybrid account increasingly marked by autobiographical reflection. That Morelli should have found it difficult to control the flow of his reflections on conduct makes sense if he acquired his social knowledge piecemeal, from personal experience; much of what he knew was context-specific and not easy to fit into a structure.

Another kind of life-writing in which Morelli engaged in the *ricordi*, the biographies of several generations of family members, is equally valuable for understanding contemporary views of individual autonomy and agency. Two aspects stand out in particular. For one, in and by itself, the choice to tell the story of the family line through biography rather than the genres of history or chronicle signals the role of the individual as acting subject. Women's agency is largely ignored in the text: only Giovanni's sisters are given full portraits, which contrast with the brief mentions about the family's other female members. Their responsibilities in educating the children are eclipsed by the emphasis on the father's conduct lessons for his sons. We learn only indirectly that the mother shouldered much of the burden of raising the children, for

---

[29] Ibid., pp. 207–14.

instance when Morelli cites the challenge of bringing up a son without the mother as one of the reasons why his widowed grandfather sent his infant son – Morelli's father – to the countryside.[30] But beyond this gender bias, the gallery of family portraits consists of fully individuated figures, with strengths and weaknesses and varying degrees of social success – not stereotyped exemplars of family tradition. This suggests that the family ethos of the *ricordi* coexisted with a strong sense of individual autonomy and agency.[31] If anything, Morelli gives precedence to the individual: it is the individual Morellis that are the heroes of the narrative; the family history is made up of a mosaic of individual *vitae*. Even in the portraits of the first ancestors on record, about whom Morelli could piece together only scraps of information that he was reluctant to embellish, there is a clear impetus to reconstruct the contours of an individual's life-story by relying on extrapolation and verisimilitude – for instance, when working out the possible social status of the first Morelli to settle in Florence.[32] Members of Giovanni di Pagolo's branch of the family receive more attention, and in particular his father. Conversely, he eschews delving into the fate of the youngest offspring of the Morellis' other branch, going back to his father's elder brother, calling it a 'distraction'.[33] This reflects the tension between two views of the family articulated in the *ricordi*, one concerned with the family line, traced back for generations, the other focused on the nuclear family of the *ricordi*'s author.[34] Attachment to family tradition reflected the individual's standpoint and priorities; the differences in length, detail, and tone between the various ancestors' *vitae* penned by Morelli reflect his individual perspective. He occasionally shifts between the conventionally favourable portrayal of ancestors and his own critical opinion of those whom he judged to have wronged *his* side of the family. A notable example is his father's elder brother, Giovanni, first introduced as 'capable' and 'wise' in both commercial operations and matrimonial strategy but subsequently denounced as 'ruthless' (*reo*) in connection with his appropriation of part of Pagolo's share of the patrimonial estate.[35]

The second revealing aspect of the biographies is to do with the manner in which one's individual worth is assessed. This too involves shifting between

---

[30] Ibid., p. 136.

[31] Cf. F. W. Kent, *Household and Lineage in Renaissance Florence: The Family Life of the Capponi, Ginori and Rucellai* (Princeton, 1977), p. 288.

[32] Branca (ed.), *Mercanti scrittori*, p. 118.

[33] 'una confusione di scritto'; ibid., p. 164.

[34] Kent, *Household and Lineage*, p. 115.

[35] Branca (ed.), *Mercanti scrittori*, pp. 133, 138.

two perspectives. The more conventional way of assessing an individual according to the results of his actions predominates. Strategic alliances contracted through marriage and holding communal office are highlighted, while time and again an individual's worth is equated with financial success: 'he bequeathed through his last will the amount of…', or a similar phrase, occurs throughout the *vitae*.[36] The last will serves as the point of articulation of two powerful ideals: individual achievement – for what better moment to measure it than at the end of a life of work – and contribution to the family line, which was the chief purpose of a testamentary bequest. Summing up one's lifetime achievement in a monetary figure made it instantly possible to compare and rank different family members. Another kind of notation invited a similar equivalence between a sum of money and the individual's worth: for each marriage into or out of the Morelli family the amount of the dowry was noted (a common practice across the *ricordi* genre). This, however, did not reflect strictly the status of the bride but also the capacity of the *pater familias* to cover this expenditure, as in the example of the dowry payments recorded in Esperon's *livre de raison* (Chapter 3). While both the *livres de raison* and the *ricordi* are awash with numbers, this kind of financial summation of personal achievement is a noteworthy development because accounting is now brought to bear on self-fashioning and personal identity.

As the *ricordanze* became a medium for articulating personal reflections, a different perspective on one's life and achievement emerges into view, complementing the attention paid to the effects of one's actions with an emphasis on good intentions, effort, and character. This perspective builds on the writer's empathy for his subject and is limited to Morelli's own biography and those of his father Pagolo and elder cousin Gualberto. Pagolo is depicted as overcoming hardship through resilience and succeeding in his affairs not by dint of money ('per forza di danari'), but through diligence and the ability to court favour and argue his case persuasively. Pagolo's success in the world is highlighted through conventional references to the amount of his testamentary bequests (perhaps exaggerated: 20,000 florins) and selection by lot to communal office, which he was prevented by death from holding. But this is overshadowed by the emphasis on how Pagolo lifted himself from his predicament through strength of character. Thus Giovanni exhorts his sons to consider where they might find the strength to carry on if they found themselves in Pagolo's shoes, facing

---

[36] Ibid., pp. 133–4. Similarly, in fifteenth-century Italian painters' contracts the artist's worth is expressed through a monetary figure; Michael Baxandall, *Painting and Experience in Fifteenth Century Italy* (Oxford, 1972), p. 19.

overwhelming odds.[37] This shows how empathy for another's struggles was transmitted to posterity through the *ricordi*; the cultural *habitus* of the urban elites was thus enriched through the attention to a more emotional side of the individual's life, even if such empathy was reserved for close family members. In portraying his father, Giovanni pushed empathy to the point of projecting the present into the past, drawing on his own experiences as an orphan to fill in the blanks and ascribing to Pagolo socioeconomic strategies that reflect his own ideas about conduct. He departed from the family records he had available to give an edulcorated version of his father's inheritance claims.[38] In Gualberto's biography, on the other hand, Morelli focuses on what he witnessed first-hand in his childhood, and the result is a particularly rounded view of an individual's efforts. Individual achievement is again brought into relief by an emotional description of the dramatic context. Not only did Gualberto succeed in providing for the women and children left behind by his father and uncle after their death during the plague, but he kept the family together despite its palpable divisions – all this while in a foreign city and in spite of his young age and inexperience.[39] Nobility of character is emphasised above all, illustrated by Gualberto's generosity to the point of self-denial. The narrative culminates with Gualberto's end, marked by the completion of the requisite rites – asking forgiveness and saying his last prayers. The dignified death is fate's final proof of Gualberto's character and conduct; this suggests that some kind of visible validation of inward character remained desirable. It is also noteworthy that fortune is described not as blind but on the contrary as handing individuals their just deserts.

Finally, in Morelli's own autobiography, conventional and written in the third-person, the emphasis falls even more clearly on good intentions. Acknowledging his failure yet to hold communal office, he expresses regret at not having been given this opportunity to make manifest his loyalty to the Guelf establishment. Clearly Morelli sensed that he could have achieved more by the age of thirty, which helps to explain why he was inclined to qualify financial success as the standard of individual achievement by careful consideration of context and individual character. Morelli's rather underwhelming self-portrait occasions one of the relatively rare expressions of hope in ego-documents, and it is interesting that hope is tied to divine agency: even if divine providence had not yet granted him the honour of holding communal office, Morelli remained confident in God's designs for his future. Like

---

[37] Branca (ed.), *Mercanti scrittori*, pp. 140–1.
[38] See Pandimiglio, 'Morelli e le strutture familiari', pp. 25, 55–6.
[39] Branca (ed.), *Mercanti scrittori*, p. 149.

Salimbene, who understood that divine help is necessary when human efforts fail, Morelli finds in divine providence a source of empowerment inasmuch as it sustains his optimism about the future.

One detail highlighted in Pagolo's biography prefigures a crucial topic in the subsequent pages of advice for posterity. Even as a boy, Pagolo negotiated special terms with the schools he frequented, seeking to avoid physical punishment and changing schools when the terms of 'the pact' were breached – a transactional approach to social relations that Giovanni Morelli fully shared.[40] He finds it remarkable that his father made the agreements without the help of an intermediary or mediator, because the normal course for building new social ties, as he makes clear in his conduct advice, was to mobilise one's existing network of partners and allies.

Agency, networks, and the social imaginary

Much of what can be gleaned from the *ricordi* about agency and the social imaginary, and particularly about the art of navigating the networks that channelled the flow of information and mutual services, comes from the pages of socioeconomic advice. The following analysis dispenses with discussing one by one Morelli's proposed remedies to the seven *danni* of his orphaned childhood,[41] focusing instead on the core tenets of his more general conduct advice, which is more relevant for the study of larger social trends. This is not to dismiss his concern that the trauma of growing up without a father might occur again in the Morelli family. This was a very real risk in the half century after the Black Death, compounded by the fact that in Tuscany men often married women a decade their junior.[42]

Morelli's vision of society is fundamentally defined by a preoccupation with the possibilities for individual strategic action, above all in the context of the support networks that held Florentine society together. This can be seen as a form of transactionalism: the interactions between social actors take place within the frame of a social relation that gives them context and meaning, yet it is the individuals' interventions and exchanges within the frame of the relation

---

[40] Ibid., p. 137.

[41] See Claudia Tripodi, 'Il padre a Firenze nel Quattrocento: L'educazione del pupillo in Giovanni Morelli', *Annali di Storia di Firenze*, 3 (2011), 29–63.

[42] Klapisch-Zuber, *Women, Family, and Ritual*, p. 28. Morelli's uncle Giovanni di Bartolomeo died in the 1363 epidemic, leaving five children behind; his father Pagolo in the epidemic of 1374, leaving four; and his cousin Bartolomeo in that of 1383, followed by his widow, a victim of the *mortalità* of 1400; Branca (ed.), *Mercanti scrittori*, pp. 133, 143, 147. Gregorio Dati too lost his father when he was still a boy.

that define its trajectory.[43] Individuals are rarely thought of outside such webs of relations, but they are endowed with the capacity to shape the relations. While social networks are paramount, they are defined by the individuals' agency, rather than the networks' structural qualities. This social vision is a consequence of the standpoint from which most of Morelli's social reflections are written, that of an instructional discourse meant to equip the individual agent – the *pater familias* of future generations – with the prerequisite social knowledge. This view of society is not detached or contemplative, as in the case of an individual with sociological inclinations led to a description of society by the pursuit of knowledge. Rather, it is articulated directly in preparation of one's interventions in the world. Morelli's reflections on Florentine society begin *in medias res*, with detailed descriptions of the manifold contexts that in his view defined the conditions for the exercise of one's social agency. This is society seen from an individual's point of view and explained for an individual's use.

At the centre of Morelli's idea of social conduct is an individual agent making calculated choices. From the very beginning of the conduct advice the first step that the young man must take is spelled out: *Prima misura te*, 'first measure yourself, who you are and of what condition and character (*natura*)'.[44] This self-assessment is not limited to moral character but must include a careful consideration of the context, as Morelli makes clear when he reiterates this imperative in the context of advice about socialising with other youths of respectable families and courting ladies: 'Above all, measure yourself (*ti misura*) in every situation, and if you cannot easily afford to perform these deeds, do not do them.'[45] The emphasis on self-knowledge means that the *pater familias* must learn from his mistakes: he must admit it to himself, for instance, if his trust in domestic servants was misplaced.[46]

This focus on the individual agent and, as discussed below, networks is not the result of Morelli's failure to perceive social classes within Tuscan society, for he clearly identified some key social groups and did so without falling back on the convention of dividing society into three or more orders. His remarks about social groups emerge organically from discussions of specific

---

[43] Compare with the merchants' transactional approach to business; Paul D. McLean and John F. Padgett, 'Was Florence a Perfectly Competitive Market? Transactional Evidence from the Renaissance', *Theory and Society*, 26:2 (1997), 209–44, esp. pp. 222–3.

[44] Branca (ed.), *Mercanti scrittori*, p. 167.

[45] Ibid., p. 195.

[46] Ibid., p. 181.

socioeconomic contexts, which suggests that they are rooted in social experience. It is then all the more significant that the social imaginary of the *ricordi* remains more about individual agency and networks. To reiterate, this is largely because for Morelli the function of social representations is directly to facilitate the passage to action. Even when agency and strategising make room for different priorities, such as the expression of one's social identity, and consequently social groups and classes are brought to the foreground, network ties remain salient. Thus, Florentines might describe themselves as members of a social class, say, the well-off but non-elite *popolo grasso* or the underprivileged *popolo minuto*; or of one of the twenty-one major, middle, and minor guilds (guild membership is given at the beginning of Morelli's portraits of his ancestors as a crucial marker of social identity). But they would also express their identity in a relational way, emphasising membership in an extended network of supporters, allies, and protectors.[47] Thus, because of his marriage to Caterina Alberti, Giovanni Morelli was identified as a supporter of the Albertis, with unwanted consequences when the fortunes of this leading family declined.

The identification of a few social groups follows economic and political criteria – the latter with respect to what Morelli saw as the elite group of the city, distinguished from the rest by their leadership role in communal affairs. Most of Morelli's attention is understandably devoted to his fellow merchants, with whom most of one's business would inevitably be conducted. The other social group that he expressly identified as such were the farmers working on the merchant's estate, the object of a digression from the main thrust of the fifth subheading, on protecting the orphans against financial losses stemming from the tutors' ineffective management.[48] Once again, this reflects the situated social imaginary of an ordinary individual. We see this clearly in Morelli's mentioning manufacturing labourers (the *ciompi*) only in passing, when the course of his communal history reaches the year of their uprising and short-lived regime,[49] even as they represented a more sizeable portion of the proletariat than their agricultural counterparts. It is simply that as a merchant, rather than owner of a textile manufacture, Morelli would not have had as many dealings with them.

---

[47] On the cultural dimension of networks, see Paul D. McLean, *The Art of the Network: Strategic Interaction and Patronage in Renaissance Florence* (Durham, NC, 2007), pp. 6–8, 34; cf. David Gary Shaw, *Necessary Conjunctions: The Social Self in Medieval England* (New York, 2005), pp. 95ff.

[48] Branca (ed.), *Mercanti scrittori*, pp. 181–2.

[49] Ibid., p. 225.

It is indicative of the importance given to individual strategic conduct and support networks that they inform even the considerations about social classes and institutions. The point Morelli ultimately wants to drive to his descendants about the farmers is that the land-owning city merchant will enter a long-time relationship with them and must know how to manage it. This relationship is not primarily defined by its legal framework or the parties' vastly disparate socioeconomic standing, as the student of classic social theory might expect, but by the gestures and transactions exchanged between them. It is these that create precedents and set the basis for future developments, can mitigate tensions arising from mutual mistrust,[50] and ultimately shape the trajectory of what remains, in Morelli's eyes, a relationship between specific individuals, notwithstanding his suspicion of agricultural workers as a group.[51] This exemplifies Morelli's transactional approach, in the sense explained above. His advice is marked by excessive prudence and generally worded in the negative: do not show the peasants signs of kindness, in demeanour or words, for they will construe it as weakness and take advantage of it in the future – a clear indication of a personal relationship with a life of its own, shaped 'from the inside' by the parties' interventions. Equally, be wary of their way of making you pay threefold for any service they render. Not surprisingly then, the reciprocity underpinning the relationship should be strictly contractual, excluding the gift exchanges recommended in relations between urban professionals.[52] The advice to evaluate each rural worker individually before hiring, inquiring into their reputation (*fama*) and habits – chattering or bragging about their loyalty – so as to sift through the candidates, shows that individual character remained fundamental even in the case of those whom Morelli perceived through their collective identity. The text leaves little doubt that from Morelli's viewpoint the farmers' group identity was defined by a set of perceived common attitudes and tactics towards their employers – in other words, by their patterns of agency rather than structural factors like socioeconomic status. Lastly, even as he warns against the harms that the landowner stands to suffer from a badly managed relationship with the peasants, Morelli makes it plain that relations with them are inevitable. There is a clear sense that one is embedded in a web of social relations as part of the normal order of society.

---

[50] See Pandimiglio, 'Morelli e la ragion di famiglia', p. 581.

[51] He is also suspicious of the urban poor who offer their services as domestic servants; Branca (ed.), *Mercanti scrittori*, p. 180.

[52] Ibid., p. 182.

Institutions were also dealt with through one's network of kin, partners, and friends. Two fundamental Florentine institutions receive significant treatment in Morelli's *ricordi*: taxation and the elections to the commune's public offices. A third is a common occurrence in Gregorio Dati's diary: the merchants' court, *Mercanzia*. Morelli's focus is on the possibilities for manipulating the fiscal and electoral rules through support networks, for example, using friends to procure a more reasonable tax assessment. This does not stem from an incapacity to think in institutional terms. Rather, the investment in the networks of friends and protectors promised a better return and thus obviated the institutionalist approach.[53] Like many a well-off Florentine, Morelli was convinced that one ought to take advantage of the subjective element built into the tax assessment procedures, which until 1427 relied on several assessments of one's fiscal worth by neighbourhood notables, from which an average was obtained.[54] Accordingly, he advises his descendants to conceal their true wealth from the neighbours' eyes by living modestly – a common strategy at the time. This advice resonates with Morelli's own practices, as candidly acknowledged in the autobiographical recollections of the *ricordi*. After the exile of the Albertis, Morelli and his brother relocated to another district in order to avoid a harsh assessment of their taxable worth by the neighbours who now viewed them with suspicion. He makes it a point to record the names of the notables who produced favourable tax assessments in the new district and notes the intercession of his brother-in-law Iacopo, who advised this move in the first place and then interceded with an assessor to procure a highly favourable tax assessment.[55] This was a crucial service, the kind that defined a relationship, and one can guess at the reasons why Morelli brought it to the attention of his descendants: already a relative by marriage, Iacopo was a connection worth maintaining, which required adequate reciprocation – and the same goes for cultivating the relationship with the assessor. That friendly relations between two families should be cultivated from one generation to the next was a point implicit in Morelli's earlier reference to the service received from a lawyer friend of Bernardo Morelli (d. 1400), whose intercession led to the renewal of the family's ancient Guelf privilege.[56]

---

[53] See Paul D. McLean, 'Patronage, Citizenship, and the Stalled Emergence of the Modern State in Renaissance Florence', *CSSH* 47:3 (July 2005), 638–64.

[54] D. Herlihy and Christiane Klapisch-Zuber, *Les Toscanes et leurs familles* (Paris, 1978), pp. 25–6.

[55] Branca (ed.), *Mercanti scrittori*, pp. 156, 233.

[56] Ibid., p. 130; for a similar example, see Molho et al., 'Genealogia', p. 239.

Moving away from the family's traditional home into a new neighbourhood was fiscally advantageous but wrought symbolic damage to one's social identity, and it is suggestive that Morelli blames it on the marriage tie that he forged with the Albertis. He is at pains to distance himself from the exiled Albertis and protests in the *ricordi* that he and his kin 'did not regret' them but shared the popular support for the movement that ousted them in 1393.[57] Yet the relationship had a life and materiality of its own: public opinion saw in the marriage tie clear evidence that the Morellis were part of the Albertis' network of supporters. So Giovanni Morelli lamented the decision to tie his fortunes to those of the Albertis: had he opted to align himself through marriage with another influential faction, he muses, he might even have received the honour of serving a term in a communal office.[58] There is a clear sense that Florentine society was made up not of dyadic ties, between two individuals or two families, but of complex social networks that channelled the flow of social and political capital, thereby procuring political office or a favourable tax assessment.

Marrying into the Albertis' orbit had not been Morelli's original plan, but the engagement to the girl he had loved since she was a child was broken by her father. Beyond the personal dimension of the drama, Morelli lamented the consequences of this failed marriage plan for his standing in society. Revealingly, he describes the whole episode as a betrayal by his future father-in-law with whom he had been negotiating. For all his attraction to the girl, the failed relationship that he describes is essentially with her father, the *pater familias* who acted on her behalf, as it was common. What Morelli found truly odious was that he had assiduously cultivated the relationship, going beyond the usual formal steps of first securing the father's promise through an intermediary and then shaking hands with him in the church in the presence of the mediator to seal the agreement.[59] A succinct but heartfelt statement dramatises precisely this personal investment in the relationship: 'in the hope of her I abandoned many fine and great marriages into which I could have entered'. Morelli's indictment goes so far as to cast strong doubts on the character of the man who betrayed him, but this notwithstanding, he acknowledges the other's strategic thinking – the fact that his decision was motivated by profit.[60]

---

[57] Branca (ed.), *Mercanti scrittori*, p. 232.

[58] Which he did for the first time only in 1409; ibid., p. 162.

[59] On mediators' role, see Anthony Molho, *Marriage Alliance in Late Medieval Florence* (Cambridge, MA, 1994), pp. 183–5.

[60] 'gli parve vantaggiare'; Branca (ed.), *Mercanti scrittori*, p. 235.

This painful recognition offers a particularly clear illustration of the calculated, instrumental nature of social networking in Florentine society.

The last section of Morelli's conduct advice emphasises the importance of cultivating relationships through active investment.[61] The didactic discourse follows an intuitive course, taking the reader –the young merchant, Morelli's heir – through each of the steps needed to forge viable social ties. Calculated selection is the first step of networking: Morelli recommends choosing allies from the powerful and respected notables connected with the city's leading faction. The underlying premise is that one is the artisan of one's support network. Morelli reviews the gestures through which one can gain the friendship of such men. Ideally one would seek the strongest possible tie, a marriage alliance. Alternatively, one could make recourse to such social overtures as offering one's aid and services and proffering praise. But in a world of shifting alliances acquiring friends and supporters was not everything, hence Morelli's emphasis on preserving and even increasing one's bond with those who had proved their worth to him ('those whom you see that love and serve you' – the ultimate test of a social relation).[62] His recommendation to go to a friend's aid without waiting for him to ask for assistance might seem to advocate altruism, but he follows it up urging to make sure to let him know of the service he has thus received. This, then, is another example of calculated investment in maintaining and consolidating social ties. Implied in the above-mentioned advice is that one must develop habits of relational thinking, so as to recognise in a social situation not directly touching one's own affairs the opportunity to intervene in favour of a friend and thus invest in the relationship. Equally, you must show appreciation for favours received (*benifici ricevuti*) and reciprocate, Morelli urges his heirs. Reciprocity involves both material and personal means: *in avere*, by using money and possessions to bestow gifts and favours, and *'n persona*, expressing profuse gratitude towards your benefactor and possibly also using your other contacts to intervene on his behalf.

The key is to engage with other merchants and professionals – 'usa e pratica con simili uomini' – and invest in social ties through gifts, favours, and friendly, honourable gestures. As already intimated, Morelli recommends cultivating a couple of connections in particular, with important people from the circles of power. Relying preferentially on a few valuable ties within one's support network is a common strategy across cultures, and we have already encountered it in Esperon's case in Chapter 3. But in Florence it made all the more sense because in the merchants' close-knit community there were only

---

[61] Ibid., pp. 200–6.
[62] Ibid., p. 202.

limited benefits to so-called 'weak ties'. The merchants' milieu was remarkably self-sufficient, both politically, with merchants controlling three of the seven major seven guilds in Florence's guild-based government, and economically – for example, trust in commercial agents in faraway ports was guaranteed by recruiting them from the cadet branches of merchant families.

Lastly, Morelli discusses a special relationship, into which the young man bereft of fatherly guidance is urged to enter with 'one or more' experienced notables. Here too, there is a well-defined objective: through careful observation the young man should pattern his behaviour on the older man so as to become a rounded person. This notwithstanding, the relationship is injected with a dose of idealism, and not just because of Morelli's own experiences as an orphan (the elderly notable, it has been noticed, is 'a father figure'[63]). The other social ties are aimed at objectives that while clearly important can nevertheless be said to serve higher, second-order goals: thus wealth and communal office, already desirable for their immediate benefits, are all the more valuable because they serve the greater goal of increasing the family's standing in the community. The aim of this particular relationship, however, is in itself an ideal: of self-realisation and individual plenitude. The inner dialogue on individual virtues is an integral part of this ideal, evidenced by the recommendation to study the classics so as to find consolation and cultivate one's intellect. But this notwithstanding, the model of the full social person is at the core about mastery of the intricacies of conduct. The reasons for advocating a solid knowledge of the scripts of contemporary sociability (*cortesia*) are strategic: 'you will do this in order to become expert' (*per diventare isperto*)'. Social identity is thus rooted in the individual's agency. For all the passionate plea to become conversant with the classics, Morelli also makes it clear that seeking inspiration from a real-life model of conduct is ultimately preferable because it is more practical.[64]

Forging network ties entailed a real risk of failure, as illustrated by Morelli's marriage to Caterina Alberti. This, at least, was a calculated risk. Morelli must have been aware that like all dominant families in recent Florentine history the Albertis might sooner or later fall from power. A marriage alliance with a family that kept its neutrality in the power struggles between the city's factions would have been safer but obviously did not hold the same promise of increase in status. Morelli's advice to his heirs to keep the middle course and avoid taking sides in the factional conflicts reveals a lesson learned from his association with the declining fortunes of the Albertis. His rationale for

---

[63] Trexler, *Public Life*, p. 171.

[64] Branca (ed.), *Mercanti scrittori*, p. 205.

self-censuring any judgmental remark in public lest it be construed as a sign of preferring one faction over its rival suggests that only the strictest apolitical stance could shield against the endemic risks stemming from factionalism. It is hard to know whom you can trust, he writes, because Florence is full of evil people ready to seize upon the slightest faux pas in order to denigrate and marginalise (or worse) their social competitors. Notwithstanding the ways in which this kind of evaluation of the other was instrumentalised, it illustrates the social hermeneutics underpinning interactions in a world that embraced prudence as a rule of conduct: one's true allegiances had to be read from small clues such as the passing joke or disparaging remark. Such risks were not calculated; rather, they stemmed from situations that were almost unavoidable. Similarly, in an example discussed above, Morelli's instructions convey a clear sense that the farmers' attempts to take advantage of the land-owning merchant are inevitable. Such risks were part and parcel of the merchant's social existence.[65]

One scenario receives ample treatment: it was an inevitable risk of doing business in Florence to receive requests for loans from bad debtors and, more generally, all manner of deceitful propositions whose only aim was to part the unsuspecting merchant from his money. Morelli quotes verbatim the lines with which shrewd business operators will inevitably approach his heirs for money, and then advises them how to parry these overtures with minimal loss to their reputation and connections. His instructional tales gain in authenticity as they depict elaborate scenarios and exemplify with quotes how the protagonists are drawn into clever exchanges: 'You'll be safe: how else do you think I'd have told you about this?' or 'Twenty men would help me in this business, but I don't want to give them this information and make them a service; but I'm glad to do it for you, because I know you.'[66] With the inclusion of these dissonant voices, the instructional discourse acquires a dialogical quality. The reasons for this were pragmatic: to address the real-life challenges facing urban professionals, the *ricordi* author had to delve into a social imaginary defined by conflicting voices and perspectives.

Such choices chart the evolution of Morelli's priorities. Unlike contemporary didactic treatises characterised by the methodical organisation of the material and scholastic distinctions, the *ricordi*'s instructional discourse unfolds in a narrative vein, relying on real-life stories to get its points across.

[65] Trust, as Gener Brucker put it, 'was a commodity in short supply' in Florence; *Living on the Edge in Leonardo's Florence: Selected Essays* (Berkeley, 2005), p. 84. And see Ulrich Beck, *Risk Society: Towards a New Modernity*, trans. Mark Ritter (London, 1992).

[66] Branca (ed.), *Mercanti scrittori*, p. 184.

Morelli had briefly tried an approach inspired by the canons of humanist prose in the opening section on the ancestral land of Mugello, which follows a conventional scheme with its threefold assessment of the beauty, goodness, and greatness of the country, each of these categories in turn subdivided into an examination of the people, landscape, and edifices. Once he turned to a discussion of conduct strategies, however, these schemas were abandoned in favour of a social discourse fundamentally rooted in the experience of Florentine society and serving practical ends. There are numerous instances in which Morelli addresses the audience directly, the better to engage them: '*tu* [you, sg.] istudi Vergilio, Boezio, Senaca'; 'you (*voi*, pl.) have seen [above] that Pagolo left four children'.[67] Once writing was used for communicating eminently practical information such marks of orality became natural. The choice of narrative rather than expository writing as a medium apt to introduce strategies calibrated for complex social contexts brings the world of everyday life into the text in colourful detail. Future Morelli generations are treated to social advice built around real situations and narrative plots, as in the example above about the carefully crafted pretexts for soliciting loans or investments.

As a crucial narrative resource, emplotment goes beyond building social advice from veridic scenarios: it also makes possible an instructional mode in which the future *pater familias* learns by being assigned a narrative role. For instance, as discussed above, he is invited to see himself as a novice merchant facing persuasive but ultimately deceptive propositions. Similarly, having recounted his father's skill and effort in salvaging the family estate after the plague of 1363 claimed the lives of his elder brothers, Morelli invites his heirs to put themselves in Pagolo's place and imagine – '*tu* considera et pensa' – how they might find the inner strength to cope with it all.[68] This instructional strategy recalls the Franciscan moral discourse explored in Chapter 1, which aimed to inculcate the habits of personal initiative by framing the reader as the protagonist of a specific scenario.

These examples illustrate how the *ricordi* enabled an instructional discourse that went beyond the traditional emphasis on morals to address in practical detail the concerns of urban professionals. As hybrid texts, the *ricordi* facilitated a significant cultural achievement, the synthesis between rigorous humanist reasoning and personal experience as a valid source of social knowledge. The marks of orality that punctuate Morelli's lessons point to a consequential phenomenon: the affirmation of everyday life into the written record as a topic that in itself merits the kind of reflection until not long ago

---

[67] Ibid., pp. 165, 199; also see Bec, *Marchands écrivains*, pp. 55–6.
[68] Branca (ed.), *Mercanti scrittori*, p. 140.

reserved for more lofty subjects like history or religion. It is in this respect that the written medium of the *ricordi* presented a key advantage over orality, since oral instructions were arguably just as effective for the mere transmission of practical knowledge to one's sons. But the effect of casting this knowledge into the fixed form of the written word was to focus reflection on what was now a more clearly expressed and defined topic, which furthermore could be reexamined because one always had a permanent record to return to.

Morelli ends his lessons on gaining friends and allies with a rhetorical twist: 'Above all, if you want to have friends and relatives, act in such a way that you do not really need them.'[69] Cash (*contanti*) is your best friend and relative, Morelli reveals – hence the emphasis on careful management of finances and maintaining a 'certain station'. This might not have come as a complete surprise to the reader: earlier Morelli advised buying the friendship of influential men with money, if one could not gain it in any other way.[70] The reader is then reassured of possessing 'a natural sense for knowing how to govern and keep yourself, according to what you are taught [here] in part'. Finally, future Morellis are urged to further educate themselves through life-long study. The seemingly contradictory remark about the limits of social networking begins to make sense in light of this renewed emphasis on self-conduct. However vital, acquiring allies and friends must be complemented by the knowledge of how to conduct oneself in society (*saperti governare*).

The importance of individual skill emerges from Morelli's emphasis on the capacity to make practical judgements tailored to changing contexts. He does not expound on a code of conduct with rules to be followed strictly but tries to cultivate in his heirs a pragmatic sense for acting strategically. No particular course of action, either involving the practices of courtesy and urban sociability, or securing the benevolence of the political regime, is so valued for itself as to be recommended as a first recourse irrespective of the circumstances. In the paragraph above it was shown how Morelli recommends hedging one's bets and relying on both social and financial capital. Other examples can be adduced to illustrate the point, perhaps none more telling than the frequent use of the conditional 'if' (*si*). Morelli's heirs are presented with several possible courses of action from which they must select the most practical according to the circumstances: 'give what remedy you think will work', he advises at one point.[71] Finding the just measure is critical. Thus Morelli recommends a marriage alliance that enhances one's social status but warns against choosing

---

[69] Ibid., p. 203.

[70] 'comperare degli amici co' tuoi danari'; ibid., p. 190.

[71] Ibid., p. 181.

a wife from too lofty a background because she might feel entitled to question the authority of the husband.[72] Going into minute details, he advises that not more than two florins should be spent on serenades in honour of one's beloved, and this should be limited to once a year, lest the young man acquire a reputation for intemperance.[73]

Morelli's major obsession went further yet: he searched for a fail-proof way to enforce one's designs from beyond the grave, so that in the event of the *pater familias*'s untimely death the underage children might be shielded from the depredations of relatives and third parties. The answer was a complex testamentary arrangement designed to limit the children's guardians' room for transgression by using incentives and determents and having them keep each other in check.[74] The view of family relations that emerges from this discussion has nothing of the idealism characterising the 'official rhetoric surrounding the Florentine family'.[75] Even if the wife passed the husband's test of her character, it would be imprudent to have total confidence in her, Morelli advises (it was common for a widow to be pressured by her birth family to remarry so that her dowry might be used to forge a new social tie[76]). As such, she should serve as guardian together with two or three relatives of the husband. While decisions required a two-thirds majority, she retained veto power as the principal guardian or conservator. To exercise some degree of influence over her decisions, Morelli recommends incentivising the widow through a conditional bequest of money requiring her not to remarry. The guardians do not have to be close family relations as long as they are reliable – another indication that the importance of late-medieval family solidarities must not be exaggerated (but Morelli advises that in cases of equally good character friends should not be preferred over relatives).[77] Lastly, Morelli's advice covered the possibility that one could not rely on one's wife or relatives. Although he generally placed his trust in negotiated interpersonal arrangements, in this case he did not shy away from recommending the institutional path of placing the children in the care of Florence's communal government, on practical grounds: because 'for many reasons the Commune is better than the family relationship or friend'. Morelli's summary of his long exposé on this topic gives an excellent illustration of a defining feature of his social advice, the range of alternative courses

---

[72] Ibid., p. 168.
[73] Ibid., p. 195.
[74] Ibid., pp. 171–5.
[75] Najemy, *History of Florence*, pp. 222 and 219–37.
[76] Klapisch-Zuber, *Women, Family, and Ritual*, pp. 123–31.
[77] More on this in ibid., pp. 68, 76–8.

of action from which his heirs should select the most appropriate according to the circumstances:

> Indeed, I believe that this path is more beneficial to the child than any other: as it was said above, the mother first, then good and wealthy relatives without reproach, or indeed friends, and finally, where these two are lacking, rely on the third, that is to say the Commune.[78]

Morelli heeded his own advice. His successive last wills, copied in the *ricordi*, show that he appointed a diverse panel of conservators for his estate and underage children, headed by the wife of his father-in-law, aided by his second wife, his sister and brother, and two others, for a total of six, as he recommends in the *ricordi*. Also on the model of his recommendations in the *ricordi*, both a two-thirds majority and the consent of the principal executor were needed for any decision. The last will was also meant to control the fate of the estate after Morelli's death, forbidding the heirs to alienate or divide the family house; the consuls of the wool guild were appointed to verify that these conditions were fulfilled.[79] Such complex arrangements were common among the merchants. At their source was a keen awareness of the potential for agency of family and partners, but they also reflect the possibilities for strategic action enabled by the development of institutional and legal structures.

The present case for strategising and calculation confirms the insights of earlier scholarship on the *ricordi*,[80] in contradistinction to a more recent argument which, acknowledging that Morelli wanted his heirs to become expert at a vast array of social exchanges, disputes that he aimed to outdo competitors by taking advantage of their naïveté.[81] Instead, it is suggested that Morelli envisaged that relations would flourish beyond calculated interest and into affective bonds, so as to mitigate the effects of the fierce competition between merchants. In this view the effectiveness of social ties rested on the performance of a formal script, a 'social ritual'. This position fails to appreciate the strength of the evidence for strategic action and presents the exceptional relation between the young man and his older mentor as indicative of Morelli's

---

[78] Branca (ed.), *Mercanti scrittori*, p. 175.
[79] Pandimiglio, 'Morelli e la continuità familiare', pp. 159–71.
[80] Bec, *Marchands écrivains*, esp. pp. 63, 328.
[81] 'there is no evidence for this point of view'; Trexler, *Public Life*, p. 170.

general outlook on social bonds. But even this relationship was anything but free of instrumental reasoning. Never mind that Morelli saw it merely as one possibility among many for advancing the young man's career – he mentions it after having detailed several other courses of action. But the aim of the relationship remained squarely to enhance one's own status by imitating, quite strategically, the conduct of the experienced man.[82] The case for 'social ritual' is weak. Morelli does not delve into detailed descriptions of the ceremonial order for visits, processions, or feasts, as we would expect of someone concerned above all with the formal aspects of social interactions. His own experience – the broken engagement – taught him that a solemn agreement could be breached if one party thought it advantageous, just as his childhood memories and stories of his father's struggles made him painfully aware that kinship and friendship ties were routinely set aside in favour of personal interests. Consequently he emphasised self-assessment, good timing, finding the right measure, and choosing between several possible courses of action according to the practical dictates of context – not the completion of a sequence of steps in the right order and the proper form.

Morelli did not imagine that his heirs' social competitors were naïve, but it does not follow that his advice lacked a strong instrumental dimension – on the contrary. For one, the advice to buy friends with money makes plain the strategic dimension of social behaviour. Morelli's key purpose was to make his descendants more adroit than their peers at manoeuvring in the social field:[83] first, precisely because he realised full well that many would try to take advantage of them, and so they needed to know how to counter such attempts, as discussed above; and second, because the recent family misfortunes meant his sons were not in the position to maintain their status by dint of a substantial fortune. It is certainly true that Morelli recommended keeping one's commitments, but this was a pragmatic course of action intended to build one's reputation and social capital; what is more, he recommended it above all in relation to valuable social connections. Reciprocity was essential, but it was asymmetrical, keeping the door open for a degree of manipulation so as to derive as much profit as possible while remaining mindful of the interests of one's partners. In this limited sense it is possible to speak of a certain altruism, but not in the strong sense of the word.

Historiographical debates can seem sterile, so it is useful to explore the larger implications of the present one. First, both the argument advanced in

---

[82] 't'ingegna di somigliarlo'; Branca (ed.), *Mercanti scrittori*, p. 205.

[83] Similar observations about Renaissance social networks in McLean, *Art of the Network*, pp. 33, 227.

these pages and the one to which it responds emphasise participation in social interactions and engagement with one's peers, and in this sense agency is central to both of them. But there is a significant difference: the earlier position reduces the individual's agency to following a culturally prescribed model of behaviour and insists that the ultimate goal of individual strategies was the common good. Morelli's case serves an overarching argument for the centrality of social ritual in the Renaissance, built from the premise that social ritual instils a feeling of community in its participants – hence the twined emphasis on Morelli's altruism and adherence to cultural forms. This reflects a particular strand of 1970s anthropology that has since been called into question.[84] The emphasis on reproducing cultural norms leaves little room for creativity and the pursuit of strategic objectives that are at odds with the prevailing values. Culture itself is conceptualised as largely homogenous. By contrast, the present argument restores the individual to the status of a moral agent and creator of culture. Morelli negotiated his way through a social imaginary defined by contradictory voices. His model of social behaviour was shaped by Florentine society and culture, but equally reflected personal experiences and served goals and priorities defined by the individual. In this sense, it represents a personal construct. The fundamental difference in the way culture is conceptualised in the present volume vis-à-vis the social-ritual approach goes back to the contrast between the two anthropological definitions discussed in the Introduction: culture as consisting of discrete building blocks such as norms and rituals, or alternatively of symbolic schemes and instructions that inform individual conduct without determining it, thus retaining a meaningful idea of human agency. Second, Morelli arrived at the social vision formulated in the *ricordi* after weighing both ideals and practical imperatives – hence the occasional hesitations and contradictions.[85] He was strongly invested in an ideal of human achievement based not on money and powerful connections but personal effort, skill, and respect for one's partners, as his emotional portraits of Gualberto and Pagolo bear witness. His aspiration for social concord seems sincere, and echoes of it made it into the conduct advice: thus, he recommends honesty as far as possible in relations with social partners. But at the end of the day his reflection on ethics and society moved in a different direction. Part of the reason Morelli yearned for good will and agreement is that he had seen little of it in Florentine society and his own family. Consequently, in his advice

---

[84] See Philippe Buc, *The Dangers of Ritual* (Princeton, 2001).

[85] One example is the nature–nurture dilemma. In the space of a few lines he acknowledges the huge formative effects of an upbringing in the city, of which his father was deprived, before taking the opposite view that Pagolo's innate virtue helped him overcome this disadvantage.

for posterity he decided to err on the side of calculated pragmatism. This is the crucial point, and it suggests that Morelli lacked the confidence that affective bonds might prevail in the competitive Florentine society.

He was hopeful, however, that the fortunes of the Morellis would turn with the next generations, and assured his family readership that the affairs of this world do not always run the same course but are bound to change.[86] It has recently been argued that this pronouncement is belied by a static vision of society, notwithstanding that this or that family might experience an episode of social mobility.[87] The changing wheel of Fortune, the figure to which humanists turned to express their sense of social instability, did not set in motion historical change. The crux of this argument is that Morelli recommends to the next generations courses of socioeconomic action steeped in his own, and even his father's, experience, about a half century removed from the *ricordi*'s intended audience.

Clearly the modi operandi proposed by Morelli are not sensitive to the possibility that his children and grandchildren might live in a fundamentally changed world. They largely did not, as it turns out: even the emergence of the Medici as the city's de facto ruling dynasty was the culmination of a trend exemplified with less success by previous leading families, such as the Albizzi. But the suggestion that this reflects a short-sighted understanding of society obscures the real reasons behind Morelli's position. There is a difference between remarking, as Morelli did, that a social scenario witnessed personally might occur again and therefore one should be prepared,[88] and holding a static vision of society. The latter view cannot be imputed to Morelli, because his social advice largely sidesteps the issue. His capital concern was with the threats that social and political instability posed to the family fortunes – something that the argument summarised above does not appreciate sufficiently. Sweeping societal change was not a premise that he retained when he sat down to write. In retrospect the implicit promissory note of Morelli's socioeconomic advice does not seem particularly ambitious, focusing as it did on preserving the family fortune. But if one takes into account the troubled recent history of the family and the relatively high degree of economic and political risk in Florentine society, his approach makes more sense. It must also be recalled that Morelli's conduct advice, where most of his views on society are expressed, was inflected by an autobiographical fixation. Small wonder then that he comes across as conservative. For him the emergence of a world in which his advice

---

[86] Branca (ed.), *Mercanti scrittori*, p. 165.
[87] Tripodi, 'Il padre a Firenze', p. 49.
[88] Branca (ed.), *Mercanti scrittori*, p. 171.

would no longer hold true must have been associated metonymically with the destabilising episodes that had marked the family's recent history. In sum, it is not, as implied in the argument cited above, that Morelli was incapable of imagining a profoundly changed society; rather, his social reflection was aimed at preserving the social order with which the fortunes of the Morellis were inextricably linked.

This social reflection was not one-dimensional. The notables who in the mid-fifteenth century acquiesced to the rise of the Medici for fear that resistance might usher in another popular government as in 1378 were committed to preserving the status quo. Morelli too was suspicious of the working poor as hired hands. From a political standpoint, however, he recognised one sole merit in the popular regime of 1378–82, the *reggimento* of workers and people of modest status: that of curbing the ambitions of the uppermost elite.[89] This gives another illustration of Morelli's relational view of society. His hope that the antagonistic relations between the oligarchy and a spirited underclass might play out to the benefit of the moderately prosperous merchant proves that he was attuned to the larger dynamics of social and political change.

Beyond human agency: 'ritual', God, and the devil

The case for religious piety and belief in divine providence has often been made in studies of late-medieval culture. Insofar as it concerns the *ricordi* this owes much to first impressions: powerful but potentially misleading. Most *ricordi* begin with an invocation of divine aid, sometimes repeated throughout the text, but this is largely formulaic, reflecting the transformation of the early record-keeping experiments into a genre with its own conventions. Surely the case for the salience of religious beliefs in texts that are otherwise dominated by mundane concerns cannot rest on this. To be clear, the question is not whether religion mattered for people like Giovanni Morelli. The urban laity were the target of preaching in the vernacular, while humanism increased the merchants' exposure to a variety of popularising religious texts. The parish was a fundamental territorial unit and the notable families took pride in arranging decorous burial places for their dead inside churches, as Morelli emphasises with respect to his family. The more intriguing issue, however, is the degree to which belief in God was woven into the fabric of everyday existence, beyond such obvious contexts as liturgical service, religious processions, and almsgiving; and, crucially, whether it shaped one's social views and behaviour (as

---

[89] Ibid., p. 162. A memorandum he drafted as magistrate articulates his concern that ordinary citizens were oppressed by the powerful; Pandimiglio, 'Morelli e la ragion di famiglia', p. 585.

discussed in Chapter 1). For example, it has been suggested that participation in the public processions of the many Florentine religious confraternities had wider social implications inasmuch as it promoted solidarity.[90] Now it has long been argued that in the merchant milieu God was approached in reciprocal terms.[91] Many a Renaissance merchant included in his accounting ledger a rubric to *Messer Domeneddio*, consisting of the pious donations through which he aimed to balance his account with God.[92] A shift of emphasis has occurred, however, in the more recent ritual-centred scholarship. It is thus important to revisit the intersections between belief in God and the variety of socioeconomic issues taken up in Morelli's text. For even if the church's moral discourse did not lead Morelli to embrace an altruistic approach to social interactions, there are indications that the merchants cultivated a special relation with the divine.

This relation emerges in full view only in specific contexts, because Morelli is drawn to reflect on divine providence by particular issues and situations. Outside such contexts the normal perspective on society in the *ricordi* is mundane, concerned chiefly with the motivations and strategies of competitors and the mechanisms that regulate social interactions and economic exchanges. This resonates with Galbert's decidedly this-worldly perspective in his first, eyewitness report on the disturbances in Bruges (Chapter 1). Occasionally, in the pages chronicling contemporary Florentine history, divine will is invoked to account for an unexpected turn of events that is difficult to rationalise in any other way and, crucially, represents such a fortunate coincidence that Morelli cannot resist seeing it as the work of divine providence. Although less conventional than the invocation of divine grace at the beginning of the *ricordi*, this reflects the traditional historiographical practice of ascribing extraordinary events to the workings of divine providence. Thus, in keeping with an old trope, God, the Holy Virgin, and St John (Florence's protector), are said to have 'permitted' the sudden death of the duke of Milan that saved the defenceless city from imminent invasion.[93] Similarly, Morelli expressed his conviction that the intervention of the lord of Piombino, who offered Florence the use of Piombino port under far more favourable terms than the city's highly disadvantageous arrangement with Paolo Guinigi of Lucca, was a

---

[90] Trexler, *Public Life*; Nicholas Eckstein, *The District of the Green Dragon: Neighbourhood Life and Social Change in Renaissance Florence* (Florence, 1995).

[91] Bec, *Marchands écrivains*, pp. 60, 276–9.

[92] Marina Gazzini, *'Dare et habere': il mondo di un mercante milanese del Quattrocento* (Firenze, 2002), p. 62.

[93] Branca (ed.), *Mercanti scrittori*, p. 264.

providential event best explained as divine punishment for Guinigi's avid pursuit of profit at the Florentines' expense. This treatment of divine intervention suggests an inclination for projecting human sentiments and emotions onto the divine: 'God became fed up, I believe, with this scornful parasite holding us at ransom.'[94]

The few instances in which divine providence emerges as a topic of more focused reflection are circumscribed by Morelli's effort to work out the implications for the individual's conduct in the world and imagine what kind of relationship the individual agent can maintain with God. In one significant context, at once biographical and didactic – it looks back to the life of Morelli's father and forward to the lessons posterity can draw from it – divine omnipotence emerges as the answer to Morelli's anxiety that fate might negate human agency. *Contra* the contemporary view, which he judged widespread, of a blind Fortune, Morelli's solution is to turn God into the guarantor of immanent justice. His conclusion is that divine reward is commensurate with individuals' merits, 'secondo i nostri meriti', in effect implying that it is prompted by the individual's deeds and character. Implicit in this is the idea of an exchange between the individual and God. And on the parallel that can be drawn between courting God's favour and winning allies, Morelli is quite explicit. He recalls how his father was 'always careful to gain (*acquistare*) the love of God, his creator, through his alms and good deeds, and then to gain the friendship of powerful men of good station'. This makes plain the similarity between earning the benevolence of social superiors and of God. Furthermore, at the same time as he urges his heirs to emulate Pagolo's ability in winning friends and supporters through courteous conduct and gifts, Morelli emphasises the importance of being 'amici di Dio', God's *friends* – a crucial term in the Renaissance social imaginary. This suggests that he conceived of the individual's relation to God as a partnership – albeit, we shall see, more special than the partnerships one entered into with fellow merchants. Lastly, Morelli finds empowering the knowledge that worldly affairs are governed not by capricious Fortune but by a just God: those who understand this fact have a distinct advantage (*vantaggio*) in their operations, because 'God wants you to help yourself'.[95] The case for self-help, so familiar to the urban professionals from their daily lives, is sanctioned here by divine providence. In sum, the kind of transactional approach to society, whereby exchanges between the participants were more important in determining the trajectory of the relationship than structural factors, also characterised one's relation with the divine.

---

[94] Ibid., p. 276.
[95] 'Dio vuole che tu t'aiuti'; ibid., p. 139.

The section of the *ricordi* dedicated to the prayers and religious meditation occasioned by the anniversary of Morelli's son's death has been celebrated for its rare insight into a lay person's mystical experience. When the connection was made with the socioeconomic contents of the *ricordi*, it was to argue that everyday life was permeated by the same ritual forms.[96] But there is ample, if more subtle, evidence that Morelli's transactional approach to social relations informed his religious experience. The following analysis focuses on the symbolic actions – prayer and meditation in front of a crucifix in his private room[97] – through which Morelli supplicated for divine mercy for his son's soul, hoping to put an end to his tormenting thoughts. The second part of the account, describing the mystical vision experienced subsequently, is less amenable to social analysis.[98] Morelli's motivation for recording it all was that it worked, the dream vision validating his hopes in the success of the religious experiment.[99] Its perceived effectiveness recommended it for transmission to posterity. The side effect is that in writing it down as a procedure that his descendants might replicate, Morelli made the entire experience look more coherent and discrete. This, however, was not a self-contained ritual but one instance of a recurrent practice of prayer and meditation: Morelli mentions the 'innumerable times' when he prayed for his son's soul.[100] One night these ongoing efforts elicited the desired result, a dream vision.

It is striking that the account dwells at great length on establishing the grounds that justify Morelli's appeal for divine aid. The sizeable first part of the narrative gives the distinct impression that Morelli is at pains to answer an underlying question, not posed as such yet answered implicitly in the arguments he makes: what is it that entitles one to ask for divine aid? On what could he found his appeal? At issue is the very premise of his religious experience. The significance of the matter can be gauged by Morelli's concern to be as comprehensive as possible: 'Again I ask you, Lord … on account of the merits and infinite gift of your most beloved nativity'; 'Ultimately, Lord, I ask it because of the merits of your holiest … passion'; 'Ultimately, I ask it of you, My Lord, through the merit of your most glorious ascension.'[101] It

[96] Trexler, *Public Life*, p. 172, and in general pp. 172–85.
[97] On the accessibility of religious images in Florence, see Megan Holmes, *The Miraculous Image in Renaissance Florence* (New Haven, 2013), p. 165.
[98] For readings informed by psychoanalysis, see references in Branca (ed.), *Mercanti scrittori*, p. 324 n. 75.
[99] Trexler, *Public Life*, p. 179.
[100] Branca (ed.), *Mercanti scrittori*, p. 303.
[101] And the list goes on; ibid., pp. 305–6.

becomes clear that establishing the framework for human–divine exchanges was the crucial step from which everything else stemmed: the prayers, ritual, and mystical vision. This framework underlies Morelli's religious experience and provides the structure in which his use of liturgical forms and religious iconography takes place.

Morelli's answer to this consuming question is not rooted in Christian theology, for all that he drew the inspiration for his elaborate prayers from contemporary religious discourse,[102] but in the urban culture of exchanges and personal relations. As the quotes above suggest, Morelli's plea to God is informed by an idea of exchange, albeit a highly asymmetrical one. He was acutely aware of the incommensurably different nature of the human individual and God, but did not let this define their relation. Rather, the relation is defined by the gestures and deeds that have been exchanged within its frame, in much the same way social ties were understood to be shaped by the parties' interactions more than the structures in which they were embedded. Engaging with the divine, however, posed special challenges, not only because it involved radical ontological difference, but also because of the Christian rhetoric of humility. Its influence is evident in Morelli's repeated acknowledgement that he is not worthy of the divine gift (*dono*). But his sense that any request, even a plea for divine aid, should be framed in a context defined by the participants' previous exchanges is so profound that he comes up with an ingenious solution: to ground his request first and foremost not in his own contribution but in the gestures of the other party – God. (Later Morelli also points to his pious deeds, albeit downplaying their weight, in line with the rhetoric of self-deprecation.) Since his good deeds are not commensurate to the task, what authorises him to court divine benevolence for his son's soul are the gifts already received from God, such as Christ's nativity and passion. This is paradoxical only to a certain point. We have to realise that what mattered most for Morelli was that one needed a legitimate position from which to engage with another party or entity, and the way to achieve this was to hearken back to a previous interaction, whatever it said about their unequal status. Other Renaissance practices reflect the same sense that reciprocal exchanges remain highly desirable even when they are clearly asymmetrical.[103] The mere fact

---

[102] See Elizabeth Bailey, 'Raising the Mind to God: The Sensual Journey of Giovanni Morelli (1371–1444) via Devotional Images', *Speculum*, 84 (2009), 984–1008, esp. pp. 985–7, 992–3.

[103] E.g., the symbolic wedding gift as the counterpart to the substantial dowry: 'more important than the material worth of these gifts … was the need that people engaged in the process of alliance felt … to make such offerings'; Klapisch-Zuber, *Women, Family, and Ritual*, p. 224.

that Morelli was consumed by a question rarely emphasised in the church's message to the laity – 'What authorises one to ask for divine aid?' – is in itself an indication that at a fundamental level his religious outlook was shaped by social notions of exchange.

Morelli's transactional approach involved more than the dyadic reciprocity emphasised in earlier scholarship. First, the divine gifts were to humanity as a whole, as Morelli makes clear, but he feels strongly that they can be invoked as part of the believer's personal relationship to God. His logic is partly that divine benevolence shown to mankind authorises the believer to ask for more; partly, perhaps, adapting the standard scholastic doctrine to his purpose, that the merits stemming from Christ and the saints' extraordinary works form a 'treasury', which individual believers can tap into for their salvation. (Here directly, through prayer; the church, however, stressed its own intercessory role, notably as distributor of indulgences.) The latter consideration seems to inform a statement such as 'Again I ask it by virtue of the merits of the worthy words and deeds of your beloved apostle St Magdalen'. But Morelli is hardly consistent on this score. He also asks for divine grace on account of 'the excellent *gift* and overwhelming joy' of Christ's 'descent into hell' where the Old Testament saints awaited him, and, immediately after, of the 'merit' stemming from a similar event, Christ's apparition to the apostles after his resurrection.[104] But it is hard to see this as the apostles' merit in the theological sense, and so the precise meaning of this term for Morelli remains unclear.

Second, Morelli went beyond dyadic reciprocity by imagining human–divine relations as part of a social network of sorts. One's personal relationship to God makes room for a nexus of relations when Morelli invokes the saints' powers of intercession: St John the Evangelist and the Holy Virgin, the latter asked to 'recommend' both him and his son's soul to God. In this context religious issues are more overtly approached through the prism of social representations. Even as Morelli remains aware of religious doctrine and accordingly presents himself as an unworthy supplicant, the influence of ideas of gift-exchange is discernible: to signal how much he desires St John's 'excellent gift' of intercession, he offers all 'the good things that I ever said or did' for the salvation of Alberto's soul.[105] He points to his offering of 'praise and reverence' to the Holy Virgin in his prayer as a modest justification for requesting her gift of intercession. Clearly in relation to the saints Morelli felt more confident to suggest a reciprocal offer, as in the contemporary model of gift-exchange, which informed his advice on social conduct. The ties between

---

[104] Branca (ed.), *Mercanti scrittori*, pp. 305–6 (emphasis added).
[105] Ibid., pp. 308–11.

the religious figures are humanised: thus St John is described as Christ's brother, the better to the make the case for his powers of intercession. This was not unusual; earlier Morelli highlighted St Catherine's special protection as the companion or associate of God's son ('isposa del Figliuolo di Dio'[106]), emphasising not the saint's exceptional devotion but her personal connection, on the model of the social networks that defined the merchants' microcosm. The cult of the saints itself had been motivated by the need to provide the laity with familiar, human protectors.[107]

Social representations of reciprocal exchanges inform not only the underlying premise of Morelli's appeal, but even his most passionate pleas. He aimed to participate emotionally in Christ's suffering on earth through intense meditation, on the model of the Franciscan ethos of initiative, so as to communicate with the divine and ensure his prayers were heard.[108] His emphasis on sincerity and emotional investment,[109] in contrast to his conduct advice advocating dissimulation and strategising, reflects the sense that with God one entered into a special relation, which demanded a different kind of engagement. But his transactional approach is once again laid bare when he addresses St Mary in language redolent of the merchants' transactions: 'by participating in your affliction, I might merit to receive the pledge (*l'arra*) of such happiness as bought back (*ricomperata*) for us by your son through his crucifixion'.[110] This recalls the Franciscans' emphasis on Christ's human nature, encouraging the laity to relate to it and take the initiative in relation to the divine (Chapter 1).

In sum, prayers, icons, and humility coexisted with an underlying transactional premise, not unlike the juxtaposition of religion and magic in the *livres de raison*. That Morelli projected onto his relation with the divine a pattern familiar from his social milieu is a remarkable finding.[111] It stands in contrast to the oft-rehearsed notion that medieval men and women saw the earthly world as a reflection of the heavenly – a notion that reproduces uncritically the formulations of medieval high culture. Studying the views of the educated laity provides a corrective to the biases inherent in the focus on elite intellectuals.

---

[106] Ibid., p. 163.

[107] Peter Brown, *The Cult of the Saints: Its Rise and Function in Latin Christianity* (Chicago, 1981), pp. 50–68.

[108] See Trexler, *Public Life*, p. 177, and Bailey, 'Raising the Mind', esp. pp. 998–1001.

[109] Sensorial experience was particularly important; see Bailey, 'Raising the Mind', pp. 993–1003.

[110] Branca (ed.), *Mercanti scrittori*, p. 308.

[111] Pandimiglio similarly notes that mundane values permeate Morelli's religious vision; 'Morelli e la ragion di famiglia', pp. 574, 601.

Morelli's case is poignant because even in a context that stands out from the overwhelmingly mundane concerns of the *ricordi*, the social world and its practices informed the relation with the divine. The larger point here is a familiar one from the last few decades of historical anthropology of the Middle Ages: while religion often played a vital role, the laity related to religious norms and beliefs in ways that foregrounded their own concerns and priorities, arising from specific social contexts.[112] Because of the intersecting trajectories of religion and social practices, analysing Morelli's religious experience in isolation from the rest of the *ricordi* is not only incomplete but potentially misleading. Equally, this experience is more than the sum of its cultural sources, broadly speaking Christian culture and the urban social imaginary, because they are synthesised in a personal construct, the work of an individual agent. The episode testifies to the laity's creative approach to religion.

The account of that night's religious experience is not only about Morelli's relation to God: it also refers to what he ultimately concluded was the devil's attempt to subvert his religious experience by infiltrating his mind and seeding paralysing doubts. The episode sheds light on an oft-misunderstood aspect of late-medieval ideas of individual autonomy in the face of non-human agency. It is particularly precious because it shows how the laity viewed and responded to notions of demonic possession. As we shall see, the episode cannot be fitted into the framework of the alleged medieval 'porous self', prone to surreptitious infiltration by spirits, that recent scholarship has set up in contrast to the modern 'buffered self'.[113] It bears emphasis that this is the only such reference in the *ricordi* and that it comes in the singular context of a mystical experience that profoundly marked Morelli's psyche; thus, however one interprets it, this episode cannot serve as the basis for generalisations.

This unusual account poses some difficulties of interpretation, but one thing seems clear: the reference to the devil emerges via a process of ascription, whereby confusing thoughts, which nevertheless are described in the text in everyday language, were finally ascribed to an external entity attempting to infiltrate Morelli's mind. As he sought rest after his prayers, Morelli felt beset by grave doubts and was unable to sleep. Later, when he recorded it in the *ricordi*, he was convinced that this moment of crisis had been the devil's work, but he acknowledges that at that time he reached this conclusion after having battled tormenting thoughts for some time – which suggests that he first tried

---

[112] See, e.g., John Arnold, *Belief and Unbelief in Medieval Europe* (London, 2005), pp. 91–6, and Jean-Claude Schmitt, *Le corps, les rites, les rêves, le temps: Essais d'anthropologie médiévale* (Paris, 2001), pp. 91–5.

[113] Charles Taylor, *A Secular Age* (Cambridge, MA, 2006), pp. 35–9.

to make sense of his predicament in this-worldly terms.[114] It is also possible that Morelli did not think of demonic possession at all that night and that it is merely an *ex post facto* rationalisation at the writing stage. Inasmuch as the narrative traces Morelli's successive states of mind in meticulous detail, there is something to be said for its authenticity. But the opposite case is arguably stronger: because he set out to write an edifying account for the benefit of his heirs, Morelli would have had good reasons to blame the doubts he experienced in the aftermath of the ritual on the devil, the better to present his religious conduct as exemplary. Furthermore, it is striking that what Morelli identifies as the main source of his confusion is a salient concern throughout the *ricordi*: the misfortunes that plagued his life from the orphaned childhood to the failed marriage plans and their repercussions. As such, while he might have sensed that these thoughts ran counter to the hopes he placed in the prayers, it is not likely that he would have found them so alien as to immediately assign them to the devil's influence. It is more probable that at the time of writing Morelli wanted to disown such doubts and thus convinced himself that the experience is best described as the devil's attempt to infiltrate his mind. Since the episode comes immediately after the account of his heart-felt pleas to God, it made narrative sense to attribute it to the opposite figure in the religious imaginary. The overall sense of the account is that the devil is a trope or figuration of doubt and despondency.

However one views the text, as an accurate report of a lived experience or as a heavily reworked account, it is crucial that Morelli does not present himself as a powerless victim, for all the initial state of confusion, but articulates a response to the threat of demonic possession. By his own account, the key moment is when he became persuaded that his mental torment was caused by an outside entity. After this, he writes, 'all that obfuscation was gone, and all that was left was to ponder what kind of fortune I enjoyed since my birth'.[115] While the ensuing reflection was also hard probing, it unfolded in a rigorous way, resonating with the merchants' structured habits of mind: thus Morelli asks in his mind the devil to 'demonstrate' its claims. What follows could just as well be described as an inner dialogue, the devil's voice – by now firmly identified as *fantasia*, an attempt to delude him – filling the role of an alter ego; the earlier list of 'seven ills' suffered by Morelli is expanded and brought to date. (This supports the hypothesis that when he decided to draft an exemplary spiritual account Morelli found it expedient to attribute his old anxieties to a figure familiar from the religious imaginary.) This approach

---

[114] Branca (ed.), *Mercanti scrittori*, pp. 311–12.
[115] Ibid., p. 312.

was in the end successful; having taken comfort in the knowledge that his life-long tribulations were not unique to him, Morelli was able to fall asleep. Subsequently his dream vision confirmed the success of his prayers and inward reflection.

Thus, the effect of ascribing mental confusion and ominous doubts to demonic possession was anything but paralysing; on the contrary, it was to dispel Morelli's doubts. The idea of possession, then, emerges as empowering – paradoxically, in light of the argument about the medieval 'porous self', but not surprising in view of our findings about the uses of the supernatural in the *livres de raison*. As a trope of the late-medieval imaginary, possession could be invoked to explain destabilising mental states; this in turn opened the way for an adequate response, for example methodical self-reflection, for which an educated professional like Morelli was well prepared. This is not to deny that people from less privileged backgrounds might have found the spectre of possession more untoward. It is significant that when possession emerges not as a motif in a literary tract but reportedly as a lived experience in a first-person account, supernatural entities are not so effective as to successfully infiltrate the self, as in the model of 'the porous self'. Human agency remains central: here, through prayer and meditation. Crucially, possession itself is circumscribed to the individual's sphere of agency. What had paved the way for demonic attack was the decrease in the individual's autonomy brought about by Morelli's own sins: 'on account of my sins, the Enemy [took] partially hold of my freedom'.[116] Yet Morelli did not see himself as a passive, disempowered target; on the contrary, he emphasises the effects of his prayer on the devil. This indicates a conception in which the individual can hold in check untoward external entities; what is more, their capacity to impinge on one's moral autonomy is limited to circumstances when one's failings render one vulnerable.

Marginalisation was a common experience in the competitive urban world evoked in Morelli's *ricordi* – so common that it had become an accepted fact to be discussed openly in a record for posterity:[117] Pagolo's upbringing in the countryside is blamed on his father's decision to save on his education,

---

[116] Ibid., p. 311.

[117] Marginalisation of the cadet brother by the elder siblings, of orphans by their distant relatives, and of the well-off but non-elite merchant by the oligarchy – as discussed above.

since he already had two grownup sons.[118] This is yet another example of the instrumental approach to family relations. Morelli and Gregorio Dati are in agreement on the best response: putting up with adversity until the moment was ripe to make a move and change things to one's benefit. Thus Morelli resigned himself to tolerate his elder brothers' machinations until he was able to go into business on his own. Dati, however, went even further in deemphasising his agency in specific contexts.

Avoiding agency: Gregorio Dati's *libro segreto*

Dati titled his record the *libro segreto*, an account that centralised crucial information from his various ledgers in order to both facilitate his management of business and family affairs and offer his heirs a clear picture thereof: 'for the sake of clarity (*chiarezza*), both mine and of those after me'.[119] The opening references to family history are gesturing towards the genre conventions of the *ricordanze*; in the same vein, he records his four marriages and some twenty-six children, of whom only eight were alive c. 1430.[120] The register entries were sometimes annual and sometimes pertaining to business deals and family events from the previous several years. The former were usually listed indiscriminately in chronological order but could also be split into income (*entrata*) and expenses (*uscita*) on separate folios, while the latter, titled *ricordanze* or *memoria*, opened with the familiar line, 'let it be recalled that'.[121] Thus the *libro segreto* combined *ricordi* and *ricordanze* in the narrow sense of the two terms, as discussed at the beginning of this chapter. There is a fair amount of overlap because the more recent entries recapitulate matters recorded previously, sometimes adding new detail. Thus, the register concludes with a chronological memorandum summarising more than four decades of Dati's life and work ('memoria di mio stato'):[122] business transactions, partnerships, and travels; marriages and children; additions to the family patrimony; and terms in various public offices. As a statement of individual achievement this is strikingly reminiscent of Pierre Esperon's memorandum, but Dati is more

---

[118] Branca (ed.), *Mercanti scrittori*, p. 136. By contrast, Pierre Esperon never admitted in his *livre de raison* that he did not marry off his younger daughter in order to save the dowry money.

[119] Gregorio Dati, *Il Libro segreto*, ed. Carlo Gargiolli (Bologna, 1869), p. 12. On his other registers, see Leonida Pandimiglio, *I Libri di famiglia e il libro segreto di Goro Dati* (Alessandria, 2006), pp. 57, 62–5.

[120] Dati, *Libro segreto*, pp. 101–4.

[121] 'ricordanza che…'; ibid., pp. 12, 16, 20, 23, 44.

[122] Ibid., p. 113.

candid about the hardships he faced and the failures he suffered. The aim is not so much to present himself as a successful individual agent as to give a clear overview of the outcomes of his life-long efforts: first for himself, but possibly also for his heirs, as Morelli argued a responsible *pater familias* should do. Lastly, Dati occasionally chose to record personal resolutions just days after they were made, the better to maintain the course of conduct he had decided upon. Such notes, very similar to diary entries, open a unique window into the individual's lived experience.

In particular, it becomes possible to study an important but largely unexplored side of human agency, which is to do with refraining from decisive action. This might involve more subtle and limited ways of exercising one's agency, for instance coping with marginalisation through endurance and resilience, as in the examples above (p. 193). While this attitude might seem passive at first, its distinguishing mark is that it requires sustained effort at self-monitoring over long periods of time, in contradistinction with the considerable but episodic concentration of individual energies for a given strategic scheme. This approach is often accompanied by the deferment of strategic action. But there is also the more radical form of placing one's agentive potential in abeyance, effectively preferring non-action over action and leaving the field open for structural effects and the agency of partners, competitors, or even supernatural entities. Once this aspect is understood, agency becomes more complicated.[123] Precious nuances come into view. The Renaissance urban elites are a case in point, because the action-oriented nature of their records can mislead the historian into imagining them as hyperbolised free agents, empowered by their money, business networks, and calculated habits of thought. The references to family conflicts, sly competitors, and social marginalisation, as above in Morelli's *ricordi*, point to the problems inherent in such a vision. More ample evidence in this respect is provided by Dati's records.

Dati's enterprising, active outlook is not at issue. From his early twenties he entered into business as a junior partner in merchant companies that were renewed yearly or every couple of years – the standard practice in Italy at the time. These were difficult beginnings, when in return for a share of the profits the junior partner had to provide his time and labour to the joint venture so as to compensate for his modest investment of capital. There are indications that Dati emerged from these experiences with a heightened awareness of the risks attendant upon various courses of action. Already in debt in 1385 when he entered his first business venture, he had to borrow his share of the capital,

---

[123] And even 'ambiguous': Debora Battaglia, 'Ambiguating Agency: The Case of Malinowski's Ghost', *American Anthropologist*, 99:3 (Sept. 1997), 505–10, at pp. 507–8.

300 florins. Business travels came with their risks: between 1390 and 1395 he was required to travel to Valencia three times and spent almost three years there, but on the second trip he was robbed and lost 250 florins of his own money. By 1395 he was short of money because, by his own admission, he had spent a lot in the hope of great profits that failed to materialise.[124] During this time he seems to have developed an appreciation for the merits of deferring or altogether avoiding action. One example concerns the financial arrangements for his second marriage and thus is not directly tied to commercial enterprises, notwithstanding that, like many Florentines, Dati treated his wife's dowry as a source of capital. In an entry for 1393, Dati wrote that his wife's cousins overvalued her trousseau by some 30 florins, adding that this was something they really should not have done; clearly the matter was not trivial. Yet he abstained from saying anything about it, *per cortesia*;[125] his restraint was calculated, because he notes that even though he invested the 900-florin dowry in his business ventures, he did not declare or insure it, in order to avoid paying taxes for it. But because he had refrained from raising the matter of the overvalued trousseau, his wife's cousins felt indebted to him and were unwilling to challenge him to insure the dowry. His approach of avoiding confrontation paid off. When he declared the dowry, almost ten years later, he was able to take advantage of the Florentine government's reprieve of back taxes for contracts declared and paid on that day.[126] In sum, having started with calculated non-intervention, Dati continued with a strategy of deferment of action, rooted in an institutional feature of the Florentine government, which periodically granted such reprieves in an effort to improve tax collection.

A couple of related examples from the realm of business are significant in that they involve not simply the deference or avoidance of overt agency but a simultaneous emphasis on resilience. In an entry of 1395, Dati recorded that in February of that year, after the term of his latest business partnership ended, he decided not to enter into a new joint venture but went into business on his own – an occurrence so rare that Dati felt the need to repeat, for more clarity, that this really meant he did not have a partner: 'per me proprio, sanza compagnia d'alcuna persona'. He relied instead on the closest and longest collaboration of his lifetime, with his brother Simone, who sold the cloth he

---

[124] Dati, *Libro segreto*, pp. 17, 29–30, 115.

[125] Ibid., p. 37.

[126] Ibid., p. 39. The dowry was declared just a week before his wife passed away, perhaps in anticipation of this event. As tutor of her children, Dati would dispute part of the inheritance with her cousins; ibid., pp. 64–8. On the Florentine dowry fund, see Molho, *Marriage Alliance*, pp. 30–8.

sent him in Valencia. This was a highly successful spell, as he acknowledges, enabling him to pay off his outstanding debts going back to a partnership that had ended in January 1393 with the withdrawal of Michele di Ser Parente; but even so, in October 1395 he ended this eight-month run and started a new partnership with his old associate, Michele. Clearly for Dati going it alone was not a viable strategy in the long run: for one thing, a partnership had the benefit of pooling more capital. He confided in the *libro segreto* that it was lack of capital that had kept him in the previous joint venture after Michele withdrew in January 1393. He had therefore made a deliberate decision to 'suffer everything for two years' (*sofferire ogni cosa*), notably serving much of this time abroad in Valencia as company agent and also putting up with Antonio di Segna, whose *malizia* was becoming apparent, but who in 1394 had advanced an impoverished Dati's share of capital.[127] Putting up with adversity until individual action became possible can be viewed as a strategy of agency abeyance and deferment, but it equally makes sense as an example of resilient behaviour, requiring self-discipline over a long stretch of time and the moral strength to sustain hope in the possibility of future decisive action. Lastly, the episode is instructive because Dati's troubles started from a business miscalculation: he accepted as part of his share of the profits of the partnership that ended in 1393 a 950-florin outstanding debt, not suspecting that recovering the money from the company's debtors would prove very difficult. Later, however, he wrote that the debt should not have been judged recoverable in the first place. But before this realisation, he was driven by the expectation of a handsome profit to acquire Michele's 600-florin share from the debts owed to the company, thus compounding his initial miscalculation (April 1395).[128] These circumstances go some way towards explaining why later on Dati opted for a risk-averse approach.

In 1406, Dati similarly opted to defer going into business and instead concentrated all his efforts on paying off debts.[129] Once again the deferment of strategic action went hand in glove with the emphasis on resilient conduct. Dati's predicament was caused by a lawsuit over business losses in Barcelona, brought before the court of the *Mercanzia* – the corporate tribunal of long-distance merchants from five of the major guilds. Dati and his partner Piero Lana lost the case (September 1405);[130] at its source was a question of personal trust, a paramount issue in the Florentine business world rooted in

---

[127] Dati, *Libro segreto*, pp. 17, 19, 28, 46.
[128] Ibid., pp. 50, 115.
[129] Ibid., pp. 80, 87.
[130] Ibid., pp. 59, 87; on the *Mercanzia*, see Najemy, *History of Florence*, pp. 110–12.

personal networks. A rival company used the same individual as their agent in Barcelona, who tried to minimise the company's liabilities at Dati and Lana's expense. Dati professes that he had been unwilling to go to court but there was no other way: in this case failure to defend his interests would have meant ruin: 'se io non mi fossi aiutato, era mio disfacimeto' – a literal reference to self-help.[131] This notwithstanding, the outcome of the case reinforced his appreciation of the merits of non-action in high-risk situations. When his partner suggested declaring bankruptcy instead of tenaciously striving to pay off the debt, he opposed this radical but perilous move. This was the root of the growing animosity between them, culminating in the lawsuit brought against Dati by Lana, shortly before his death in 1411. By now edified about the perils of litigation, Dati settled with Lana's heirs.[132]

In these cases the abeyance of agency is largely calculated; one anthropological model describes it as a strategy for coping with risk by de-emphasising one's involvement.[133] This both resonates with and qualifies the idea of the Renaissance merchant as a strategic agent. The merchants were not so enslaved to their entrepreneurial instincts as to believe that decisive intervention was always the right answer. Facing adversity, their response was not to redouble their efforts; rather, they saw the merits of concentrating on the alternative pattern of conduct, everyday resilience. An apposite contrast is provided by Max Weber's Protestant entrepreneurs, characterised by compulsive work habits and acquisitiveness.

The 1406 episode is more complex because it also involved value judgements. Dati stresses that although Lana argued for declaring bankruptcy so as to minimise their financial losses, he opposed it because it would bring shame (*vergogna*). Dati would rather be deprived of wealth than honour (*onore*).[134] This resonates with a different anthropological explanation, which emphasises the moral dimension of placing one's agency in abeyance.[135] But Dati's case suggests that the two anthropological models are not mutually exclusive. The key point is that the values evoked as the rationale for Dati's decision reflected business ethics, in which pragmatism was more salient than in other ethical systems. The merchant's honour was predicated on keeping his word, fulfilling

---

[131] Dati, *Libro segreto*, p. 80.

[132] Ibid., p. 90.

[133] Michael Herzfeld, 'Pride and Perjury: Time and Oath in the Mountain Villages of Crete', *Man*, new ser., 25:2 (1990), 305–22.

[134] Dati, *Libro segreto*, p. 87.

[135] Hirokazu Miyazaki, 'Faith and Its Fulfilment: Agency, Exchange and the Fijian Aesthetics of Completion', *American Ethnologist*, 27:1 (2000), 31–51, at pp. 42–3.

contractual obligations, and paying off debts on time.[136] Thus gained, honourable reputation brought financial credit, which in the fast-growing Florentine economy, as in modern economies, was more valuable than material assets. Dati makes clear that in 1406 his biggest problem was the difficulty of finding credit because of the lost court case, the suspicions raised by Simone's business dealings in Barcelona, and the envy and rumours kindled by many.[137] In sum, the decision to de-emphasise one's agency could be motivated by both strategic and ethical considerations.

Lastly, that the abeyance of agency could on occasion be staged and manipulated suggests that it had an established place in the repertoire of Renaissance social strategies. One such episode is narrated in the *ricordi* of Buonaccorso Pitti. In 1399 he was captain of Pistoia and became involved in a dispute with the Florentine communal government, which demanded that he turn over a thief arrested in Pistoia. Pitti refused and asked that the jurisdictional privileges of Pistoia be respected; in the *ricordi* he emphasises his commitment to the vows he made to the people of Pistoia when he took up office.[138] He narrowly avoided exile for his obstinacy when a resolution to this effect was two votes short in Florence, but after his relatives and friends counselled him to comply lest the resolution be put to the vote again, he finally reconsidered his position. Having summoned the priors of Pistoia and informed them of the prospects he faced, he put the matter in their hands, asking them to decide what he should do, while reiterating his willingness to suffer exile rather than infringe Pistoia's jurisdictional rights. He concluded by subtly hinting at a face-saving solution: the thief's transfer to Florence should be approved by the priors. Pitti's speech had the intended effect, as the priors, 'with tears and sighs', expressed their gratitude for what he had done and agreed that it was prudent to acquiesce in Florence's demand. Pitti's strategy ensured his good relations with the Pistoiesi through the remainder of his term in office. His success rested on the theatrical ability to devise and act out a script of disempowerment.[139]

---

[136] See Gene Brucker, *Living on the Edge in Leonardo's Florence: Selected Essays* (Berkeley, 2005), p. 87.

[137] Dati, *Libro segreto*, p. 87.

[138] Branca (ed.), *Mercanti scrittori*, pp. 414–15.

[139] On Pitti as a man of action, see Catherine Pineau-Harvey, 'Jeu, ouverture sociale et diplomatie: à propos de Bonaccorso Pitti', *Bibliothèque d'Humanisme et Renaissance*, 63:1 (2001), 33–45.

Memoranda or 'notes to self'

The *libro segreto* includes two personal memoranda, dated 1404 and 1412, which articulate Dati's designs for his future conduct. Their interest for the historian lies in the fact that Dati is much less concerned with what actions he should undertake than with what he ought to refrain from doing. The first memorandum, dated 1 January 1404, consists of three closely connected resolutions: to refrain from work on Church holidays, spend Fridays in chastity, and remember God every day through alms or prayers.[140] The second memorandum, of 3 May 1412, similarly consists of two personal commitments. Dati first expressed his surprise and satisfaction at having been drawn by lot to serve as Standard-bearer of the Militia Company, one of the advisory colleges of the Signoria, the chief magistracy of the communal government. Previously he had not known whether his name was among those eligible for office, since this was known only to the scrutiny committee that selected the eligible citizens and to the *accoppiatori*, the powerful officials in charge of the extractions,[141] but he had wanted to hold office because of the honour it brought. He thanked God for sending him the inspiration to pay his debts just a quarter of an hour before his name was drawn for office, thus avoiding ineligibility. Finally, now that he realised he could be elected again for office, Dati put into writing his commitment to refrain from manipulating the future elections in his favour. Henceforth he would not ask anyone to intercede for him, but leave it to those in charge of this matter and accept the offices for which his name would be drawn. Immediately below this resolution, Dati recorded in the *libro segreto* a second one, reached on the same day of 3 May 1412 and similarly pertaining to the realm of public life:

> Furthermore on the said day, knowing myself powerless to resist sins, I resolve, for the good and assurance of my conscience, never to accept, if I were drawn for it, any office of rector, which would have the power to judge the blood.[142]

---

[140] Dati, *Libro segreto*, pp. 68–71.

[141] See Baron, *Crisis*, vol. 1, p. 140 n. 5 (note text in vol. 2, p. 506); John M. Najemy, *Corporatism and Consensus in Florentine Electoral Politics, 1280–1400* (Chapel Hill, NC, 1982), p. 273. Previously, Dati had served in a lesser magistracy; Dati, *Libro segreto*, p. 79.

[142] 'Ancora detto dì dilibero per bene e sicurtà della mia coscienza, sentendomi debole a risistere a' peccati, di non volere mai, se io fossi tratto, accettare alcuno uficcio di rettore, che abbia balìa di giudicare sangue'; Dati, *Libro segreto*, p. 73.

With the exception of the third resolution of 1404, which emphasises action (remembering God every day), Dati's decisions are clearly about refraining from behaviour that he might normally have engaged in. Two of the promises of 1404 are an expression of traditional Christian abstemious practices, and as such might not appear remarkable. The 1412 resolutions, however, reflect an ordinary individual's self-imposed limits on his sociopolitical agency – a rare occurrence in the premodern record. The political background for the 1412 resolutions goes back to the so-called politics of consensus that developed in Florence after the defeat of the popular government in 1382. Although more citizens were eligible for public office, Florentine political life became dominated by members of the major guilds, and particularly those from the families of Florence's traditional elite, who controlled the electoral system. The *borsellino*, or little bag, grouped the names of just a few citizens loyal to the regime who were given preference at each extraction for office. At one election in 1393 the chief magistrates were even handpicked, in effect being appointed directly.[143] The crucial point in the 1412 memorandum is that Dati could have turned to his network of kin, business associates, and friends, as was the common practice, in order to influence in his favour the purportedly impartial election system, and have his name drawn for office. The best indication that he gave this option careful consideration is that in the memorandum he set a financial penalty every time he would break the promise; clearly the temptation to become involved in the electoral machinations was very real, at a time when the practice of *borsellino* extractions was a hotly debated issue. As discussed above, by this time communal offices were coveted largely because they brought family honour and prestige. Enlarged eligibility for public office did not translate into the power to implement policies, because the non-elite communal officers were pressured to follow the leadership of the elite.

Dati's memoranda have not escaped the notice of modern scholarship, but the discussion has focused largely on what his decision to refrain from manipulating the elections reveals about political trends in Florence.[144] The resolutions, however, are first and foremost about an individual's conduct and sense of personhood. Through them, Dati hoped to produce an effect on himself, not on others,[145] although he anticipated that his decision to refrain from

---

[143] Najemy, *Corporatism and Consensus*, pp. 276–7.

[144] Ibid., p. 303; Claudio Varese, *Storia e politica nella prosa del Quattrocento* (Torino, 1961), p. 73.

[145] For Renaissance pacts involving several family members, see Dale Kent and F. W. Kent, 'A Self Disciplining Pact Made by the Peruzzi Family of Florence (June 1433)', *Renaissance Quarterly*, 34:3 (1981), 337–55.

work on holidays would affect his employees. This personal dimension is particularly clear in the 1404 resolutions, which marked a life-changing spiritual turn. The diary entry sets up the decisions within the overall context of Dati's life and personal development: by way of prefacing the resolutions he refers to the forty years since his birth, spent with little regard to God's commandments. He was really forty-two, but 'forty was the age at which individuals were supposed to convert and prepare for death'.[146] This recalls how Salimbene situated his life-changing decision to join the Franciscans at another critical moment of one's life, the completion of the first 'three lustres'. However conventional, this chronology reflects the effort to invest with meaning an event by emphasising not its specific circumstances but its place within the arc of one's life.

It was essential for Dati's designs that the resolutions were expressed as self-standing memoranda in his personal ledger. The memoranda of 1404 and 1412 were written down on the same folio of the diary, which opened with an account of his second wife's inheritance.[147] Thus, in 1412, when he wrote down his new commitments, Dati chose to go back to the folio where the resolutions of 1404 were recorded – a decision that evinces the profound unity of the two memoranda. Although the act of making a resolution denotes an active outlook, Dati's limited confidence in his own resilience is made clear by his provisions in the event he failed to live up to his intentions. His self-imposed penalties for every such lapse were moderate but not trivial, reaching one gold florin in alms to the poor in 1404 and two gold florins in the first resolution of 1412; the exception is the second resolution of 1412, with its hefty twenty-five florins. But how exactly did Dati think that the lapses might come to pass?

First, because of special circumstances: as he put it in 1404, if necessity forced him to work on holidays. Second, through forgetfulness: 'I have made this recording the better to bear in mind the resolution,' he says; or, 'if it shall happen that I fail, by not realising it or by not remembering it.' The last remark indicates an awareness that with time he might neglect his commitments, presumably because other things will by then be at the forefront of his mind. This suggests that Dati was worried about more than sheer forgetfulness; he understood that his priorities could change over time. This is particularly clear in his other rationale for writing down the 1404 resolution: not only as an aid to memory but also so that he would be embarrassed or ashamed (*per mia confussione*) if he broke his promise.[148] This value-laden language suggests he

---

[146] Trexler, *Public Life*, p. 73.

[147] On fol. 9; more on this in Pandimiglio, 'Pigliate esempro', p. 168.

[148] Dati, *Libro segreto*, p. 69.

envisaged that a transgression might come about not just through forgetfulness or neglect but also because of something more dramatic.

Dati realised he might deliberately break his resolution. It was this kind of deliberate transgression that ought to make him ashamed. He intended the resolutions as an instrument whereby he might change himself into a better moral agent, but he was aware that with time he could also change for the worse. He might even change so much that he would no longer share the ideals that defined him at the moment when he made his commitments. In short, Dati contemplated the possibility of radical personal change: that with the passing of time his older self might re-emerge to replace his self of 1404. (He may even have contemplated the emergence of a new self with a different configuration of priorities and values.) The crucial point, however, is that he hoped the change would not be so complete that the values he embraced in the resolutions would no longer resonate with the later Dati, provided they could be forcefully evoked – hence his statement that any transgression should make him ashamed. To meet the challenges that the 'lapsed self' or a new self might pose to the ideal of conduct enshrined in the resolutions, he relied on the written memorandum and its powerful language. In this sense, the penalties are a disincentive against the temptation to change his mind deliberately. This is clearer in 1412, when there is no reference to forgetfulness, and the suspicion that the future self could endanger the resolutions is evident. Dati acknowledges that at some point the temptation to accept an appointment as rector might be hard to resist; such a decision, it bears emphasis, would only be taken after careful deliberation.[149]

In sum, as written records of the resolutions the memoranda were an essential part of the self-imposed limits on individual agency. Placing one's agency in abeyance entailed the affirmation of a different form of agency, that of the written memorandum, which in this sense emerges as an actant. This is not to impose a modern construct on premodern culture. Belief in the efficacy of forms was common in Renaissance Florence – recall Morelli's use of prayer. Relics were similarly believed to produce effects in the world, along lines familiar from the *livres de raison*. Richard Trexler points out that for Florentines 'diplomacy at a distance had every chance of success if done according to the best *form*' (emphasis added). Thus, in his history of Florence Dati 'noted with obvious satisfaction that the decline of Visconti rule in Milan coincided to the hour in 1403 with the first act of Florence's celebration of the feast of San Giovanni'.[150]

---

[149] Ibid., p. 73.

[150] Trexler, *Public Life*, p. 289.

The success of Dati's schemes was predicated on the autonomy of the written word.[151] By virtue of being fixed in writing the memoranda would not be affected by whatever evolution Dati might experience; through their agency his resolutions could be affirmed against the agency of his future self. But this autonomy also posed specific problems. Dati understood very well that once written down the memoranda escaped his control. If they ended up in someone else's hands they could be held against him if his intentions were construed as akin to contractual obligations. To avoid this contingency he made sure to specify in the 1404 memorandum that his resolutions were not vows but propositions that he intended to keep to the best of his ability. This is close to what at the end of the thirteenth century John Peter Olivi described as indeterminate vows, 'less a promise to do a series of specific things than a promise to embark on a certain path toward an envisaged goal'.[152] This calculated statement in a moment of moral pathos speaks to the fusion of pragmatic rationality and spiritual aspirations.

As the foregoing analysis suggests, moral values were essential for the success of Dati's designs. Both the moral confusion (*confussione*) of the 1404 memorandum and the disgrace (*vergogna*) of the 1412 reference the same set of values, roughly equivalent to modern notions of shame. Dati hoped that the memoranda would spark an emotional reaction and thus curtail the intentions of the future self before they were put into practice. Similar cases have been documented, as medievalists investigating the past of emotions have focused largely on their instrumentalisation in political and social contexts. The instrumental use of emotions is certainly an important theme, but it also raises questions about the authenticity of individual behaviour and offers only a partial account of social emotions, leaving out those dimensions of emotive experience that are not circumscribed by strategic reasoning. Dati's resolutions bring into view the substantive and expressive sides of emotions: the fact that through emotions we make manifest our identity, feelings towards someone else, and profound attachment to specific values. This fundamental dimension of moral emotions should not be dismissed simply because Dati envisaged a pragmatic purpose for them. If the moral language of the memoranda did not reflect his authentic sense of being, no moral effect could be hoped for in case of future lapses and the whole textual arrangement would be meaningless. We would be in the presence of one's elaborate attempt to delude oneself.

[151] See Jack Goody, *The Logic of Writing and the Organisation of Society* (Cambridge, 1986), p. 129 and *The Power of the Written Tradition* (Washington, DC, 2000), pp. 10–11.

[152] David Burr, *The Spiritual Franciscans: From Protest to Persecution in the Century after Saint Francis* (University Park, PA, 2001), p. 52.

Notwithstanding the foregoing argument about the text's authenticity by virtue of its nature as a private record, one might still be tempted to dismiss the moral justifications of Dati's decisions as mere rhetoric. The *Libro segreto* is not a late-life memoir, but a delay of even several days between an event and its recording raises the possibility of reworking and embellishment. We can only speculate about Dati's thought process in 1412 during the five days between the election and the resolutions. But it needs to be emphasised that the diary entry is not an *ex post facto* rationale, a tardy attempt to make sense of an earlier decision. The diary entry for 3 May 1412 *is* Dati's resolution. And it is so because the diary entry is a memorandum, a speech act but in writing, that is, a speech to oneself recorded for future reference with the intention to remind its author not just of the general substance of the decision but also of the motivations behind it. By attending to the text's function as a personal memorandum we can see that Dati was sincere and the values of the resolutions were lived values.[153]

This exceptional text also opens a window into the motivations behind Dati's resolutions – a central question in the anthropological models about the abeyance of agency. His motivations reflect the cultural construction of agency, considering that his decision was shaped by the culture and society of Renaissance Florence. But cultural influences notwithstanding, Dati's individual agency is evident in the fusion of moral and practical reasoning reflecting his own priorities, as the memorandum of 1412 bears witness.

The idea of making resolutions is rooted in the forms of Christian life, specifically the taking of vows, not just by the clergy but also by the laity: vows of pilgrimage or, as in Dati's case, of almsgiving. The moral dimension of the first resolution of 1412 is obvious in the references to the Christian theology of vices and virtues: thus, involvement in partisan electoral practices is equated with the vice of ambition ('il vizio della ambizione'). Ambition was not one of the traditional seven vices, but the late-medieval period witnessed an extension of the earlier list, to which new vices were now added.[154] Furthermore, Dati's reference to the 'insatiable appetite (*lo insaziabile appetito*) which the more it has the more it desires' is consistent with the widespread idea, going back to the early fathers of the Church, that excess leads to excess and one vice spills over into another. The connection between desire and ambition resonates with that between natural impulse and *superbia* (pride) in the *Fiore di*

---

[153] See Charles Taylor, *Philosophical Papers* (2 vols, Cambridge, 1985), vol. 2, pp. 25–7.

[154] Richard Newhauser, *The Treatise on Vices and Virtues in Latin and the Vernacular*, Typologie des Sources du Moyen Âge Occidental 68 (Turnhout, 1993), pp. 124–5. On ambition in medieval culture, see Alexander Murray, *Reason and Society in the Middle Ages* (Oxford, 1985), pp. 81–109.

virtù, a popular vernacular treatise on vices and virtues, even though the term is not used explicitly in Dati's memorandum. In the *Fiore di virtù*, suffering (*sofferenza*, a vernacular echo of *patientia*) is seen as the greatest virtue, in opposition to the drive that stems from natural impulse and makes people lustful, proud, and wrathful.[155] Of the different types of vain behaviour identified in the *Fiore di virtù*, the desire for more status and honour than becomes one and the ingratitude vis-à-vis favours received in the past are quite close to one of Dati's rationales for not meddling with elections:[156] 'so that I may not be ungrateful'. A similar discussion of pride is offered by another popular vernacular treatise on the vices and virtues, the thirteenth-century *Trattato di virtú e di vizí*, authored by a Florentine.[157] Even if Dati's resolution may not have been directly shaped by the body of medieval treatises on vices and virtues, their tenets filtered down. Beyond books, Dati may have been influenced by his brother, Leonardo, prior of a Dominican church in Florentine and preacher and lecturer on theology.[158] At any rate, *superbia* is a theme present in Dati's history of Florence and his annotations on the commentary of Dante's *Inferno*.[159]

In light of this connection with the Christian moral ideals, Dati's resolution emerges as a 'strong evaluation', an expression of the durable values around which he organised his existence.[160] But there is also evidence of calculated pragmatism, much like in the examples from Dati's business and family affairs analysed above. The memorandum is equally explicit on this: the whole point of staying away from the networks of political patronage was to avoid the political debts that one usually incurred in the process.[161] Dati feared he could become the slave of his pleas for political support and therefore resolved to avoid them altogether and live as a free man: 'libero e non servo per prieghi'.[162] The troubled history of Florentine politics in the preceding decades suggests that protection and preferment to office came at a heavy price, requiring in

---

[155] Bruto Fabricatore (ed.), *Fiore di Virtù*, 3rd edn (Napoli, 1870), p. 94.

[156] Dati, *Libro segreto*, pp. 101–2.

[157] Bono Giamboni, *Il Libro de' vizî e delle virtudi e il trattato di virtú e di vizí*, ed. Cesare Segre (Torino, 1968), pp. 141–2.

[158] On Leonardo, see Paolo Viti, 'Leonardo Dati', in Massimiliano Pavan (ed.), *Dizionario biografico degli italiani* (vol. 33, Roma, 1987), pp. 35–40.

[159] Andrew P. McCormick, 'Toward a Reinterpretation of Goro Dati's *Storia di Firenze*', *Journal of Medieval and Renaissance Studies*, 13:2 (1983), 227–50, at p. 239.

[160] Taylor, *Philosophical Papers*, vol. 1, pp. 18–21.

[161] See Trexler, *Public Life*, pp. 27–30.

[162] Dati, *Libro segreto*, p. 73.

return one's full support, even in conspiracies or street fighting. Although these were extreme scenarios that might not have been at the forefront of Dati's mind, the resolution clearly aimed to avoid onerous obligations that could have significant social repercussions. Dati implies this much, recalling that during the few days between his election and the recording of the resolution he thought back to the adversities he faced after the business debacle in Barcelona in 1405. This evocation serves as a backdrop or preface to the memorandum, suggesting that risk-avoidance emerged as a priority for Dati. The point bears emphasis because it shows how personal experience informs agency, something that emerges very clearly from self-narratives covering a long span of one's life.

A similar convergence of moral and practical imperatives can be discerned in the second resolution of 1412. Dati shunned the office of rector because it might occasion the perpetration of mortal sin through its power to pass death sentences – *giudizio di sangue*, a term also used in the general sense of homicide. But risk-avoidance might also have played a role in his decision. The first two decades of the fifteenth century witnessed growing concern with the administration of the Florentine dominion. The consultative assemblies of the 1410s debated the problems raised by the rectors appointed by Florence to the towns of Tuscany. Contemporary reports analysed by Gene Brucker convey an overall picture of the rectors' abuses, spoliation, and corruption. Consequently, the rectors also came under pressure from both the subjects of the dominion as well as their patrons and supporters in Florence; accusations of partisanship against them were frequent.[163] We have seen above the troubles that Buonaccorso Pitti ran into as captain of Pistoia. Another episode from Pitti's *ricordi* similarly illustrates the sorts of problems Dati may have had in mind when he made the resolution. As *podestà* of Montepulciano, Pitti fined a local 600 florins. He was then instructed at the intervention of the defendant's powerful supporters from Florence to revoke the sentence or incur a fine of 1,000 florins. He complied.[164] Pitti came from an aristocratic family and was one of the city's chief diplomats, with connections at the papal and imperial courts. That he should find himself under such pressure over a fine says much about the risks that Dati might run in passing a death-sentence as rector. In sum, although the memorandum does not give pragmatic reasons for the

---

[163] Gene Brucker, *The Civic World of Early Renaissance Florence* (Princeton, 1977), pp. 216–22; Lauro Martines, *Lawyers and Statecraft in Renaissance Florence* (Princeton, 1968), pp. 221–3.

[164] Branca (ed.), *Mercanti scrittori*, pp. 490–1; Laura De Angelis, 'Territorial Offices and Officeholders', in William Connel and Andrea Zorzi (eds), *Florentine Tuscany: Structures and Practices of Power* (Cambridge, 2000), pp. 165–82, at pp. 175–80.

decision to refuse appointments as rector, there is much to suggest the practical advantages of this decision for someone who on the same day resolved to avoid conflicts and stay away from networks of political patronage.

The convergence of moral and practical considerations in Dati's memoranda is noteworthy. The historian would be hard pressed to prioritise one over the other. Previous scholarship emphasised the renunciation of profits in favour of strict adherence to religious norms as 'typical of Dati's mentalité'.[165] But ignoring strategic motivations in favour of purely moral ones is as misleading as dismissing the moral language of the memoranda as mere rhetoric. The point is that Dati did not renounce public life, in which case he would have resolved to refuse new elections to office altogether. He simply redefined the terms of his involvement in communal politics, distancing himself from dubious electoral practices.

Lastly, the memorandum of 1412 is particularly interesting for the original position on the relation between divine providence and human agency. Writing just days after one of his long-time hopes, election to communal office, was fulfilled, Dati registers his gratitude towards the political system set up by the elite of great families,[166] a system that had just worked for him. The confidence he places in it stems from this sense of reciprocity. By vowing to leave his election for future offices 'to those in charge of this matter', Dati at once de-emphasised his involvement in electoral politics and emphasised the role of the elite families that controlled the elections. He simultaneously placed his agency in abeyance and reaffirmed the agency of the political elite. Furthermore, these two moves went together with his third endeavour, to follow the designs that God had for him. The juxtaposition of these three elements – abeyance of individual agency and emphasis on collective agency of social superiors and on divine providence – is quite clear in the text:

> As regards the extractions for the Commune's offices, I have resolved and decided that from now on *I should never solicit anyone, but leave it to those in charge of this matter, and according to what God wills for me* (emphasis added).[167]

This is very different from the doctrine of free will, which, as we have seen, emphasised the role of human agency in actively cooperating with divine

---

[165] Bec, *Marchands écrivains*, p. 155.

[166] Najemy, *Corporatism and Consensus*, pp. 301, 303.

[167] 'mi sono proposto e diliberato che da ora inanzi per ufici di Comune che s'abiano a fare o a squittinare, mai non debo pregare alcuno, ma lasciare fare a chi fia sopracciò, e seguiti quello che a Dio piace che di me sia'; Dati, *Libro segreto*, p. 72.

providence and stressed the merits of the individual who raised himself to become God's *cooperator*. That was the position ultimately embraced by Galbert of Bruges, who wrote that God's plan for the punishment of Count Charles's assassins involved divine causation and human actions, the former prompting the latter (Chapter 1). Dati, who in the *Libro segreto* invoked God's aid frequently, was familiar with this view. In his *Storia di Firenze* he refers to divine providence, for instance to show that God was on the Florentines' side in their conflict with Pisa and Milan.[168] He comes close to the traditional views of human cooperation with divine providence when he endeavours to account for Florence's success by means of both a this-worldly explanation (*ragione naturale*) and a theological explanation emphasising divine grace.[169] And while he grants that human *virtù* is capable of opposing misfortune, he explicitly states that nothing worthy can be acquired without divine grace.[170] The approach that he took in his personal life in 1412 – that is, his lived, rather than merely professed, values – departed radically from the orthodox position. In the memorandum it is the abeyance of individual agency that opens up a space for the unfolding of the divine plan; only through self-imposed limits on his freedom of action – the very opposite of active cooperation – would Dati fulfil God's designs.

There are echoes here of the 1404 resolutions, which focused on the Christian practice of abstaining from sinful behaviour. But their scope was limited: chastity on Fridays and refraining from work on church holidays. The resolution of 1412 was far more consequential because it affected a fundamental dimension of social existence: appointment to office, the pinnacle of participation to public life. By extension there was even more at stake, because involvement in the networks of political patronage to secure election to office was not fundamentally different from the social and business networking that was so pervasive in Florence; at times the two could be difficult to distinguish because friends and business partners were commonly called upon to procure political favours. Thus, what Dati renounced was an ingrained part of the urban professionals' life. His exceptional renunciation indirectly points to what was the norm: a worldview characterised by the tension between human and divine agency. In this worldview the individual is not an instrument of providence whose highest achievement is to subordinate his efforts to the divine plan as God's 'coadjutor', in the theologian's language, or as an actant, in

---

[168] Dati, *Storia*, p. 118; McCormick, 'Toward a Reinterpretation', p. 239; also see Bec, *Les marchands écrivains*, p. 160.

[169] Dati, *Storia*, pp. 54–6; Varese, *Storia e politica*, p. 77.

[170] Dati, *Storia*, p. 56; Bec, *Marchands écrivains*, p. 77.

the idiom of action theory. Rather, it is an autonomous agent whose objectives and modus operandi are often at odds with the divine precepts – hence Dati's exceptional decision to make way for the unfolding of the divine plan by placing his agency in abeyance, as a gesture of gratitude for the 'divine inspiration' to pay his debts and avoid ineligibility. This indicates a relationship with the divine built on reciprocity; his promise of exemplary conduct makes sense as counter gift. What is more, his gesture was not purely spiritual: as discussed above, practical reasons also weighed heavily. This resonates with Morelli's idea of engaging with the divine by emphasising the exchanges between the two parties.

Religious ethics played a significant role, alongside practical considerations, in Dati's decisions about his future conduct. But to acknowledge the cultural construction of agency is not to reduce the acting subject to little more than an exemplar of culture, his conduct an instantiation of the values and attitudes characteristic of its microcosm. One is struck by Dati's original take on the issue of human and divine agency, in contrast to traditional models. Equally personal was the fusion of pragmatic and moral imperatives. In sum, Dati's mode of acting upon the world was a personal construct. Even the act of imposing specific limits on his agency denotes a great deal of personal creativity. This aspect has been at the centre of a debate between two leading sociologists, Margaret Archer and Jon Elster. Elster sees the *The Odyssey* episode where Ulysses ties himself to the ship's mast the better to resist the Sirens' call as a case of overcoming weakness of will (*akrasia*) through clever tactics. But Archer argues that the whole episode emphasises the moral agent's initiative even as he seemingly disempowers himself:

> Ulysses needs to be a morally active agent to ask his sailors to bind him to the mast so that he can hear the Sirens without being drawn to his doom by them. However, if he is such an agent, then there is more to him than a programmed robot. [...] For one thing, the Classical Sea Captain's manual did not contain the instruction 'Immobilise yourself when in the vicinity of beguiling Sirens', because roles cannot be scripted for every contingency.[171]

In Dati's case self-interpretation was crucial. His commitment to align his conduct more closely to Christian ethics was accompanied by specific provisions rooted in his self-knowledge; notably, he envisioned he might break his commitment, not just through moral weakness but also because of the dictates of necessity (*caso molto necessario*). That he did so in one instance, for

---

[171] Margaret Archer, '*Homo economicus, Homo sociologicus,* and *Homo sentiens*', in Margaret Archer and Jonathan Tritter (eds), *Rational Choice Theory: Resisting Colonization* (London, 2000), pp. 36–56, at p. 53.

very good reasons, is further proof of the individual's role in renegotiating his relation to culture and society.

In 1422 Dati took up the office of *podestà* in the territory, in effect breaking the second resolution of 1412. This departure from the resolutions was not, however, the expression of a radical personal change. Rather, it was his response to an extraordinary circumstance. The record of this event is quite different from the entries about Dati's other public offices. Whereas Dati would normally note that he was drawn for office ('fui tratto a l'uficio, etc.') he now stated that he *accepted* the office, and explained the reason why: to run away from the plague: 'Podestà del Montale e Agliana accettai per fuggire la mortalità'.[172] The atypical wording makes sense in light of Dati's memorandum. In 1422 he was very much aware of his earlier resolution, recorded in the same diary just a few folios before, and felt the need to explain the violation – first of all to himself, but perhaps to his family posterity as well.[173] In the spirit of the ideals he articulated in 1412, he added that the six-month term of office brought him little wealth but a great deal of gratitude from the locals. There is no record of a donation to the poor in the amount of twenty-five gold florins.[174]

The grassroots view of society afforded by the *ricordi* brings us closer to the concerns of the laity: the social imaginary centred on networks and the possibilities for strategic action helps to put into perspective the top-down social taxonomies of medieval intellectuals, notably 'the three orders'. When one looks beyond the literary productions of the intellectual elites, the medieval worldview appears much less dominated by the imperatives of coherence and hierarchy, and more concerned with the practical challenges confronting individual agents in everyday life.

The foregoing examination has qualified the notion of the hyper-active Renaissance merchant. In addition to socioeconomic achievement, Morelli highlighted character as a measure of one's worth. Both Morelli and

---

[172] Dati, *Libro segreto*, p. 106.

[173] In the written text 'contradictions become more "obvious" and more "exact" when placed side by side'; Goody, *Logic of Writing*, p. 163, and *Power of the Written Tradition*, pp. 142–3.

[174] On Dati's term at Montale, see De Angelis, 'Territorial Offices and Officeholders', p. 169 n. 23. Dati's other appointments in 1413 and 1417 did not carry the power to pass death-sentences. When he served again in Florence there is no indication that he procured his election through illicit tactics.

particularly Dati show that pragmatism, in the latter's case combined with a personal approach to religion, occasionally recommended everyday resilience or even non-action over decisive intervention. It is this emphasis on pragmatic reasoning that defines the *ricordi*, more than other prominent features of their social imaginary, such as the preference for a transactional, network-oriented approach to the detriment of institutional channels. The thrust of Morelli's conduct advice, in which he summed up a vast body of contemporary social knowledge, was the cultivation of the capacity to select the appropriate modus operandi according to social context. This explains the striking diversity of courses of action presented in his *ricordi*. Conversely, there is little evidence of highly scripted social interactions, as in the ritual-centred interpretation. So pragmatic was Morelli that in specific circumstances he saw the merits of turning to institutions instead of the network of family and friends, notwithstanding his overall preference for the transactional approach. It was an approach that both Morelli and Dati extended, in their different ways, to the realm of the individual's relation to the divine. The relation between the authors' calculated outlook and the frequent but terse references to God has been a central issue since the early explorations of the *ricordi*, but the references were rarely contextualised, leading to partial and potentially misleading findings. In his prayers and meditation Morelli drew on religious forms and material culture, but appropriated them within a framework of human–divine relations based on reciprocal exchanges. It was this framework that gave meaning to his religious experience, and it was derived not from religion but from social interactions. The ways in which Morelli and Dati engaged with the divine represented personal constructs – an aspect that is overlooked in scholarship that emphasises cultural influences, for instance in the form of religious and social ritual, over the individual's agency in selecting and transforming them. What is more, the individual's agency in balancing the competing imperatives of a complex society is not sufficiently appreciated even in scholarship that highlights the merchants' pragmatic outlook. The synthesis between the demands of business and family, or profit and Christian ethics,[175] was achieved through personal, sometimes dramatic, efforts – recall how Morelli painstakingly made the case that he was entitled to ask for divine favour. Even when practical and ethical imperatives converged, as in Dati's case, the synthesis thus achieved could only be sustained through the ingenious drafting of personal memoranda. Lastly, the focus on agency in the present analysis offers a corrective to the idealised image of the Renaissance family in a good deal of scholarship on the *ricordi*. Any account of the 'ragion di

---

[175] Branca (ed.), *Mercanti scrittori*, p. xxi.

famiglia', the family matters that are central in the *ricordi*, would be misleading if it failed to include the tensions, marginalisation, and conflicts that as often as not defined relations between members of the same family. The economy of human relations underpinning Morelli's arrangements for the family succession is fundamentally defined by the concern with individuals' potential for agency. Social standing and family fortune could be lost if the capacity for strategising of less powerful but skilled competitors was ignored. Agency, more than power, provides the accurate conceptual focus for making sense of the Renaissance urban microcosm.

A recurrent theme in this and the preceding chapter, both dealing with texts traditionally labelled 'family books', is that self-assertion, for example in the form of claiming personal initiative for a course of action and stressing its effectiveness, emerged not in opposition to family values but in direct relation to them. Morelli acknowledges with some regret that his family, which unlike others could legitimately boast its ancient ancestry, as yet lacked a chronicle. But inasmuch as this absence brought into relief his founding gesture as the author of the family *ricordanze*, it offered an avenue for asserting individual agency. Similarly, Dati made it plain that he was the first in his family to hold public office. This kind of self-assertion was open first and foremost to the *pater familias*: in the *ricordi* it is a function of his authorship of a record intended to memorialise the family past for the next generations. But it shows that achievement in the service of the family was a source of self-worth (compare with Esperon's memorandum in Chapter 3). While this observation might seem banal, it offers a corrective to both the line of argument that arrives at the modern individual ethos by subtracting it from traditional, community values, and the one that seizes on attachment to family values in order dispute the affirmation of the individual before the modern era.

Record-keeping was instrumental in the exercise of individuals' agency in all the ego-documents analysed in this volume, but with Dati the personal memorandum functioned as an actant, the success of his designs depending on the agency of the written text. Morelli's text evinces the potential of the *ricordi* as the medium for articulating social reflections and passing them on to posterity. His conduct advice is unparalleled in scope and detail – to find something comparable one must look beyond the *ricordi* and into the conduct literature, to Paolo da Certaldo's *Libro di buoni costume*, for example.[176] But the contrast is particularly striking with the *livres de raison*. Of the French legal professionals and merchants who turned to record-keeping the better to manage their business and family affairs, some found in the nascent genre of

[176] Ibid., pp. 1–99.

livres de raison the opportunity to pass on consequential but essentially limited advice to the family posterity: some general prudent guidelines about investment or marriage, and the occasional list of potions, invocations, and spells. They must have sensed that many other important lessons about social and economic conduct were too context-bound adequately to be rendered into written advice. By contrast, Morelli – and to a lesser degree a few other Florentine writers of *ricordanze* – felt that complex guidelines for action could put down into writing, covering a vast array of contingencies. Beyond the greater levels of literacy in Florence, the explanation lies in the tremendous confidence in the uses of writing instilled by humanism. This feature is famously illustrated by its leading exponents: Petrarch extolled the power of eloquent speech to move the minds and hearts, and Coluccio Salutati, chancellor of the Florentine commune, injected classical rhetoric into diplomatic correspondence.[177] Closer to the world of *ricordanze* authors, in the *Libro di buoni costume* and other vernacular conduct treatises, the twined concerns for literary style and moral rectitude increasingly made room for social and economic pragmatism. The comparison with Bartolomeo da San Concordio's earlier *Ammaestramenti degli antichi*, an excellent example of both careful organisation of the material according to scholastic distinction and concern for the ethics of conduct, evinces the distance travelled by Italian conduct literature, notwithstanding the faint impression of formalism owed to humanist learning in Morelli's *ricordi*. This conduct literature also existed in France (see the next chapter), but was not as widespread or disposed to sacrifice literary style in favour of practical advice. Directed at a limited family audience, the advice in the Florentine *ricordanze* was formulated more directly, which helped the authors make the next logical step, rooted in their personal experience of how critical social context was, and embark on the task of devising elaborate schemes of action for complex social scenarios. The *ricordi* authors remained *in medias res*, unlike, for instance, Leon Battista Alberti in his dialogue *On the Family*, where the discussion turns theoretical with the protagonists debating how one might start life from scratch, by selecting according to rigorous criteria the ideal land where one might settle.[178] Morelli's pragmatism was of course limited; he let himself be carried away by the text's promise of exorcising the spectre of an orphaned childhood through detailed, fail-proof strategies. Eager to extend

---

[177] Petrarch, *De sui ipsius et multorum ignorantia*, ed. L. M. Capelli (Paris, 1906), pp. 68–70; English translation in Ernst Cassirer, Paul Oskar Kristeller, and John Herman Randall (eds), *The Renaissance Philosophy of Man* (Chicago, 1948), pp. 104–5; Coluccio Salutati, *Political Writings*, ed. Stefano U. Baldassarri and trans. Rolf Bagemihl (Cambridge, MA, 2014).

[178] Alberti, *The Family*, pp. 52–3.

to the realm of everyday life the patterns of organising knowledge familiar from humanist literature, Morelli and his peers did not pause in the process to reflect on the inherent limits of written instructions. While this was first tried in texts circulating within family circles, it remains a highly consequential development because it stands at the roots of the Western tradition of handbooks and guides about societal and practical matters, still amply illustrated today in print and online.

5

A Gendered Social Imaginary: The Vernacular Literature on Social Conduct

ALL THE ACTIONS TAKEN BY individuals are informed by a set of representations, ideas, and expectations shared across society, about how social interactions should unfold, what strategies are known to succeed, which kinds of conduct are socially approved and which are regarded as illegitimate. As discussed in the Introduction, the sum of these everyday representations constitutes the social imaginary. Significant aspects of it have already been encountered in the previous chapters, such as the strategic perspective informing the politics of the Amiénois aristocracy and the underlying sense in both the *livres de raison* and the *ricordi* that calculation, attention to detail, and diversified investments are the keys to socioeconomic success. But in addition to such widely shared beliefs, each milieu is characterised by specific social views and attitudes. Thus Salimbene's Franciscan ideal of witty exchanges and Galbert's notarial emphasis on proper form in collective political action reflect particular subcultures and even individual preferences, but these were not divorced from the larger social imaginary.

This chapter examines two texts in the bourgeoning late-medieval genre of vernacular conduct literature,[1] approached here as ego-documents because both include significant references to the authors' personal experiences. Because their authors were not professional writers but educated bourgeois who took up the quill in specific contexts, the texts resonate with the sections on social conduct in the *livres de raison* and *ricordanze;* they go further by dramatising the burden of responsibility bearing on the *pater familias*, which leads to an exacerbated sense of individual agency and an unwillingness to acknowledge the contributions of women and social inferiors. What sets the conduct texts apart is their decidedly prospective, indeed programmatic outlook: the authors articulate their aspirations about how social relations should function, starting

---

[1] On which see Alice Hentsch, *De la littérature didactique du Moyen Âge: s'adressant spécialement aux femmes* (Cahors, 1903).

with the domestic space and moving to society in general. This is a crucial, if somewhat elusive, dimension of the social imaginary, because action is rooted in one's prior desires and dreams of engaging with the world. The texts' conduct advice is fundamentally gendered and informed by a keen awareness of the potential for agency of the seemingly disempowered subaltern, which include women as well as servants and labourers. Consequently, a systematic effort is made to control who has access to parts or all of the model of individual empowerment through reason, self-discipline, and work.

Notwithstanding the autobiographical framing, neither writer gives his name in the text. We know the name of the first, Jehan or Jacques Bruyant, only because fifty years later the second author identifies him as the source of the text he copies wholesale in his own work. This close relationship between the texts affords a rare opportunity to understand how the social vision of a modest bourgeois (Bruyant) was read and appropriated by someone from more or less the same milieu. In his *Chemin de povreté et de richesse*, 'The path to poverty and riches' (c. 1342), Bruyant uses the medium of the allegorical poem to articulate a model of conduct predicated on pragmatic rationality, work, and self-discipline in response to the socioeconomic instability brought about by what we now recognise as the growth crisis of European society. His aim is a moderate but secure social standing. The text is remarkable for its vision of a society built around work, epitomised by the *chastel de Labour*. Populated not by knights but by 'more than a hundred thousand labourers', the castle subverts the hierarchy of the traditional imaginary of the three orders. What is more, the text offers a moment of genuine dialogism when the character of *maistre Barat* ('Deceit'), the personification of the *arrivistes* who rely on fraud and sycophancy, defends his own path to success. The author's genuine engagement with a competing model of conduct speaks to a complex social imaginary in which alongside widely shared representations there is room for conflicting views. The *Ménagier de Paris* (c. 1393) is similarly concerned with the socioeconomic realities of the fourteenth century but focuses on the domestic sphere. It is a conduct manual dedicated to a young wife by her bourgeois husband with the aim of instructing her about marriage and household. Few late-medieval texts are as rich in material relevant for the study of human agency. The *Ménagier* is fundamentally about behaviour and action: the effects of corporeal interventions within the household or in the city; the form and timing of social action; the sense of authorisation and legitimation of the individual's actions. Ultimately, the text is all about directing people to act or refrain from exercising their agentive potential.

The social representations that inform everyday exchanges and the theories of the elites are two different matters; to return to a classic example, 'the imaginary of the three orders', much emphasised by medievalists over the last decades, was an elite construct that did not become part of popular culture. The gulf between high theory and the everyday attitudes of the general population could not easily be bridged in the age before widespread literacy and print culture, but some degree of mutual influence was normal. Literate bourgeois engaged in social reflection, such as Bruyant and the author of the *Ménagier*, were in an intermediate position. The social issues they engaged with in their writing reflect concerns and attitudes that were shared more widely; thus Bruyant gestures explicitly towards the world of labourers and even the *Ménagier*'s author strives to understand their habits, if only to counter them more effectively. But their social reflection is first of all circumscribed by their own microcosms – and so must be the conclusions we draw from the texts. Their learned culture was shaped more by vernacular literature than scholastic social thought. Bruyant relied in very large measure on the *Roman de la rose*, whose encyclopaedic excursuses familiarised a vernacular audience with the hot issues of political debate. The *Ménagier*'s author was familiar with a wider range of vernacular texts and through them with classical culture, but he draws on them mostly to lend his work a pretence of literary erudition. If literary allusions were ancillary, both authors' views were fundamentally shaped by their specific social context and lived experiences. With the *Chemin* and even the more erudite *Ménagier* we are some distance away from the intellectual milieu of professional writers like Christine de Pizan, whose vernacular treatise on conduct becoming the wives of bourgeois and artisans gave central place to prudence,[2] a key scholastic notion that is conspicuously absent from the *Chemin*. For that matter, of the church intellectuals' sociomoral discourse only a few elements came to play a structuring role in the *Chemin* and the *Ménagier*, and even these were appropriated and reworked for the authors' purposes: the scheme of seven virtues paired with as many vices, which had become pervasive throughout the vernacular conduct literature, and in the case of the *Ménagier* the relatively recent theology of individual confession. This does not prevent occasional ideological alignments: Bruyant's view of Fortune resonates with the traditional theological point that all receive their just deserts, in opposition to the fourteenth-century literary trope of a blind *Fortuna* whose wheel turns erratically.

More broadly, the valorisation of work and practical reason in both texts reflects cultural trends ushered in by the period of urban revival and economic growth until the late thirteenth century and epitomised by the semantic shift

---

[2] 'femmes mariees aux hommes des mestiers' and 'femmes des laboureurs'; Christine de Pizan, *Le livre des trois vertus*, ed. Charity Canon Willard and Eric Hicks (Paris, 1989).

of Latin *labor* from connotations of pain and suffering to a more positive conception of work, evoking the idea of a lucrative activity.[3] The fact that *laboratores* ('those who work') were included in the theory of the three orders alongside the clergy and the military aristocracy amounted to an acknowledgement of the social function of individuals engaged in productive activities.[4] The reflection on the paths to *povreté* and *richesse* became a necessity in an increasingly commercialised society that saw the disparity between the poor and the rich widen and legal disputes about labour multiply.[5] Moral theologians too eventually took note of the changing world. William of Auvergne, the thirteenth-century bishop of Paris, placed the city at the centre of his vision of the ideal society.[6] While individual dispositions such as the appetite for acquisitiveness were still condemned, implied justifications were offered for recent economic practices;[7] from the fourteenth century the scholastics' criticism of sociopolitical inequalities became muted.[8] The Franciscan Bonaventure highlighted the usefulness of different kinds of work, while the Dominican Thomas Aquinas defended the merits of manual labour and enshrined in his influential theological synthesis

[3] Jacques Le Goff, 'Le travail dans les systèmes de valeur de l'Occident médiéval', in Jacqueline Hamesse and Colette Muraille-Samaran (eds), *Le travail au Moyen Âge: une approche interdisciplinaire* (Louvain-la-Neuve, 1990), pp. 7–21, at pp. 13–17.

[4] Initially *laboratores* designated an economic elite of prospering peasants; Jacques Le Goff, *Time, Work, and Culture in the Middle Ages*, trans. Arthur Goldhammer (Chicago, 1980), pp. 56–7. On the gradual acceptance of the new meaning of *labor* by church intellectuals, see Jacqueline Hamesse, 'Le travail chez les auteurs philosophiques du 12e et du 13e siècle: Approche lexicographique', in Jacqueline Hamesse and Colette Muraille-Samaran (eds), *Le travail au Moyen Âge: une approche interdisciplinaire* (Louvain-la-Neuve, 1990), pp. 115–27, at pp. 123–7.

[5] Sharon Farmer, *Surviving Poverty in Medieval Paris: Gender, Ideology, and the Daily Lives of the Poor* (Ithaca, NY, 2002), esp. pp. 16–23, 34–6; Jacques Foviaux, 'Discipline et réglementation des activités professionelles à travers les arrêts du Parlement de Paris (1257–1382)', in Jacqueline Hamesse and Colette Muraille-Samaran (eds), *Le travail au Moyen Âge: une approche interdisciplinaire* (Louvain-la-Neuve, 1990), pp. 185–200.

[6] Jacques Le Goff, *The Medieval Imagination*, trans. Arthur Goldhammer (Chicago, 1988), pp. 177–80.

[7] Ian P. Wei, 'Paris Theologians and Responses to Social Change in the Thirteenth Century', in Hans-Joachim Schmidt (ed.), *Tradition, Innovation, Invention: Fortschrittsverweigerung und Fortschrittsbewusstsein in Mittelalter* (Berlin, 2005), pp. 195–209.

[8] Philippe Buc, *L'Ambiguïté du livre: prince, pouvoir, et peuple dans les commentaires de la Bible au Moyen Age* (Paris, 1994), pp. 309–403.

the view of human activity that raised man to the status of God's *cooperatorem*.⁹ Both, however, had to counter the criticism that their recently founded orders abandoned the monastic ideal of *industria*, epitomised by the manual labour of the Benedictines and Cistercians; both continued to regard the active life as inferior to philosophical study.¹⁰ Lastly, a more rationalist attitude was fostered by a series of cultural trends towards self-empowerment.¹¹ Reason had been the central idea of the twelfth-century humanist movement, before its vernacular personification reached a broad audience through the *Roman de la rose*. Notwithstanding its disciplinary aims, confession, since 1215 prescribed at least once a year to all believers, stimulated self-reflection.¹²

A changing social imaginary:
the *Chemin de povreté et de richesse*

Written in the first-person singular, the *Chemin* opens with the quotation of a proverb, 'Leave a fool to his own and he'll think of how to provide for himself,'¹³ from which the moral is drawn that, as taught in the Scriptures and experienced by the narrating author, 'souffisance' is the perfect richness. To substantiate this maxim, the narrator presents a personal vision experienced shortly after his marriage. Lying awake in his bed at night, his wife sound asleep, the newlywed (the author's narrative alter ego) receives the visit of four characters: *Besoing* (Need), *Neccessité* (Necessity), *Souffrete* (Want), and *Disette* (Scarcity). Their terrible appearance, illustrative of the real-life ills they

---

⁹ Christian Wenin, 'Saint Bonaventure et le travail manuel', in Jacqueline Hamesse and Colette Muraille-Samaran (eds), *Le travail au Moyen Âge: une approche interdisciplinaire* (Louvain-la-Neuve, 1990), pp. 141–55, at pp. 151–5; Philippe Delhaye, 'Quelques aspects de la doctrine thomiste et néo-thomiste du travail', in Jacqueline Hamesse and Colette Muraille-Samaran (eds), *Le travail au Moyen Âge: une approche interdisciplinaire* (Louvain-la-Neuve, 1990), pp. 157–75, at pp. 164–9.

¹⁰ Penn R. Szittya, *The Antifraternal Tradition in Medieval Litterature* (Princeton, 1986), esp. pp. 47–8; Wenin, 'Bonaventure', p. 152; Delhaye, 'Quelques aspects', p. 162; Farmer, *Surviving Poverty*, pp. 44–7.

¹¹ See John Arnold, *Belief and Unbelief in Medieval Europe* (London, 2005), pp. 144–5; on the 'arithmetical mentality', see Alexander Murray, *Reason and Society in the Middle Ages*, 2nd edn (Oxford, 1985), pp. 162–210; on self-discipline and calculation in vernacular preaching, see Daniel Lesnick, *Preaching in Medieval Florence: The Social World of Franciscan and Dominican Spirituality* (Athens, GA, 1989).

¹² Karma Lochrie, 'Desiring Foucault', *Journal of Medieval and Early Modern Studies*, 27:1 (1997), 3–16.

¹³ Cf. Samuel Singer (ed.), *Thesaurus Proverbiorum Medii Aevi* (13 vols, Berlin, 1995–2002), vol. 8, p. 403.

personify, makes a powerful impression on him as he suffers their physical 'assault'. They are joined by two others of their kin, *Pensée* (Concern) and *Soussi* (Worry), and then by *Desconfort* (Distress) and his daughter, *Désespérance* (Despair). The latter in particular vituperates about the hardships of life and conjures up the spectre of destitution. On the verge of losing control of his mind and body, the author is rescued by the arrival of *Raison*, whose lessons aim to help the newlywed lead a good life. He is first instructed to guard against the vices with the aid of the virtues. *Mesure*, *Raison*'s sister, is introduced; *Raison* then explains that by taking the path of diligence, going right, instead of the road of poverty and sloth, going left, the protagonist can reach the *manoir de Richesse*. This is the path that guards against the reversals of Fortune, prone to hurl down those it had previously raised to riches. With the aid of *Entendement* (Understanding) the newlywed ponders *Raison*'s wisdom, but another character, a lawyer, *maistre Barat* (Fraud), interjects his own lessons about the path to success in life, rebuking *Raison*. *Barat* explains that deception, not honesty, can earn you prosperity; conversely, reciprocity and altruism are unprofitable and thus pointless. The protagonist is now tempted to follow the path indicated by *Barat*, but *Entendement* and *Raison* address him again and finally convince him. He proclaims his allegiance to *Raison* and enters the road of diligence, arriving at the *chastel de Labour*, an obligatory point of passage to *Richesse*. He encounters *Soing* (Care) as gate-keeper and the castellan *Travail* (Work) with his wife, *Peine* (Toil), and convinces them of his desire to work diligently. He joins the multitude of workers in the castle (*plus de cent mille ouvriers*) and works in earnest in his chamber the whole night. He dines in the labourers' modest fashion and is invigorated by this simple way of life, with only such rest as necessary. Edified as to the benefits of the life of work and sobriety, he takes his leave and is once again in his home, eager to share the vision with his wife, insisting that it is not a dream.[14] But to her it makes no sense and she rebukes him for his meaningless imaginings (*fantasie*). This occasions some remarks on women's failure to understand such consequential lessons about life, because they are incapable of self-discipline. The poem ends with the protagonist once again in his bed, reflecting on his vision and praying that he may reach his *souffisance*.

In the *Ménagier* Bruyant is identified as a former royal notary at the Châtelet, a minor office created in 1301 and subordinated to the *prevôt*, the official in charge of administration and justice in Paris. The documentary record does not support this assertion but the *Chemin* is permeated by legal culture and it

---

[14] 'ma vision qui n'est pas songe'; Jérôme Pichon (ed.), *Le Ménagier de Paris*, vol. 2 (Paris, 1846), p. 41, col. 2. There is also a recent edition of the text: Glynnis M. Cropp (ed.), *La Voie de Povreté et de Richesse: Critical Edition* (Cambridge, 2016).

may be that Bruyant served at the Châtelet temporarily or in a related capacity.[15] He might have received some university training but it is unlikely that he graduated; the poem's autobiographical references suggest that Bruyant lived a difficult life of work and modest achievement.[16] His rudiments of scholastic thought – the structure of syllogism, for example – were inspired, like the use of allegory and personifications, by the hugely popular *Roman de la rose*,[17] while the common medieval trope of life as an individual's journey and the motif of choosing at the crossroads are shared with Guillaume de Deguileville's *Pèlerinage de la vie humaine* and Salimbene's chronicle. The *Ménagier*'s author, an educated bourgeois who cites a plethora of literary works but nevertheless not an intellectual, makes Bruyant appear quite unsophisticated by comparison.

Reason and the individual's chemin

The combination of focus on the individual and keen awareness of his embeddedness in society and culture is a defining characteristic of the text. While theological reflection traditionally emphasised the psychological dimension of the individual's conduct in society, the *Chemin* follows its protagonist in his social interactions: working to earn his living, offering and receiving advice, or simply greeting others on the street. In effect, Bruyant's reflection is carried out through an examination of the individual's position in the social space. For example, poverty and deceit are not viewed broadly as societal ills but as personal challenges that each individual must overcome.

Personal experience represented a crucial source of Bruyant's social reflection. That he dedicated the thrust of his argument to the active life of work and moderation, a subsidiary topic in the *Roman* – fewer than a hundred lines – suggests that his reading was sensitive to those topics that resonated with his social experience, however marginal these may have been in the *Roman*.[18] The

---

[15] Pierre-Yves Badel, *Le roman de la Rose au XIVe siècle: étude de la réception de l'oeuvre* (Geneva, 1980), p. 361.

[16] In his other known work, a prayer, Bruyant identifies himself as *clerc*, rather than *maistre*; Arthur Långfors, 'Jacques Bruyant et son poème, *La voie de povreté et de richesse*', *Romania*, 65 (1918–19), 49–83, at p. 75; on the autobiographical character of the *Chemin*, see Badel, *Roman de la Rose*, pp. 354–61; more generally, Laurent Brun, 'Jacques Bruyant', *Archives de littérature du Moyen Age* (http://www.arlima.net/il/jacques_bruyant.html).

[17] Pichon (ed.), *Ménagier*, vol. 2, p. 28, col. 1; Armand Strubel (ed.), *Le roman de la Rose: édition d'après les manuscrits BN 12786 et BN 378* (Paris, 1992), lines 12143–50. On the 'querelle de la Rose', the debate surrounding the *Roman*, see Christine McWebb (ed.), *Debating the Roman de la rose: A Critical Anthology* (London, 2007).

[18] Strubel (ed.), *Roman de la Rose*, lines 4971–5020, 5037–96.

newlywed's predicament is from the beginning socioeconomic, with moral considerations introduced only subsequently, in contradistinction with the flourishing genre of *Voie d'Enfer* and *Voie de Paradis*. It is immediately apparent that the poem's personifications do not signify abstract ideas but refer to specific social attitudes and economic practices: thus *Avarice* stands for usury, falsity, deception, cheating, and fraud. Bruyant is so specific in detailing the real-life attitudes embodied by the personifications that his rich descriptions largely obviate the signifying work of allegory.[19] Like similar vernacular texts, the *Chemin* marks an evolution from the general categories and broad typologies of the previous, largely moral, discourse about the estates of society (*de statibus mundi*).[20]

The text's defining social referentiality is evident in the allusions to men who rose to great heights through ambition and then suddenly lost their life and estate. Although not mentioned by name, famous examples of this social scenario included Pierre de la Broce, Philip III's *chambellan*, Enguerran of Marigny, Philip IV's chief minister, and Pierre Remi, Charles IV's treasurer – all ambitious men who rose from modest backgrounds to power and wealth and then lost it all overnight. Their trials and executions found a large echo in French public opinion and were discussed, as in the *Chemin*, under the trope of Fortune's wheel. The *Chemin* echoes the *Complainte de Pierre de la Broce*, although a direct influence cannot be proved.[21] Bruyant assures his readers that such reversals of Fortune are everyday occurrences, which suggests that

---

[19] *Usure, Faulx-traictié, Déception, Tricherie, Fraude*; Pichon (ed.), *Ménagier*, vol. 2, p. 12, col. 2. On allegory in late-medieval culture, see Philippe Maupeu, *Pèlerins de vie humaine: Autobiographie et allégorie narrative, de Guillaume de Deguilleville à Octovien de Saint-Gelais* (Paris, 2009), pp. 25–8.

[20] See Jean Batany, 'Norms, types, et individus: la présentation des modèles sociaux au XIIe siècle', in Danielle Buschinger (ed.), *Littérature et société au Moyen Âge: Actes du colloque des 5 et 6 mai 1978* (Amiens, 1978), pp. 177–200.

[21] Achille Jubinal (ed.), *La complainte et le jeu de Pierre de la Broce, chambellan de Philippe-le-Hardi* (Paris, 1835); William Chester Jordan, 'The Struggle for Influence at the Court of Philip III: Pierre de la Broce and the French Aristocracy', *French Historical Studies*, 24:3 (2001), 439–68, at pp. 448, 459–62. Bernard Guenée, *Une meurtre, une société: L'assasinat du duc d'Orléans, 23 novembre 1407* (Paris, 1992), pp. 74–5, shows that references to Broce's fall were not always by name. For the vernacular texts covering Marigny's fall, including the *Roman de Fauvel*, which may have inspired Bruyant, see Jean Favier, *Un roi de marbre: Philippe le Bel, Enguerran de Marigny* (Paris, 2005), pp. 577–9, 705–39, and Långfors, 'Bruyant', pp. 58–61. For Remi, see Olivier Canteaut, 'Confisquer pour redistribuer: la circulation de la grâce royale d'après l'exemple de la forfaiture de Pierre Remi (1328)', *Revue Historique*, 658 (2011), 311–26.

they were familiar with other, less spectacular, examples.²² Historians have sometimes regarded Marigny's case as the symptom of larger social trends, specifically the resistance of the nobility to the rise of *novi homines* who proved instrumental in the centralisation of the French state.²³ Bruyant too did not see such events as isolated dramas but believed that they spoke to a state of affairs in French society. Yet he emphasises the direct relevance of such personal histories for the ordinary bourgeois, mirroring in this respect the medieval literature on conduct. The condition of those who fall from status is depicted in emotional terms that can resonate broadly. These men are despondent ('ont les cuers si amatis'), disoriented ('ne scevent quel part ils aillent'), their personal histories likely to end at the scaffold.²⁴ That they remain nameless, although the audience would have been put in mind of notorious cases like Marigny's and Remi's, suggests Bruyant's intention to generalise their experiences and make them relevant for people from his social class. Thus, as the epitome of the scrupleless *arriviste*, *Barat* is almost lavish, but within the limits of liberal professionals. He is not a larger-than-life character like Marigny; rather, he reflects the transposition into a bourgeois milieu of the nexus of socioeconomic and moral issues most famously illustrated by Marigny's career.

The point is not that Bruyant was incapable of grasping social dynamics; quite the opposite impression emerges from the text. But he preferred to stress the individual aspect of the historical dramas. His option reflects the goal of articulating a conception about the path to social success from the standpoint of a moderately placed bourgeois. The fall of overly ambitious great men is a lesson that can edify even modest people, who are urged to draw on such examples, quite instrumentally, for their own endeavours: 'Great self-discipline achieves he / Who uses another to correct himself.'²⁵ Underlying this view, as well as the proverb highlighted in the poem's opening line, is the intuition that

---

²² 'On le puet chascun jour véoir'; Pichon (ed.), *Ménagier*, vol. 2, p. 21, col. 2. On communication channels in late-medieval France, see Veronika Novák, 'La source du savoir: publication officielle et communication informelle à Paris au début du XVᵉ siècle', in Claire Boudreau et al. (eds), *Information et société en Occident à la fin du Moyen Age* (Paris, 2004), pp. 151–63.

²³ Favier, *Roi de marbre*, pp. 513–14, 738–9.

²⁴ Pichon (ed.), *Ménagier*, vol. 2, p. 21, col. 2. *Raison* sounds a similar warning: 'tu mesmes seras pendus / Corporelment, par aventure, / A grant angoisse et à laidure'; ibid., vol. 2., p. 30, col. 2.

²⁵ 'Beau chastiement met en lui / Qui se chastie par autrui'; ibid., vol. 2, 20, col. 1. On the contrary in the *Roman* reversals of Fortune are welcome because they build character and reveal one's true friends; Strubel (ed.), *Roman de la Rose*, lines 4834–956.

social change depends on the choices and efforts of ordinary individuals. Some indirect confirmation of this comes from the absence of any references to the king of France, the agency ultimately tasked with remedying societal wrongs in late-medieval texts such Philippe de Mézières's *Songe du vieil Pèlerin* or Jean Gerson's *Vivat rex*.

Central to the text is the model of the self-reflexive individual defined by his relationship to *Raison*, which stands largely for practical rationality. Internalising practical reason is the key imperative.[26] What characterises decision making is judicious reflection. A contrast is drawn between thinking per se and the kind of methodical, goal-oriented deliberation epitomised by *Raison*. The former does not, in itself, have positive connotations. Before *Raison*'s arrival, *Pensée* plunges the newlywed into a kind of compulsive, self-absorbing rumination that destabilises the individual and renders him incapable of reaching a solution to his existential dilemmas.[27] No matter how probing, such scrutiny remains counterproductive if not aided by the mental habits of reason. True to its etymology, *Pensée* literally weighs on the newlywed's chest. This is not so much thinking as worrying; tellingly, it is followed by *Soussy*. Consequently, the newlywed laments that 'on my own I shall never reach the manor where Prosperity dwells'.[28] Fatalism crops in until *Raison* enters the stage.[29] Bruyant emphasises that the road to poverty is so short that the instant you step on it you have already arrived at the destination.[30] What is more, the men who have strayed from the right path cannot find the way back unaided by *Raison*. Their efforts to think of a solution on their own end up in *grant mérencolie*.[31] Such hopelessness is tied not to a crisis of society, but to the individual's loss of confidence in his capacities. Once internalised, however, reason is an autonomous faculty that can rebuke the individual's nefarious urges. It empowers him by banishing insidious thoughts that could infiltrate his mind.[32] Thus, while the poem dramatises the moment of decision through the same narrative trope

---

[26] 'dedens moi senti ainsi / Raison la sage que j'aim si / Que tousjours en mon cuer demeure'; Pichon (ed.), *Ménagier*, vol. 2, p. 33.

[27] Ibid., vol. 2, p. 5, col. 2.

[28] 'par moy ne puet estre attaint / Le manoir où Richesse maint'; ibid., vol. 2, p. 7, col. 2.

[29] '… qui au Deable veult aler, / Riens ne vault longuement attendre / Noyer ne puet, cil qui doit pendre'; ibid., vol. 2, p. 7, col. 2.

[30] 'il est assez court / Tant soit-il ort et desrivé / Car on est tantost arrivé / […] Droit au manoir où il s'adresse / C'est assavoir chez Povreté'; ibid., vol. 2, pp. 19–20.

[31] Ibid., vol. 2, p. 18, col. 2.

[32] Ibid., vol. 2, p. 19, col. 1.

of the crossroads we have encountered in Salimbene'a autobiography, it also makes clear that reason needs to be exercised constantly, together with diligence and moderation. Hence the shift of emphasis, after the moment of decision, on perseverance.[33] The *chastel de Labour* functions as a supplement to the bifurcating paths of poverty and riches in order to emphasise that the individual's life journey is not simply a matter of making one crucial decision: it goes on with further trials.

Self-discipline becomes crucial. At the castle, the newlywed is warned against the temptation of prolonged rest and urged to match his sensible words with actions.[34] Through the verb *agencer* (to place in good order, to array) the path of diligence is depicted as an efficacious arrangement – structured action, we might say – that leads to social status.[35] The narrative offers a model for cultivating self-discipline, as the protagonist's resolve is tested successively by the castle's guardians, all while stressing that perseverance is the prerequisite for success.[36] The case for reason is validated not only through its logical coherence but also through direct proof, as if in a court of law; its importance is indicated deictically: the newlywed informs *Raison* of his final decision after an intriguing pause, so as to prove with his actions that he internalised the wisdom of reflecting three times before pronouncing on a matter. Similarly, another such pause is underscored visually in one of the *Chemin*'s manuscripts: a blank space of two lines, the only one of its kind, is inserted right after the protagonist confesses that he was almost persuaded by *Barat*'s deceitful speech and just before *Entendement* arrives to offer his counsel.[37]

This cerebral approach does not, however, dispense with sentiments, emotions, and the body, but aims to subordinate them to reason. To begin at the narrative level, the poem makes of its rational model of conduct an

---

[33] Ibid., vol. 2, p. 32, col. 2; p. 36, col. 1; pp. 39–40.

[34] 'Amis, dist Peine, c'est bien dit / Fay que le fait s'accorde au dit'; ibid., vol. 2, p. 37, col. 2.

[35] Ibid., vol. 2, p. 20, col. 2. *Mesure*, *Raison*'s sister, is described as well-ordered ('bien ruillée') and indispensable for self-conduct: 'Ainsi de soy s'occist Nature / Se ne la *gouverne* Mesure'; ibid., vol. 2, p. 16, col. 1 (emphasis added). The late-medieval idea of *gouverner* denotes both management and following a *chemin*; see Michel Foucault, *Security, Territory, Population: Lectures at the Collège de France, 1977–1978*, ed. Michel Senellart (New York, 2007), pp. 108–9, 121.

[36] 'persévérer sans retraire'; Pichon (ed.), *Ménagier*, vol. 2, pp. 36–8.

[37] Ibid., vol. 2, pp. 32–3; Paris, BN, MS français 808, fol. 63v. For the transition to inquest and the corollary emphasis on proof in late-medieval legal culture, see Claude Gauvard,*"De grace especial": Crime, état et société en France à la fin du Moyen Ag*e (Paris: Publications de la Sorbonne, 1991).

ethos upheld through pathetic descriptions and pleas. The adherence to the principles of reason is described as a personal, heartfelt investment; 'turn a cold shoulder to [*Barat*] and love me', *Raison* urges the newlywed.[38] Similarly, servants are urged to love their masters with a sincere heart and serve them loyally, even as it is made clear that this is the key for gaining their reward.[39] In other words, the individual is empowered to deploy his emotions according to necessity. Furthermore, the signs of emotion should be recognised in others as well, and prompt an appropriate response – for instance a strategy of avoidance and deferment, as in Gregorio Dati's case (Chapter 4): even if you are right, there is no point in trying to talk sense to your superior when he is enraged.[40] Agency acquires an emotional dimension. The aspiration to put feelings into the service of reason is evident in the injunction to deny any sympathy to the poor, who, in an exacerbation of the ethos of rational choice and self-discipline, are denounced as themselves responsible for their predicament.[41] Behind this radical view of individual responsibility we can detect Bruyant's emotional investment. Determinism, in the form of the invocation of fate to explain failure, is dismissed as self-victimisation and apology for the individual's flaws of intellect and character.[42] At a time when the traditional idea of a blind Fortune was being questioned, Bruyant was unequivocal. For him Fortune brings people their just deserts; only the timing of its retribution remains unforeseen.[43] The point is that by adopting this stance Bruyant would have reinforced his belief in the individual's capacity to affect his life chances.

Care of the body enables specific forms of action – a pragmatic conception with which Bruyant once again departs from the traditional negative view of the body, still present in contemporaneous texts such Deguileville's *Pèlerinage*

---

[38] 'Met le doncques en non chaloir / Et m'aimes'; Pichon (ed.), *Ménagier*, vol. 2, p. 31, col. 1.

[39] Ibid., vol. 2, p. 22; see Susan Broomhall, 'Emotions in the Household', in Susan Broomhall (ed.), *Emotions in the Household, 1200–1900* (New York, 2008), pp. 1–37.

[40] Pichon (ed.), *Ménagier*, vol. 2, p. 23, col. 2.

[41] Ibid., vol. 2, p. 20, col. 1.

[42] 'Et prennent en leur meschéance / Par ce parler, glorifiance / Et s'excusent de leur méffait'; ibid., vol. 2, p. 18, col. 2.

[43] Cf. Guenée, *Une meurtre, une société*, pp. 79–82; Élisabeth Crouzet-Pavan, 'La pensée médiévale sur la mobilité sociale, XIIe–XIVe siècle', in Sandro Carocci (ed.), *La mobilità sociale nel medioevo* (Rome, 2010), pp. 69–96, at pp. 83–4. Bruyant's Fortune is subordinated to the principles of justice and reason: Pichon (ed.), *Ménagier*, vol. 2, p. 18, col. 2; p. 28, col. 1.

de la vie humaine.⁴⁴ Unlike Deguileville, Bruyant is far from pitting the body against the mind. For instance, the rationale for the advice to wake up early is to have enough time to work on the task at hand, but it is also the mark of the man who spurns sloth, *paresse*. Physical work without strength of character and perseverance remains insufficient for attaining prosperity.⁴⁵ Work ethic is tied to physical activity and nourishment. Sensations like the pleasant fatigue at the end of a day of work in the *chastel*, or satiety after the frugal lunch with the labourers, become sources of the protagonist's positive emotional and spiritual outlook.⁴⁶ They provide the physical validation of his rational choice for a life of moderation and work. Furthermore, body posture is important because it signifies social status: among the benefits of the life organised according to reason is that one can stand upright in front of everyone, 'sans traire le cul arriére', and speak boldly.⁴⁷ Human dignity is not simply cultivated inwardly but meant to be affirmed in society. On the contrary, for *Barat* body techniques are just an instrument of deception: in dissimulation, facial expression is as important as speech.⁴⁸ Furthermore, Bruyant brings the techniques of the body into the social sphere by proposing a new subcategory of the vice of gluttony, namely *Male-bouche* (bad-mouthing). *Male-bouche* stands for embellishing rumours (*Surdit*) and spreading calumnies (*Mesdit*), speaking rashly (*Hastiveté*), disgracefully (*Pautonnerie*), or blasphemously (*Maugréerie*).⁴⁹ By adding *Male-bouche* as a branch of gluttony Bruyant links a technique of the body, refraining from culinary excesses, to a mode of acting in society that preserves social ties by avoiding gossip.

Rationality itself, far from being an inward affair shielded from the attrition of everyday existence, is affected by the material conditions bearing on

---

⁴⁴ In which 'le corps est [ton] adversaire'; Guillaume de Deguileville, *Pèlerinage de la vie humaine*, ed. J. J. Stürzinger (London, 1893), p. 198; and see Karin Ueltschi, *La Didactique de la chair: approches et enjeux d'un discours en français au Moyen Age* (Geneva, 1993).

⁴⁵ Pichon (ed.), *Ménagier*, vol. 2, p. 39, col. 2.

⁴⁶ Ibid., vol. 2, pp. 38–9.

⁴⁷ Ibid., vol. 2, p. 29, col. 2.

⁴⁸ 'Des dens doit rire et non de cuer'; ibid., vol. 2, p. 26, col. 2.

⁴⁹ Ibid., vol. 2, p. 13, col. 2. Bruyant seems original: the examples cited in *Dictionnaire du Moyen Français*, s.v. Malebouche, do not indicate an association with gluttony. In the *Roman de la rose Malebouche* is simply a threat to lovers' secrets; Strubel (ed.), *Roman de la Rose*, lines 3509–25, 3566–74. In *La somme le roi* the discussion of vices includes an eighth section, 'Dou pechié de la langue', which is nevertheless more traditional; Edith Brayer and Anne-Françoise Leurquin-Labie (eds), *La somme le roi par frère Laurent* (Paris, 2008).

the body. The newlywed's initial fall into moral despondency results from the increasing pressures on his body perpetrated by the concerted 'assault' of *Pensée, Soussi*, and the rest. His reasoning is impaired and his will perverted because his body has been infected by them.[50] The personifications of need, penury, and discomfort convey the daily experience of the individual whose efforts to organise his social existence are frustrated by the concrete conditions of living. The close connection between the body and intellect is also manifest in the vices' dual offensive, physical and psychological: 'You wretch! What will you do? How will you pay your debts?'[51] The gradation of the narrative, in which *Désespérance* enters the stage immediately after the vices' assault, puts forth the idea that despondency, though eminently a condition of the mind, settles in when material conditions facilitate it. The implications are ultimately social: the newlywed is tempted to get by wrong what he cannot by right, with fatal consequences.

In sum, Bruyant's discussion of vices and virtues retains some traditional psychological considerations but brings a novel emphasis on social context. Virtues such as abstinence and sobriety are not only cultivated as part of a moral–aesthetic ideal of the human person, but also serve important social functions. Through them, specifically by exercising the mental habits and techniques of the body introduced under the aegis of *Raison* and *Mesure*, the individual equips himself for participating in the life of society.

The social imaginary

As the foregoing discussion has suggested, the individual at the centre of Bruyant's vision is embedded in a rich social imaginary. Bruyant's views do not have the coherence of a system, for one because he was not an elite intellectual searching for terminological precision: for example, 'the path to prosperity' is also described as the way of diligence, moderation, and reason. Everyday speech offers the proverb with which the poem opens and the words of wisdom about how to serve. Even the fundamental choice between the two paths is described through an everyday-life metaphor: 'Leave the bran and take the flour.'[52] On the other hand, Reason's discourse is underpinned by two crucial notions in late-medieval legal practice, test and proof. The effort to dramatise decision-making should be viewed against the backdrop of a social imaginary in which conflicting imperatives inform one's course of action. In

---

[50] Pichon (ed.), *Ménagier*, vol. 2, p. 6, col. 1.
[51] Ibid., vol. 2, p. 7, col. 1.
[52] 'Laisses le bren et pren la fleur'; ibid., vol. 2, p. 17, col. 1.

effect, Bruyant reaches his conclusions through a confrontation of both religious and social arguments.

To begin with, if the ancient ideal of moderation surfaces as a key component of Bruyant's fresh social vision, it is because the lessons of the recent past have suggested its potential usefulness. Tellingly, the description of *Souffisance* and *Convoitise* includes references to the demise of great estates through reversals of Fortune. *Convoitise* is the defining characteristic of those who amass wealth compulsively only to lose it overnight. Thus, if 'souffisance ... est parfaicte richesce',[53] it is in good measure because Bruyant's observation of society has revealed that the opposite path does not lead to success. What is more, the life of work is itself presented as the right choice on both spiritual and this-worldly grounds.[54] At a time when shift from *courtoisie* to *civilité* involved the 'disjunction of manners and ethics',[55] Bruyant makes the secular world a standard in its own right for validating the good life. As we shall see, he takes this view to its logical consequences and treats seriously even those who hold radically different views. Since he saw the world as an autonomous instance for judging one's life and achievements, is it surprising that Bruyant decided to take up the quill and intervene in the debate on these topics? Through his poem, Bruyant both articulates for himself a position on social issues and begins to disseminate it, aware that his achievements are measured against the social views that carry the day. All this is not remarkable: medieval social values reflected custom and consensus as well as a down-to-earth appreciation for finding workable solutions to the challenges of an expanding society.[56] But with the *Chemin* we see how a modest Parisian professional took up the defence of worldly values as positive in themselves. What is more, Bruyant preserves his moral commitments, and while his pragmatic outlook is not simply the effect of religious beliefs, as with Max Weber's Protestant capitalist, the *Chemin* should not be reduced to a this-worldly ethos either. *Raison*'s advice is structured according to the two fundamental Christian commandments (Matthew 22. 36–40). Moreover, eschatological concerns are invoked as a last argument for the life of diligence and

---

[53] Ibid., vol. 2, p. 4, col. 1; p. 42, col. 2.

[54] 'Tu en pues à grant bien venir / Selon Dieu et selon le monde'; ibid, vol. 2, p. 24, col. 1.

[55] Jorge Arditi, *A Genealogy of Manners: Transformations of Social Relations in France and England from the Fourteenth to the Eighteenth Century* (Chicago, 1998), pp. 4–5, 54–85.

[56] Susan Reynolds, *Kingdoms and Communities in Western Europe, 900–1300*, 2nd edn (Oxford, 1997) pp. 13–21, 42–7, 141–7; Murray, *Reason and Society, pp. 81–109.*

moderation: the fate of *Barat*'s followers, it is made clear, is eternal damnation.⁵⁷ *Raison*'s speech emphasises the convergence of religious and practical considerations: 'Tu vois que mon salaire est double'.⁵⁸ In sum, Bruyant treats religious ethics and social behaviour as autonomous but insists that both be taken into account.

In one sense, however, the religious appears decentred by the affirmation of worldly values. The *Chemin* proposes a model of relating to religious values that reflects the laity's social dispositions. In a typical example of pragmatic rationality, the newlywed is asked to weigh carefully the two options and decide for the more profitable course of action. Even as regards the moral merits of each ideal of conduct, Bruyant's decision-making model is predicated on the principles of calculation and profit. There are certainly precedents for this, but perhaps not very many: notably, the preachers of the first crusade made the case for the expedition on both moral grounds and through a rhetoric of profit that resonated with the laity's values.⁵⁹

On the other hand, his moral commitments leads him to search for a more profound explanation behind the socioeconomic upheavals. In the process, he formulates a personal perspective on the relation between reason and moderation. The parvenus' unexpected loss of their fortunes is not put down to a gross business miscalculation; similarly, Bruyant dismisses accident as an explanation because he wants to emphasise the consequences of the life choice of acquisitiveness. Once embraced, cupidity leads one to push further and further in an effort to compulsively increase one's wealth, no matter how much has been already amassed; sooner or later, the fall comes unavoidably and for Bruyant there is little point in searching for the spark that finally triggered it. It had been in the making ever since one entered the path of cupidity, and in this sense this path is also, from the very beginning, the path of poverty. The arrivistes' error is fundamentally moral.

While moderation is emphasised, the key point is that is also adjusted to the specific circumstances of Bruyant's milieu. *Souffisance* is redefined as an ideal of moderate prosperity and security.⁶⁰ It is hardly subsistence as

---

[57] Pichon (ed.), *Ménagier*, vol. 2, pp. 31–2.

[58] Ibid., vol. 2, p. 30, col. 1.

[59] Hans Eberhard Mayer, *The Crusades*, trans. John Gillingham, 2nd edn (Oxford, 1988); cf. Matthew 13. 44–6. Also see Steven A. Epstein, 'Economics in Dante's Hell', in Iris Shagrir et al. (eds), *In Laudem Hierosolymitani: Studies in Crusades and Medieval Culture in Honour of Benjamin Z. Kedar* (Aldershot, 2007), pp. 437–46, at p. 440.

[60] It brings a modest but guaranteed return (*chevance*); Pichon (ed.), *Ménagier*, vol. 2, p. 22, col. 1. Bruyant once again departs from the *Roman*, in which poverty is

the medieval clergy understood it. What Bruyant fears is losing status – an understandable concern if he was indeed a bureaucrat – and ending up among the lower classes. This relates him to the 'shamed-face poor', professionals and artisans facing the threat of downward mobility.[61] Despite rejecting the ambition to get rich, Bruyant could not banish a certain fascination with the lifestyle of the aristocracy, witness his choice of the castle as the poem's key site, understandable if he indeed worked at the Parisian Châtelet, and of the *manoir de Richesse*. *Povreté* may not have a stable meaning in the *Chemin*, but one thing it is not is destitution. Two decades after the great famine of 1315, for Bruyant living in poverty, hideous though it is, is not risking starvation but simply not being well-nourished. What defines it first and foremost is the loss of *estat*, having to forgo one's desires and not being well-at-ease in society – a decidedly bourgeois idea of poverty.[62]

The realisation that society was becoming increasingly complex and conflicted informs the confrontation between *Raison* and *Barat*, the latter exemplifying the profit mentality permeating the late-medieval imaginary. The slick lawyer makes it clear that taking advantage of others through flattery, deceit, and fraud is the shortest and most effective path to opulence, and rejects the moderate achievement advocated by *Raison*.[63] In the end this approach is condemned vehemently, as the protagonist chooses reason. Yet in the first place, when *Barat* argues his points against *Raison*, a coherent case is made, preserving all the while the unapologetically instrumentalist tone that is *Barat*'s defining mark. The author's articulate exposition of *Barat*'s model of conduct, followed by a critique that is anything but dismissive, offer a brief moment of dialogism. While a character named *Baraz* makes a passing appearance in the *Roman*, Bruyant's originality is to turn it into a lawyer and have it address the audience at length.[64] Even as he was strongly opposed to *Barat*'s way, Bruyant sensed that neither dismissing nor caricaturing it would do. His statement about 'taking the better of two paths' implies that *Barat*'s

---

idealised by Reason; Strubel (ed.), *Roman de la Rose*, lines 4887–5020; 11273–9.

[61] See Michel Mollat, *Les pauvres au Moyen âge: étude sociale* (Paris, 1978), pp. 190–1, 198–202, and Richard Trexler, 'Charity and the Defence of Urban Elites in the Italian Communes', in Frederick Cople Jaher (ed.), *The Rich, the Wellborn, and the Powerful: Elites and Upper Classes in History* (Urbana, IL, 1973), pp. 64–109.

[62] Pichon (ed.), *Ménagier*, vol. 2, 19, col. 2.

[63] Ibid., vol. 2, pp. 24–7.

[64] Strubel (ed.), *Roman de la Rose*, lines 11901–10. Cf. Mikhail Bakthin, *The Dialogic Imagination*, trans. Caryl Emerson and Michael Holquist (Austin, 1981).

model is an option in its own right,[65] like the life of moderation and reason. Bruyant's case for 'la meilleure' choice acknowledges implicitly that the two options are after all comparable. He was probably led to this nuanced approach by the realisation that increasingly broader circles were becoming more open to the tough socioeconomic thinking epitomised by *Barat*. Bruyant must have encountered and pondered the worth of such views enough times to be able to articulate them clearly. We may call this a doubling of perspective, the sign of a genuine engagement with otherness. Bruyant first thought 'with' the scrupleless lawyers or entrepreneurs and then against them. He even reworked and integrated in his own model of conduct elements of self-interested materialism. A few of *Raison*'s instructions echo *Barat*'s advice. Both emphasise individual strength and hard work, the importance of fine speech and manners in social interactions, and promise not just wealth but also social standing; finally, both are disparaging of the poor. But on the whole *Barat*'s approach remains radically at odds with the ideals of reason and moderation. While *Raison* emphasises discernment, the elision of any distinction between good and bad thinking is *Barat*'s attribute and completes the picture of compulsion that characterises the *arrivistes*.[66]

The endeavour to understand different perspective and articulate a programme that can be shared broadly reflects the effort to adapt to a changing society. The text registers the advances of the culture of *civilité*, advising to greet people on the streets, be 'courtois et amiables', and avoid disputes (*tencions ne noises*) because they are counterproductive.[67] The related advice to listen attentively and think carefully before offering one's opinion is part of the model of the calculated individual, shared with similar with late-medieval advice books. This attitude is recommended because of its perceived effectiveness in gaining cultural capital: 'in this way you shall be held as wise'.[68] Overall, the risk- and conflict-averse advice and the emphasis on negotiation

---

[65] Pichon (ed.), *Ménagier*, vol. 2, p. 17, col. 1.

[66] *Barat* too recommends a determined attitude; however, in his case this is badly misguided: 'Que tu faces hardiement / Quanque tu auras empensé / *Soit bien pensé ou mal pensé* (emphasis added); ibid., vol. 2, p. 26, col. 2.

[67] Ibid., vol. 2, pp. 16–17; Norbert Elias, *The Civilising Process*, rev. edn, trans. Edmund Jephcott (Oxford, 2000), esp. pp. 47–8, 87–8; John Gillingham, 'From *Civilitas* to Civility: Codes of Manners in Medieval and Early Modern England', *Transactions of the Royal Historical Society*, 6th ser., 12 (2002), 267–89.

[68] Pichon (ed.), *Ménagier*, vol. 2, p. 16, col. 2; Thor Sundby (ed.), *Brunetto Latinos Levnet og Skrifter* (Copenhagen, 1869), pp. xciii–xciv, xcvii. Cf. Pierre Bourdieu, 'The Forms of Capital', in John G. Richardson (ed.), *Handbook of Theory of Research for the Sociology of Education* (New York, 1986), pp. 241–58.

and cultivating social ties resonates with the socioeconomic *habitus* of urban professionals.⁶⁹ Conscious that people like him were often cast in socially subordinate positions, Bruyant recommends treating even the 'menus' or 'small' people kindly.

Lastly, the advice received by the newlywed on the possibility of entering the service of a social superior can be linked to the little we can surmise about Bruyant's own work in a hierarchical bureaucracy in which the good will of superiors and protectors counted for much. The advice offered to the struggling young bourgeois is geared towards advancing his career by securing the reward and support of his employer; self-discipline and hard work are subordinated to this purpose. The practical instructions are organised around three easy-to-remember *significations*, which focus on techniques of the body: one should have the back of a donkey (*dos de asne*) to perform his workload, a cow's ears (*oreilles de vache*) to listen dutifully, and a pig's snout (*groing de purcel*) to gulp his master's bread. The last two pieces of wisdom also suggest a model of deferential sociability, and Bruyant adds that one must be of good cheer (*en bon gré*) and bear hardships willingly.⁷⁰ Such mundane tropes suggest he envisaged an audience sensitive to down-to-earth imagery, probably a class of aspiring professionals from modest backgrounds.

The castle of labour

The social imaginary comes into full view with the castle of labour. This is where Bruyant is at his most innovative, appropriating the aristocratic castle in the service of a discourse about work, thus elevated to the status of an esteemed activity. By turning the castle into a site of productive activities rather than military or administrative, and by populating it with a mass of labourers, the poem subverts the hierarchy of social functions enshrined in the tripartite imaginary inherited from the previous centuries, which relegated *laboratores* to the bottom rung. This subversion is captured with visual force in an early-fifteenth-century illuminated manuscript of the poem, which depicts the castle as a traditional medieval fortress but devoid of knights or squires: its denizens are now workers and craftsmen, present not to build the castle,

---

⁶⁹ Later this found more appeal among the aristocracy as well; Thierry Dutour, 'La noblesse et la ville dans l'espace francophone à la fin du Moyen Âge: État de la question et propositions de réflexion', in Thierry Dutour (ed.), *La noblesse et la ville dans l'espace francophone (XIIe–XVIe siècles)* (Paris, 2010), pp. 17–58, at pp. 19–22.

⁷⁰ See Murray, *Reason and Society*, pp. 107–9.

which is already finished, but to inhabit it and engage in physical work.[71] The idea of a working woman (Toil), dressed in a decidedly proletarian outfit but raised to the status of castellan's wife, is similarly subversive.[72] The novelty of the *chastel de Labour* is brought into relief by the comparison with the *Castle of Perseverance* (c. 1400–25), a Middle English morality play in which the castle is simply the symbol of evil lordship and sin. Although this text too is a commentary on the social order, it does not endeavour to rework the traditional view of society.[73] Even among the late-medieval texts engaged in rethinking the traditional social imaginary by emphasising personal merit or the role of the bourgeoisie, the castle of labour appears as quite original.[74]

Our assessment of the *chastel* depends on how we read its allegory: do the 'more than one hundred thousand workers' amount to the vision of a whole society based on labour? Alternatively, does the allegory simply signify the life of work becoming a bourgeois? For *le chastel de Labour* is more allegorical than what precedes it in the poem. Conversely, judged by the standards that the text set, the imaginary of the *chastel* is less transparent and referential. There is a good dose of realism in the rigorous treatment of *Barat*'s immoral but hard-headed principles, because Bruyant recognised that many found the materialistic approach appealing. But in staging the castle of labour the imagination runs more freely. This is not only because a whole new social space is created, whereas previously the text merely describes existing socioeconomic realities, debating only which path should be chosen. The castle of labour

---

[71] Philadelphia, Free Library, Rare Book Department, MS Widener 1, fol. 61v; miniatures reproduced in P. A. B. Widener, *A Catalogue of the More Important Books, Autographs and Manuscripts in the Library of George C. Thomas* (Philadelphia, 1907), pp. 18–19.

[72] Pichon (ed.), *Ménagier*, vol. 2, p. 37, col. 1.

[73] Milla B. Riggio, 'The Allegory of Feudal Acquisition in *The Castle of Perseverance*', in Morton W. Boomfield (ed.), *Allegory, Myth, and Symbol* (Cambridge, MA, 1981), pp. 187–208, at pp. 189–94, 208.

[74] See Otto Gerhard Oexle, 'Perceiving Social Reality in the Early and High Middle Ages: A Contribution to a History of Social Knowledge', in Bernhard Jussen (ed.), *Ordering Medieval Society: Perspectives on Intellectual and Practical Modes of Shaping Social Relations* (Philadelphia, 2001), pp. 92–143, at p. 118; Dutour, 'La noblesse et la ville', pp. 24–8; Bernard Ribémont, 'Ville et noblesse au regard de la littérature médiévale', in Thierry Dutour (ed.), *La noblesse et la ville dans l'espace francophone (XIIe–XVIe siècles)* (Paris, 2010), pp. 221–44, at pp. 230–34; Boris Bove, 'L'image de soi dans le jeu des normes sociales aux XIIIe et XIVe siècles: l'exemple de la bourgeoisie parisienne', in Marie-France Auzépy and Joël Cornette (eds), *Des images dans l'histoire* (Saint-Denis, 2008), pp. 179–213, at pp. 200–1.

strikes us as less real because its allegory gestures towards a totalising social imaginary – and falls short.

In part, this vision proceeds from real-life premises like the material that precedes it; notably, it extols the value of labour. But the more sophisticated allegory of the *chastel*, in a text in which specific social references render allegory transparent, creates a strange effect. It makes the castle appear, by comparison, too artificial and schematic to pass for a realistic vision of a new society. Its portrayal remains so absorbed by the ethos of labour that it offers little else in the way of social reform. Although the text spotlights the labourers' active and frugal lifestyle, it pays attention to them only inasmuch as they can inspire the author's narrative alter ego. Some form of individualism lingers even as Bruyant tries to move towards a fuller vision of society: his is the only individualised activity in the castle, as the protagonist works in his chamber by candlelight – studying and writing, no doubt, as Bruyant would in his legal practice. Exactly what kinds of manual work the multitude of labourers engage in is beyond the poem's purview. By contrast, the painter of the miniatures that accompany the text in one manuscript gave visual poignancy to the castle of labour with the kind of detail that Bruyant leaves out: he pictured builders, woodworkers, and smiths engaged in their own crafts inside the castle (see Plate 3). Bruyant lacked the motivation to engage in a detailed depiction of the labourers and their manual crafts, because his focus was on his own milieu. Labour is first and foremost an ethos that poses great appeal for Bruyant personally, and only subsequently the founding principle of a reformed society. Similarly, he offers no account of how reason can be acquired in the first place: he hints that the *sens naturel* is sufficient, but this cannot explain why so many fail to make the expected choice.[75] This is the mindset of the educated person whose only challenge ahead is to turn reason into a practical faculty.

This individualist attitude becomes understandable if we consider that the text is inflected by a discourse of self-justification. From the beginning, Bruyant volunteers the testimony of his own life of modest material gain.[76] Later, another personal avowal goes beyond the parameters that define the experiences of the narrative alter ego and must be viewed as an autobiographical statement by the author:

---

[75] Pichon (ed.), *Ménagier*, vol. 2, p. 27, col. 2.

[76] 'I can vouch through my own example / For I have earned a modest living (*chevissance*)'; ibid., vol. 2, p. 4, col. 1. This is a direct statement from the aged Jacques Bruyant; subsequently, however, the narrative 'I' refers to the newlywed, the author's younger alter ego.

Plate 3. Le chastel de Labour. Reproduced by permission of The Free Library, Rare Book Department, Philadelphia (MS Widener 1, fol. 61v).

Worrying has troubled many a heart
And it still does, every day
No one really knows it unless he experiences it
As I have despite myself
In sufferance, labour, and anxiety.[77]

Here Bruyant addresses his readers directly, putting the fiction of the narrative alter-ego aside, so as to vouch with his own real-life experiences for the validity of the poem's social discourse. More generally, Bruyant emerges as a man who had to fight to stay afloat in society. He has a clear grasp of the plight of the young professional. *Barat* and Bruyant's narrative alter-ego differ starkly in their economic success, the former dressed in a fur-lined coat and accompanied by an assistant and a valet, the latter on the verge of selling his robe to pay debts.[78] Bruyant would have encountered quite a few legal professionals of *Barat*'s ilk. He resented their ability to rise in status through fraud or by courting the favour of the magnates who controlled the bureaucracy in which he too probably served.[79] Small wonder that he argues passionately for a modest estate and denounces those who take risks in seeking ever larger fortunes. The ethos of the *chastel de Labour* reassures him of the value of hard work. By associating *Barat* with the parvenus who get rich and then lose everything, Bruyant could convince himself that some of the sly lawyers who got rich practising his trade would eventually share this fate. It might be that as the incarnation of the social vices *Barat* even served to exorcise Bruyant's fears about his own weakness in the face of temptation. Thus, underlying the social vision based on general principles we encounter the individual's preoccupation with his particular lifeworld.

Notwithstanding Bruyant's focus on issues directly relevant to him, his social perspective achieves a modicum of inclusiveness through the invention of the *chastel de Labour*. The *chastel* opens the way for labourers into the social thought of the urban middle class. Even if Bruyant's aim was to appropriate a work ethos that could help him sustain the mode of socioeconomic agency he

---

[77] 'Soussy a maint cuer esmayé / Et encor tous les jours esmaie / Nul ne le scet qui ne l'essaye / Ainsi com j'ay fait maugré moi, / En paine en travail et esmoy'; ibid., vol. 2, p. 6, col. 2. This personal statement only makes sense within the lifeworld of an experienced individual, Bruyant the empirical author; it does not resonate with the narrative world of the newlywed.

[78] Ibid., vol. 2, p. 24, col. 2.

[79] While the *Chemin* is not political, it bears some resemblance to vernacular texts on societal reform, e.g., Henri Moranvillé (ed.), 'Le songe véritable, pamphlet politique d'un Parisien du XVe siècle', *Mémoires de la Société de l'histoire de Paris*, 17 (1890), 217–438.

embraced, the inclusion of the *cent mille ouvriers* remains significant. Despite his anxieties about the urban poor, Bruyant's appreciation for the value of work builds a bridge to the social class of labourers. If his narrative alter-ego can fraternise with them, it is not because Bruyant believes that social distinctions should be abolished for good, but because he shares with them a positive view of work. The significance of the *chastel* lies in the affirmation of work as socially meritorious, and even capable of mitigating class divides. The reception of the *Chemin* in the fourteenth and fifteenth centuries turned out to be largely a matter of appropriating its message about work.

From moral agent to actant: gendered conduct in the *Ménagier de Paris*

How was the *Chemin* read? The twelve extant manuscripts – including three of the *Ménagier* – offer important clues about the reception of a text that proved surprisingly popular considering the complexity of its argument and its non-professional author. Social conduct and particularly marriage advice are central themes in a manuscript in which the *Chemin* is included alongside a *Conseil de mariage* and two *enseignemens a son fils* (advice for one's son, a popular genre); the subtitles added in this manuscript emphasise the protagonist's status as a newlywed or *nouvel mesnagier*.[80] The *Chemin* was regarded as a conduct text in three other manuscripts, where it is associated with collections of moral sentences and translations of moral texts like Albertano da Brescia's tale of Melibee (also copied in the *Ménagier*) and Jacques de Cessoles's treatise about social order viewed through the game of chess.[81] Other manuscripts reveal an association with poetic works, including *Le roman de la rose*.[82] In 1499 Pierre Gringore published *Le chastel de labour*, copying and reworking Bruyant's text.[83] With the *Ménagier*'s author we can even home in on what an ordinary bourgeois thought was the *Chemin*'s central message. The whole point of inserting the *Chemin*'s text in the section on household management and work ethic (*regard au labour*) was to demonstrate the importance of

---

[80] Paris, IRHT, microfilm of Stockholm, Kungliga biblioteket, MS Vu 23, fols 2–7v, 12v, 14, 24–7.

[81] London, British Library, MS Royal 19 C XI, and MS Royal 19 B IV; Berkeley, Bancroft Library, MS 173.

[82] Paris, BN, MS français 808, fols 51–72; Ms français 1563, fols 203–21, which reflects the 'querelle de la Rose': the *Chemin*'s personifications are underlined, signalling an interest in allegory in the tradition of the *Roman*.

[83] Charles Oulmont, *La poésie morale, politique et dramatique à la veille de la Renaissance: Pierre Gringore*, repr. (Geneva, 1975), pp. 96–107.

diligence and *parseverance*. This explicit statement suggests that the *Ménagier*'s author was well aware that other interpretations were possible and wanted to anchor the meaning of the text he copied wholesale into his own work. His was a highly interested reading of the *Chemin*. To understand his reasons we must examine his textual project.

Scholars have seen in the *Ménagier*'s household and young wife in need of guidance a narrative pretext, and rightly so; but a narrative pretext need not be unreal. The author, who most likely came from the haute bourgeoisie, alludes to the fact that his work will circulate first among his entourage,[84] which is likely the reason he did not find it necessary to give his name in the text (a common practice, as we have seen with the *Chemin*). This circle of friends and relatives would have been startled by an elaborately fictionalised young wife, particularly since the author puts much stock in the veracity of the anecdotes he reports.[85] But even if this was fiction, the author's attention to its details and coherence suggests that verisimilitude remained crucial; consequently, the present approach is to bracket the dilemma of literary fiction versus autobiographical realism and see how the text can be read so as to account for its dual nature.

The *Ménagier* consists of three books or *distinctions*, of which the first is dedicated to the topic of loving God and one's husband and offers advice on attending Mass, making confession, and the vices and virtues. In the second part of the first *distinction*, the focus shifts to the wife's duties toward her husband, with articles on how to obey him and care for his person. To illustrate these themes, several stories are inserted, along with *exempla* from biblical, classical, and recent history. Microeconomic advice is offered in the second *distinction*, on household management, emphasising 'regard au labour' by the inclusion in its first article of the *Chemin*. The remaining articles deal with gardening, managing servants, and arranging festive dinners. How to behave in society is the theme of the third *distinction*; the author intended to write three chapters – on society games, hawking, and arithmetic and number games – but only the second was completed (it is inserted into the second *distinction*). Advice about the wife's conduct in public is interspersed throughout the text.

Beyond this elaborate structure, the literary ambitions of the *Ménagier* are evident in the numerous quotes and paraphrases from vernacular literature,

[84] Georgine Brereton and Janet M. Ferrier (eds), *Le Ménagier de Paris: A Critical Edition* (Oxford, 1981), 1.4.1. A conjectural attempt to identify him as a petty aristocrat is unconvincing; Nicole Crossley-Holland, *Living and Dining in Medieval Paris: The Household of a Fourteenth-century Knight* (Cardiff, 1996), pp. 4–7.

[85] See Janet M. Ferrier, 'A Husband's Asides: The Use of the Second Person Singular in *Le Ménagier de Paris*', *French Studies*, 31:3 (1977), 257–67, at p. 257.

not to mention the wholesale copying of entire texts, like the *Chemin* and the story of Melibee.[86] Together with the religious sources and influences, this suggests that in this model of conduct moral and aesthetic commitments were as important as practical matters. The author's interest in the moral and aesthetic aspects of conduct is understandably startling for the practical-minded modern reader, but it becomes more readily understandable if we consider that the *Ménagier* exemplifies not so much medieval conduct as the medieval practice of *writing* conduct, whose cultural logic shaped the text's approach to domestic relations. Many of its aspects make less sense if the aim was simply to instruct the author's wife about running the household: the lengthy excursuses and the propensity to expatiate on the rationale of everyday practices, the erudite references and verbatim copying of entire texts. The objective professed in the prologue is that by reading the treatise the wife might teach herself, without turning to her husband every time. Indirectly, this suggests that oral instructions were the norm. Oral advice would have been the most direct way to instruct the wife about household management, complemented by written lists as an aid to memory.[87] Hands-on demonstration seems particularly effective for those everyday tasks in which the techniques of the body play the most crucial role. These range from keeping the chambers and clothes clean to gardening to the art of maturing wine in barrels. Mastery of such practices 'falls on the other side of words'. The written word is an inefficient mode of inculcating them.[88]

This tension was not altogether lost on the author, who on occasion resorts to drawing – providing, for instance, a small figure to indicate the angle at which oak grafts need to be sharpened.[89] But on the whole the treatise exudes confidence in the power of writing, and the author himself becomes fully immersed in the practice of writing conduct – much like Giovanni Morelli in his *ricordi* (Chapter 4). He indicates that his wife might in turn use the text to instruct (*endoctriner*) others: her lady friends (*amies*) and especially her daughters ('et par especial voz filles').[90] He acknowledges other sources of instruction, such as oral advice from neighbours and family. But this is proposed as a complement to his text, not the other way around. Even religious and literary authorities

---

[86] Brereton and Ferrier (eds.), *Ménagier*, pp. xxx–xxxix; Gina L. Greco and Christine M. Rose (trans.), *The Good Wife's Guide* (Ithaca, NY, 2009), pp. 13–28.

[87] Brereton and Ferrier (eds.), *Ménagier*, 2.2, 2.3.15, 2.4.

[88] Ibid., 1.7.3–5, 2.2, 2.3.11–15; Pierre Bourdieu, *Outline of a Theory of Practice*, trans. Richard Nice (Cambridge, 1977), pp. 17–9.

[89] Brereton and Ferrier (eds.), *Ménagier*, 2.2.43.

[90] Ibid., 1.4.1.

are mentioned as possible sources whereby the wife might learn more, that is, by building on the advice in his treatise.[91] Notably, he points out that his wife has a *grant adventaige* over the women who came before her,[92] because they did not have the benefit of a work like the one he pioneers – an effective way of drawing attention to his own merits. This is an important statement for understanding the element of self-representation entailed in the author's project. The *Ménagier* can be viewed partly as an exercise in self-representation through the fashioning of an exemplary household,[93] which is identified as the author's own home but also put forth as a model of domestic order that others might copy. This would have affirmed his merits not just as a literary author, but also as the artisan of a workable model of domestic organisation. Furthermore, the author makes reference to husbands' wagers on their wives' obedience,[94] evidence of a bourgeois milieu in which men's competition for honour was predicated on a shared ideal of domesticity. In this world of competitive male sociability, the writing of the treatise would have represented a response to cultural pressures and a strategic effort to gain cultural capital by posing as the architect of the perfectly run household.[95]

But while the text articulates a model of household organisation that in principle could be implemented, there is nothing to suggest that the test of its achievement would have been others' ability to put this programme into practice. Vast and elaborate, the *Ménagier* is more of an encyclopaedic treatise than a manual. Most of its pages offer *theoretical* discussions of *practical* knowledge. On the one hand, the author was in touch with some elements of scholastic culture, as intimated above: he gives Latin quotes, favours structured arguments, and is eager to explain points of doctrine.[96] On the other hand, it bears emphasis that these elements coexist with a real-life framing manifest in anecdotes from personal experience and references to Parisian markets. The author clearly displays an appreciation for a worldly lifestyle, which includes

---

[91] Ibid., Prologue 3, 1.2.1, 1.3.118.

[92] Ibid., 2.1.2.

[93] Cf. Arnold, *Belief and Unbelief*, p. 151. Glen Burger, *Conduct Becoming: Good Wives and Husbands in the Later Middle Ages* (Philadelphia, 2018), came too late to my attention to engage with its findings.

[94] Brereton and Ferrier (eds.), *Ménagier*, 1.6.27, 40–3.

[95] See Bourdieu, 'Forms', pp. 247–50.

[96] Thus, the prologue has a clearly organised table of contents, the second *distinction* begins with a recapitulation of material, while a biblical rationale is offered for the structuring principles of the first *distinction* and the symbolism of Mass is discussed at length in 1.3.2–16.

games, wagers, and feasts; his references to the entertainments and modes of socialisation of bourgeois women indicate the influence of the culture of *civilité*.[97] And he was an observer of men's psychology who pondered what consequences their natural inclinations might have on domestic relations.[98] On occasion, his extraordinary preoccupation with the details of everyday life emerges rather free of the mediation of religious or literary categories. Thus, the inclusion of quasi-magical healing formulas would have seemed suspect to an orthodox mind, notwithstanding their use in conjunction with prayers.[99] In sum, the text reflects the influence of different cultural traditions and the author's different orientations.[100] This complexity is reflected in the author's use of a combination of didactic modes, as discussed below.

The construction of a normative discourse

A good deal of the *Ménagier*'s advice comes in the form of norms and rules, which are generalised, decidedly moral, and integrated into a hierarchical structure. The Prologue's table of contents amounts to a hierarchical list of general injunctions: to live chastely, love your husband, obey him, and keep his secrets. (This notwithstanding, in the Prologue's summary of contents one can already see that a few articles are more about how to accomplish certain tasks than about what kinds of conduct are meritorious; in other words, they are more practical than moral and read more like specific instructions than general rules).[101] The reliance on norms to model behaviour is not surprising in the context of medieval religious culture, because the Christian moral discourse was defined by its universalising claims. Revealingly, the author turns the fundamental Christian commandments (Matthew 22. 36–40) into the cornerstones of his moralising discourse, with some adaptation: loving God (and thus gaining the salvation of the soul) and loving and pleasing the husband are 'les deux choses plus principalment neccessaires', 'the two most fundamentally necessary things'.

---

[97] Brereton and Ferrier (eds), *Ménagier*, 1.4.15, 1.6.1; Gillingham, 'From *Civilitas* to Civility'.

[98] Brereton and Ferrier (eds), *Ménagier*, 1.6.31, 43; see Broomhall, 'Emotions in the Household'.

[99] Brereton and Ferrier (eds), *Ménagier*, esp., 1.7, 2.3; see Delaurenti, *Puissance*.

[100] Cf. Roberta L. Krueger, 'Identity Begins at Home: Female Conduct and the Failure of Counsel in *Le Ménagier de Paris*', *Essays in Medieval Studies*, 22 (2005), 21–39, at p. 22.

[101] See Brereton and Ferrier (eds), *Ménagier*, 1.2, 1.9, 2.2–5.

That such principles and rules are insufficient for sociomoral instruction had long been apparent, and the *Ménagier* follows the medieval tradition of complementing the general norms with anecdotes and examples.[102] Like the *exempla* of church writers,[103] these stories serve moral purposes by illustrating the real-life side of the general principles. It is a notable feature of the *Ménagier* that in relating a diversity of anecdotes, it emphasises the consequences of women's errant behaviour, the better to dissuade the young wife from acting on her will. Both the general norms and the *exempla* reflect the author's moral commitments. Furthermore, by demonstrating his capacity to embody in the treatise a moral-religious ideal, the references to Christian ethics would have also served the goal of producing a respectable treatise that would earn him esteem. Since many anecdotes come from translations of classical works, they would have buttressed the *Ménagier*'s credentials as an erudite work.

The author relies on two other devices as well: a multitude of specific, detailed instructions (*not* general rules) and long lists of practical information. The two are closely related: thus the precise instructions about gardening are organised in a long list in which the first article is introduced with a *primo* and subsequent ones with '*nota* que' or *item*.[104] Such itemised lists are by and large flat and stand in contrast to the hierarchy of moral principles. Some display a sense of structure: thus various gardening tasks are ordered more or less according to the season when they must be performed. But others, like the recipes and menus piled one after another,[105] reveal more of a spirit of indiscriminate accumulation than a discerning logic. The elaborate menus inspired by the feasts of the aristocracy were listed more for literary effect, as a display of the author's wealth of knowledge,[106] thus serving the aims of self-representation. In the more austere bourgeois homes such exquisite banquets would have been rare: the author explicitly warns the wife against attending the festivities of aristocrats or mingling with the wayward courtiers from the aristocracy.[107]

The recourse to precise instructions reflects an attention to material details that makes the *Ménagier*, even more than the *Chemin*, a notable example of the affirmation of everyday life in late medieval society.[108] Remarkably knowl-

---

[102] Ferrier, 'Seulement'.

[103] Brémond et al., *L'exemplum*, esp. pp. 50–7, 79–84.

[104] Brereton and Ferrier (eds), *Ménagier*, 2.2.

[105] Ibid., 2.4–5.

[106] Cf. Brereton and Ferrier, 'Introduction', pp. l–liii.

[107] Brereton and Ferrier (eds), *Ménagier*, Prologue 2; 1.5.1.

[108] See Taylor, *Sources*, pp. 212–17; Brereton and Ferrier, 'Introduction', pp. l–lv.

edgeable about domestic tasks, the author sensed that not only wives but also husbands could benefit from his advice. Thus, in the guise of instructions to *maistre* Jehan, the household steward, he offers practical information that corresponds to male gender roles – for instance, about horses and farming; and on occasion he addresses husbands about their duties.[109]

The text's eclecticism extends beyond the diverse didactic modes it employs; the central imperative of its normative discourse, the wife's obedience to the husband, is itself the resultant of different sets of concerns: practical, moral, and even aesthetic. Together they reflect the complex late-medieval social imaginary, including the tensions within it. To begin with, the Christian doctrine of gender relations underlies the concern with the wife's docility, but while the author quotes the crucial biblical passages in support of man's preeminence,[110] he is able to put aside, on occasion, the traditional lament about women's moral weaknesses and voice moderate optimism that the treatise can be instrumental in training them to overcome their limits.[111] On the other hand, as intimated above, his general intransigence can be read as a strategy for gaining cultural capital in a bourgeois milieu in which men competed on their wife's obedience. What is more, economic concerns had a significant role. The bourgeois wife occupied a key place in the domestic economy, as the husband was often required by his business to delegate household responsibilities to her. In this context, her freedom of action raised concerns. Keeping the wife's agentive potential in check became a priority. On the whole we witness a fascinating imbrication of practical and moral considerations in defence of the husband's authority. The wife's obedience is emphasised on moral grounds, as a way of making manifest her devotion towards the husband; the situations that require it are made to seem unimportant.[112] Extended to the whole range of domestic activities, the doctrine of the husband's authority reaffirms the subordination of the wife even in the smallest matters, which are judged not on their own modest significance but as test cases of a moral principle.[113] Yet elsewhere the practical importance of numerous small tasks is stressed, from making the house comfortable for the hardworking husband to defending his reputation to supervising the servants. These examples reflect a concern with

---

[109] Brereton and Ferrier (eds), *Ménagier*, 2.3.10, 19–39; 1.5.26; 1.8.10.

[110] Ibid., 1.6.6, citing Eph. 5. 22–4.

[111] Ibid., 1.5.24, 1.6.41.

[112] Ibid., 1.6.2, 30.

[113] Ibid., 1.6.22.

the material effects of women's work.[114] And then there is the adamant rejection of any exchange between the spouses that might indicate the husband is in any way accountable to the wife – literally that husbands should give wives 'an account and rationalisation' of their actions: ('la raison et sens de leur maris').[115] While the text does not lose sight of the practical consequences of women's empowerment, in this particular case a deep moral concern is again brought to the fore. It centres on the sense of authorisation for, and ownership of, one's actions.

The wife's subordination to the husband furthermore reflects an aesthetic appreciation for 'the proper order of things'. The entire text, through its elaborate structure, is the testimony of a profound interest in aesthetic form. More specifically, this aesthetic dimension is reflected in the author's attention to conduct in public and thus to the role of witnesses of the wife's behaviour. He narrates with approval a husband's elaborate scheme to convince the neighbours that his runaway wife was actually returning home from a meritorious pilgrimage.[116] In the anecdotes about wagers on women's obedience, witnesses play a crucial role as arbiters and are then expected to testify to the reputation of the well-obeyed husband. Thus we can detect, as part of the concern for keeping status in society, an appreciation for how things look from the point of view of an audience (as with Salimbene in Chapter 1). The emphasis shifts to the *perception* of women's behaviour as an instantiation of the ideal form of domestic relations.[117]

In the domestic sphere as well, the wife occupies her position in a complex order in which all servants have their well-defined place. The sense of hierarchy is reflected in the epithet bestowed upon the wife: *sovereign* master of the household ('souverain maistre de vostre hostel') but only *after* (*après*) the husband.[118] In the fourteenth century, the novel word *souverain* was closer to the etymological sense of 'superior' (from the Latin *superanus*), with its visual and spatial connotations, and thus reflects an idea of order that is also aesthetic. Similarly, as regards the servants' position, it is noteworthy that on occasion the author is not concerned with exactly what tasks they perform; these are

---

[114] Ibid., 1.7, 2.3.1–8; Roberta L. Krueger, '"Nouvelles choses": Social Instability and the Problem of Fashion in the *Livre du Chevalier de la Tour Landry*, the *Ménagier de Paris*, and Christine de Pizan's *Livre de Trois Vertus*', in Kathleen Ashley and Robert L. A. Clark (eds), *Medieval Conduct* (Minneapolis, 2001), pp. 49–85, at pp. 64–5.

[115] Brereton and Ferrier (eds), *Ménagier*, 1.6.19.

[116] Ibid., 1.8.12.

[117] Cf. Arnold, *Belief and Unbelief*, pp. 147–8.

[118] Brereton and Ferrier (eds), *Ménagier*, 2.3.6, 2.4.

listed in a general way. The point is simply that the servants be occupied, 'one up here, the other down there', and that they busy themselves earning their pay.[119] This does not reflect a practical concern but an ideal of industriousness and order to which the servants must conform for its own sake.

At other times, aesthetic concerns converge with pragmatic goals. In the instructions on how to make confession, the author insists on a precise, comprehensive formula,[120] signalling the importance of using those exact words for the success of the sacrament, which is capital for one's salvation. This reflects not only an aesthetic appreciation for ceremonial, as with the attention he pays to the ritual of Mass, but also the sense that the completion of a formalised sequence of speech acts is crucial for producing the intended effects. This emphasis on the effectiveness of form is a more general characteristic of medieval perspectives on action, from liturgical to legal contexts.[121] Its presence in the manual on domestic conduct of a non-professional writer is noteworthy inasmuch as it documents the influence of this model on the literate bourgeois milieu.

One source of tension within the social imaginary that informed the imperative of obedience to the husband affords us an opportunity to understand how a non-elite individual responded to cultural models. Notwithstanding the thesis of the woman's obedience to the man and the uses to which it was put, the Christian doctrine entailed a potentially empowering ideal of the individual person, even inasmuch as it prescribed social roles.[122] But this ideal conflicted with the author's intentions about the wife's role, notwithstanding that, confident of his well-organised programme of domestic relations, he occasionally affords his wife empathic regard, explaining for instance how she can find consolation and even use her powers of persuasion to pacify a mischievous husband.[123] The venerable tradition of writings on the vices and virtues articulated a normative discourse at once restraining – its crux was refraining from certain practices on ethical grounds – and potentially empowering. Even if it relegated practical considerations in favour of moral imperatives, it nevertheless placed the individual in the centre and offered a model of self-empowerment by indicating how one can counteract perilous influences (exemplified by the vices) with the aid of moral principles

---

[119] Ibid., 2.3.16.

[120] Brereton and Ferrier (eds), *Ménagier*, 1.3.37–47, 71–4.

[121] Alain Boureau, *La loi du Royaume: Les moines, le droit et la construction de la nation anglaise (XIe–XIIIe siècles)* (Paris, 2001), pp. 73–5.

[122] Arnold, *Belief and Unbelief*, pp. 144–5.

[123] Brereton and Ferrier (eds), *Ménagier*, pp. xxviii–xxx, 1.9.

(introduced under the aegis of the virtues). As we have seen, Bruyant's *Chemin* is a good example of a text that draws on the tradition of vices and virtues to articulate the ideal of the rational, autonomous individual agent. A key normative feature of late-medieval religious culture, individual confession, instituted a dialogue between the confessor and the individual believer. However asymmetric – power and authority were on the side of the confessor – and informed by a rigorous moral system and a probing method of inquiry about its transgressions, this dialogue invited the believers' participation and prompted them to examine their deeds methodically, if only to relate them to moral categories.[124] It thus stimulated a 'hermeneutics of the self', albeit one in which guilt played a key role.[125] Self-reflection, even if initiated under the strict guidance of the confessor, proved crucial for the individual's sense of moral and social agency.

But these trends towards individual autonomy favoured men far more than women.[126] The *Ménagier*'s author was certainly committed to a programme that limited the wife's agentive potential. The proliferation of detailed instructions suggests that he grasped women's capacity for acting autonomously. Admittedly, he wanted the wife to internalise certain principles. But in other respects the treatise simply instructs her to remember and execute mechanically specific instructions. In this sense reflection and rationalisation are discouraged. No matter the consequences of her actions, the wife will always be excused and even praised if she dutifully seeks the husband's instructions, even under extraordinary circumstances.[127] It is instructive to compare the *Ménagier*'s directives for making confession with those in *La somme le roi*, a popular moral treatise on which the author relied. In *La somme* there are clear elements of the hermeneutics of the self, like the injunction to reflect on one's life – 'recourder ta vie' – and recall how many times one has harboured sinful thoughts.[128] By contrast, the *Ménagier* instructs the wife to reproduce a standard formula

---

[124] Alexander Murray, 'Counselling in Medieval Confession', in Peter Biller and A. J. Minnis (eds), *Handling Sin: Confession in the Middle Ages* (York, 1998), pp. 63–77, at pp. 75–7.

[125] Lochrie, 'Desiring Foucault'.

[126] For women confession was both 'a potential source of female empowerment' and 'a mechanism of disempowerment'; Dyan Elliot, 'Women and Confession: From Empowerment to Pathology', in Mary C. Erler and Maryanne Kowaleski (eds), *Gendering the Master Narrative: Women and Power in the Middle Ages* (Ithaca, NY, 2003) pp. 31–51, at p. 40. On women's empowerment, see Sharon Farmer, 'Persuasive Voices: Clerical Images of Medieval Wives', *Speculum*, 61:3 (1986), 517–43.

[127] Brereton and Ferrier (eds), *Ménagier*, 1.6.25.

[128] Brayer and Leurquin-Labie (eds), *La somme*, p. 119.

encompassing all the imaginable forms of the seven sins, paying almost no attention to whether she committed any, some, or all of these transgressions.[129] This is an exhortation to confess, in the exact words that are put into her mouth, a precise list of infractions grouped under specific headings (avarice, envy, etc.) – not to reflect on one's experiences and discern whether some of them fall within specific moral categories. Self-reflection is thus obviated; the sense of responsibility for one's actions, which is a source of awareness about one's agentive potential, is replaced by a general notion of guilt. All this brings into focus the author's priorities. His interest in discouraging women from self-reflection becomes clear if we recall that he was not ignorant of the idea of confession as a hermeneutical practice. He acknowledges that contrition is the prerequisite for confession and that one should recall the circumstances of one's transgressions, including the inner motivation,[130] but immediately abandons this line of thought in favour of the ready-made formulas. Furthermore, his use of anecdotes and *exempla* is not geared towards moral edification, which implies reflection; instead, it seeks to eliminate any doubt about the perils of straying from the path prescribed in the text. Marshalled one after another, the stories aim to overwhelm the audience with cases of domestic insubordination and their dire repercussions on the female perpetrators. This last aspect is invariably emphasised as the moral of the story.

We return to his reading of the *Chemin*, which now appears profoundly shaped by the same concern with women's potential to act autonomously. The poem clearly made an impression on the *Ménagier*'s author, who copied it in lieu of his own words of advice on hard work, relying on the *Chemin* to demonstrate 'qu'est diligence et qu'est parseverance', 'what diligence and perseverance are all about'.[131] The *Chemin* certainly extols the value of labor, particularly with the crucial scene of the *chastel de Labour*, but even a cursory reading makes plain the centrality of *Raison*, the main allegorical character of the poem. Why then did the *Ménagier*'s author not draw the wife's attention to reason, alongside labour and perseverance, as one of the lessons to be learned from the *Chemin*? The answer is certainly that *Raison* empowers the protagonist to live a meaningful social existence; equipped with the tools of practical

---

[129] Exceptionally, one is enjoined to mention how frequently one has lusted; Brereton and Ferrier (eds), *Ménagier*, 1.3.103; introspection is suggested in passing in 1.3.1; also see Ferrier, 'A Husband's Asides', p. 260.

[130] Brereton and Ferrier (eds), *Ménagier*, 1.3.20–5.

[131] Ibid., 2.1.6.

reason, the bourgeois emerges in the *Chemin* as an autonomous agent. Clearly this was not the *Ménagier*'s design for the young wife.[132]

Conduct literature and the livres de raison

Some of the issues highlighted in the previous pages, about control, accountability, and work within the domestic sphere, have a familiar ring – we have already encountered them in connection with the *livres de raison*. The *Ménagier*'s author did not leave us a *livre de raison*, but keeping such a register was not unusual in his milieu; we know of at least one case in which notes like those in the *livres* were made in the manuscript of a conduct book,[133] and, as we have seen with Esperon and Benoist, the *livres* occasionally included advice. Such points of convergence call for a brief comparison between the family socioeconomic records and the domestic conduct literature of fourteenth-century France. To begin with, this comparison validates some of the *Ménagier*'s claims to verisimilitude, for instance as regards domestic helpers like Master Jehan the steward (*le despensier*), who is instructed to keep a 'papier de la despense' or account book about the servants' employment in the household; this recalls the accounting records of the *livres*.[134] Similarly, the *Ménagier*'s use of lists as a device for organising practical information reflects a late-medieval practice that can be abundantly documented from the *livres de raison*. More significantly, the evidence of both the *livres de raison* and the Italian *ricordi* corroborate the *Ménagier* with respect to the coexistence among the late-medieval urban middle strata of an emphasis on Christian devotion and a meticulous concern for material aspects. Both kinds of texts, personal records and domestic treatises, speak to a widely shared aspiration to accommodate the tough-minded socioeconomic pragmatism needed to secure the prosperity of the family with the religious values that largely defined late-medieval culture. Both several *livres de raison* and the *Ménagier* open with religious considerations and incorporate prayers in their text, before articulating a conservative and risk-averse socioeconomic perspective. The Massiot family's *livre*

---

[132] The exception that confirms the rule: comparing the woman to a chess player who must reflect carefully before making a move. Significantly, this refers to the time *before* a woman remarries, i.e., when she is without a husband; Brereton and Ferrier (eds), *Ménagier*, 1.8.13.

[133] Kathleen Ashley, 'The *Miroir des Bonnes Femmes:* Not for Women Only?', in Kathleen Ashley and Robert L. A. Clark (eds), *Medieval Conduct* (Minneapolis, 2001), pp. 86–105, at pp. 90–1.

[134] Brereton and Ferrier (eds), *Ménagier*, 2.3.5; cf. Louis Guibert (ed.), *Nouveau recueil de registres domestiques limousins et marchois* (2 vols, Paris, 1895), vol. 1, pp. 59, 74, 103.

de raison even offers instructions about attending Mass similar to those in the *Ménagier*. But the appeal of eclecticism leads both the *livres* and the *Ménagier* to juxtapositions that the church found profoundly suspicious: the *livres*' mix of healing prayers and magical potions and invocations finds its counterpart in the *Ménagier*, which instructs that the formula *abgla, abgli, alphara, asy* should be recited together with three *Pater Nosters*.[135]

Equally relevant are the differences between the texts. Orally transmitted knowledge, though certainly important in the *Ménagier*, plays a greater role in the *livres*.[136] Occasionally, an episode like the one recorded by the merchant Gérald Massiot reveals significant cultural distinctions. Massiot was so touched by the sermon of a preaching friar that he summarised it in his *livre de raison* for the moral instruction of the family.[137] For him, the sermon represented a remarkable cultural event, whereas for the *Ménagier*'s author the equivalent role was played by his literary encounters with an array of sources. On the crucial issue of socioeconomic advice, the *livres* are selective and pragmatic, their instructions more clearly tailored to the authors' specific circumstances: canon law and notarial formulas were copied down in the *livres* of the jurists Guillaume d'Erquis and Pierre Esperon, while the *livre* of the Massiot merchants featured advice on drawing business contracts. As discussed in Chapter 3, Esperon emphasised the applicability of lessons verified *per experienciam* and preferred not to delve into issues perceived as too complex and context-specific adequately to be explained in writing. In this respect the comparison with the *livres* brings into relief the *Ménagier*'s originality. Its literary interests and tendency to theorise daily conduct seem all the more remarkable in light of the *livres de raison*, and particularly its underlying premise that detailed written rules and instructions can encompass all the domains of life (cf. Morelli's programme for the instruction of his heirs in Chapter 4).

On the key issue of gendered social conduct, and particularly women's possibilities to act autonomously, the *livres de raison* and the *Ménagier* are closely aligned. They share a male-oriented instructional discourse aimed at ensuring the success of the *caput familias* as an autonomous agent acting upon the world in pursuit of the family's prosperity; its corollary in the *Ménagier* are the injunctions aimed at restraining and subordinating the wife (see below).

---

[135] Brereton and Ferrier (eds), *Ménagier*, 2.3.37–8.

[136] On literacy and orality, see Brigitte Bedos-Rezak, 'Civic Liturgies and the Urban Records in Northern France, 1100–1400', in Barbara A. Hanawalt and Kathryn L. Reyerson (eds), *City and Spectacle in Medieval Europe* (Minneapolis, 1994), pp. 34–55, at p. 41.

[137] Louis Guibert (ed.), *Livres de raison, registres de famille et journaux individuels, limousins et marchois* (Paris, 1888), pp. 113–14.

What is more, the *Ménagier*'s misgivings about women's status within the marriage are rooted in late-medieval ideas of social accountability of which the *livres de raison*, with their meticulous tallies of kinship and affinity ties, gifts, counter-gifts, and services rendered, are the perfect expression. At a time when accountability was becoming more and more important, both socially and institutionally, the head of the family considered himself accountable to his male heirs but not to his wife. In the *livres de raison* the duty to act as a responsible administrator of the dowry surfaces as a legal obligation rather than an internalised moral duty, while women's domestic labour remains unacknowledged. Occasionally, one sought to dispense with the socially and legally accepted requirement. The advice received in writing from an ancestor and copied in Benoist's *livre de raison* recommends a marriage contract to circumvent local custom and prevent the widow from claiming half of the estate.[138] The *Ménagier*'s author echoed such sentiments. While he took seriously the event of his wife's remarrying after his death and advised her on how to treat her future husband, he makes no reference to her dowry, although this was a chief consideration in the remarrying of widows. I suggest this is because in respect to her dowry the wife would emerge as a partner to whom the husband owes an account – an idea that he vehemently opposes. Unrestrained by customary law, the *Ménagier* could go further in denying the wife a well-defined set of rights. The unlikely story, a version of which is narrated in the farce *Le cuvier*, of the couple who write their respective rights in a *cedule*, a private deed, to which the wife adheres strictly with dire repercussions on her,[139] aims to discredit precisely the idea of marriage as a more equal partnership. For the *Ménagier*'s author the wife is not a full moral person and the husband should not be accountable to her – 'acoustumé a rendre compte de ses vouloirs a sa femme' or 'in the habit of justifying his designs to his wife'[140] – or appear in such a light publicly. This status is confirmed by the absence of advice about cultivating social ties: social agency – acting on the family's behalf in the social arena – remained the husband's prerogative.

---

[138] Louis Guibert (ed.), 'Le livre de raison de Etienne Benoist', *Bulletin de la Société Archéologique et Historique du Limousin*, 29 (1881), 225–318, at pp. 250–2.

[139] Brereton and Ferrier (eds), *Ménagier*, 1.6.11–12; Christine M. Rose, 'Glossing Griselda in a Medieval Conduct Book: *Le Ménagier de Paris*', in Ewa Ciszek and Łukasz Hudomięt (eds), *The Propur Langage of Englische Men* (Frankfurt, 2008), pp. 81–103, at pp. 92–7.

[140] Brereton and Ferrier (eds), *Ménagier*, 1.6.19.

Actants and agents; the agency of the subaltern

The *Ménagier*'s focus on agency should be quite clear by now, from the formal aspects of action to the strategic possibilities opened by pragmatic literacy to the individual's sense of accountability and effectiveness in the world. What is more, the text emphasises the wife's material dependence on the husband and justifies his preeminent status and the demand to attend to his desires by his role as provider for the family. While this certainly brings economic power into the spotlight, it becomes subsequently apparent that in contrast with the wife's domesticity, the husband's depiction as busy seeking lucrative deals, working late, and travelling long distances amounts to the definition of two spheres of agency, the former subordinated to the latter.[141] This division of labour, and its consequences for the spouses' different status, is spelled out clearly: 'serve and arrange that [your husband] is served in your home. And you can rely on him in outside matters, because if he is a good man he will put more effort and hard work in these than you can wish'.[142] Lastly, the wife's dependence is also portrayed as a personal need for the husband's affection and moral support,[143] which calls for an analysis informed by social scientific models of personhood.

Actor–network theory arguably offers the conceptual scheme that captures most suggestively the position of the *Ménagier*'s wife in relation to the husband, from the crucial perspective of their different models of agency. In the text the *caput familias* is imagined as the source of initiatives, plans, and microstrategies, while the wife must simply act out his instructions in precise detail. She is responsible for her actions but only within the strict parameters set by her husband's designs. In a sense, it might be argued that even in the model envisaged by the author she retains some degree of agency, if by agency one means strictly the capacity to generate effects in the world. The merits of this inclusive view of agency notwithstanding, there is a heuristic case for foregrounding those aspects of agency revolving around reflexivity, intentionality, and strategies. From this angle one can see clearly that in the *Ménagier* the *pater familias* emerges as a social actor in a way in which the wife does not. Unlike the autonomous agent embodied by the husband, the *Ménagier*'s wife resembles most closely an actant – a term used in actor–network theory to designate an entity that produces effects in the world but whose reflexivity can be bracketed analytically. Put simply, an actant is something that acts; it is

---

[141] Ibid., 1.7.1.
[142] Ibid., 1.7.6.
[143] Ibid., 1.6.32.

a figuration of action more than an assignation of initiative or strategising.[144] The notion captures the contrast in the *Ménagier* between the husband as a full moral agent and the wife imagined as executing his instructions mechanically.[145] Another pair of concepts from actor–network theory seems apposite; thus, Bruno Latour distinguishes between a mediator and an intermediary:

> An *intermediary* ... is what transports meaning or force without transformation: defining its inputs is enough to define its outputs. [...] *Mediators*, on the other hand ... transform, translate, distort, and modify the meaning or the elements they are supposed to carry. [...] No matter how apparently simple a mediator may look, it may become *complex*; it may lead in multiple directions which will modify all the contradictory accounts attributed to its role.[146]

As evident in the repeated injunctions to fulfil the husband's orders exactly and without delay, the author envisaged for the wife the role of an intermediary and was apprehensive about her potential for acting as a complex mediator. The view of women as self-reflexive agents does surface in some well-defined contexts, for one because the wife's capacity to internalise general principles builds the dispositions required for executing effectively the husband's precise instructions. This adamant effort to prevent women from acting according to their own will affords us the opportunity to grasp their real potential for agency in late-medieval society – a topic to which we now turn through an exploration of the microstrategies that can be gleaned from the *Ménagier*.

The unavoidable necessity of delegating to the wife a measure of control over the management of the household posed a challenge to the author, which he tried to meet by devising a scheme in which important aides like *maistre* Jehan are at once subordinated to the wife and meant to keep in check her initiatives, usually in the guise of offering her assistance. And yet the author's reluctance to delegate this vital responsibility even with the precaution of including the top aides in the process is evident in the concluding remark on the topic: 'You should nevertheless inform me in private about these matters and act by my counsel, for you are too young and can easily be deceived by

---

[144] Bruno Latour, *Reassembling the Social: An Introduction to Actor–Network-Theory* (Oxford, 2005), pp. 46–7, 54–5.

[145] For a more charitable view of the *Ménagier*'s designs for women, see Glenn Burger, 'Laboring to Make the Good Wife Good in the *Journées Chrétiennes* and *Le Ménagier de Paris*', *Florilegium*, 23:1 (2006), 19–40, at p. 36.

[146] Latour, *Reassembling the Social*, p. 39.

your own people.'[147] Dame Agnes is explicitly charged with not only serving but also instructing (*endoctriner*) her young mistress.[148]

And still the *Ménagier*'s author feared the disruption of his ideal household. By his own account, his anxieties about women's self-assertion were shared widely in his milieu. To impress upon the wife the importance of obeying the husband, he invokes the behaviour of the men of his day, specifically their apprehension vis-à-vis women's assertiveness, and if he wanted to remain credible he could not have exaggerated too much.[149] Disempowered by structural conditions that favoured the husband, both economically and legally, the wife retained the capacity to subvert the husband's orders through clever tactics, manoeuvring between his injunctions, and manipulating his structural power through her agency. The author's examples in this respect reflect observed patterns of behaviour among contemporary women and come across as realistic.[150] In one example, the wife explores in conversation the husband's intentions in a particular matter and once she realises they are different from hers changes the topic so that she might act on her own designs with the excuse that he never made his intentions known. To the author this seems an appalling thing, meant to 'trick, deceive, and test her husband' ('barater, decevoir et essaier son mary');[151] but it was a strategy employed by numerous women, including, as he experienced personally, one of his wife's cousins. Another example denounces a wife's delays in matters where the husband has issued a clear restriction. She waits until the husband is absorbed by work and either forgets his injunction or leaves on a journey, then she proceeds according to her own designs, relying on his neglectfulness – and wrongly so, the author emphasises, assuring the audience that in the end the husband realises his wife's deception.[152]

Such examples hinge on the manipulation of time, a tactic which, as discussed in the previous chapters, is preferred by the disempowered and subaltern, who are unable to control the field of play and consequently make tactical use of the timing of their own actions to subvert the schemes of social superiors and establish themselves as partners in a dialogue of power. Inasmuch as her actions are monitored and the tactics of shrewd women exposed, the *Ménagier*'s wife receives a similar treatment to the servants and workers, even as she is herself warned against their clever negotiation tactics, in which the timing

[147] Brereton and Ferrier (eds), *Ménagier*, 2.3.4.
[148] Ibid., 2.3.7.
[149] Ibid., 1.6.31.
[150] Ibid., 1.6.19–20, 23, 27, 31, 39–42, 45–6, 62.
[151] Ibid., 1.6.46–7.
[152] Ibid., 1.6.62.

of action is of the essence. This recalls how the author intended to control the household servants and the wife alike by having them control each other, in an economy of human relations in which the wife is clearly included with the subaltern. Hired for several days to perform heavy work in the household, the labourers' subterfuge is to avoid a firm agreement on their compensation in the first place, promising to settle for the remuneration their employer will deem appropriate once the task is completed. Their tactic is to overcharge the bill at the end, claiming that more work was needed than initially anticipated and threatening a scandal that would give their employers *male renommee* or bad reputation. Even servants are in the habit of gossiping and speaking ill of their former employers (in fact a microstrategy for putting pressure on their masters).[153] The issue was clearly sensitive at the time, as the *Chemin* confirms, albeit from the employee's perspective, warning that in service one must gain the benevolence of one's master or risk being defamed (*diffamer*) by him and thus rendered unemployable.[154] The *Ménagier*'s author too is adamant that labourers are not really in any position to dictate terms, because they have only their wages and are always looking for employment.[155] Thus the house's mistress, aided by her chief servants, can frustrate their tactics if she knows how to act. The emphasis here is not on power, because the text makes clear that economic power is all on the side of the bourgeois household, but on the subaltern's actions and capacity to improvise new social scenarios. Similarly, the admonitions to execute the husband's orders without delay, particularly in the case of gardening when not only the precise time of the year but even the duration of specific procedures is essential,[156] reflect the realisation that many tasks depend on the individual. They do not require control of resources, like money and household goods, but only her own time.

The subaltern's agency pushed the author to explore their world and habits, if only the better to counter their tactics. This was a hermeneutics of suspicion in which tests play an important role. In selecting valets and chambermaids their inward dispositions and personal histories must be ascertained through examination and inquiry. Thus the wife and *maistre* Jehan are instructed to select workers who seem *paisibles*, calm and amiable – in contrast with the workers' usual hard bargaining. The bourgeois misgivings vis-à-vis the working poor take the form of the suspicion that every such person is the possessor of a hidden truth about himself or herself – an idea that had a remarkable posterity

---

[153] Ibid., 2.3.2, 2.3.5.

[154] Pichon (ed.), *Chemin*, 23, col. 1.

[155] Jean-Pierre Leguay, *La rue au Moyen Âge* (Rennes, 1984), pp. 141–3.

[156] Brereton and Ferrier (eds), *Ménagier*, 2.2.3.

in the early modern period.¹⁵⁷ That truth should be extracted through investigation before a decision is made to employ them, because 'were they without stain, they would be mistresses and not maids – which I can also say about the men'.¹⁵⁸ Banal tasks are used to test whether the wife has internalised the crucial lessons of obedience and discipline. Conversely, in a typical example of the effort to preserve women's subordinate status, the possibility that the wife might put the husband to the test is denounced through an anecdote in which a wife is severely punished by her husband for having attempted to test his tolerance.¹⁵⁹

However biased, this effort to understand the perspective of social inferiors is significant because it shows how the social imaginary impinged on the text. This can also be seen in the case of women's conduct in public. Body posture and small changes in a woman's attire were a great source of anxiety for the author,¹⁶⁰ not only because of their public dimension and element of self-representation but because their medium of expression, the woman's own body, cannot be easily appropriated by men. The behaviour of some bourgeois women made the author realise that the model of conduct he advocated could not be taken for granted. It was not a hegemonic *doxa* from which one might err but which was not contested in principle. The 'rebellious women' who asserted themselves in public or inside the house had a sense of purpose – stimulated perhaps by the example of women who in the late Middle Ages reached more significant socioeconomic positions.¹⁶¹ Perhaps in his effort to rebuke their conduct the author makes it seem more programmatic than it was; but even if the concepts that he imputes to them – 'auctorité, maistrise et seignourie': 'authority, dominion, and lordship'¹⁶² – were his own, the overall sense is that such women acted as autonomous agents, fashioning their own behaviour. They offered defences that irritated the author because it justified their self-fashioning by appealing to the same moral ground that he claimed:

---

[157] When 'the other' was thought of 'in terms of secrets awaiting discovery'; Elizabeth Hanson, *Discovering the Subject in Renaissance England* (Cambridge, 1998), p. 2.

[158] Brereton and Ferrier (eds), *Ménagier*, 2.3.5.

[159] Ibid., 1.6.48–60.

[160] Ibid., 1.2.1.

[161] Claudia Opitz, 'Life in the Late Middle Ages', in Christiane Klapisch-Zuber (ed.), *A History of Women in the West*, vol. 2, *Silences of the Middle Ages* (Cambridge, MA, 1992), pp. 267–317, at pp. 292–304; André Chédeville, Jacques Le Goff, and Jacques Rossiaud, *La ville en France au Moyen Âge: Des Carolingiens à la Renaissance*, rev. edn (Paris, 1998), pp. 348–9.

[162] Brereton and Ferrier (eds), *Ménagier*, 1.6.19.

to the charge that they dressed too informally, they would answer that they were too humble to care for their appearance. In another example, the wife might act symbolically to affirm her self-worth, purposively disregarding the command to put a token in safekeeping to make the point that the husband ought to have done her the honour (*honneur et reverence*) of conveying its special significance.[163] Such dissenting voices pushed the author into a dialogue of sorts. He is conscious that the young wife, ignoring his warnings against gossiping with other women, will find in their milieu a different model of conduct, and he realises that a compelling case must be made against it. Note that his treatment of such occurrences is vehement but not dismissive. His rebuttal of the women who use the excuse of humility for their studied sartorial negligence is visceral: they are plainly lying (*elles mentent*);[164] yet he devotes a lengthy paragraph to meticulously exposing their pretence. Sometimes he feels the need to make the case for his demands. Particularly on key issues such as the wife's obedience he writes in a persuasive mode, arguing his case at great length. As intimated above, many of the stories and anecdotes marshalled to this end fall short of the standards of rational demonstration. Their reasoning is often strained, the better to prove the author's point and dispel any doubts. But indirectly this indicates the perceived need to make the strongest possible case for an issue that was clearly contested, otherwise such vast reserves of persuasion would not have been required.[165] On rare occasions, the author concedes a point. He realises that the games and wagers about wives' obedience, which some women resisted, are morally objectionable, and justifies them simply through men's need for entertainment.[166] The acknowledgement of a possible contestation and the sense that an explanation is necessary resonate with the idea of a dialogue, albeit more limited than in the *Chemin*.

Lastly, the author's anxieties about women's agency are reflected in the choice of the narrative strategy on which to found the text's instructional discourse. From the very beginning the narrative figure of the wife is constructed as young, inexperienced, and by her own admission uneducated,

---

[163] Ibid., 1.1.10; 1.6.22.

[164] Ibid., 1.1.10.

[165] The increased number and tone of texts about women in the late Middle Ages has been interpreted as indicating women's diminishing status; Didier Lett, *Famille et parenté dans l'Occident médiéval, V^e–XVe siècle* (Paris, 2000), pp. 172–5. But equally such writings may have been a reaction to women's affirmation in society.

[166] Brereton and Ferrier (eds), *Ménagier*, 1.6.43

therefore eager to be taught.[167] The emphasis on the wife's ignorance reveals the author's awareness of how crucial the claim to a monopoly of moral and practical knowledge was for his programme of domestic relations. While the author does not relinquish the initiative for writing the text, he emphasises that it answers her own pleas for guidance and instruction. This framing serves the important function of precluding possible contestations of his authority and resistance to his propositions; in effect, it transforms the young wife's figure from a potential dissenter into an advocate of his programme. But in seeking to create the appearance of a consensus, the author indirectly reveals that in reality things were quite different. That this discursive strategy seemed necessary confirms his concern over women's potential to contest patriarchal claims to knowledge and act autonomously. Ironically, then, at the moment the *Ménagier*'s wife briefly emerges as a moral agent, her voice reaching us if only indirectly, she lends support to the husband's designs. The explanation is that her silence on this matter would have seemed portentous, in a world in which women remain a source of concern because of their agency.

A late-medieval social imaginary characterised by conflicting voices irrupts in both the *Chemin* and the *Ménagier*, as the two bourgeois, accidental authors, seek solutions to the hot issues of the day: social status and mobility, gender relations and domestic roles, and work. Central to both texts is the model of the individual agent empowered by practical reason and self-discipline. Who could embody the model remained a contested issue; Bruyant gestures towards the world of labourers, whereas the *Ménagier*'s author is adamant in his efforts to curtail their agency. Both deny it to women – the *Ménagier* systematically so – and thus individual autonomy remains a male model; on the whole the bourgeois wife is aligned with the socially subaltern. One significant way in which the social imaginary impinges on the texts is reflected in the anxieties that men of dominant socioeconomic status felt vis-à-vis the potential of the subaltern to subvert their designs through strategic action. The *Ménagier* strives to deprive the wife of power, but in so doing suggests the ways in which medieval women, although subject to socioeconomic domination and seemingly disempowered, were able to produce effects in the world through persuasion, assertive dress and body posture, and socioeconomic microstrategies. This finding serves as a corrective to a common approach among medievalists: empathising with the plight of the subaltern,

---

[167] Cf. Krueger, 'Identity Begins at Home', p. 23.

from medieval peasants to the urban proletariat to women, but displaying little appreciation for their agentive potential. In part this is the result of operating with a traditional understanding of power, but it also reflects a preference for medieval normative sources, often produced by the intellectual elite for the purposes of the political elite's ideal of self-representation. But in texts emanating from the educated bourgeoisie, such as the *Chemin* and the *Ménagier* or, in Chapter 4, Morelli's *ricordi*, the emphasis on social order emerges precisely as a response to a fluid and conflicted society. This casts the obsession with hierarchy in late-medieval sociopolitical treatises in a different light: not as a factual description of social relations but as a programmatic effort to prevent autonomous action by the subaltern. To what degree this was achieved in practice remains an open question. To return to the *Ménagier*, the excursuses and literary references meant to assert the author's erudition were not apt to create a clear-cut discourse. The text presents the reader with a range of ideas. The wife is warned against the perils of an aristocratic lifestyle yet the mini-treatise on hawking provides her with an example of the bourgeoisie's fascination with the nobility's way of life. For all the author's efforts to force different sources into a hegemonic *doxa* of obedience, diligence, and modesty, the potential for different interpretations persists. When he mentions the castle described in the *Chemin*, does he refer to the *chastel de Labour* or the *manoir de Richesse*?[168] Judged by its professed rationale of providing the wife with a text whereby she might educate herself according to the author's precepts, the treatise would not seem very effective.

---

[168] The latter reading is preferred by Greco and Rose in their introduction to *The Good Wife's Guide* (p. 51), but the former is just as plausible.

Conclusions

THESE CONCLUDING REMARKS relate the findings of the different case studies to each other so as to evince some larger patterns, to be tested by future research. The limitations of the case-study approach have been mitigated here by the analysis of contexts more rarely brought together in the same monograph, from the seigneuries of northern France to merchants and humanism in Florence, and from self-narratives in Latin to conduct literature in French. But far more work on agency in medieval society is needed before generalisations can be advanced.

Throughout this volume agency has been a vehicle for the exploration of a set of crucial issues for how people understood and planned their involvement in society. These range from shared representations about social interactions to socioeconomic strategies to individuals' sense of effectiveness in the world. They belong to the realm of practice and are often left out in studies that focus on social structures, be they systems of beliefs (the Christian view of human affairs as divinely ordained) or political order ('feudalism'). Ego-documents opened alternative entry points into Western European society c. 1100–1450, from the autobiographical insertions in chronicles to the registers of town notables and middle-rank aristocrats. The pairing of a construct more rarely used in medieval studies with an equally underexplored category of medieval sources has been particularly effective for understanding the individual's experience of the world. The social imaginary reconstructed from private records and vernacular experiments in conduct literature has taken us much closer to the laity's concerns than the doctrinarian writings of church intellectuals. This matters because of what one might call, with slight hyperbole, historians' battle for the soul of medieval culture: not infrequently the views that obtained within high intellectual circles are presented as '*the* medieval culture', although only the most salient parts thereof even reached a sizeable audience in the age before print and mass schooling, let alone be accepted by the lay majority with its more down-to-earth priorities. By contrast, the present analysis has spotlighted the lived values and strategic choices defined and recorded by the protagonists themselves in their *livres de raison* and *ricordi*. Even the terse evidence of thirteenth-century charters has been used to reconstruct local politics from the perspective of aristocrats concerned with building sociopolitical networks rather than obeying the rules of fief-holding.

The interest in how individuals experienced medieval society is not merely moral or aesthetic – a case of intellectual curiosity where some appreciation

Conclusions 261

for individuals' self-understanding makes a nice if not particularly insightful complement to our knowledge of history. Rather, the present focus on agency offers a corrective to the findings of structural approaches. The contrast between foregrounding agency as opposed to structure maps onto another one, between history from the grassroots and from above. As discussed in the Introduction, agency forms a recursive relation with structure. But whereas feudal relations or the rise of bourgeois dynasties are often viewed as an *explanans*, a historical form playing such a major structuring role that historians invoke it to explain social practices, they have been approached here as an *explanandum*, a development whose genesis and functioning need to be accounted for by attending to the interests and actions of a variety of agents. In making the case for how sociopolitical structures were created through human actions the present focus on agency has been heuristic. Certainly, the patterns of action and thought analysed were shaped by structural conditions such as the unequal distribution of resources; moreover, social forms normally viewed as constraints on action, from holding in fief to cultural models such as Christian divine providence, played a more complex structuring role that also enabled specific strategies. This notwithstanding, foregrounding agency has evinced how sociopolitical structures, notably in the case of a sizeable territorial unit such as the seigneurie of Picquigny, were built through individual agents' strategies and exchanges within flexible social networks. The book has spotlighted individuals' creative reworking and appropriation of received ideas and norms, from liege homage to divine intervention to the moral panoply of vices and virtues.

Not infrequently it became apparent that the structural picture of society needs to be amended because it fails to take into account how the dominant sociocultural forms were transformed in practice through individual agency. This is the case of the views of divine and human agency worked out in the context of their own lifeworlds by educated members of the urban middle strata, such as Galbert, Salimbene, Esperon, Morelli, and Dati. These views reflected one's personal synthesis of moral values and strategic objectives and were often at odds with church doctrine. The sources surveyed here are more detailed than for other periods and social groups – the early Middle Ages and the peasantry, for example. Notwithstanding the limits of the evidence in such cases, there remains something inadequate in abstracting from the general structures a sense of how social relations and economic exchanges worked in practice. Similarly, the obvious reality that individuals engaged with the key moral–religious norms and the material culture of Christianity does not imply that their approach was in line with church doctrine. More important than the constitutive elements of religious life, material culture included, was the mental framework in which they were fitted and which gave them meaning, as well as the logic underlying their use in specific contexts. The foregoing analyses of the writings of educated urban notables have shown that their moral–religious sentiments, and crucially the way they related to God, were informed by the experience of social exchanges and their sense of agency as individuals.

The larger argument of this book is that agency, more than power, offers the conceptual focus for making sense of the later Middle Ages. This argument restates the perspective of the historical actors themselves: although keenly aware of the power inherent in land, money, and the emerging institutions, they were even more concerned with the individual's potential for strategic action and manipulation – a function of individual skill and practical reasoning that could be improved through the 'techniques of the self'. This is most evident in the attention to the agency of the seemingly disempowered. To curb the agentive potential of subaltern groups, the urban middle strata of Florence and Paris relied on effective arrangements and schemes – what has been termed here an 'economy of human relations' – more than institutions. This opens a different perspective on the emphasis on order and hierarchy in texts and images emanating from the late-medieval political and intellectual elites: not as a description of social practice but as an effort to control it through literary and visual rhetoric. Human capital, from self-knowledge to habits of strategic action honed over years of social exchanges, trumped structural power, that is to say, power derived from the control of resources. Some of the actions taken by the lords of Picquigny can be read in the same register: for instance, Gérard's intervention to prevent local aristocrats from entering his rivals' orbit was motivated by concerns over the latter's network-building capabilities rather than a sense that they could match his financial or landed resources. Land and money were, of course, highly important, and as such subject to careful inventorying and accounting, which, however, focused on how resources were used and exchanged as part of the agents' strategies. Self-knowledge and social skills were paramount to Morelli. Salimbene, the scion of a well-off family who ended up as a Franciscan friar with practically no material possessions, became invested in an ideal of the autonomous individual empowered by his knowledge, skills, and the capacity to forge social ties. Medievalists are obviously much more familiar with power, but the present case for agency resonates with our general knowledge of the later Middle Ages. Agency is an analytical tool attuned to the more fluid medieval realities, characteristic of a less structured society with slowly developing institutions. This is not to deny the importance of structural factors, but many medievalists would accept that comparatively speaking in medieval society power emanated from human capital and actions to a greater degree than in the modern world. They ought also to accept the corollary point that agency, a construct focused on the links between self-knowledge, individual action, and power, should play a larger role in the study of medieval society.

A few more thoughts on the implications for medievalists' work of the present case for agency may be apposite, considering that the matter remains contentious. Indeed, even when it is recognised that individuals were more concerned with their competitors' potential for strategic action than with structural power rooted in inequalities of status or distribution of resources, there is a tendency to downplay the significance of this finding because individual courses of action do not seem the proper object of historical inquiry. This scepticism is in part grounded in the notion that 'people always do whatever works', ignoring that individuals' modes of acting upon the world are constructed culturally and differ widely across historical contexts; and in part reflects empirical problems. Shifting the emphasis from structures and power to agency is arguably more challenging than moving from the macro- to the microhistorical level, because it is not immediately clear with what to replace the familiar building blocks of historical writing. After all, part of the appeal of social class, the state, or religion is that as discrete entities they facilitate historians' efforts at synthesis. Yet this challenge should not be exaggerated; one obvious answer is to identify patterns of conduct and strategic action starting from individual cases. This is radically different from inferring the individual's experience from the general structural conditions, themselves reconstructed from normative sources. The medieval evidence does make it possible to write histories centred on social practices and networks rather than state institutions or political structures, but such studies are on the whole rather rare. This does not have to be so, as suggested by the example of modern history. Subversive practices and alternative social networks are crucial in the study of colonial societies or the Communist regimes of Eastern Europe, to the point of displacing as the fundamental blocks of historical analysis the putatively all-important institutions and ideology. While scholars of twentieth-century history find it important to investigate how much fiction there was in the institutions and ideology of the Eastern bloc and rethink the constitutive elements of their historical accounts accordingly, medievalists are more reluctant to question the role of the dominant structures of the medieval world, from the Church to lordship, and test whether more convincing histories can be told by foregrounding social practices, networks, and strategies.

Ego-documents have been chosen for this study because of their richness as sources for individual conduct, but the pairing of agency and ego-documents bore fruit in a rather unexpected way when a common pattern emerged from the different case studies. Writing and record-keeping were means of acting upon the world – not just for the emerging bureaucratic governments but for private individuals, aristocrats or bourgeois. From the careful assessment of resources to the ratification of gains through legal documents, a range of strategies were predicated on documentary practices. Literacy went hand in hand with numeracy; this hybridisation is best illustrated by the ample use of lists in both the *livres de raison* and the *ricordi*. Accounting was essential in a world of reciprocity, gift exchange, and support networks. The most powerful indication in this respect is the concern with (asymmetric) reciprocity even in one's relation to God. Even ostensibly narrative texts such as Tarneau's local chronicle are informed by an accounting logic. The accounting of the *livres de raison* and the *ricordi* charts the effects of written accountability, with roots in commercial practices and the new techniques of governance, on the traditional responsibility of the *pater familias*. Accountability for one's management of the family patrimony was apt to reinforce one's sense of effectiveness in the world, which became a fundamental building block of personal identity. It was moreover not limited to the intellectual elites. The self-narratives analysed here were not penned by high intellectuals, but nevertheless within them self-fashioning involved a fair deal of textual creativity in recasting the events of one's life in a favourable light, from Salimbene to Esperon.

This notwithstanding, in a study based wholly on textual evidence one risks being misled into making exaggerated claims about the role of the written word. In particular, to see in the rise of self-narratives evidence of 'the discovery' of the individual is to fall prey to a textual bias. Several ego-documents display a similar trajectory from more conventional types of writing to increasingly personal notations: Tarneau began to insert notes on family events in his local chronicle, Morelli moved from family history to the diary-style record of a spiritual experience, and Esperon and Dati started their registers to keep tabs on business and family matters and then included personal memoranda. That such leaps were made with relative ease suggests a strong interest in self-reflection among educated townsfolk. Once the practice of keeping track of business and family affairs in a register got off its feet, there was a good chance that personal reflections would find their way into the text. This confirms the basic intuition that self-reflection did not start with keeping a private register or writing a family chronicle but preceded them. But if writing did not force the merchants or legal professionals to ask themselves for the first time fundamental questions about identity and social conduct, it made it possible to articulate their intuitions and make them available for re-examination, tackle more complex subjects, and transmit more effectively their knowledge of society to their grandchildren.

Indeed, the advantages to be reaped from the mastery of pragmatic literacy extended into the near future. Once written down, conduct advice was protected from the hazards of oral transmission and could be examined more critically. Granted, specific strategies might be rendered obsolete by social change and backfire. But once written down in vivid detail the imperatives of self-knowledge and self-discipline offered an edge over social competitors. Put simply, the knowledge of society and human nature thus transmitted increased the cultural capital of literate families. In this sense the socioeconomic advice of the *livres de raison*, the *ricordi*, and even the vernacular conduct texts amounted to a set of intergenerational promissory notes, if not always of increase, at least of preservation of the family's social standing. While the concept of promissory notes is used by historians and sociologists mostly in relation to the public sphere and institutional programmes of reform, most notably modernisation,[1] it is noteworthy that here they pertain to the domestic sphere, and rather than envisaging widespread societal advancement were aimed at protecting the interests of bourgeois families. A case of both resemblance and discrepancy, this leads us to the connection between late-medieval social change and the emergence of European modernity, particularly as it concerns questions of agency.

As discussed in the Introduction, human agency is central to the definition of modernity in substantive rather than merely chronological terms, as a time of sweeping historical change;[2] the medieval notion of 'modern' was likewise characterised by optimism and confidence in human energies.[3] The affirmation of the individual has been a cornerstone of European modernity, highlighted by the philosopher Charles Taylor, a leading theorist of both modernisation and agency, as 'the finest achievement of modern civilisation'.[4] Some of the key findings of the present study speak directly to this issue, beginning with the personal investment in a model of individual autonomy in practically all the case studies analysed. Not merely an ideal but often fully functional in practice, from Salimbene to Morelli and Bruyant to Esperon, the autonomous individual agent was empowered by knowledge, self-discipline, and pragmatic rationality – all salient attributes of the modern subject, from Max Weber to

---

[1] Björn Wittrock, 'Modernity: One, None, or Many? European Origins and Modernity as a Global Condition', *Daedalus*, 129:1 (2000), 31–61, at pp. 36–8.

[2] Ibid., p. 39; Shmuel N. Eisenstadt, 'Some Observations on Multiple Modernities', in Domenic Sachsenmaier, Jens Riedel, and Shmuel N. Eisenstadt (eds), *Reflections on Multiple Modernities* (Leiden, 2002), pp. 29–31.

[3] See R. W. Southern, *Medieval Humanism and Other Studies* (Oxford, 1970), pp. 32, 49–50.

[4] Charles Taylor, *The Ethics of Authenticity* (Cambridge, MA, 1992), pp. 2–4.

the theorists of 'multiple modernities'. Bruyant's idea of the calculated individual capable of affecting his feelings so as to achieve social objectives remains a prominent concern of modern social thought.[5] The salience of individualism in our contemporary society notwithstanding, even a summary comparison suggests that medieval texts like the *Chemin* and the *Ménagier* were even more concerned with the individual. We place more emphasis on institutions; indeed, the tension between individual autonomy and the modern proliferation of impersonal bureaucracies was well captured by Weber.[6]

The *livres de raison*, the *ricordi*, and the vernacular conduct literature prompt us to re-examine some recent assertions of radical cultural difference between medieval and modern society. Charles Taylor contrasts the modern 'buffered' or bounded self with the earlier 'porous' self, characterised by vulnerability to surreptitious infiltration by external forces that take control of the mind and body.[7] Meaningful non-human agents were certainly part of medieval culture, but Taylor generalises from cases of possession and does not explain how belief in 'the porous self' functioned in practice. The cases analysed here, however, reveal how ordinary people situated themselves vis-à-vis ideas about the self's porosity. We have seen Morelli's robust response; as far as Bruyant is concerned, evil spirits did not register on his otherwise cautious psyche, which suggests that such threats did not seem real. We have discerned, however, an anxiety in the face of subversive external forces, personified in the *Chemin* by the vices, whose insidious influence can destabilise the individual. But what makes their assault so egregious is that it transgresses a personal space that is imagined precisely as bounded. The *Chemin* formulates a self-empowering programme for coping with such subversive threats, emphasising reason and self-discipline. While a few verses illustrate the concern that mental dispositions like compulsiveness can infiltrate the individual's psyche, they also express the belief that armed with the tools of reason the individual can prevent this

---

[5] Notably rational choice theory, which on the whole is quite different from Bruyant's ideas; Simon J. Williams, 'Is Rational Choice Theory "Unreasonable"? The Neglected Emotions', in Margaret Archer and Jonathan Tritter (eds), *Rational Choice Theory: Resisting Colonization* (London, 2000), pp. 59–61.

[6] Max Weber, *The Protestant Ethic and the Spirit of Capitalism*, trans. Talcott Parsons, repr. (Mineola, 2003), pp. 180–2. On late-modern institutions, see Ulrich Beck, Anthony Giddens, and Scott Lash, *Reflexive Modernisation: Politics, Tradition, and Aesthetics in the Modern Social Order* (Cambridge, 1994), pp. 59–60. As regards the individual in medieval society, compare the present argument with, e.g., Harald Kleinschmit, *Understanding the Middle Ages: The Transformation of Ideas and Attitudes in the Medieval World* (Woodbridge, 2000), pp. 63, 76–88.

[7] Charles Taylor, *A Secular Age* (Cambridge, MA, 2007), pp. 35–9.

transgression. Ultimately, the protagonist's home sustains the allegorical siege. The *livres de raison* similarly reveal the instrumental use of magical invocations and potions, whereas for Taylor the possibility of such 'counter-manipulation' is the prerogative of the modern self.[8]

Other developments highlighted in studies of modernisation, such as the valorisation of labour and everyday life, the rise of the vernacular, and the advances of pragmatic literacy, have been well documented in this book. Rather than rehearse these findings, the following pages will elaborate on the paradigm of modernity that underlies the present argument – bearing in mind that the focus remains squarely on making sense of the medieval evidence, not on an exegesis of modernisation theory,[9] a topic so vast that would require multiple volumes.

Because historians' work is so profoundly defined by the search for historical difference,[10] all talk of precedents and precursors is likely to be contentious, with the other side in the debate seeking to minimise them the better to highlight the significance of the change from the preceding period. All the more important, then, to get the tone of the argument right. The case for the medieval roots of European modernity is persuasive,[11] but its limitation is the inherent tendency to represent the period before the moment of 'birth' or 'origin' as essentially static.[12] The view of an early modernity originating in the later Middle Ages can potentially cause a disservice to the nuanced understanding of social change in the preceding period, say, before the twelfth century. Another kind of criticism of the historical origins approach

---

[8] From the early Middle Ages beliefs in supernatural agencies served to reassure individuals and communities that they could influence the natural world; see, e.g., Paul Edward Dutton, 'Thunder and Hail over the Carolingian Countryside', in Del Sweeney (ed.), *Agriculture in the Middle Ages: Technology, Practice, and Representation* (Philadelphia, 1995), pp. 112–37.

[9] The fundamental difference in the definition of modernity might be, as Charles Taylor argues, between culturalist and evolutionist accounts; 'Two Theories of Modernity', in Dilip Parameshwar Gaonkar (ed.), *Alternative Modernities* (Durham, NC, 2001), pp. 172–96.

[10] Paul Veyne, 'The Inventory of Differences', *Economy and Society*, 11:2 (1982), 173–98.

[11] Shmuel N. Eisenstadt, 'Multiple Modernities', *Daedalus*, 129:1 (2000), 1–30; Wittrock, 'Modernity: One, None, or Many?'; Shmuel N. Eisenstadt and Wolfgang Schluchter, 'Introduction: Paths to Early Modernities – A Comparative View', *Daedalus*, 127:3 (1998), 1–18.

[12] Daniel Lord Smail, 'Genealogy, Ontogeny, and the Narrative Arc of Origins', *French Historical Studies*, 34:1 (2011), 30–5.

highlights the perils of seeing 'false continuities' over the *longue durée*.[13] In this view, the problem with origins is not that they fail to go back long enough in history, but that they reach too far, misrepresenting the role of swift, radical transformations. This critique resonates with the view of modernisation as a time of accelerated change on multiple planes. In view of both these critiques, one needs to be open to a more radical possibility implied in the concept of 'multiple modernities', and approach the modernising trends in late-medieval society as a process with its own dynamic and cultural logic, one of several movements of social innovation and modernisation in history. Having said this, because these trends were manifest in the period immediately preceding the age known in European history as 'early modern', the historian must also be sensitive to the continuities (as well as the mutations) with the sixteenth to eighteenth centuries. The *livres de raison* are a good example of a medieval socioeconomic record that became widespread in the early modern period, and it is a limitation of the present study that it cannot follow through these sources the trajectory of the autonomous individual agent from the fourteenth to the eighteenth century. To reiterate, the point is not to redraw historical periodisation, claiming the thirteenth and fourteenth centuries for early modernity. Rather, it is to reflect from a longer historical perspective on a cluster of crucial developments documented to varying degrees across several centuries, from the late-medieval to the modern period.

One hurdle is a very literal reading of the evidence. Thus, because the language of late-medieval social reflection by the likes of Jacques Bruyant, the modest clerk, is traditional, one is tempted to regard it as alien to modernity; yet despite the dissonance with the present-day social idiom, the substance of late-medieval social thought remains relevant for the history of modernity. In particular, we must appreciate the sense of one's own worth and the self-confidence manifest in Bruyant's project to rethink society starting from his personal experiences. This is the sign of a modern outlook. To fashion a sense of his life and achievements, Bruyant went as far as envisaging the kind of society that could nurture his identity – supplanting in the process the social imaginary of the three orders with the more modern castle of labour. He wrote during what we now perceive as the crisis of European economy since the late thirteenth century, keenly aware of social changes such as the rise of unscrupulous *arrivistes*; similarly, the fourteenth-century epidemics are present in Esperon's and Morelli's records. This puts into perspective their shared aversion to risk. The *Chemin* has rather little on upward social mobility but that is because for

---

[13] Paul Veyne, *Quand notre monde est devenu chrétien (312–394)* (Paris, 2007), pp. 249–50, 266–8.

people in Bruyant's situation avoiding economic demise was the top priority.[14] The coexistence of fascination with aristocratic models and fear of ending up among the poor characterises the modern middle-class experience as well.[15] Their nostalgia for a simpler world should not overshadow the crucial fact that both Bruyant and Morelli articulated programmes aimed at moving forward under difficult conditions. Like many a late-medieval reformist, Bruyant took the path of introducing change under the prudent aegis of tradition.[16] But rather than fall back on traditional ideas about moderation and diligence, he adapted them to a changing society.

Because forward-looking, innovative ideas were mixed with tradition and a prudent economic outlook, the modernity of the late-medieval social imaginary inevitably falls short of the expectations of historians in search of retrospective teleology. For example, the advances in record-keeping and accounting since the twelfth century are mostly studied in relation to the development of state institutions, an association that lends them an air of general societal progress. The present findings suggest that on the contrary mastery of numbers and the written word represented a strategic asset that strengthened urban notables' hand vis-à-vis social subalterns and in the long run contributed to the rise of bourgeois dynasties in towns and cities.[17] As already intimated, the social models and promissory notes articulated in

[14] Cf. Élisabeth Crouzet-Pavan, 'La pensée médiévale sur la mobilité sociale, XIIe–XIVe siècle', in Sandro Carocci (ed.), *La mobilità sociale nel medioevo* (Rome, 2010), pp. 69–96, at pp. 94–5; on the early fourteenth-century socioeconomic background, see Sandro Carocci, 'Introduzione: la mobilità sociale e la "congiuntura del 1300": Ipotesi, metodi d'indagine, storiografia', in Sandro Carocci (ed.), *La mobilità sociale nel medioevo* (Rome, 2010), pp. 1–37, esp. pp. 7–14, 36.

[15] See Sherry Ortner, *Anthropology and Social Theory: Culture, Power, and the Acting Subject* (Durham, NC, 2006), pp. 25, 31–2.

[16] Beryl Smalley, 'Ecclesiastical Attitudes to Novelty, c. 1100–1250', in Derek Baker (ed.), *Church, Society and Politics: Papers Read at the Thirteenth Summer Meeting and the Fourteenth Winter Meeting of the Ecclesiastical History Society* (Oxford, 1975), pp. 113–31, at p. 99; Philippe Contamine, 'La crise de la royauté française au XIVe siècle: réformation et innovation dans le *Songe du vieil Pelerin* (1389) de Philippe Mézières', in Hans-Joachim Schmidt (ed.), *Tradition, Innovation, Invention: Fortschrittsverweigerung und Fortschrittsbewusstsein in Mittelalter* (Berlin, 2005), pp. 361–79; Odd Langholm, 'The Medieval Schoolmen (1200–1400)', in Todd Lowry and Barry Gordon (eds), *Ancient and Medieval Economic Ideas and Concepts of Social Justice* (Leiden, 1998), pp. 439–501.

[17] See Nicole Lemaître, *Le scribe et le mage: Notaires et société rurale en Bas-Limousin aux XVIe et XVIIe siècles* (Ussel, 2000), for the use of literacy and accounting to establish a monopoly on credit by a dominant family in a backwater town of early-modern Limousin.

ego-documents are directly at odds with the generous, 'egalitarian' (generally speaking) modernisation projects of the late eighteenth century. For some, notably Morelli and the *Ménagier*'s author, the point of socioeconomic advice was to empower the bourgeois in his dealings with farmers and servants. It is tempting to conceptualise agency as resistance to dominance, but in some cases it is this equivalence that needs to be resisted. Notwithstanding the political marginalisation experienced by Morelli and Dati, or Tarneau's deferential stance towards the aristocracy, they all aimed to consolidate their economic basis and move up the social ladder, rather than contest the sociopolitical order (Bruyant is a somewhat different case). The *Ménagier*'s author came strongly on the side of tradition. He was concerned that Bruyant's model of the calculated, self-reliant man might be appropriated by a woman and used to subvert the authority of the *pater familias*. Accordingly, he made clear to his young wife that the *Chemin* should be read for its praise of work. But this selfsame author who took a conservative stance on gender relations saw himself as an innovator through the writing of an unprecedented treatise.[18] By contrast, Bruyant resigned himself to the fact that women cannot grasp the import of his conduct advice. His text lacks the political agenda of late-medieval vernacular treatises, not unlike the *livres de raison*, in which the emphasis on socioeconomic accounting rarely leaves room for political reflections. It might be that sociopolitical reflection became more inclusive the more remote it got from the author's lifeworld. Thus Brunetto Latini, a respectable intellectual who authored a vernacular translation of Aristotle's *Ethics* and a *Tesoretto* that can be compared in some ways with the *Chemin*,[19] stressed the common good as a civic and economic ideal.

The point to make about a late-medieval social imaginary riven with contradictions is that engaging critically with the issues that characterise modernity is in itself a sign of modernity. We should not dismiss the outcome of this engagement simply because it does not approximate to our entrenched ideas about modernity. That educated laymen rather than high intellectuals

---

[18] Cf. Stephen Greenblatt's observation that a modern society is not necessarily a more altruistic one; *Renaissance Self-Fashioning: From More to Shakespeare* (Chicago, 1980), pp. 224–8.

[19] See John M. Najemy, 'Brunetto Latini's *Politica*', *Dante Studies*, 112 (1994), 33–51, at pp. 42–6, and Cary J. Nederman, 'Commercial Society and Republican Government in the Latin Middle Ages: The Economic Dimensions of Brunetto Latini's Republicanism', *Political Theory*, 31:5 (2003), 644–63; on civic consensus in the later Middle Ages, see Anthony Black, 'The Individual and Society', in J. H. Burns (ed.), *The Cambridge History of Medieval Political Thought, c. 350–1450* (Cambridge, 1988), pp. 588–606, at pp. 596–7.

drew on the tradition of vices and virtues to articulate a model of the autonomous individual agent, empowered by the internalisation of the principles of reason, diligence, and moderation, shows the potential of medieval cultural resources to foster social change. It may seem clichéd, but a fourteenth-century allegorical poem brings up issues that remain relevant in contemporary social thought; there is no good reason, anyway, to exclude history that is more than two hundred years old from informing our understanding of humanity. Thus, in the *Chemin*, the most relevant for the history of modernity of all the ego-documents analysed here, Bruyant was able to emphasise self-discipline and work ethic but reject uncontrollable acquisitiveness, in contrast with the compulsiveness of the modern capitalist, well-known through Max Weber's work.[20] That Bruyant's narrative alter-ego's solidarity with the labourers is rooted in his own plight speaks directly to the recent argument in moral philosophy for vulnerability as a fundamental human experience on which a more fair society can be built.[21]

Similarly, Giovanni Morelli's social views are entirely apposite in the context of the ongoing debate about what society consists of, besides individuals – 'individual humans' being first-year university students' unreflective answer to this question; social science professors try to problematise this answer by pointing to structures like social classes and cultural norms as fundamental constituents of social reality. Recently some of the underlying assumptions of social theory have been called into question, particularly the tendency to view 'the social' as already constituted by such fundamental building blocks as classes and institutions. This assumption leaves out the perennial work of reconfiguring and reconstituting the social world through ever-changing networks that link a variety of actors, human and non-human.[22] Now Morelli's social universe was first and foremost populated by individual agents, from fully individuated characters who stand out through their exemplary conduct to what he considered minor family members, including many of the women. But beyond individuals, Morelli's worldview was built not around classes and

---

[20] 'the *summum bonum* of this ethic, the earning of money ... is thought of so purely as an end in itself, that from the point of view of the happiness of, or utility to, the single individual, it appears entirely transcendental. ... Man is dominated by the making of money, by acquisition as the ultimate purpose of his life'; Weber, *Protestant Ethic*, p. 53.

[21] Alasdair MacIntyre, *Dependent Rational Animals: Why Human Beings Need the Virtues* (London, 1999).

[22] Bruno Latour, *Reassembling the Social: An Introduction to Actor–Network–Theory* (Oxford, 2005), esp. 4–8, 64–74.

institutions but webs of relations. This makes him modern in a sense not fully appreciated until the recent advances of sociology.

The depiction of the castle of labour in an illuminated manuscript of the *Chemin* is suggestive of the complex nature of late-medieval social change (see Plate 3). The visual representation of labourers populating an otherwise recognisably aristocratic castle, complete with gatehouse and drawbridge, evinces the inevitable tensions of social innovation. The image epitomises the poem's dual temporal orientation: anchored in tradition by the pull of cultural conventions, which, on the other hand, are reworked to formulate a social programme that in good measure reveals a forward-looking, modern vision. Such tensions and contradictions are an indicator of change. In a study of early modern subjectivity, Elizabeth Hanson shows that new forms of knowledge surface as 'improvisations around the fissures between the material conditions of life and the conceptual resources' of a culture. Thus, novel perspectives emerge 'not as principles from which a world order can be derived, but as contradictions in discourse and social practice'.[23] All the more important, then, to include in the history of a complex historical transition the situated worldviews of men like Bruyant, Morelli, Dati, or Esperon.

---

[23] Elizabeth Hanson, *Discovering the Subject in Renaissance England* (Cambridge, 1998), p. 3.

Bibliography

Manuscript sources

Amiens

ADS, MS 3 G 405 (microfilm 2 MI 38/1)
ADS, MS 13 H 4, Collectanea omnium bonorum quae in possessionem huius monasterii de Gardo, acquisitione et pietate fidelium, olim deuenere
ADS, MS 65 H 88 (microfilm 2 MI 38/6), Cartulary of Paraclet
BM, MS 781, Cartulaire de l'abbaye de Saint-Jean des Prémontrés d'Amiens

Limoges

ADHV, MS 1 G 8, Register of the bishop of Limoges titled 'Ac singularem'
ADHV, MS 1 G 9, Cartulary of the bishop of Limoges titled 'O Domina'
ADHV, MS 1 G 11, Cartulary of the bishop of Limoges titled 'Tuae hodie'
ADHV, MS 1 G 12, Livre des hommages
ADHV, MS 1 G 14, Livre des hommages
ADHV, MS 1 G 162, Agreement between the bishop of Limoges and the church of Saint-Junien
ADHV, MS 1 G 163
BFM, MS 6, Registre d'Aimeric et Gérald Tarneau, notaires à Pierre Buffière

Paris

AN, Q^1 1620
AN, R^1 634, dossier 4
AN, MS R^1 672, Cartulary of Picquigny
AN, MS R^1 675, dossier 1, Livre des stages
BA, MS 5259, MS de M. Du Cange etiqueté B
BN, MS français 808
BN, MS français 1563
BN, MS latin 17758, Cartulaire 'noir' de Corbie
IRHT, microfilm of Stockholm, Kungliga biblioteket, MS Vu 23

Philadelphia

The Free Library, Rare Book Department, MS Widener 1

Edited primary sources

Arbellot, François (ed.), *Chronique de Maleu, chanoine de Saint-Junien: Suivié de documents historiques sur la ville de Saint-Junien* (Saint-Junien and Paris, 1847).

Archambault, Paul (trans.), *A Monk's Confessions: The Memoirs of Guibert of Nogent* (University Park, PA, 1996).

Baird, Joseph L., Giuseppe Baglivi, and Giovanni Robert Kane (trans.), *The Chronicle of Salimbene de Adam* (Binghamton, NY, 1986).

Baldwin, John W. (ed.), *Les registres de Philippe Auguste* (Paris, 1992).

Beauvillé, Victor de (ed.), *Recueil de documents inédits concernant la Picardie* (4 vols, Paris, 1860–81).

Bonnet, Marie Rose (ed.), *Livres de raison et de comptes en Provence: Fin du XIVe siècle–début du XVIe siècle* (Aix-en-Provence, 1995).

Bono Giamboni, *Il Libro de' vizî e delle virtudi e il trattato di virtú e di vizî*, ed. Cesare Segre (Torino, 1968).

Bonvesin de la Riva, *De magnalibus urbis Mediolani*, ed. M. Corti (Milan, 1974).

Branca, Vittorio (ed.), *Mercanti scrittori: ricordi nella Firenze tra Medioevo e Rinascimento* (Milan, 1986).

—— *Merchant Writers: Florentine Memoirs from the Middle Ages and Renaissance*, trans. Murtha Baca (Toronto, 2015).

Brayer, Edith, and Anne-Françoise Leurquin-Labie (eds), *La somme le roi par frère Laurent* (Paris, 2008).

Brereton, Georgine, and Janet M. Ferrier (eds), *Le Ménagier de Paris: A Critical Edition* (Oxford, 1981).

Brucker, Gene (ed.), *Two Memoirs of Renaissance Florence: The Diaries of Buonaccorso Pitti and Gregorio Dati*, trans. Julia Martines, repr. (Prospect Heights, IL, 1991).

Buonaccorso Pitti, *Cronica*, ed. Alberto Bacchi della Lega (Bologna, 1905).

Cassirer, Ernst, Paul Oskar Kristeller, and John Herman Randall (eds), *The Renaissance Philosophy of Man* (Chicago, 1948).

Christine de Pizan, *Le livre des trois vertus*, ed. Charity Canon Willard and Eric Hicks (Paris, 1989).

Coluccio Salutati, *Political Writings*, ed. Stefano U. Baldassarri and trans. Rolf Bagemihl (Cambridge, MA, 2014).

Cropp, Glynnis M. (ed.), *La Voie de Povreté et de Richesse: Critical Edition* (Cambridge, 2016).

Delisle, Leopold (ed.), *Catalogue des actes de Philippe Auguste* (Paris, 1856).

—— *Recueil des historiens des Gaules et de la France* (24 vols, Paris, 1869–1904).

Estienne, J. (ed.), *Chartes de l'hôpital et de la ville d'Albert (Encre)* (Amiens, 1942).

Fabricatore, Bruto (ed.), *Fiore di Virtù*, 3rd edn (Napoli, 1870).

Galbert of Bruges, *De multro, traditione et occisione Karoli comitis Flandriarum*, ed. Jeff Rider, CCCM 131 (Turnhout, 1994).

—— *The Murder of Charles the Good*, trans. James Bruce Ross (Toronto, 1967, orig. 1959).
Giovanni di Pagolo Morelli, *Ricordi*, ed. Vittorio Branca (Firenze, 1956).
Gregorio Dati, *Istoria di Firenze*, ed. Giuseppe Manni (Firenze, 1735).
—— *Il Libro segreto*, ed. Carlo Gargiolli (Bologna, 1869).
Guibert de Nogent, *Autobiographie*, ed. and trans. Edmond-René Labande (Paris, 1981).
Guibert, Louis (ed.), 'Le livre de raison de Etienne Benoist', *Bulletin de la Société Archéologique et Historique du Limousin*, 29 (1881), 225–318.
—— *Livres de raison, registres de famille et journaux individuels, limousins et marchois* (Paris, 1888).
—— *Nouveau recueil de registres domestiques limousins et marchois* (2 vols, Paris, 1895).
—— *Documents, analyses de pièces, extraits et notes relatifs à l'histoire municipale des deux villes de Limoges* (2 vols, Limoges, 1897–1902).
Guillaume de Deguileville, *Pèlerinage de la vie humaine*, ed. J. J. Stürzinger (London, 1893).
Iohannis de Caulibus, *Meditaciones vite Christi*, ed. M. Stallings-Taney, CCCM 153 (Turnhout, 1997).
Jacopo de Voragine, *Legenda Aurea*, ed. Th. Graesse, 3rd edn (Osnabrück, 1965).
Jubinal, Achille (ed.), *La complainte et le jeu de Pierre de la Broce, chambellan de Philippe-le-Hardi* (Paris, 1835).
Legendae S. Francisci Assisiensis saeculis XIII et XIV conscriptae, Analecta Franciscana 10 (Quaracchi, 1941).
Leon Battista Alberti, *The Family in Renaissance Florence: Book III*, trans. Renée Neu Watkins (Prospect Heights, IL, 1994).
Leroux, A., and A. Bosvieux (eds), *Chartes, chroniques et mémoriaux pour servir à l'histoire de la Marche et du Limousin* (Tulle and Limoges, 1886).
Muratori, Ludovico Antonio (ed.), *Rerum Italicarum Scriptores*, 1st ser. (25 vols, Milan, 1723–51).
Opuscula Sancti Patris Francisci Assisiensis (Quaracchi, 1949).
Pandimiglio, Leonida (ed.), *I Libri di famiglia e il libro segreto di Goro Dati* (Alessandria, 2006).
Petit, Joseph (ed.), *De Libro Rationis Guillelmi de Erqueto* (Paris, 1900).
Petrarch, *De sui ipsius et multorum ignorantia*, ed. L. M. Capelli (Paris, 1906).
Pichon, Jerôme (ed.), *Le Ménagier de Paris* (2 vols, Paris, 1846).
Pirenne, Henri (ed.), *Histoire du Meurtre de Charles le Bon, Comte de Flandre (1127–1128), par Galbert de Bruges* (Paris, 1891).
Prarond, Ernest (ed.), *Le cartulaire du comté de Ponthieu* (Paris, 1898).
Rather of Verona, *The Complete Works*, ed. and trans. Peter Reid (Binghamton, NY, 1991).
Roux, J. (ed.), *Cartulaire du chapitre de la cathédrale d'Amiens* (2 vols, Amiens, 1905–12).

Scalia, Giuseppe (ed.), *Salimbene de Adam: Cronica*, CCCM 125–6 (2 vols, Turnhout, 1998).
Strubel, Armand (ed.), *Le roman de la Rose: édition d'après les manuscrits BN 12786 et BN 378* (Paris, 1992).
Sundby, Thor (ed.), *Brunetto Latinos Levnet og Skrifter* (Copenhagen, 1869).
Teulet, Alexandre (ed.), *Layettes du Trésor des Chartes* (2 vols, Paris, 1863–6).

Secondary literature

Alberzoni, Maria Pia, 'Un mendicante di fronte alla vita della Chiesa nella seconda metà del Ducento: Motivi religiosi nella Cronaca di Salimbene', in Giovanna Petti Balbi (ed.), *Salimbeniana: Atti del convegno per il VII centenario di Fra Salimbene* (Bologna, 1991), pp. 7–34.
Alcoff, Linda, 'Cultural Feminism versus Post-Structuralism: The Identity Crisis in Feminist Theory', in Nicholas B. Dirks, Geoff Eley, and Sherry Ortner (eds), *Culture / Power / History: A Reader in Contemporary Social Theory* (Princeton, 1994), pp. 96–122.
Algazi, Gadi, 'Introduction: Doing Things with Gifts', in Gadi Algazi, Valentin Groebner, and Bernhard Jussen (eds), *Negotiating the Gift: Pre-modern Figurations of Exchange* (Göttingen, 2003), pp. 9–27.
Andenmatten, Bernard, *La maison de Savoie et la noblesse vaudoise (XIIIe–XIVe s.): Supériorité féodale et autorité princière* (Lausanne, 2005).
Anderson, Benedict, *Imagined Communities*, rev. edn (London, 1991).
Archer, Margaret, *Culture and Agency: The Place of Culture in Social Theory*, rev. edn (Cambridge, 1996).
—— *Being Human: The Problem of Agency* (Cambridge, 2000).
—— '*Homo economicus*, *Homo sociologicus*, and *Homo sentiens*', in Margaret Archer and Jonathan Tritter (eds), *Rational Choice Theory: Resisting Colonization* (London, 2000), pp. 36–56.
—— *Structure, Agency, and the Internal Conversation* (Cambridge, 2003).
Archer, Margaret, and Jonathan Tritter, 'Introduction', in Margaret Archer and Jonathan Tritter (eds), *Rational Choice Theory: Resisting Colonization* (London, 2000), pp. 1–17.
Arditi, Jorge, *A Genealogy of Manners: Transformations of Social Relations in France and England from the Fourteenth to the Eighteenth Century* (Chicago, 1998).
Arnold, John, *Belief and Unbelief in Medieval Europe* (London, 2005).
Asad, Talal, *Formations of the Secular: Christianity, Islam, Modernity* (Stanford, CA, 2003).
Ashley, Kathleen, 'The *Miroir des Bonnes Femmes*: Not for Women Only?', in Kathleen Ashley and Robert L. A. Clark (eds), *Medieval Conduct* (Minneapolis, 2001), pp. 86–105.
Aurell, Martin (ed.), *La parenté déchirée: les luttes intrafamiliales au Moyen Âge* (Turnhout, 2010).

Autrand, Françoise, *Naissance d'un grand corps de l'état: Les gens du Parlament de Paris, 1345–1454* (Paris, 1981).
Badel, Pierre-Yves, *Le roman de la Rose au XIVᵉ siècle: étude de la réception de l'oeuvre* (Geneva, 1980).
Bagge, Sverre, Michael H. Gelting, and Thomas Lindkvist (eds), *Feudalism: New Landscapes of Debate* (Turnhout, 2011).
Baglivi, Giuseppe, and Joseph L. Baird, 'Salimbene and Il Bel Motto', *American Benedictine Review*, 28:2 (1977), 201–9.
Bailey, Elizabeth, 'Raising the Mind to God: The Sensual Journey of Giovanni Morelli (1371–1444) via Devotional Images', *Speculum*, 84 (2009), 984–1008.
Bakhtin, Mikhail, *The Dialogic Imagination*, trans. Caryl Emerson and Michael Holquist (Austin, 1981).
Baldwin, John W., *The Government of Philip Augustus: Foundations of French Royal Power in the Middle Ages* (Berkeley, 1986).
Balestracci, Duccio, *The Renaissance in the Fields: Family Memoirs of a Fifteenth-Century Tuscan Peasant*, trans. Paolo Squatriti and Betsy Merideth (University Park, PA, 1999).
Baron, Hans, *The Crisis of the Early Italian Renaissance* (2 vols, Princeton, 1955).
Barthélemy, Dominique, *La société dans le comté de Vendôme, de l'an mil au XIVᵉ siècle* (Paris, 1993).
—— *Deux ages de la seigneurie banale: Coucy (XIᵉ–XIIIᵉ siècle)*, 2nd edn (Paris, 2000).
Batany, Jean, 'Norms, types, et individus: la présentation des modèles sociaux au XIIᵉ siècle', in Danielle Buschinger (ed.), *Littérature et société au Moyen Âge: Actes du colloque des 5 et 6 mai 1978* (Amiens, 1978), pp. 177–200.
Battaglia, Debbora, 'Ambiguating Agency: The Case of Malinowski's Ghost', *American Anthropologist*, 99:3 (1997), 505–10.
Baxandall, Michael, *Painting and Experience in Fifteenth Century Italy* (Oxford, 1972).
Bec, Christian, *Les marchands écrivains: affaires et humanisme à Florence, 1375–1434* (Paris, 1967).
Beck, Ulrich, *Risk Society: Towards a New Modernity*, trans. Mark Ritter (London, 1992).
Beck, Ulrich, Anthony Giddens, and Scott Lash, *Reflexive Modernisation: Politics, Tradition, and Aesthetics in the Modern Social Order* (Cambridge, 1994).
Bedos-Rezak, Brigitte, 'Civic Liturgies and the Urban Records in Northern France, 1100–1400', in Barbara A. Hanawalt and Kathryn L. Reyerson (eds), *City and Spectacle in Medieval Europe* (Minneapolis, 1994), pp. 34–55.
—— *When Ego Was Imago: Signs of Identity in the Middle Ages* (Leiden, 2011).
Bedos-Rezak, Brigitte Miriam, and Dominique Iogna-Prat (eds), *L'Individu au Moyen Age: Individuation et individualisation avant la modernité* (Paris, 2005).
Behrmann, Thomas, 'The Development of Pragmatic Literacy in the Lombard City Communes', in Richard Britnell (ed.), *Pragmatic Literacy: East and West, 1200–1330* (Woodbridge, 1997), pp. 25–41.

Berkhofer, Robert, *Day of Reckoning: Power and Accountability in Medieval France* (Philadelphia, 2004).
Bertrand, Paul, *Les écritures ordinaires: Sociologie d'un temps de révolution documentaire (entre royaume de France et Empire, 1250–1350)* (Paris, 2015).
Bianchi, Luca, '*Prophanae novitates et doctrinae peregrinae*: la méfiance à l'égard des innovations théoriques aux XIIIe et XIVe siècles', in H.-J. Schmidt (ed.), *Tradition, Innovation, Invention: Fortschrittsverweigerung und Fortschrittsbewusstsein im Mittelalter* (Berlin and New York, 2005), pp. 211–29.
Biget, Jean-Louis, and Jean Tricard, 'Livres de raison et démographie familiale en Limousin au XVe siècle', *Annales de démographie historique* (1981), pp. 321–63.
Billac, Emmanuelle, *Une famille de vassaux des vicomtes de Rochechouart (1260–1388): les Prunh* (Limoges, 1990).
Bisson, Thomas N., *The Crisis of the Twelfth Century: Power, Lordship, and the Origins of European Government* (Princeton, 2009).
Black, Anthony, 'The Individual and Society', in J. H. Burns (ed.), *The Cambridge History of Medieval Political Thought, c. 350–1450* (Cambridge, 1988), pp. 588–606.
Bouchard, Constance Brittain, *Holy Entrepreneurs: Cistercians, Knights, and Economic Exchange in Twelfth-century Burgundy* (Ithaca, NY, 1991).
Boudon, Raymond, *Raison, bonnes raisons* (Paris, 2003).
Boulet-Sautel, Marguerite, 'Le droit romain et Philippe Auguste', in Robert-Henri Bautier (ed.), *La France de Philippe Auguste: Le Temps des Mutations* (Paris, 1982), pp. 489–502.
Bourdieu, Pierre, *Outline of a Theory of Practice*, trans. Richard Nice (Cambridge, 1977).
—— 'The Forms of Capital', in John G. Richardson (ed.), *Handbook of Theory of Research for the Sociology of Education* (New York, 1986), pp. 241–58.
Boureau, Alain, *La loi du Royaume: Les moines, le droit et la construction de la nation anglaise (XIe–XIIIe siècles)* (Paris, 2001).
—— *De vagues individus: la condition humaine dans la pensée scolastique* (Paris, 2008).
Bove, Boris, 'L'image de soi dans le jeu des normes sociales aux XIIIe et XIVe siècles: l'example de la bourgeoisie parisienne', in Marie-France Auzépy and Joël Cornette (eds), *Des images dans l'histoire* (Saint-Denis, 2008), pp. 179–213.
Bratman, Michael E., *Shared Agency: A Planning Theory of Acting Together* (Oxford, 2014).
Brémond, Claude, Jacques Le Goff, and Jean-Claude Schmitt, *L'exemplum*, 2nd edn (Turnhout, 1996).
Britnell, Richard, 'Pragmatic Literacy', in Richard Britnell (ed.), *Pragmatic Literacy: East and West, 1200–1330* (Woodbridge, 1997), pp. 3–25.
Brooke, Rosalind, *Early Franciscan Government: Elias to Bonaventure* (Cambridge, 1959).

Broomhall, Susan, 'Emotions in the Household', in Susan Broomhall (ed.), *Emotions in the Household, 1200–1900* (New York, 2008), pp. 1–37.
Brown, Elizabeth A. R., 'The Tyranny of a Construct: Feudalism and Historians of Medieval Europe', *American Historical Review*, 79:4 (1974), 1063–88.
—— *Customary Aids and Royal Finance in Capetian France* (Cambridge, MA, 1992).
Brown, Peter, *The Cult of the Saints: Its Rise and Function in Latin Christianity* (Chicago, 1981).
Brucker, Gene, *The Civic World of Early Renaissance Florence* (Princeton, 1977).
—— '"The Horseshoe Nail": Structure and Contingency in Medieval and Renaissance Italy', *Renaissance Quarterly*, 54 (2001), 1–19.
—— *Living on the Edge in Leonardo's Florence: Selected Essays* (Berkeley, 2005).
Buc, Philippe, *L'Ambiguïté du livre: prince, pouvoir, et peuple dans les commentaires de la Bible au Moyen Age* (Paris, 1994).
—— *The Dangers of Ritual* (Princeton, 2001).
—— *Holy War, Martyrdom, and Terror: Christianity, Violence, and the West* (Philadelphia, 2015).
Bull, Marcus, *Eyewitness and Crusade Narrative: Perception and Narration in Accounts of the Second, Third, and Fourth Crusades*, Crusading in Context (Woodbridge, 2018).
Burger, Glenn, 'Laboring to Make the Good Wife Good in the *Journées Chrétiennes* and *Le Ménagier de Paris*', *Florilegium*, 23:1 (2006), 19–40.
—— *Conduct Becoming: Good Wives and Husbands in the Later Middle Ages* (Philadelphia, 2018).
Burr, David, *The Spiritual Franciscans: From Protest to Persecution in the Century after Saint Francis* (University Park, PA, 2001).
Busija, Edith C., Hugh M. O'Neill, and Carl P. Zeithaml, 'Diversification Strategy, Entry Mode, and Performance: Evidence of Choice and Constraints', *Strategic Management Journal*, 18:4 (1997), 321–7.
Bynum Walker, Caroline, 'Franciscan Spirituality: Two Approaches', *Medievalia et Humanistica*, 7 (1976), 195–7.
—— 'Did the Twelfth Century Discover the Individual?', *Journal of Ecclesiastical History*, 31:1 (1980), 1–17.
Camporesi, Piero, *Bread of Dreams: Food and Fantasy in Early Modern Europe*, trans. David Gentilcore (Chicago, 1989).
Canteaut, Olivier, 'Confisquer pour redistribuer: la circulation de la grâce royale d'après l'exemple de la forfaiture de Pierre Remi (1328)', *Revue Historique*, 658 (2011), 311–26.
Carocci, Sandro, 'Introduzione: la mobilità sociale e la "congiuntura del 1300": Ipotesi, metodi d'indagine, storiografia', in Sandro Carocci (ed.), *La mobilità sociale nel medioevo* (Rome, 2010), pp. 1–37.
Chabot, Isabelle, 'Reconstruction d'une famille: Les Ciuriani et leurs *Ricordanze* (1326–1429)', in Jean-André Cancellieri (ed.), *La Toscane et les Toscanes autour de la Renaissance: Cadres de vie, société, croyances* (Aix-en-Provence, 1999), pp. 137–60.

Chakrabarty, Dipesh, 'The Time of History and the Time of Gods', in Lisa Lowe and David Lloyd, *The Politics of Culture in the Shadow of Capital* (Durham, NC, 1997), pp. 35–60.

Chartier, Roger, 'The Practical Impact of Writing', in Roger Chartier (ed.), *A History of Private Life*, vol. 3, *Passions of the Renaissance*, trans. Arthur Goldhammer (Cambridge, 1989), pp. 111–61.

Chédeville, André, Jacques Le Goff, and Jacques Rossiaud, *La ville en France au Moyen Âge: Des Carolingiens à la Renaissance*, rev. edn (Paris, 1998).

Chenu, M. D., *L'éveil de la conscience dans la civilisation médiévale* (Paris, 1969).

Chevalier, Bernard, 'Le pouvoir par le savoir: le renouvellement des élites urbaines en France au début de l'âge moderne (1350–1550)', in Claude Petitfrère (ed.), *Construction, reproduction et répresentations des patriciats urbains de l'Antiquité au XXᵉ siècle* (Tours, 1999), pp. 73–81.

Cheyette, Frederic, 'Giving Each His Due', repr. in Lester K. Little and Barbara H. Rosenwein (eds), *Debating the Middle Ages: Issues and Readings* (Oxford, 1998), pp. 170–9.

—— *Ermengard of Narbonne and the World of the Troubadours* (Ithaca, NY, 2001).

Ciappelli, Giovanni, 'La memoria degli eventi storici nelle ricordanze private fiorentine del Tre-Quattrocento', in Claudia Bastia and Maria Bolognani (eds), *La memoria et la città: Scritture storiche tra Medioevo ed Età Moderna* (Bologna, 1995), pp. 123–50.

—— *Memory, Family, and Self: Tuscan Family Books and Other European Egodocuments* (Leiden, 2014).

Cicchetti, Angelo, and Raoul Mordenti, *I libri di famiglia in Italia* (2 vols, Roma, 1985–2001).

Clanchy, Michael, *From Memory to Written Record: England 1066–1307* (Oxford, 1993).

—— *Abelard: A Medieval Life* (Oxford, 1997).

Constable, Giles, *Three Studies in Medieval Religious and Social Thought* (Cambridge, 1995).

Contamine, Philippe, 'La crise de la royauté française au XIVᵉ siècle: réformation et innovation dans le *Songe du vieil Pelerin* (1389) de Philippe Mézières', in Hans-Joachim Schmidt (ed.), *Tradition, Innovation, Invention: Fortschrittsverweigerung und Fortschrittsbewusstsein in Mittelalter* (Berlin, 2005), pp. 361–79.

Crespi, Franco, *Social Action and Power* (Oxford, 1992).

Crossley-Holland, Nicole, *Living and Dining in Medieval Paris: The Household of a Fourteenth-century Knight* (Cardiff, 1996).

Crouzet-Pavan, Élisabeth, 'La pensée médiévale sur la mobilité sociale, XIIᵉ–XIVᵉ siècle', in Sandro Carocci (ed.), *La mobilità sociale nel medioevo* (Rome, 2010), pp. 69–96.

Cusato, Michael F., '*Esse ergo mitem et humilem corde, hoc est esse vere fratrem minorem*: Bonaventure of Bagnoregio and the Reformulation of the Franciscan Charism', in Giancarlo Andenna, Mirko Breitenstein, and Gert

Melville (eds), *Charisma und religiöse Gemainschaften im Mittelalter* (Münster: 2005), pp. 343–82.
Czaja, Karin, 'The Nuremberg *Familienbücher*: Archives of Family Identity', in Marco Mostert and Anna Adamska (eds), *Uses of the Written Word in Medieval Towns: Medieval Urban Literacy II* (Turnhout, 2014), pp. 325–38.
Dalarun, Jacques, *François d'Assise ou le pouvoir en question: Principes et modalités du gouvernement dans l'ordre des Frères mineurs* (Paris, 1999).
D'Alatri, Mariano, *La Cronaca di Salimbene: Personaggi e tematiche* (Roma, 1988).
—— 'La religiosità popolare nella Cronaca di fra Salimbene', *Collectanea Franciscana*, 60:1–2 (1990), 175–90.
Davidson, Donald, 'The Individuation of Events', in Donald Davidson, *Essays on Actions and Events*, 2nd edn (Oxford, 2001), pp. 163–80.
Davis, Natalie Zemon, *The Gift in Sixteenth-Century France* (Madison, 2000).
De Angelis, Laura, 'Territorial Offices and Officeholders', in William Connel and Andrea Zorzi (eds), *Florentine Tuscany: Structures and Practices of Power* (Cambridge, 2000), pp. 165–82.
Débax, Hélène, *La féodalité languedocienne, XIe–XIIe siècles: Serments, hommages et fiefs dans le Languedoc des Trencavel* (Toulouse, 2003).
—— 'L'Aristocratie languedocienne et la société féodale: Le témoignage des sources (Midi de la France: XIe et XIIe siècles)', in Sverre Bagge, Michael H. Gelting, and Thomas Lindkvist (eds), *Feudalism: New Landscapes of Debate* (Turnhout, 2011), pp. 77–100.
De Beer, Francis, *La conversion de saint François selon Thomas de Celano* (Paris, 1963).
De Certeau, Michel, *L'invention du quotidian*, repr. (2 vols, Paris, 1990).
Dekker, Rudolf (ed.), *Egodocuments and History: Autobiographical Writing in Its Social Context since the Middle Ages* (Hilversum, 2002), pp. 7–15.
Deladreue, L. E., 'Histoire de l'abbaye de Lannoy, ordre de Cîteaux', *Mémoires de la Société académique d'archéologie, sciences et arts du département de l'Oise*, 10 (1878), 405–84, 569–696.
Delaurenti, Béatrice, *La puissance des mots, "Virtus Verborum": Débats doctrinaux sur le pouvoir des incantations au Moyen Âge* (Paris, 2007).
Delhaye, Philippe, 'Quelques aspects de la doctrine thomiste et néo-thomiste du travail', in Jacqueline Hamesse and Colette Muraille-Samaran (eds), *Le travail au Moyen Âge: une approche interdisciplinaire* (Louvain-la-Neuve, 1990), pp. 157–75.
Delisle, Leopold (ed.), 'Chronologie des baillis et des sénéchaux royaux depuis les origines jusqu'à l'avénement de Philippe de Valois', in Leopold Delisle (ed.), *Recueil des historiens des Gaules et de la France* (24 vols, Paris, 1869–1904), vol. 24, pp. *15–*385.
Demangeon, Albert, *La plaine picarde* (Paris, 1905).
Desbonnets, Théophile, *From Intuition to Institution: The Franciscans*, trans. Paul Duggan and Jerry du Charme (Chicago, 1988).

Desbordes, Jean-Michel, 'Les origines de Pierre-Buffière (Haute-Vienne)', *Revue archéologique du Centre de la France*, 17:3–4 (1978), 169–76.
Duby, Georges, *La société aux XIe et XIIe siècle dans la region mâconnaise* (Paris, 1953).
—— 'The "Youth" in Twelfth-century Aristocratic Society', repr. in Frederic Cheyette (ed.), *Lordship and Community in Medieval Europe: Selected Readings* (New York, 1968), pp. 198–209.
—— *Les trois ordres ou l'imaginaire du féodalisme* (Paris, 1978).
Du Cange, Charles du Fresne, *Glossarium Mediae et Infimae Latinitatis*, new edn by Léopold Favre (10 vols, Niort, 1883–7).
Dumont, Louis, *Essays on Individualism: Modern Ideology in Anthropological Perspective* (Chicago, 1986).
Dutour, Thierry, 'La noblesse et la ville dans l'espace francophone à la fin du Moyen Âge: État de la question et propositions de réflexion', in Thierry Dutour (ed.), *La noblesse et la ville dans l'espace francophone (XIIe–XVIe siècles)* (Paris, 2010), pp. 17–58.
Dutton, Paul Edward, 'Thunder and Hail over the Carolingian Countryside', in Del Sweeney (ed.), *Agriculture in the Middle Ages: Technology, Practice, and Representation* (Philadelphia, 1995), pp. 112–37.
Dyer, Christopher, *An Age of Transition? Economy and Society in England in the Later Middle Ages* (Oxford, 2005).
Eckstein, Nicholas, *The District of the Green Dragon: Neighbourhood Life and Social Change in Renaissance Florence* (Florence, 1995).
Eisenstadt, Shmuel N., 'Multiple Modernities', *Daedalus*, 129:1 (2000), 1–31.
—— 'Some Observations on Multiple Modernities', in Domenic Sachsenmaier, Jens Riedel, and Shmuel N. Eisenstadt (eds), *Reflections on Multiple Modernities* (Leiden, 2002), pp. 29–31.
Eisenstadt, Shmuel N., and Wolfgang Schluchter, 'Introduction: Paths to Early Modernities – A Comparative View', *Daedalus*, 127:3 (1998), 1–18.
Elias, Norbert, *The Civilising Process*, rev. edn, trans. Edmund Jephcott (Oxford, 2000).
Elliott, Dyan, 'Women and Confession: From Empowerment to Pathology', in Mary C. Erler and Maryanne Kowaleski (eds), *Gendering the Master Narrative: Women and Power in the Middle Ages* (Ithaca, NY, 2003), pp. 31–51.
Epstein, Steven A., 'Economics in Dante's Hell', in Iris Shagrir et al. (eds), *In Laudem Hierosolymitani: Studies in Crusades and Medieval Culture in Honour of Benjamin Z. Kedar* (Aldershot, 2007), pp. 437–46.
Epurescu-Pascovici, Ionuț, 'Local Politics, Social Networks, and Individual Agency in a Northern French *Seigneurie*: Picquigny and Its lords, c. 1190–1250', *Studies in Medieval and Renaissance History*, 3rd ser., 7 (2010), 53–166.
Erler, Mary C., and Maryanne Kowaleski, 'A New Economy of Power Relations: Female Agency in the Middle Ages', in Mary C. Erler and Maryanne Kowaleski (eds), *Gendering the Master Narrative: Women and Power in the Middle Ages* (Ithaca, NY, 2003), pp. 1–16.

Eve, Michael, 'Qui se ressemble s'assemble? Les sources d'homogénéité à Turin', in Maurizio Gribaudi (ed.), *Espaces, temporalities, stratifications: exercises sur les réseaux sociaux* (Paris, 1998), pp. 43–69.

Evergates, Theodore, *Feudal Society in the Baillage of Troyes under the Counts of Champagne, 1152–1284* (Baltimore, 1975).

Farmer, Sharon, 'Persuasive Voices: Clerical Images of Medieval Wives', *Speculum*, 61:3 (1986), 517–43.

—— *Surviving Poverty in Medieval Paris: Gender, Ideology, and the Daily Lives of the Poor* (Ithaca, NY, 2002).

Favier, Jean, *Un roi de marbre: Philippe le Bel, Enguerran de Marigny* (Paris, 2005).

Fawtier, Robert, *The Capetian Kings of France*, trans. Lionel Butler and R. J. Adam (New York, 1960).

Ferrier, Janet M., 'A Husband's Asides: The Use of the Second Person Singular in *Le Ménagier de Paris*', *French Studies*, 31:3 (1977), 257–67.

—— '"Seulement pour vous endoctriner": The Author's Use of *Exempla* in *Le Ménagier de Paris*', *Medium Aevum*, 48 (1979), 77–89.

Flint, Valerie, *The Rise of Magic in Early Medieval Europe* (Princeton, 1991).

Flora, Holly, *The Devout Belief of the Imagination: The Paris 'Meditationes Vitae Christi' and Female Franciscan Spirituality in Trecento Italy* (Turnhout, 2009).

Fontaine, Laurence, and Jürgen Schlumbohm, 'Household Strategies for Survival: An Introduction', in Laurence Fontaine and Jürgen Schlumbohm (eds), *Household Strategies for Survival, 1600–2000: Fission, Faction, and Cooperation, International Review of Social History*, supplement 8 (Cambridge, 2000), pp. 1–18.

Foote, David, 'Mendicants and the Italian Communes in Salimbene', in Donald Prudlo (ed.), *The Origin, Development, and Refinement of Medieval Religious Mendicancies* (Leiden, 2011), pp. 197–238.

Fossier, Lucie, and Olivier Guyotjeannin, 'Cartulaires français laïques: seigneuries et particuliers', in Olivier Guyotjeannin, Laurent Morelle, and Michel Parisse (eds), *Les Cartulaires: Actes de la table ronde organisée par l'Ecole nationale des chartes* (Paris, 1993), pp. 379–410.

Fossier, Robert, *La terre et les hommes en Picardie jusqu'à la fin du XIIIe siècle* (2 vols, Paris, 1968).

—— *Hommes et villages d'Occident au Moyen Âge* (Paris, 1992).

Foucault, Michel, *L'hérmeneutique du sujet* (Paris, 2001).

—— *Security, Territory, Population: Lectures at the Collège de France, 1977–1978*, ed. Michel Senellart (New York, 2007).

Foviaux, Jacques, 'Discipline et réglementation des activités professionelles à travers les arrêts du Parlement de Paris (1257–1382)', in Jacqueline Hamesse and Colette Muraille-Samaran (eds), *Le travail au Moyen Âge: une approche interdisciplinaire* (Louvain-la-Neuve, 1990), pp. 185–200.

Franceschi, Franco, and Josiane Tourres, 'La mémoire des laboratores à Florence au début du XVe siècle', *Annales: Histoire, Sciences Sociales*, 45:5 (1990), 1143–67.

Frugoni, Chiara, *Francesco e l'invenzione delle stimmate* (Turin, 1993).
Fulbrook, Mary, and Ulinka Rublack, 'In Relation: The "Social Self" and Ego-Documents', *German History*, 28:3 (2010), 263–272.
Ganshof, François-Louis, *Feudalism*, trans. Ph. Grierson, repr. (Toronto, 1996).
Garnier, M. J., 'Dénombrement du temporel de l'éveché d'Amiens, en 1301', *Mémoires de la Société des Antiquaires de Picardie*, 2nd ser., 7 (1860), 107–310.
Gatto, Lodovico, 'Il sentimento cittadino nella *Cronica* di Salimbene', in *La coscienza cittadina nei comuni italiani nel Duecento* (Todi, 1972), pp. 365–94.
Gauvard, Claude, *"De grace especial": Crime, état et société en France à la fin du Moyen Age* (Paris: Publications de la Sorbonne, 1991).
Gazzini, Marina, *'Dare et habere': il mondo di un mercante milanese del Quattrocento* (Firenze, 2002).
Geary, Patrick, 'Living with Conflicts in Stateless France: A Typology of Conflict Management Mechanisms, 1050–1200', repr. in Patrick Geary, *Living with the Dead in the Middle Ages* (Ithaca, NY, 1994), pp. 125–62.
Geertz, Clifford, *The Interpretation of Cultures: Selected Essays* (New York, 1973).
Giddens, Anthony, *Central Problems in Social Theory* (Berkeley, 1979).
—— *Social Theory and Modern Sociology* (Stanford, CA, 1987).
Gillespie, Michael Allen, *The Theological Origins of Modernity* (Chicago, 2008).
Gillingham, John, 'From *Civilitas* to Civility: Codes of Manners in Medieval and Early Modern England', *Transactions of the Royal Historical Society*, 6th ser., 12 (2002), 267–89.
Gilson, Etienne, *The Spirit of Mediaeval Philosophy, Gifford Lecture Series, 1931–2*, trans. A. H. C. Downes (New York, 1944).
Gimpel, Jean, *The Medieval Machine: The Industrial Revolution of the Middle Ages* (New York, 1976).
Goldmann, Catherine, 'La seigneurie de Fontenay-le-Marmion (Calvados): analyse d'une comptabilité seigneuriale (1377–1380)', in *Seigneurs et seigneuries au Moyen Age* (Paris, 1993), pp. 275–87.
Goodich, Michael, 'The Multiple Miseries of Dulcia of St Chartier (1266) and Cristina of Wellington (1294)', in Michael Goodich (ed.), *Voices from the Bench: The Narratives of Lesser Folk in Medieval Trials* (New York, 2006), pp. 99–126.
Goody, Jack, *The Logic of Writing and the Organisation of Society* (Cambridge, 1986).
—— *The European Family: An Historico-Anthropological Essay* (Oxford, 2000).
—— *The Power of the Written Tradition* (Washington, DC, 2000).
Granet, Vital, *Histoire de la ville de Saint-Junien* (Saint-Junien, 1926).
Granovetter, Mark, 'The Strength of Weak Ties', *American Journal of Sociology*, 78:6 (1973), 1360–80.
Greco, Gina L., and Christine M. Rose (trans.), *The Good Wife's Guide* (Ithaca, NY, 2009).
Greenblatt, Stephen, *Renaissance Self-Fashioning: From More to Shakespeare* (Chicago, 1980).

Grenier, Pierre-Nicolas, *Introduction à l'histoire générale de la province de Picardie*, ed. Ch. Dufour and J. Garnier (Amiens, 1856).
Grubb, James, 'Libri privati e memoria familiare: esempi dal Veneto', in Claudia Bastia and Maria Bolognani (eds), *La memoria et la città: Scritture storiche tra Medioevo ed Età Moderna* (Bologna, 1995), pp. 63–72.
Guenée, Bernard, *Une meurtre, une société: L'assasinat du duc d'Orléans, 23 novembre 1407* (Paris, 1992).
Guerreau, Alain, *Le féodalisme: un horizon théorique* (Paris, 1980).
Guillemain, Bernard, 'Philippe Auguste et l'épiscopat', in Robert-Henri Bautier (ed.), *La France de Philippe Auguste: Le temps des mutations* (Paris, 1982), pp. 365–84.
Gurevich, Aaron, 'Réprésentations et attitudes à l'égard de la propriété pendant le haut Moyen Age', *Annales: Économie, Sociétés, Civilisations*, 27:3 (1972), 523–47.
—— *Historical Anthropology of the Middle Ages*, trans. Jana Howlett (Chicago, 1992).
—— *The Origins of European Individualism*, trans. Katharine Judelson (Oxford, 1995).
Guyotjeannin, Olivier, *Salimbene de Adam: Un chroniqueur franciscain* (Turnhout, 1995).
—— 'French Manuscript Sources, 1250–1330', in Richard Britnell (ed.), *Pragmatic Literacy: East and West, 1200–1330* (Woodbridge, 1997), pp. 51–71.
Hallam, Elizabeth M., and Judith Everard, *Capetian France, 987–1328*, 2nd edn (Harlow, 2001).
Haluska-Rausch, Elizabeth, 'Transformations in the Powers of Wives and Widows near Montpellier, 985–1213', in Robert F. Berkhofer III, Alan Cooper, and Adam J. Kosto (eds), *The Experience of Power in Medieval Europe* (Aldershot, 2005), pp. 153–68.
Hamesse, Jacqueline, 'Le travail chez les auteurs philosophiques du 12e et du 13e siècle: Approche lexicographique', in Jacqueline Hamesse and Colette Muraille-Samaran (eds), *Le travail au Moyen Âge: une approche interdisciplinaire* (Louvain-la-Neuve, 1990), pp. 115–27.
Hanawalt, Barbara, *The Ties That Bound: Peasant Families in Medieval England* (Oxford, 1986).
Hankins, James, 'The *Baron Thesis* After 40 Years and Some Recent Studies of Leonardo Bruni', *Journal of the History of Ideas*, 56:2 (1995), 309–38.
Hanson, Elizabeth, *Discovering the Subject in Renaissance England* (Cambridge, 1998).
Hautefeuille, Florent, 'Livre de compte ou livre de raison: le registres d'une famille de paysans quercynois, les Guitards de Saint-Anthet (1417–1526)', in Natacha Coquerie, François Menant, and Florence Weber (eds), *Écrire, compter, mesurer: vers une histoire de rationalités pratiques* (Paris, 2006), pp. 242–6.
Heidegger, Martin, *Being and Time*, trans. John Macquarrie and Edward Robinson (New York, 1962).

Hentsch, Alice A., *De la littérature didactique du Moyen Âge: S'adressant spécialement aux femmes* (Cahors, 1903).
Herlihy, D., and Christiane Klapisch-Zuber, *Les Toscanes et leurs familles* (Paris, 1978).
Herzfeld, Michael, 'Pride and Perjury: Time and Oath in the Mountain Villages of Crete', *Man*, new ser., 25:2 (1990), 305–22.
Holmes, Megan, *The Miraculous Image in Renaissance Florence* (New Haven, 2013).
Homans, George, 'Social Behavior as Exchange', *American Journal of Sociology*, 63:6 (1958), 597–606.
Hudson, John, 'Anglo-Norman Land Law and the Origins of Property', in George Garnett and John Hudson (eds), *Law and Government in Medieval England and Normandy: Essays in Honour of Sir James Holt* (Cambridge, 1994), pp. 198–222.
Hüwelmeier, Gertrud, 'Gendered Houses: Kinship, Class, and Identity in a German Village', in Victoria Goddard (ed.), *Gender, Agency, and Change: Anthropological Perspectives* (London, 2000), pp. 122–41.
Hyams, Paul R., 'Homage and Feudalism: A Judicious Separation', in Natalie Fryde, Pierre Monnet, and Otto Gerhard Oexle (eds), *Die Gegenwart des Feudalismus* (Göttingen, 2002), pp. 13–49.
Jauss, Hans Robert, *Pour une esthétique de la reception*, trans. Claude Maillard (Paris, 1978).
Jeay, Madeleine, *Le commerce des mots: L'usage des listes dans la littérature médiévale (XIIe–XVe siècles)* (Geneva, 2006).
Jordan, William Chester, 'The Struggle for Influence at the Court of Philip III: Pierre de la Broce and the French Aristocracy', *French Historical Studies*, 24.3 (2001), 439–68.
Kapferer, Bruce, "Transactional Models Reconsidered', in Bruce Kapferer (ed.), *Transactions and Meaning: Directions in the Anthropology of Exchange and Symbolic Behavior* (Philadelphia, 1976), pp. 1–22.
—— 'Agency, or Human Agency', in Thomas Barfield (ed.), *Dictionary of Anthropology* (Oxford, 1997).
Kaye, Joel, *Economy and Nature in the Fourteenth Century* (Cambridge, 1998).
Keane, Webb, 'From Fetishism to Sincerity: On Agency, the Speaking Subject, and Their Historicity in the Context of Religious Conversion', *CSSH* 39:4 (1997), 674–93.
—— 'Religious Language', *Annual Review of Anthropology*, 26 (1997), 47–71.
—— 'Self-Interpretation, Agency, and the Objects of Anthropology: Reflections on a Genealogy', *CSSH* 45:2 (2003), 222–48.
Kelly, H. A., 'Canon Law and Chaucer on Licit and Illicit Magic', in Ruth Mazo Karras, Joel Kaye, and E. Ann Matter (eds), *Law and the Illicit in Medieval Society* (Philadelphia, 2008), pp. 211–24.
Kent, Dale, and F. W. Kent, 'A Self Disciplining Pact Made by the Peruzzi Family of Florence (June 1433)', *Renaissance Quarterly*, 34:3 (1981), 337–55.

Kent, F. W., *Household and Lineage in Renaissance Florence: The Family Life of the Capponi, Ginori and Rucellai* (Princeton, 1977).
Kieckhefer, Richard, *Magic in the Middle Ages* (Cambridge, 1989).
Klapisch-Zuber, Christiane, *Women, Family, and Ritual in Renaissance Italy*, trans. Lydia G. Cochrane (Chicago, 1985).
—— 'Comptes et mémoire: l'écriture des livres de famille florentins', in Caroline Bourlet and Annie Dufour (eds), *L'Écrit dans la société médiévale: Divers aspects de sa pratique du XIe au XVe siècle* (Paris, 1991), pp. 251–8.
—— 'Les archives de famille italiennes: le cas florentin, XIVe–XVe siècles', in *L'autorité de l'écrit au Moyen Âge* (Paris, 2009), pp. 361–78.
Klein, Elka, 'Good Servants, Bad Lords: The Abuse of Authority by Jewish Bailiffs in the Medieval Crown of Aragon', in Robert F. Berkhofer III, Alan Cooper, and Adam J. Kosto (eds), *The Experience of Power in Medieval Europe* (Aldershot, 2005), pp. 59–72.
Kleinschmit, Harald, *Understanding the Middle Ages: The Transformation of Ideas and Attitudes in the Medieval World* (Woodbridge, 2000).
Koziol, Geoffrey, 'The Dangers of Polemic: Is Ritual Still an Interesting Topic of Historical Study?', *Early Medieval Europe*, 11:4 (2002), 367–88.
—— 'Is Robert I in Hell?', *Early Medieval Europe*, 14 (2006), 233–68.
Krueger, Roberta L., '"Nouvelles choses": Social Instability and the Problem of Fashion in the *Livre du Chevalier de la Tour Landry*, the *Ménagier de Paris*, and Christine de Pizan's *Livre de Trois Vertus*', in Kathleen Ashley and Robert L. A. Clark (eds), *Medieval Conduct* (Minneapolis, 2001), pp. 49–85.
—— 'Identity Begins at Home: Female Conduct and the Failure of Counsel in *Le Ménagier de Paris*', *Essays in Medieval Studies*, 22 (2005), 21–39.
Långfors, Arthur, 'Jacques Bruyant et son poème, *La voie de povreté et de richesse*', *Romania, 65 (1918–19), 49–83*.
Langholm, Odd, 'The Medieval Schoolmen (1200–1400)', in Todd Lowry and Barry Gordon (eds), *Ancient and Medieval Economic Ideas and Concepts of Social Justice* (Leiden, 1998), pp. 439–501.
Latour, Bruno, *The Pasteurisation of France*, trans. Alan Sheridan and John Law (Cambridge, MA, 1988).
—— *We Have Never Been Modern*, trans. Catherine Porter (Cambridge, MA, 1993).
—— *Reassembling the Social: An Introduction to Actor–Network-Theory* (Oxford, 2005).
Layder, Derek, 'Power, Structure, and Agency', *Journal for the Theory of Social Behaviour*, 15:2 (1985), 131–49.
Lazzerini, Lucia, 'Fra Salimbene predicatore', in Giovanna Petti Balbi (ed.), *Salimbeniana: Atti del convegno per il VII centenario di Fra Salimbene* (Bologna, 1991), pp. 133–41.
Lebreton, Marie-Madeleine, 'Eudes de Chateauroux', in M. Viller et al. (eds), *Dictionnaire de spiritualité: ascétique et mystique, doctrine et histoire* (17 vols, Paris, 1932–95), vol. 4:2, pp. 1675–8.

Lecler, André, *Dictionnaire historique et géographique de la Haute Vienne* (Marseille, 1976).
Ledieu, Alcius, 'La carte de commune de Molliens-Vidame', *Cabinet historique de l'Artois et de la Picardie*, 8 (1893–4), 156–201.
Leff, Gordon, 'The Franciscan Concept of Man', in Ann Williams (ed.), *Prophecy and Millenarianism: Essays in Honour of Marjorie Reeves* (Harlow, 1980), pp. 219–37.
Le Goff, Jacques, *Time, Work, and Culture in the Middle Ages*, trans. Arthur Goldhammer (Chicago, 1980).
—— *The Medieval Imagination*, trans. Arthur Goldhammer (Chicago, 1988).
—— 'Le travail dans les systèmes de valeur de l'Occident médiéval', in Jacqueline Hamesse and Colette Muraille-Samaran (eds), *Le travail au Moyen Âge: une approche interdisciplinaire* (Louvain-la-Neuve, 1990), pp. 7–21.
—— *Saint Francis of Assisi*, trans. Christine Rhone (London, 2004).
Leguay, Jean-Pierre, *La rue au Moyen Âge* (Rennes, 1984).
Le Jan-Hennebicque, Régine, 'Aux origines du douaire medieval (VIe–Xe siècle)', in Michel Parisse (ed.), *Veuves et veuvage dans le haut Moyen Age* (Paris, 1993), pp. 107–22.
Lemaître, Nicole, *Le scribe et le mage: Notaires et société rurale en Bas-Limousin aux XVIe et XVIIe siècles* (Ussel, 2000).
Lesnick, Daniel, *Preaching in Medieval Florence: The Social World of Franciscan and Dominican Spirituality* (Athens, GA, 1989).
Lett, Didier, *Famille et parenté dans l'Occident médiéval, V^e–XVe siècle* (Paris, 2000).
Levi, Giovanni, *Inheriting Power: The Story of an Exorcist*, trans. Lydia Cochrane (Chicago, 1988).
—— 'On Microhistory', in Peter Burke (ed.), *New Perspectives on Historical Writing*, 2nd edn (University Park, PA, 2001), pp. 97–119.
Lochrie, Karma, 'Desiring Foucault', *Journal of Medieval and Early Modern Studies*, 27:1 (1997), 3–16.
MacDonald, Scott, 'Aquinas's Libertarian Account of Free Choice', *Revue Internationale de Philosophie*, 52 (1998), 309–28.
Macfarlane, Alan, *The Origins of English Individualism* (Cambridge, 1979).
MacIntyre, Alasdair, *Dependent Rational Animals: Why Human Beings Need the Virtues* (London, 1999).
Magnani S.-Christen, Eliana, 'Transforming Things and Persons: The Gift *pro anima* in the Eleventh and Twelfth Centuries', in Gadi Algazi, Valentin Groebner, and Bernhard Jussen (eds), *Negotiating the Gift: Pre-modern Figurations of Exchange* (Göttingen, 2003), pp. 269–84.
Magnou-Nortier, Elisabeth, 'La féodalité en crise: Propos sur "Fiefs and Vassals" de Susan Reynolds', *Revue historique*, 600 (1996), 253–348.
Mahmood, Saba, 'Feminist Theory, Embodiment, and the Docile Agent: Some Reflections on the Egyptian Islamic Revival', *Cultural Anthropology*, 16:2 (2001), 202–36.

Malo, Henri, *Un grand feudataire: Renaud de Dammartin et la coalition de Bouvines* (Paris, 1898).
Martin, John Jeffries, *Myths of Renaissance Individualism* (New York, 2004).
Martines, Lauro, *Lawyers and Statecraft in Renaissance Florence* (Princeton, 1968).
Matsusaka, John G., 'Corporate Diversification, Value Maximization, and Organizational Capabilities', *Journal of Business*, 74:3 (2001), 409–31.
Maupeu, Philippe, *Pèlerins de vie humaine: Autobiographie et allégorie narrative, de Guillaume de Deguilleville à Octovien de Saint-Gelais* (Paris, 2009).
Mauss, Marcel, 'Les techniques du corps', *Journal de Psychologie*, 32 (1936), 271–93.
Mayer, Hans Eberhard, *The Crusades*, trans. John Gillingham, 2nd edn (Oxford, 1988).
McCormick, Andrew P., 'Toward a Reinterpretation of Goro Dati's *Storia di Firenze*', *Journal of Medieval and Renaissance Studies*, 13:2 (1983), 227–50.
McInerny, Ralph, 'Action Theory in St Thomas Aquinas', in Albert Zimmermann (ed.), *Thomas von Aquin: Werk und Wirkung im Licht neuerer Forschungen* (Berlin, 1988), pp. 13–22.
McLean, Paul D., 'Patronage, Citizenship, and the Stalled Emergence of the Modern State in Renaissance Florence', *CSSH* 47:3 (2005), 638–64.
—— *The Art of the Network: Strategic Interaction and Patronage in Renaissance Florence* (Durham, NC, 2007).
McLean, Paul D., and John F. Padgett, 'Was Florence a Perfectly Competitive Market? Transactional Evidence from the Renaissance', *Theory and Society*, 26:2 (1997), 209–44.
McNamer, Sarah, 'The Origins of the *Meditationes vitae Christi*', *Speculum*, 84:4 (2009), 905–55.
McNay, Lois, *Gender and Agency: Reconfiguring the Subject in Feminist and Social Theory* (Cambridge, 2000).
McWebb, Christine (ed.), *Debating the Roman de la rose: A Critical Anthology* (London, 2007).
Miller, Maureen C., 'Religion Makes a Difference: Clerical and Lay Cultures in the Courts of Northern Italy, 1000–1300', *American Historical Review*, 105:4 (2000), 1095–1130.
Miyazaki, Hirokazu, 'Faith and Its Fulfilment: Agency, Exchange and the Fijian Aesthetics of Completion', *American Ethnologist*, 27:1 (2000), 31–51.
Molho, Anthony, *Marriage Alliance in Late Medieval Florence* (Cambridge, MA, 1994).
Molho, Anthony, et al., 'Genealogia, parentado e memoria storica a Firenze nel XV secolo', in Claudia Bastia and Maria Bolognani (eds), *La memoria et la città: Scritture storiche tra Medioevo ed Età Moderna* (Bologna, 1995), pp. 253–70.
Mollat, Michel, *Les pauvres au Moyen âge: étude sociale* (Paris, 1978).
—— *Jacques Coeur ou l'esprit d'entreprise au XVe siècle* (Paris, 1988).

Morelle, Laurent, 'La notice des plaids generaux de Corbie: une revision', in Elisabeth Mornet (ed.), *Campagnes médiévales: l'homme et son espace: études offertes à Robert Fossier* (Paris, 1995), pp. 573–86.

Morsel, Joseph, 'La construction sociale des identites dans l'aristocratie franconienne aux XIVe et XVe siècle: Individuation ou identification?', in Brigitte Miriam Bedos-Rezak and Dominique Iogna-Prat (eds), *L'Individu au Moyen Age: Individuation et individualisation avant la modernité* (Paris, 2005), pp. 79–100.

Morrison, Karl, *Understanding Conversion* (Charlottesville, VA, 1992).

Mostert, Marco, 'Some Thoughts on Urban Schools, Urban Literacy, and the Development of Western Civilisation', in Marco Mostert and Anna Adamska (eds), *Writing and the Administration of Medieval Towns: Medieval Urban Literacy I* (Turnhout, 2014), pp. 337–48.

Mouysset, Sylvie, *Papiers de famille: Introduction à l'étude des livres de raison (France, XVe–XIXe siècle)* (Rennes, 2007).

Murray, Alexander, *Reason and Society in the Middle Ages*, 2nd edn (Oxford, 1985).

—— 'Counselling in Medieval Confession', in Peter Biller and A. J. Minnis (eds), *Handling Sin: Confession in the Middle Ages* (York, 1998), pp. 63–77.

—— 'Missionaries and Magic in Dark-Age Europe', repr. in Lester K. Little and Barbara H. Rosenwein (eds), *Debating the Middle Ages: Issues and Readings* (Oxford, 1998), pp. 92–104.

Najemy, John M., *Corporatism and Consensus in Florentine Electoral Politics, 1280–1400* (Chapel Hill, NC, 1982).

—— 'Brunetto Latini's *Politica*', *Dante Studies*, 112 (1994), 33–51.

—— *A History of Florence, 1200–1575* (Oxford, 2006).

Nederman, Cary J., 'Commercial Society and Republican Government in the Latin Middle Ages: The Economic Dimensions of Brunetto Latini's Republicanism', *Political Theory*, 31:5 (2003), 644–63.

Newhauser, Richard, *The Treatise on Vices and Virtues in Latin and the Vernacular*, Typologie des Sources du Moyen Âge Occidental 68 (Turnhout, 1993).

Newmann, William M., *Les Seigneurs de Nesle en Picardie, XIIe–XIIIe siècle* (Paris, 1971).

—— *Le personnel de la cathédrale d'Amiens* (Paris, 1972).

Nieus, Jean-François, 'Un exemple précoce de répertoire féodal: le livre des fiefs de la châtellenie d'Encre (nord de la France, ca. 1245)', *Bulletin de la Commission Royale d'Histoire*, 168 (2002), 1–70.

—— *Un pouvoir comtal entre Flandre et France: Saint-Pol, 1000–1300* (Bruxelles, 2005).

—— 'Avant-Propos', in Jean-François Nieus (ed.), *Le vassal, le fief et l'écrit: pratiques d'écriture et enjeux documentaries dans le champ de la féodalité (XIe–XVe siècle)* (Louvain-la-Neuve, 2007), pp. 5–9.

—— 'Les quatre travaux de maître Quentin (1250–1276): cartulaires de Picquigny et d'Audenarde, *Veil rentier* d'Audenarde et *Terrier l'évêque* de

Cambrai. Des écrits d'exception pour un clerc seigneurial hors normes?', *Journal des Savants* (2012), 69–119.
—— '"Et hoc per meas litteras significo": Les débuts de la diplomatique féodale dans le nord de la France (fin XIIe–milieu XIIIe siècle)', *Cahiers de civilisation médiévale*, 58 (2015), 43–64.
Novák, Veronika, 'La source du savoir: publication officielle et communication informelle à Paris au début du XVe siècle', in Claire Boudreau et al. (eds), *Information et société en Occident à la fin du Moyen Age* (Paris, 2004), pp. 151–63.
Oberman, Heiko, 'Via Antiqua and Via Moderna: Late-Medieval Prologomena to Early Reformation Thought', *Journal of the History of Ideas*, 48:1 (1987), 23–40.
Oexle, Otto Gerhard, 'Perceiving Social Reality in the Early and High Middle Ages: A Contribution to a History of Social Knowledge', in Bernhard Jussen (ed.), *Ordering Medieval Society: Perspectives on Intellectual and Practical Modes of Shaping Social Relations* (Philadelphia, 2001), pp. 92–143.
Opitz, Claudia, 'Life in the Late Middle Ages', in Christiane Klapisch-Zuber (ed.), *A History of Women in the West*, vol. 2, *Silences of the Middle Ages* (Cambridge, MA, 1992), pp. 267–317.
Origo, Iris, *The Merchant of Prato: Francesco di Marco Datini, 1335–1410* (New York, 1957).
Ortner, Sherry, 'Theory in Anthropology since the Sixties', *CSSH* 26:1 (1984), 126–66.
—— 'Thick Resistance: Death and the Cultural Construction of Agency in Himalayan Mountaineering', *Representations*, 56 (1997), 135–62.
—— *Anthropology and Social Theory: Culture, Power, and the Acting Subject* (Durham, NC, 2006).
Ott, John S., review of Heather J. Tanner, *Families, Friends, and Allies: Boulogne and Politics in Northern France and England, c. 879–1160* (Leiden, 2004), *Speculum*, 81:2 (2006), 615–16.
Oulmont, Charles, *La poésie morale, politique et dramatique à la veille de la Renaissance: Pierre Gringore*, repr. (Geneva, 1975).
Ourliac, Paul, 'Législation, coutumes et coutumiers au temps de Philippe Auguste', in Robert-Henri Bautier (ed.), *La France de Philippe Auguste: Le Temps des Mutations* (Paris, 1982), pp. 471–87.
Pandimiglio, Leonida, 'Giovanni di Pagolo Morelli e la ragion di famiglia', in *Studi sul Medioevo Cristiano* (2 vols, Rome, 1974), vol. 2, pp. 553–608.
—— 'Giovanni Morelli e le strutture familiari', *Archivio Storico Italiano*, 136 (1978), 3–88.
—— 'Giovanni di Pagolo Morelli e la continuità familiare', *Studi Medievali*, 3rd ser., 22 (1981), 128–81.
—— 'Pigliate esempro di questo caso: l'inizio della scrittura di Bonaccorso Pitti', *Lettere italiane*, 40:2 (1988), 161–73.
Pàsztor, Edith, 'L'esperienza francescana nella *Cronica* di Salimbene', in *Salimbene da Parma. Curiosità umana ed esperienza politica in un francescano di*

sette secoli fa: Studi in occasione delle celebrazioni nel VII centenario della morte di Fra Salimbene da Parma (1221–1287), Zenit Quaderni, Supplemento al IV numero del 1987 (Bologna, 1987), pp. 13–21.

Pellegrini, Luigi, 'Istituzione francescana e quotidianità conventuale nell'ideale umano di Salimbene', in Giovanna Petti Balbi (ed.), *Salimbeniana: Atti del convegno per il VII centenario di Fra Salimbene* (Bologna, 1991), pp. 158–73.

Petti Balbi, Giovanna, 'Lignagio, famiglia, parentela in Salimbene', in Giovanna Petti Balbi (ed.), *Salimbeniana: Atti del convegno per il VII centenario di Fra Salimbene* (Bologna, 1991), pp. 35–47.

Pezzarossa, Fulvio, 'La tradizione Fiorentina della memorialistica', in Gian-Mario Anselmi, Fulvio Pezzarossa, and Luisa Avellini (eds), *La 'memoria' dei 'mercatores': Tendenze ideologiche, ricordanze, artigianato in versi nella Firenze del Quattrocento* (Bologna, 1980), pp. 39–149.

Philips, Mark, *The Memoir of Marco Parenti: A Life in Medici Florence* (Princeton, 1987).

Pichot, Daniel, 'Une famille de la petite aristocratie du Bas-Maine', in Elisabeth Mornet (ed.), *Campagnes médiévales: l'homme et son espace: études offertes à Robert Fossier* (Paris, 1995), pp. 477–80.

Picquigny: le château-fort, la collégiale, la ville (Amiens, 1987).

Pineau-Harvey, Catherine, 'Jeu, ouverture sociale et diplomatie: à propos de Bonaccorso Pitti', *Bibliothèque d'Humanisme et Renaissance*, 63:1 (2001), 33–45.

Poppi, Antonino, 'Fate, Fortune, Providence, and Human Freedom', in Charles Schmitt et al. (eds), *The Cambridge History of Renaissance Philosophy* (Cambridge, 1988), pp. 641–67.

Provero, Luigi, 'Vassallaggio e reti clientelari: Una via per la mobilità', in Sandro Carocci (ed.), *La mobilità sociale nel medioevo* (Roma, 2010), pp. 437–51.

Renoux, Annie, 'Aux sources du pouvoir châtelain de Geoffroi "seigneur de Mayenne, le plus fort homme du Maine" (c. 1040–1098)', in Dominique Barthélemy and Olivier Bruand (eds), *Les pouvoirs locaux dans la France du centre et de l'ouest (VIIIe–XIe siècles): Implantation et moyens d'action* (Rennes, 2004), pp. 61–89.

Reynolds, Susan, *Fiefs and Vassals: The Medieval Evidence Reinterpreted* (Oxford, 1994).

—— *Kingdoms and Communities in Western Europe, 900–1300*, 2nd edn (Oxford, 1997).

Ribémont, Bernard, 'Ville et noblesse au regard de la littérature médiévale', in Thierry Dutour (ed.), *La noblesse et la ville dans l'espace francophone (XIIe–XVIe siècles)* (Paris, 2010), pp. 221–44.

Richard, Jean, *Saint Louis: Roi d'une France féodale, soutien de la Terre sainte* (Paris, 1983).

Ricoeur, Paul, 'The Model of the Text: Meaningful Action Considered as Text', in Paul Ricoeur, *From Text to Action*, trans. Kathleen Blamey and John B. Thompson (Evanston, IL, 1981), pp. 144–67.

—— *Time and Narrative*, trans. Kathleen McLaughlin and David Pellauer (3 vols, Chicago, 1984–8).
Rider, Jeff, *God's Scribe: The Historiographical Art of Galbert of Bruges* (Washington, DC, 2001).
—— '"Wonder with Fresh Wonder": Galbert the Writer and the Genesis of the *De multro*', in Jeff Rider and Alan V. Murray (eds), *Galbert of Bruges and the Historiography of Medieval Flanders* (Washington, DC, 2009), pp. 13–38.
Rigby, Stephen, 'Approaches to Pre-industrial Social Structure', in Jeffrey Denton (ed.), *Orders and Hierarchies in Late Medieval and Renaissance Europe* (Toronto, 1999), pp. 6–25.
Riggio, Milla B., 'The Allegory of Feudal Acquisition in *The Castle of Perseverance*', in Morton W. Boomfield (ed.), *Allegory, Myth, and Symbol* (Cambridge, MA, 1981), pp. 187–208.
Rigon, Antonio, 'Mendicant Orders and the Reality of Economic Life in Italy in the Middle Ages', in Donald Prudlo (ed.), *The Origin, Development, and Refinement of Medieval Religious Mendicancies* (Leiden, 2011), pp. 241–75.
Roest, Bert, *A History of Franciscan Education (c. 1210–1517)* (Leiden, 2000).
Rose, Christine M., 'Glossing Griselda in a Medieval Conduct Book: *Le Ménagier de Paris*', in Ewa Ciszek and Łukasz Hudomięt (eds), *The Propur Langage of Englische Men* (Frankfurt, 2008), pp. 81–103.
Rubenstein, Jay, *Guibert of Nogent: Portrait of a Medieval Mind* (London, 2002).
Ruiz, Teofilo, *From Heaven to Earth: The Reordering of Castillian Society, 1150–1350* (Princeton, 2004).
Ryan, Magnus, 'Feudal Obligation and Rights of Resistance', in Natalie Fryde, Pierre Monnet, and Otto Gerhard Oexle (eds), *Die Gegenwart des Feudalismus* (Göttingen, 2002), pp. 51–78.
Sahlins, Marshall, *Islands of History* (Chicago, 1985).
—— *Apologies to Thucydides: Understanding History as Culture and Vice Versa* (Chicago, 2004).
Schmitt, Jean-Claude, 'Religion, Folklore, and Society in the Medieval West', repr. in Lester K. Little and Barbara H. Rosenwein (eds), *Debating the Middle Ages: Issues and Readings* (Oxford, 1998), pp. 376–88.
—— *Le corps, les rites, les rêves, le temps: Essais d'anthropologie médiévale* (Paris, 2001).
—— *Le corps des images: Essais sur la culture visuelle au Moyen Âge* (Paris, 2002).
—— *La Conversion d'Hermann le Juif: Autobiographie, Histoire, et Fiction* (Paris, 2003).
Schuchman, Anne M., 'The Lives of Umiliana de' Cerchi: Representations of Female Sainthood in Thirteenth-Century Florence', *Essays in Medieval Studies*, 14 (1997), 15–28.
Segatto, Filiberto, 'Un'immagine quattrocentesca del mondo: la *Sfera* del Dati', *Atti della Academia Nazionale dei Lincei. Memorie. Classe di Scienze morali, storiche e filologiche*, 8th ser., 26:4 (1983), 147–82.
Senn, Felix. *L'institution des vidamies en France* (Paris, 1907).

Severino, Gabriella, 'Storia, genealogia, autobiografia: il caso di Salimbene da Adam', in *Cultura e Società nell'Italia Medievale* (2 vols, Roma, 1988), vol. 2, pp. 775–93.

Shaw, David Gary, *Necessary Conjunctions: The Social Self in Medieval England* (New York, 2005).

Shogimen, Takashi, *Ockham and Political Discourse in the Late Middle Ages* (Cambridge, 2007).

Signori, Gabriela, '"Family Traditions": Moral Economy and Memorial "gift-exchange" in the Urban World of the Late Fifteenth Century', in Gadi Algazi, Valentin Groebner, and Bernhard Jussen (eds), *Negotiating the Gift: Pre-modern Figurations of Exchange* (Göttingen, 2003), pp. 285–318.

Singer, Samuel (ed.), *Thesaurus Proverbiorum Medii Aevi* (13 vols, Berlin, 1995–2002).

Smail, Daniel Lord, 'Genealogy, Ontogeny, and the Narrative Arc of Origins', French Historical Studies, 34:1 (Winter 2011), 30–5.

Smalley, Berryl, 'Ecclesiastical Attitudes to Novelty, c. 1100–1250', in Derek Baker (ed.), *Church, Society and Politics: Papers Read at the Thirteenth Summer Meeting and the Fourteenth Winter Meeting of the Ecclesiastical History Society* (Oxford, 1975), pp. 113–31.

Southern, R. W., *Medieval Humanism and Other Studies* (Oxford, 1970).

Stark, Laura, *Peasants, Pilgrims, and Sacred Promises: Ritual and the Supernatural in Orthodox Karelian Folk Religion* (Helsinki, 2004).

Stein, Robert, 'Death from a Trivial Cause: Events and Their Meanings in Galbert of Bruges's Chronicle', in Rider and Murray (eds), *Galbert of Bruges and the Historiography of Medieval Flanders* (Washington, DC, 2009), pp. 200–14.

Stone, Mark, 'Augustine and the Discovery of the Will', *Medieval Perspectives*, 3.1 (1990), 261–70.

Strathern, Marilyn, *The Gender of the Gift* (Berkeley, 1988).

Szittya, Penn R., *The Antifraternal Tradition in Medieval Litterature* (Princeton, 1986).

Taylor, Charles, *Philosophical Papers* (2 vols, Cambridge, 1985).

—— *Sources of the Self* (Cambridge, 1989).

—— *The Ethics of Authenticity* (Cambridge, MA, 1992).

—— 'Two Theories of Modernity', in Dilip Parameshwar Gaonkar (ed.), *Alternative Modernities* (Durham, NC, 2001), pp. 172–96.

—— *Modern Social Imaginaries* (Durham, NC, 2004).

—— *A Secular Age* (Cambridge, MA, 2006).

Thomas, Keith, *Religion and the Decline of Magic* (London, 1971).

Tourtier, Chantal de, 'Les seigneurs de Picquigny, vidames d'Amiens et leur famille: des origines à la fin du XIVe siècle', *Positions des theses, École nationale des chartes* (1954), pp. 135–8.

—— 'Le péage de Picquigny au Moyen Age', *Bulletin philologique et historique*, 1 (1960), 271–94.

Trexler, Richard, 'Charity and the Defence of Urban Elites in the Italian Communes', in Frederick Cople Jaher (ed.), *The Rich, the Wellborn, and the Powerful: Elites and Upper Classes in History* (Urbana, IL, 1973), pp. 64–109.
—— *Public Life in Renaissance Florence* (New York, 1980).
Tricard, Jean, 'La mémoire des Benoist: livre de raison et mémoire familiale au XVe siècle', in Bernard Guillemain (ed.), *Temps, mémoire, tradition au Moyen Age* (Aix-en-Provence, 1983), pp. 119–40.
—— 'Qu'est-ce qu'un livre de raison Limousin du XVe siècle?', *Journal des savants* (1988), pp. 263–76.
—— 'Confiscation et conaissance d'une seigneurie: l'état de "biens et héritages" du seigneur de Veyrac en 1378', in *Seigneurs et seigneuries au Moyen Age* (Paris, 1993), pp. 123–39.
—— 'Livres de raison et presence de la bourgeoisie dans le campagnes limousines (XIVe–XVe siècle)', in Elisabeth Mornet (ed.), *Campagnes médiévales: l'homme et son espace: études offertes à Robert Fossier* (Paris, 1995), pp. 709–22.
—— *Les campagnes limousines du XIVe au XVIe siècle: originialité et limites d'une reconstruction rurale* (Paris, 1996).
—— 'Maladies et médicines en Limousin à la fin du Moyen Age', in Elisabeth Mornet and Franco Morenzoni (eds), *Milieux naturels, espaces sociaux: études offertes à Robert Delort* (Paris, 1997), pp. 741–9.
—— 'Les livres de raison français au miroir des livres de famille italiens: pour relancer une enquête', *Revue historique*, 307:4 (2002), 993–1011.
Tripodi, Claudia, 'Il padre a Firenze nel Quattrocento: L'educazione del pupillo in Giovanni Morelli', *Annali di Storia di Firenze*, 3 (2011), 29–63.
Ueltschi, Karin, *La Didactique de la chair: approches et enjeux d'un discours en français au Moyen Age* (Geneva, 1993).
Van Caenegem, R. C., 'Galbert of Bruges on Serfdom, Prosecution of Crime, and Constitutionalism (1127–28)', in Bernard S. Bachrach and David Nicholas (eds), *Law, Custom, and the Social Fabric in Medieval Europe* (Kalamazoo, MI, 1990), pp. 89–112.
Varese, Claudio, *Storia e politica nella prosa del Quattrocento* (Torino, 1961).
Vauchez, André, *Francesco d'Assisi e gli Ordini mendicanti* (Assisi, 2005).
Vecchio, Silvia, 'Valori laici e valori francescani nella "Cronica" di Salimbene da Parma', in Giovanna Petti Balbi (ed.), *Salimbeniana: Atti del convegno per il VII centenario di Fra Salimbene* (Bologna, 1991), pp. 254–65.
Verdier, Pascale, 'La construction d'une seigneurie dans la Champagne du XIIIe siècle: Renier Acorre, seigneur de Gouaix (1257–1289)', in *Seigneurs et seigneuries au Moyen Age* (Paris, 1993), pp. 99–110.
Veyne, Paul, 'The Inventory of Differences', *Economy and Society*, 11:2 (1982), 173–98.
—— *Writing History: Essay on Epistemology*, trans. Mina Moore-Rinvolucri (Middletown, CT, 1984).
—— *Did the Greeks Believe in Their Myths?*, trans. Paula Wissing (Chicago, 1988).

—— 'Foucault Revolutionises History', in Arnold Davidson (ed.), *Foucault and His Interlocutors* (Chicago, 1997), pp. 146–82.
—— *Quand notre monde est devenu chrétien (312–394)* (Paris, 2007).
Violante, Cinzio, 'Motivi e carattere della *Cronica* di Salimbene', *Annali della Scuola Normale Superiore di Pisa: Lettere, Storia, e Filosofia*, 22 (1953), 108–54.
Viti, Paolo, 'Leonardo Dati', in Massimiliano Pavan (ed.), *Dizionario biografico degli italiani* (vol. 33, Roma, 1987), pp. 35–40.
Walker, Simon, *Political Culture in Later Medieval England*, ed. Michael J. Braddick (Manchester, 2006).
Weber, Max, *The Protestant Ethic and the Spirit of Capitalism*, trans. Talcott Parsons, repr. (Mineola, 2003).
Weber, Wolfgang, and Nicky Hayes, *Everyday Discourse and Common Sense: The Theory of Social Representations* (New York, 2005).
Wei, Ian P., 'Paris Theologians and Responses to Social Change in the Thirteenth Century', in Hans-Joachim Schmidt (ed.), *Tradition, Innovation, Invention: Fortschrittsverweigerung und Fortschrittsbewusstsein in Mittelalter* (Berlin, 2005), pp. 195–209.
Wellman, Barry, 'Structural Analysis: From Method and Metaphor to Theory and Substance', in Barry Wellman and S. D. Berkowitz (eds), *Social Structures: A Network Approach* (Cambridge, 1988), pp. 19–61.
Wenin, Christian, 'Saint Bonaventure et le travail manuel', in Jacqueline Hamesse and Colette Muraille-Samaran (eds), *Le travail au Moyen Âge: une approche interdisciplinaire* (Louvain-la-Neuve, 1990), pp. 141–55.
Wessell Lightfoot, Dana, *Women, Dowries and Agency: Marriage in Fifteenth-century Valencia* (Manchester, 2013).
West, Delno C., Jr., 'The Education of Fra Salimbene of Parma', in Ann Williams (ed.), *Prophecy and Millenarianism: Essays in Honuor of Marjorie Reeves* (Harlow, 1980), pp. 191–215.
White, Stephen D., 'Service for Fiefs or Fiefs for Service: The Politics of Reciprocity', in Gadi Algazi, Valentin Groebner, and Bernhard Jussen (eds), *Negotiating the Gift: Pre-modern Figurations of Exchange* (Göttingen, 2003), pp. 63–98.
—— 'Pactum ... legem vincit et amor judicium: The Settlement of Disputes by Compromise in Eleventh-century Western France', repr. in Stephen D. White, *Feuding and Peace-making in Eleventh-century France* (Aldershot, 2005), pp. 281–308.
Wickham, Chris, *Community and Clientele in Twelfth-century Tuscany: The Origins of the Rural Commune in the Plain of Lucca* (Oxford, 1998).
—— 'Le forme del feudalesimo', in *Il feudalesimo nell'alto medioevo* (Spoleto, 2000), pp. 15–52.
—— 'Fama and the Law in Twelfth-Century Tuscany', in Thelma Fenster and Daniel Lord Smail (eds), *Fama: The Politics of Talk and Reputation in Medieval Europe* (Ithaca, NY, 2003), pp. 15–26.
Widener, P. A. B., *A Catalogue of the More Important Books, Autographs and Manuscripts in the Library of George C. Thomas* (Philadelphia, 1907).

Williams, Simon J., 'Is Rational Choice Theory "Unreasonable"? The Neglected Emotions', in Margaret Archer and Jonathan Tritter (eds), *Rational Choice Theory: Resisting Colonization* (London, 2000), pp. 59–61.
Williams Lewin, Alison, 'Salimbene de Adam and the Franciscan Chronicle', in Sharon Dale, Alison Williams Lewin, and Daniel J. Osheim (eds.), *Chronicling History: Chroniclers and Historians in Medieval and Renaissance Italy* (University Park, PA, 2007), pp. 87–100.
Wittrock, Björn, 'Early Modernities: Varieties and Transitions', *Daedalus*, 127:3 (1998), 19–40.
—— 'Modernity: One, None, or Many? European Origins and Modernity as a Global Condition', *Daedalus*, 129:1 (2000), 31–61.

Web-based sources

Alarcón, Enrique (ed.), *S. Thomae de Aquino Opera Omnia*
https://www.corpusthomisticum.org/iopera.html
Brun, Laurent, 'Jacques Bruyant', *Archives de littérature du Moyen Age*
http://www.arlima.net/il/jacques_bruyant.html
Herlihy, David, Christiane Klapisch-Zuber, R. Burr Litchfield, and Anthony Molho (eds), *Online Catasto of 1427*, version 1.3, machine-readable data file based on D. Herlihy and C. Klapisch-Zuber, *Census and Property Survey of Florentine Domains in the Province of Tuscany, 1427–1480* (Providence, RI, 2002)
http://cds.library.brown.edu/projects/catasto/main.php
Pandimiglio, Leonida, 'E in fine ci sono le "Ricordanze"?', *Testo e Senso*, 12 (2011)
http://testoesenso.it/article/view/46

Index

accountability 2, 11
  of *pater familias* 23, 120, 122, 126, 215, 245, 251, 264
  See also accounting
accounting 119–20, 126, 128, 131–2, 152, 155, 157–8, 165, 184, 249, 262, 264
action theory 12–21
  actor-network-theory 252–3, 271
  actant 4, 202, 212, 208, 232, 252
  habitus 13, 16–7, 147
  in medieval studies 10, 12–14, 263
  methodological individualism 8
agency
  abeyance of 3, 16, 24, 31, 153, 194, 196–8, 202, 204, 207–9
  co-acting 2, 90
  collective 9, 23, 33–5, 87–9, 126–7, 170, 207, 215
  cultural construction of 15, 113, 117, 145, 190, 204–5, 209, 260, 263
  definition 2, 4
  judicial paradigm of 2, 53, 127
  non-human 3–4, 11, 22, 57, 149–51
  vs. power 3, 8, 11, 15–6, 25, 62, 115, 135, 254–5, 262
  of social subalterns 17, 170, 183, 254–6, 258
  strategic 2, 5, 8, 10–2, 15–7, 55, 62, 69–70, 79 n. 49, 89, 92, 95, 109, 113, 117, 120, 167–70, 172, 177, 179–80, 196–8, 207, 212, 241, 252–4, 258, 260–2
  and structure 3, 11, 13–8, 52, 115, 138, 140, 151, 160 n. 23, 168, 170, 185, 187, 194, 254, 260–3, 271
  techniques of the body 13–5, 48 n. 57, 226–8, 233, 240, 256
  See also individual agent, self-interpretation
Ailly-sur-Somme 70–1, 73, 75, 84, 106
Albertano da Brescia 238
Alberti family 160, 169, 171–2, 174
Albizzi family 182

alms 55, 183, 185, 199, 201, 204
Amiens 60, 75, 82
Amiens, bishop of 63, 65, 91, 95–6, 98–101, 108–11, 113–4, 118
Amiens, castellan of 63, 74–6, 88–9, 94–5, 105, 108–10
Amiens, chapter of 68, 93, 107, 110–2
Amiens, *vidame* of 63, 65, 95–6
  See also under Picquigny family
Aquinas, Thomas 17 n. 41, 29, 218
  See also under free will
Archer, Margaret 18, 209
autobiography 4, 21–2, 162–3, 166, 171–2, 215–6, 221, 235, 237
  autobiographical inserts in histories 40–56, 124–5
  twelfth-century revival 27–8
autonomous moral agent *see* individual agent

Bartolomeo da San Concordio 213
Beauval 73, 75, 85, 88–9, 95, 109, 117
Benoist, Etienne 122, 151, 153, 251
Bonaventure, St 50, 218
Bourdieu, Pierre 16–8, 147
Bruges 31–6, 184
  siege of castle 31–3
Brunetto Latini 270

cartularies 21, 60–1
  of Picquigny *see* Picquigny, cartulary of
  private cartularies 23, 119, 127, 153–4
Castle of Perseverance 234
Châlucet 123–6, 131
Champagne, county of 76, 80 n. 52
Charles IV, king of France 222
Charles the Good, count of Flanders 27, 31–2, 35–7, 208
charters 34, 67–77, 80–8, 93–4, 96, 100, 105–6, 108–10, 113, 117–8, 122–3, 131, 136, 138, 141, 154, 157, 260

300   Index

charters (*continued*)
  chirograph   88
  See also cartularies
Chastel de Labour   25, 216, 225, 233–8
Châtelet, court of   220–1, 231
Chemin de povréte et de richesse   24–5, 219–39, 266
  allegory   13, 219–20, 222, 227–9
    Barat   225, 231–2, 237
    Raison see under rationality
  dialogism   231–2
  reception   238–9
  social imaginary   215–38
  See also *Chastel de Labour*, Jacques Bruyant
Christine de Pizan   217
chronicles   22, 27, 39–40, 49, 55, 57, 119, 264
  local   122–3, 127, 157, 184
ciompi   170
civilising process   6, 116, 232 n. 67
  civilité   229, 232, 242
  curialitas   55–6
  See also under Picquigny, lordship of
Clairy-Saulchoix   70–1, 75, 84, 94, 99, 104, 106
Coluccio Salutati   213
conduct literature   5, 24, 121, 157, 159, 161–3, 168–70, 174–7, 212–7, 232–3, 238–41, 243–4, 247, 249–50, 265
  See also *livres de raison*; *ricordi*
confession   7, 219, 239, 246–8
Corbie, abbey of   73, 84 n. 62, 88
crusades   29–30, 90–1, 100, 118

Dati, Gregorio   24, 158–9, 193–212, 261
  agency abeyance   194–210
  business ventures   194–8
  Libro segreto   193, 204
    memoranda   193–4, 199–210
  offices held   199, 210
Dati, Leonardo   159 n. 21, 205
divine providence   1, 4, 8, 22, 29–31, 35–40, 48, 57, 150, 166–7, 183–8, 199, 207–9, 211, 260–1

dowries   68 n. 20, 90–1, 102, 106, 108, 138–9, 143, 145–6, 165, 178, 187 n. 103, 193 n. 118, 195, 251
dream visions   47–9, 186, 220
Dreux of Saint-Sauflieu   84–5, 92–3, 97, 117

ego-documents   4–9, 32, 68, 126, 215
  definition   4
  See also autobiography, cartularies, *livres de raison*, *ricordi*
Elias of Cortona, Franciscan minister general   45, 52
emotions   20 n. 59, 34–5, 166, 185, 189, 203, 225–7, 266
  hope   54, 106, 161, 166, 186, 191, 196, 202–3
Enguerran de Marigny   222–3
Erembalds   31–7
Esperon, Pierre   130–51, 261
  background   130–1
  livre de raison   130–1, 133, 138–40, 142–5, 147–51
    advice for posterity   150–1
    miraculous remedies   147–51
    self-fashioning   143–5
    support network   135–42
everyday life   8, 12, 17, 20, 28, 38, 58, 144–5, 163, 175–6, 183, 186, 210, 214–5, 227–8, 240–6, 267
excommunication   88 n. 84, 112
exempla   239, 243, 248

family   30, 53–4, 119, 156–7, 159, 178–9, 181, 193, 211–3, 240, 249–52, 264–5
  conflicts and marginalisation   7, 10, 192–4, 211–2
  Familienbücher   5
  histories   156, 161, 164
  and individual   9–10, 23, 40, 44, 49, 121–2, 164–5, 212, 215
  See also *livres de raison*, kinship, *ricordi*
Fano   41–2, 45–6, 52
feudal relations   85–6, 115–6, 116 n. 181
  criticism of   78–9
  definitions   77–8

historiography 10, 61–3
  See also under Picquigny, lordship of
fiefs 61, 77–81, 83, 86, 115–6
Flanders 6, 27, 31–8, 75–6
  See also Bruges, Charles the Good,
    William Clito
Florence 153–60, 164, 166–75, 178–9,
    181–5, 194–202, 262
  guilds 174, 200
  institutions 158, 171, 178, 195–6, 199
  politics 158, 172–5, 182–4, 199, 200,
    205–6
  social groups 169, 183
  See also ciompi; Dati, Gregorio;
    Mercanzia; Morelli, Giovanni; Pitti,
    Buonaccorso; ricordi
Fortune 166, 182, 185, 217, 220, 222, 226
franchise charters 88, 122
Francis, St 46–51, 53
Franciscan Order 40–59
  convents 40–2, 45, 55
  criticism of 55–6
  rule 42, 47
  See also Francis, St; Meditaciones
    vite Christi; Ockham, William;
    Salimbene de Adam of Parma
free will
  Thomas Aquinas 29, 30 n. 7, 39 n. 31
  Augustine 38, 42
  Galbert of Bruges 38–9
  Gregorio Dati 207–8
  individual as God's coadjutor 8, 30,
    207–8, 219
  Salimbene of Parma 42, 49
Fulk of Querrieux 95–6

Galbert of Bruges 22, 31–9, 124, 184,
    208, 261
  autobiographical references 32
  redactions of De multro 32–3, 35–7
  this-worldly view of history 32–5, 37
gender relations 25, 121–2, 139, 144–5,
    163–4, 215–6, 220, 238–9, 241, 244–7,
    250–8, 270
Gerardo of Modena 45, 48, 56
Gertrude, countess of Holland 34–5

Ghibellines 157
gift-exchange 55–7, 83, 138–9, 144 n. 105,
    170, 173, 186–8, 209, 251, 264
Giles of Clairy 94–5
Giddens, Anthony 14, 17–8
Guelfs 157, 171
Guibert of Nogent 29–31
Guido de Adam of Parma 45, 48
Guillaume de Deguileville 221
Guillaume d'Erquis 119 n. 3, 250

habitus see under action theory
hagiography 22, 32–4, 37–9, 47, 51–2,
    58
Hallelujah movement 46
Hangest 89, 104, 106, 108
homage 13, 141, 261
  See also under Picquigny, lordship of
humanism 5–6, 25, 154–5, 159, 161, 176,
    182–3, 213, 219, 265
Hundred Years War, the 23, 121, 123–4,
    131, 137–8, 151

imitatio Christi 46–7
individual agent 8–9, 28–9, 39, 42–8,
    54–5, 88, 117, 145, 167–8, 181, 190,
    209–10, 230, 247–9, 256, 265–6
  buffered self 190, 266–7
  self-fashioning 27–8, 43, 46, 48, 52,
    58, 93, 125, 145, 165, 200, 202, 205, 207,
    241, 256, 264, 268
  vulnerability 219–22, 271
  See also agency, self-interpretation
individual, myths 28–9, 264
Italy 40–1, 45–9, 54–6, 155
  urban values 49, 52–3, 55
  See also Florence, Parma, Pistoia,
    Venice

Jacques Bruyant 216–7, 220–4, 226–38,
    261
  background 220–1, 233
  See also Chemin de povréte et de
    richesse
Jacques de Cessoles 238
Jean d'Anneux 56

Jean Gerson 224
Jean of Fourdrinoy 107, 117
Joachimism 58
John Peter Olivi 203

kinship 91, 96, 105–6, 115, 137–8, 172, 180, 195
Klapisch-Zuber, Christiane 155 n. 9, 157, 160 n. 23
knights 14, 25, 34, 36, 38, 61, 75, 79, 81–2, 84, 88–9, 91, 94, 115, 118, 127, 141, 216, 233

labour 122, 144–5, 169, 216–8, 233–5, 238–9, 251–2, 255, 271
   valorisation of 216, 218, 227, 234, 237, 248–9, 267
   See also Chastel de Labour
La somme le roi 227 n. 49, 247
last wills 102, 134–5, 165, 179
legal profession 53, 56, 77, 94, 121, 127–8, 137–8, 141–2, 151 n. 135, 152, 212, 228, 235, 237
   See also notaries
Leon Battista Alberti 156, 213
letters 4, 22, 41, 54, 65, 124
libro segreto 154–5, 193
Limoges 122 n. 10, 128, 138, 141
   siege of 124–5
Limoges, bishop of 131, 133
   Hugh of Magnac 140
Limoges, viscount of 124
lists 69–70, 74–5, 106, 117, 119, 132, 142–3, 148–50, 162, 213, 242–3, 248
literacy 6, 60, 68–9, 77, 115, 119–22, 126–8, 131, 141–2, 147–8, 152, 154–8, 201–3, 212–3, 217, 252, 264–5
   See also autobiography, cartularies, charters, chronicles, letters, *livres de raison*, *ricordi*
livres de raison 23–4, 119–51, 249–51
   advice for posterity 121, 151
   early modern 120
   family events 119, 128, 130
      births 128
   origins 119, 127
   See also Benoist, Etienne; Esperon, Pierre; Guillaume d'Erquis; Massiot family; Tarneau, Gérald
lordship 60–3, 263
   See also Picquigny, lordship of
Lucca 184

magic 121, 147–51, 242, 250, 267
Martino of Fano 45, 56
Martino of Parma, bishop of Mantua 54
Mass 147, 149, 239, 241 n. 96, 246, 250
Massiot family 148, 151, 249–50
Mathaeus Platearius 147
Medici 182–3
   Filigno de' 157
Meditaciones vite Christi 50–1
Melibee, story of 240
memoranda 5, 24, 126, 130, 143–6, 199–207, 210–2, 264
Ménagier de Paris 24–5, 216–7, 238–59
   aims 239–42
   instructional discourse 241–9, 256–9
   sources 221, 239–40
   wife's status 244–8, 250–4
   women's agency 253–8
Mercanzia 171, 196
microhistory 3, 62, 86, 115, 263
Milan 184, 202, 208
mills 88, 92, 97–9, 104, 107, 110
modernity 25–6, 58, 145, 265–71
   definition 25, 265, 267 n. 9
   multiple modernities 26
Molliens-Vidame 74, 88–9, 94–5, 106, 108
Morelli, Giovanni 24, 156, 158–93, 209–14, 261
   advice for posterity 161–3, 168, 170–1, 173–7
   autobiographical episodes 162, 166–7
   marriage 172, 174
   biographies of family members 159, 163–7
   last will 179
   religious experiences 186–92

writing of the *ricordi* 156–61, 174–7
Morelli, Pagolo 164–67, 176, 181, 185, 192
Mugello 160, 163, 176
Murray, Alexander 6 n. 13, 150

networks 69, 79, 89–97, 101, 105–7, 135–42, 167–70, 173–5, 177, 188–9, 200, 205–8, 210–1, 260–4
 'weak ties' 139–40
notaries 27, 32, 34–5, 37, 122, 127, 136, 220
Nuremberg 5

Ockham, William 58
Odo of Chateauroux, bishop of Tusculum 100
orality 176, 240, 250
Orville 73

Paolo da Certaldo 212
Paris 5, 24, 136, 220, 229, 231, 237 n. 79, 241, 262
 bishop of 218
 university of 55
Parma 41, 43, 45–6, 49, 54, 56
Petrarch 213
Philip II, king of France 65, 75
Philip III, king of France 222
Philip IV, king of France 222
Philippe de Mézières 224
Picquigny, cartulary of 22–3, 65, 67–8, 70, 72, 77, 83 n. 66, 108
Picquigny family 64
 Enguerran, *vidame* of Amiens 63–5, 69, 89–99, 108, 110, 115–8
 personal initiatives 91–2, 95–6
 support network 90–7
 Gérard II, *vidame* of Amiens 90–1, 94
 Gérard III, *vidame* of Amiens 63–5, 67, 69, 99–118
 acquisitions 102–5
 disputes 108–14
 Gérard of Ailly 96, 115
 Jean, *vidame* of Amiens 67, 112
 Margaret 90–1, 115
 Matilda 91

matrimonial alliances 105–6
Picquigny, lordship of 22–3, 63–118
 aids (*auxilia*) 81–3
 castle 65, 67, 69–71, 74–6, 84, 86–7, 90, 100
 courtly society 75–6, 90, 116
 estages 67, 69–76
 feudal relations 79–81, 85–6, 90, 115–6, 116 n. 181
 homages 67, 70–5, 79–81, 83–7, 89, 115
  circular 85, 117
  'joint liege' 84–5, 116–7
 sesterage 102, 113–4, 118
 See also Picquigny family
Pierre-Buffière 122–9
 raids on 123–4
 See also Tarneau, Gérald
Pierre de la Broce 222
Pierre Gringore 238
Pierre Remi 222
pilgrimage 138, 150
pious donations 95, 97–101, 107, 184
Pisa 41, 43, 48, 208
Pistoia 198
Pitti, Buonaccorso 156–7, 198
plague 131, 149, 163, 167 n. 42, 176, 210,
Poitiers, bishop of 133, 140
Ponthieu, county of 90–1, 114 n. 77
possession 220, 266–7
 demonic 57, 190–2
prayer 4, 24, 121, 131, 147–50, 166, 186–8, 191–2, 199, 202, 211, 221 n. 16, 242, 249–50
preaching 7, 50, 56, 100, 183, 205, 219 n. 11, 230, 250
promissory notes 24, 182, 265
Provence 54, 120, 151

Ratherius of Verona 28
Raoul de Cambrai 118
rationality 13, 19, 117, 120, 184, 197, 203, 216, 219, 224–7, 230, 247, 257, 265
 Raison 220, 224–6, 228–32, 248
rational choice theory 15, 29, 266 n. 5

reciprocity 11, 55–6, 86, 107, 117, 157, 170–1, 173, 180, 187 n. 103, 207, 220, 264
　in relation to the divine 56–7, 184–5, 187–9, 209, 211
　See also transactionalism
ricordanze see ricordi
ricordi 24, 153–213
　definition 153–8
　See also Dati, Gregorio; Morelli, Giovanni; Pitti, Buonacorso
Rochechouart 138, 141, 150
Romagna 40
Roman de la rose 217, 219, 221, 223 n. 25, 227 n. 49, 230 n. 60, 231, 238

Saint-Junien 130–8, 140–2, 149
　disputes with bishop of Limoges 140–1
　local elites 140–2
Saint-Pol, county of 63 n. 10, 83, 84 n. 67, 88, 89 n. 87
Saint-Sauflieu 74, 76, 84–5, 89, 92–3, 96–7, 106, 117
saints, cult of 136, 150, 184, 188–9, 202
　See also Francis, St
Salimbene de Adam of Parma 22, 39–59, 125, 261
　autobiographical episodes 48, 52, 54–5
　chronicle 39–40, 56–7
　family 42, 44, 49, 52–4
　　See also Guido de Adam of Parma
　narrative strategies 43–6
　religious conversion 39–42, 44–6
self-interpretation 4, 15, 18–9, 21, 33, 209, 211, 246–8, 265
　reflexivity 3, 9, 13, 18, 145, 224, 252–3
Sens 55
social imaginary 19–20, 169, 175–6, 179–83, 215–38, 270–2
　definition 19–20, 216–7
　forward looking 215–6, 232, 234–8, 268–70
　See also Chastel de Labour, Chemin de povréte et de richesse

Somme, river 22, 63, 65, 88, 92–3, 97, 107, 109–12
speech 125, 225, 228, 230, 232
　as mode of agency 42–3, 46, 48, 54, 55, 198, 204, 213, 246
strategies, socioeconomic 102, 104, 132–4, 167–70, 195–7, 264
　timing of 17–8, 134–5, 254–5
subaltern social groups 97, 169–70, 183, 254–6, 258

Tarneau, Gérald 122–30
　autobiographical references 124–6
　legal mindset 125–7
　support network 124, 128
taxes 23, 162, 171, 195
　relief tax 81–2
　taille 122–5, 127, 131
　tolls 65, 73, 112
Taylor, Charles 1 n. 1, 19–20, 25, 69, 190 n. 113, 205 n. 160, 265–7
theodicy 36–7
theology 39, 42–3, 187–8
　adapting to societal change 218–9
　of gender 244, 246
　See also confession, divine providence, free will, theodicy, vices, virtues
three orders, the 20, 210, 216–8, 268
transactionalism 2, 11, 19, 167–8, 170, 186, 188–9, 211

Venice 155–6
Veyne, Paul 35 n. 23, 39, 268 n. 13
vices 162, 204–5, 217, 227–8, 230, 239, 247
Vignacourt, lordship of *see* Amiens, castellan of
virtues 162, 174, 204–5, 217, 220, 228, 239, 246–7
　See also Raison

Weber, Max 197, 229, 265–6, 271
William Clito, count of Flanders 34
William of Auvergne, bishop of Paris 218
William of Saint-Amour 55–6
William of Ypres 36

www.ingramcontent.com/pod-product-compliance
Lightning Source LLC
Chambersburg PA
CBHW051601230426
43668CB00013B/1939